M000266383

The Big Instant Pot Cookbook

Simple and Delicious Recipes for Beginners and Advanced Users

Martha Romero

Table of Contents

Introduction 9

Fundamentals of Instant Pot 10

    What Is Instant Pot............................ 10
    Benefits of Using Instant Pot 10
    First Use 10
    Main Functions of Instant Pot 11
    Buttons and User Guide of Instant Pot 15
    Accessories of Instant Pot 16
    Cleaning and Maintenance of Instant Pot.. 17
    Troubleshooting 17
    Meals Cooking Time in Instant Pot 18

Breakfast 19

    Ham and Hash 19
    Cheddar Egg Puff............................. 19
    Avocado Toast with Boiled Egg 19
    Feta Frittata 20
    Bacon-Cheddar Egg Bites 20
    Maple Steel-Cut Oats 20
    Brown Sugar Quinoa 20
    Creamy Oatmeal 21
    Coconut Oatmeal............................. 21
    Blueberry- Oatmeal 21
    Breakfast Biscuits and Gravy................. 21
    Breakfast Grits 22
    Vegetable Egg White.......................... 22
    Vanilla Bean Yogurt 22
    Creamy Pumpkin Yogurt...................... 23
    Blueberry French Toast Bake................. 23
    Banana Oatmeal.............................. 23
    Sausage Pancake Bites........................ 24
    Denver Omelet................................ 24
    Egg Kale Casserole 24
    Raspberry Steel Cut Oatmeal Bars 25
    Blueberry Quinoa Porridge 25
    Buckwheat Granola........................... 25
    Cinnamon Oatmeal Muffins 26
    Chocolate Oatmeal........................... 26
    Banana Date Porridge 26
    Banana Walnut Oats 26
    Artichoke Egg Casserole 27
    Almond Granola 27
    Pumpkin Quinoa 27

Poppy Seed Oatmeal Cups..................... 28
Apple Steel Cut Oats........................... 28
Berry Steel Cut Oats........................... 28
Banana Bites 28
Cinnamon Breakfast Loaf 29
Vegetable Breakfast Bowls 29
Root Vegetable Casserole 29
Strawberries Quinoa Porridge................. 30
Eggs with Asparagus 30
5-Ingredient Oatmeal 30
Loaded Bacon Grits 31
Ham Cheese Egg Bites 31
Sausage Spinach Quiche 31
Blueberry Coffee Cake 32
Chocolate Chip Banana Bread 32
Vanilla Yogurt with Granola 33
Biscuit Dumplings and Gravy 33
Ham Cheese Omelet........................... 33
Egg Bites 34

Snacks & Appetizers.......................... 35

    Unsweetened Applesauce 35
    Classic Hummus 35
    Refried Beans 35
    Classic Black Beans 35
    Cilantro-Lime Brown Rice 36
    Coconut Brown Rice.......................... 36
    Feta Chickpea Salad 36
    Potato Pea Salad............................. 37
    Cider Collard Greens......................... 37
    Garlicky Brussels Sprouts 37
    Cinnamon Acorn Squash 38
    Mashed Potato and Cauliflower.............. 38
    Honey Sweet Potatoes 38
    Cinnamon Raisin Granola Bars 38
    Almond Butter Chocolate Chip Granola Bars
    39
    Hot Cauliflower Bites 39
    Nacho Cheese Sauce 39
    Buffalo Chicken Dip 40
    Spinach Artichoke Dip........................ 40
    Sweet Potato Hummus........................ 40
    Cauliflower Hummus.......................... 40
    Black Bean Dip 41

White Bean Dip 41
Tamari Edamame 41
Cinnamon Almonds..........................42
Lentil Balls 42
Quinoa Energy Balls..........................42
Broccoli Bites 43
Hard-Boiled Eggs............................43
Avocado Hummus............................43
Avocado Deviled Eggs 44
Cauliflower Queso with Bell Pepper 44
Lemon Eggplant in Vegetable Broth........44
Garlic Collard Greens in Vegetable Broth..45
Sweet Potatoes with Maple Syrup 45
Dijon Brussels Sprouts 45
Jalapeño Peppers with Cashews.............46
Simple Lentil-Walnut Dip 46
Spiced Potatoes Dip 46
Corn with Tofu Crema 47
Beet Hummus 47
Garlic Baby Potatoes 47
Creamed Spinach with Cashews 48
Polenta with Mushroom Ragù 48

Beans, Pasta & Grains 49

Chickpea Mushrooms 49
Chickpea Salad 49
Homemade Three-Bean Salad 49
Cannellini Bean Salads 50
Salty Edamame..............................50
Garlicky Black-Eyed Pea Soup 50
Dill Black-Eyed Peas.........................51
Black Bean Sliders 51
Beans with Tomato and Parsley 52
Black Beans with Corn and Tomato Relish 52
White Bean Soup.............................52
Creamy White Bean Soup 53
Herbed Lima Beans..........................53
Greek Navy Bean Soup......................53
Three-Bean Chili.............................54
White Bean Barley Soup 54
Bean and Lentil Chili 54
Chili-Spiced Beans...........................55
Lima Bean Soup 55
Vegetarian Loaf..............................55
Chickpea Soup 56
White Bean Soup with Kale 56
White Bean Cassoulet 56

Toasted Orzo Salad 57
Beefsteak Tomatoes with Cheese 57
Pasta with Marinated Artichokes.............57
Couscous with Tomatoes 58
Couscous with Crab 58
Pepper Couscous Salad 58
Pasta Primavera...............................59
Rotini with Red Wine Marinara 59
Couscous with Olives 59
Bowtie Pesto Pasta Salad 60
Israeli Pasta Salad.............................60
Rotini with Walnut Pesto 60
Tomato, Arugula and Feta Pasta Salad 61
Mixed Vegetable Couscous 61
Toasted Couscous with Feta..................61
Pasta with Chickpeas and Cabbage 62
Dill Pasta Salad...............................62
Angel Hair Pasta with Spinach and White
Wine 62
Tahini Soup..................................63
Marinara Spaghetti with Mozzarella Cheese
....63
Spaghetti with Meat Sauce 63
Avgolemono 64
Zesty Couscous 64

Chicken and Poultry 65

Chicken Enchiladas............................65
Chicken Pot Pie 65
Chicken with Potatoes and Peas 65
Chicken Wings 66
Chicken Dumplings...........................66
Mushroom and Chicken Sausage Risotto.. 67
Chicken Tikka Masala.........................67
Spiced Coconut Chicken 68
Roasted Chicken with Tomatoes 68
Stuffed Turkey Breast........................69
Penne and Turkey Meatballs 69
Duck with Vegetables 70
Teriyaki Wing 70
Chicken-Stuffed Sweet Potatoes 71
Makhani Chicken.............................71
Stuffed Chicken Parmesan....................71
Mustard-Braised Chicken 72
Chicken Penne Puttanesca....................72
Italian Sausage Ragu with Polenta 72
Chicken Burrito Bowls 73

Faux-Tesserae Chicken Dinner...............73
Quinoa–Stuffed Peppers 74
Chicken with Black Bean Garlic Sauce......74
Game Hens with Garlic 75
Wine Glazed Whole Chicken 75
Seasoned Chicken 76
Italian Chicken..............................76
Thai Chicken 76
Spicy Chicken Wings 77
Hot Wings 77
Lime Chicken Wings 77
Sesame Chicken 78
Salsa Verde Chicken 78
Sriracha Chicken 78
8-Ingredient Chicken 78
Chicken Coconut Curry 79
Chicken Curry 79
Chicken Cacciatore 79
Chicken Nachos.........................80
Chicken Piccata 80
Chicken Adobo 80
Chicken Congee 81
Chicken Puttanesca......................81
Chicken with Potatoes 81
Chicken Drumsticks 82
Chicken Tomato Drumsticks 82
Teriyaki Chicken 82
Buffalo Chicken 83
Crack Chicken 83
Pina Colada Chicken 83
Orange Chicken.........................83
Apricot Chicken 84
Shredded Chicken Breast.................84
Shredded Chicken with Marinara...........84
Lemon Mustard Chicken with Potatoes.....85
BBQ Chicken with Potatoes 85
Creamy Chicken with Bacon 85
Cajun Chicken with Rice 86
Mojo Chicken Tacos 86
Roasted Tandoori Chicken.................86
Salsa Chicken 87
Cream Cheese Chicken 87
Coca Cola Chicken 87
Hunter Chicken 87
Olive Chicken............................88
Chili Lime Chicken 88
Ginger Chicken 89

Fish and Seafood.................................90
Calamari with Pimentos.....................90
Curried Halibut Steaks 90
Carp Pilaf 90
Tilapia Fillets with Mushrooms..............91
Shrimp in Tomato Sauce 91
Trout Salad 91
Tuna Fillets with Eschalots...................92
Chunky Tilapia Stew 92
Haddock Fillets with Black Beans 92
Foil-Packet Fish with Aioli 93
Baked Fish with Parmesan..................93
Salmon Steaks with Kale Pesto Sauce 93
Parmesan Cod with Basmati Rice...........94
Butter Grouper 94
Tuna, Ham and Pea Chowder 94
Ocean Trout Fillets 95
Red Snapper in Mushroom Sauce 95
Portuguese-Fish Medley 95
Prawns with Basmati Rice...................95
Tuna Fillets with Onions 96
Haddock Fillets with Steamed Green Beans
....................................96
Greek-Shrimp with Feta Cheese 96
Indian Kulambu 97
Cod Fish with Goat Cheese 97
Crab Dip 97
Creole Gumbo 98
Blue Crabs with Wine and Herbs...........98
Sausage and Prawn Boil 98
Sole Fillets with Vegetables 99
Louisiana-Seafood Boil...................99
Southern California Cioppino................99
Fish and Vegetables 100
Japanese Seafood Curry.................. 100
Spicy Thai Prawns 100
Haddock Curry........................ 101
Tuna and Asparagus Casserole............ 101
Spinach-Stuffed Salmon.................. 101
Steamed Tilapia with Spinach 102
Codfish with Scallions 102
Teriyaki Fish Steaks 102
Fish Tacos............................ 103
Halibut Steaks with Wild Rice............. 103
Shrimp Scampi with Carrots 103
Orange Sea Bass........................ 104
Prawn Dipping Sauce..................... 104

Tilapia Fillets with Peppers 104
Greek-Style Fish 105
French Fish En Papillote 105
Seafood Quiche with Colby Cheese 105
Spanish Paella 106
Crabs with Garlic Sauce 106
Butter dipped Lobster Tails 106
Mussels in Scallion Sauce 106
Saucy Red Snapper 107
Shrimp Salad 107
Crab Sliders 107
Vietnamese-Fish 108
Fish and Couscous Pilaf 108
Salmon on Croissants 108
Tuna Steaks in Lime- Sauce 109
Beer-Steamed Mussels 109
Fish Paprikash 109
Mahi-Mahi Fish with Guacamole 110
Halibut Steaks with Tomatoes 110
Mayo Shrimp Salad 111
Risotto with Sea Bass 111
Fish Mélange 111
Fish Burritos 111
Saucy Clams 112
Sole Fillets with Pickle 112

Soups 113

Black Bean Soup with Avocado Salsa 113
Tomato Soup 113
Cauliflower and Potato Soup 113
Broccoli and Leek Soup 114
Matzo Ball Soup 114
Chicken Noodle Soup 115
French Onion Soup 115
Butternut Squash Soup 116
Sweet Potato Kale Soup 116
Ham Bone Soup 117
Chicken Tortilla Soup 117
Lentil and Tomato Soup 117
Vegetable Wild Rice Soup 118
Noodle Soup 118
Minestrone Soup 118
Beef Soup with Vegetables 119
Acorn Squash Soup 119
Pinot Grigio Soup 119
Creamy Clam Chowder 120
Cod Tomato Soup 120

Beef Stroganoff Soup 120
Cheesy Broccoli Soup 121
Sage Onion Soup 121
Meatball Noodle Soup 121
Chipotle Chili Soup 122
Corn and Chicken Soup 122
Kidney Bean Chicken Soup 122
Sweet Potato Soup with Swiss Chard 123
Turkey and Basmati Rice Soup 123
Beef Barley Soup 124
Peppery Ground Pork Soup 124
Lima Bean Soup 124
Lobster Bisque 124
Seafood Chowder with Bacon 125
Potato Chowder 125
Halibut Chowder 126
Red Lentil Spinach Soup 126
Chicken Vegetable Soup 126
Farmhouse Soup 127
Tomato Vegetable Soup 127
Hang Wau Soup 127
Minty Asparagus Soup 128
Zucchini Quinoa Soup 128
Shrimp Vegetable Bisque 128
Borscht Soup 129
Alfredo Ditalini Soup 129
Hamburger Soup 129
Sausage and Cabbage Soup 130
Duck Millet Soup 130

Stews 131

Beef Potato Stew 131
White Chicken Chili 131
Beef Peas Stew 131
Italian Beef Stew 132
Bosnian Pot Stew 132
Chickpea Stew 132
Sausage and Bean Stew 133
Chicken Stew with Apples 133
Chicken and Shrimp Gumbo 133
Steak Kidney Bean Chili 134
Marsala Fish Stew 134
Bœuf À La Bourguignonne 135
Hungarian Beef Goulash 135
Pork Chile Verde 135
Italian Beef Ragù 136
Brunswick Stew 136

Traditional Polish Stew 136
Vegan Pottage Stew........................ 137
Mulligan Stew 137
Irish Bean Cabbage Stew.................. 137
Rich Chicken Purloo 138
Almond Lentil Vegetable Stew 138
Catalan Shellfish Stew..................... 138
Beef and Potato Stew...................... 139
Hungarian Chicken Stew................... 139
Indian Bean Stew 139
Mediterranean Chicken Stew 140
Seafood Vegetable Ragout 140
Spanish Olla Podrida 140
Basque Squid Stew 141
Slumgullion Stew 141
Lentil Vegetable Hotpot 141
Vegetarian Ratatouille 142
French Pot-Au-Feu........................ 142
Chicken Fricassee with Wine 142
Barley Pottage 143
Hyderabadi- Lentil Stew 143
Kentucky Burgoo.......................... 143
Thai Curry Stew 144
Oyster Stew with Chorizo 144
Lentil Curry Stew.......................... 145

Stocks & Sauces 146

Chicken Stock............................. 146
Vegetable Stock 146
Beef Bone Broth 146
Spicy Chicken Bone Broth 146
Homemade Ketchup....................... 147
Sweet and Tangy Barbecue Sauce........ 147
Marinara Sauce 147
Puttanesca Sauce 148
Broccoli Pesto 148
Onion Gravy 148
Mango-Apple Chutney 149
Cranberry Sauce 149
Cinnamon Applesauce 149
Orange and Lemon Marmalade 150
Triple-Berry Jam 150
Apple Butter 150
Vegetable Broth 151
Oil-Free Marinara Sauce 151
Maple Barbecue Sauce 151
Fresh Tomato Ketchup 152

Hot Pepper Sauce........................... 152
Nut-Free Cheese Sauce...................... 152
Applesauce................................. 152
Strawberry Compote 153
Bone Broth 153
Pork Broth 153
Mushroom Broth 154
Chicken Stock.............................. 154
Chicken Feet Stock......................... 154
Turkey Stock 154
Fish Stock 155
Seafood Soup Stock 155
Herb Stock 155
Homemade Salsa 155
Bolognese Sauce 156
Cranberry Apple Sauce 156
Tabasco Sauce............................. 156
Vegan Alfredo Sauce 156
Tomato Basil Sauce 157
Caramel Sauce 157
Mushroom Gravy Sauce 157
Chili Sauce 158
White Sauce 158
Strawberry Applesauce 158

Vegetables & Side Dishes 159

Dandelion Greens........................... 159
Greek-Style Peas 159
Braised Eggplant........................... 159
Roasted Spaghetti Squash................... 160
Tomato Basil Soup 160
Artichokes Provençal 160
Hearty Minestrone Soup 161
Spaghetti Squash with Mushrooms 161
Artichoke Soup 161
Green Beans with Tomatoes and Potatoes
.... 162
Cabbage Soup 162
Eggplant Caponata 162
Pureed Cauliflower Soup 163
Spicy Corn On the Cob...................... 163
Gingered Sweet Potatoes 163
Zucchini Pomodoro......................... 164
Burgundy Mushrooms 164
Wild Mushroom Soup....................... 164
Stuffed Acorn Squash 165
Herbed Potato Salad........................ 165

Steamed Cauliflower with Herbs 165
Maple Dill Carrots 166
Ratatouille.. 166
Steamed Broccoli 167
Boiled Cabbage 167
Vegetable Cheese Sauce..................... 167
Purple Cabbage Salad 167
Steamed Cauliflower 168
Saucy Brussels Sprouts and Carrots 168
Simple Spaghetti Squash..................... 168
Baked Sweet Potatoes......................... 168
Lemony Cauliflower Rice..................... 169
Lemony Steamed Asparagus 169
Lemon Garlic Red Chard 169
Ginger Broccoli and Carrots................. 169
Spinach Salad with Quinoa................. 170
Curried Mustard Greens...................... 170
Cheesy Brussels Sprouts and Carrots 170
Garlic Green Beans 171
Simple Beet Salad 171
Spinach Salad with Beets.................... 171
Mashed Sweet Potatoes...................... 172
Mashed Cauliflower............................. 172

Desserts 173

Pumpkin Pie Bites................................ 173
Gooey Chocolate Chip Cookie Sundae.... 173
Berry Almond Crisp.............................. 173
Mango Sticky Rice 174
Stuffed Baked Apple À La Mode 174
Cinnamon-Vanilla Rice Pudding............. 174
Carrot Cake with Cream Cheese Frosting 175
Vanilla Crème Brulee........................... 175
Crème Caramel (Purin)....................... 176
Bread Pudding with Rum Sauce 176
Brown Butter–Cinnamon Rice Treat....... 176
Molten Chocolate Lava Cake................. 177
Cherry Cheesecake Bites 177
Key Lime Pie.. 177
White Chocolate Crème Brûlée 178
Dairy-Free Rice Pudding 178
White Chocolate–Lemon Pie 178
Chocolate Peanut Butter Popcorn 179

Stuffed Apples 179
Vanilla Bean Custard 179
Peach Cobbler 179
Lemon Bars.. 180
Carrot Date Cake 180
Berry Almond Bundt Cake 181
Brownies... 181
Banana Pudding Cake 181
Coconut Cake 182
Apple Crisp 182
Blueberry Crisp 182
Cinnamon Apples 183
Cinnamon Pineapple 183
Banana Chocolate Chip Bundt Cake 183
Warm Caramel Apple Dip 183
Pumpkin Pudding 184
Orange Walnut Coffee Cake 184
Caramelized Plantains.......................... 184
Blueberry Pudding Cake 185
Maple Pecan Pears 185
Strawberry Chocolate Chip Cakes 185
Red Velvet Cake 186
Apple Bundt Cake................................ 186
Banana Sundae with Strawberry Sauce . 187
Peanut Butter Pudding 187
Zucchini Cake...................................... 187
Blueberry Almond Cakes 188
Chocolate Rice Pudding 188
Walnut Brownies 188

4 Weeks Meal Plan 189

Week 1... 189
Week 2... 189
Week 3... 190
Week 4... 190

Conclusion 191

Appendix 1 Measurement Conversion Chart..192

Appendix 2 Recipes Index 193

Instant Pot is a versatile multi-use pressure cooker. You can call it with another name, "genius or miracle pot." It is a secret weapon in your kitchen. Instant Pot is a great kitchen appliance for busy people and helps them to save time, energy, and money. No doubt, Instant Pot can change the way of life.

Cooking with Instant Pot is super easy and fun. Everyone is excited and enjoys the versatility and ease of getting mouthwatering and creative meals on the dining table in a hurry. It is a great cooking appliance that saves you many hours every week.

With this Instant Pot cooking appliance, you can cook flavorful, healthy, and quick meals with little effort. It comes with various cooking functions, cooking accessories, and user-friendly operating buttons. In this cookbook, you will get delicious and healthy recipes. You can prepare them at any time or on any occasion.

The Instant Pot makes our life easier. It cooks food in very less time. You can spend many hours with your family. You can prepare any meal like chicken, beef, lamb, pork, vegetables, appetizer, soup, stews, dips, sauces, grains, beans, rice, yogurt, fish/seafood, dessert, snacks, and many more. You don't need any other appliance because it offers all cooking functions.

It is safe to use and easy to understand. It provides the families and households with everything they need from the Instant pot, but at the accurate settings and possible size. Let's find out more about this wonderful Instant Pot cooking appliance that can make you fall in love with cooking all over again!

HAPPY COOKING!!!

Fundamentals of Instant Pot

What Is Instant Pot

The Instant Pot is a wonderful kitchen appliance. It comes with two smart programs: Pressure cooking includes steam, pressure cook, porridge, soup/broth, rice, meat/stews, bean/chili, etc. No pressure cooking includes slow cook, sauté, yogurt, and keep warm, etc. It comes with useful accessories, including the top lid, bottom lid, inner pot, cooker base, steam rack, condensation collector, and control panel. It has user-friendly operating buttons. Using Instant Pot cooking appliance, prepare chicken, beef, lamb, pork, seafood, vegetables, dessert, appetizer/snacks, soups/broth, yogurt, beans, rice meals. It makes life comfortable.

The Instant Pot is wonderful for the family budget. You didn't need to bring a complex shopping list. In this cookbook, you will find simple and common ingredients for each recipe. You can create different meals using your favorite ingredients and spices.

Benefits of Using Instant Pot

Here are some benefits of using the Instant Pot:

Time, Money, and Energy Saving Pot:
Pressure cooking is one of the most affordable ways to cook large budget-friendly foods. It saves your time and takes your some hours in the week. It doesn't allow you to bring complex shopping for cooking meals. You will spend 4 to 5 hours with your family and cook food within 1 hour. You didn't need to purchase separate kitchen appliances such as pans/skillet, rice cooker, steamer, or slow cooker. It is the best pot for busy people. In the morning, you can prepare breakfast in very little time. Then, you can go on your work.

Multi-Functions:
The Instant Pot offers many useful functions such as steam, pressure cook, porridge, soup/broth, rice, meat/stews, bean/chili, slow cook, sauté, yogurt, and keep warm, etc. Now, you can prepare any meal using these cooking functions. Using this cooking appliance, you will get tender, healthy, and delicious meals.

Cool Accessories:
When you purchase this appliance, you will have some cool accessories, which you can use in everyday cooking. The accessories include a steam rack, inner pot, cooker base, condensation collector, top lid, etc. It is an excellent way to get started cooking. You don't need to purchase additional accessories before you start cooking. The cleaning process of these accessories is super easy.

Safe to Use:
High pressure or high temperature can make you afraid of using this appliance, especially children. However, Instant Pot has created a safety mechanism, which almost certainly guarantees that the appliance will continue to cook without any problems. There is nothing that kids and adults should be afraid of. The best way is to read about this appliance before cooking. I added all information, including safety tips, in my cookbook. You can read it before cooking food.

First Use

When you purchase an Instant Pot appliance, remove all the cooker and accessories packaging.

Cleaning before First Use:
Remove the inner pot from the cooker base and rinse it with hot and soapy water. Wash with warm and clean water and use a soft cloth or dry the exterior of the pot or you can put the inner pot in the dishwasher.

Wipe the heating element with a soft cloth before returning the inner pot to the cooker base. Make sure that there are no dust and package particles present. The inner pot is a main part of the Instant Pot. The food is placed into the inner pot, not directly in the cooker base.

If you see the deformed or damaged inner pot, return it because it will cause personal injury or damage the appliance.

Install Condensation Collector:
Dry the inner pot, cooker base, and accessories before returning to the main unit. When all parts are inserted in the main pot, install the condensation collector at the rear of the cooker by aligning the top of the collector and press in. When done, place the steam release handle on the lid.

Before Using Instant Pot:
If you want to remove the lid, hold the handle, turn the lid counterclockwise, and lift the lid. Remove the inner pot from the main unit. Place food and liquid into the inner pot according to the recipe instructions. Place the steam rack if using the steam cooking function onto the bottom of the inner pot first. Wipe outside of the unit and make sure that there is no food debris on the bottom side of the inner pot.

Return the inner pot to the unit and rotate slightly. Check and make sure that the sealing ring rack is completely set on the inner side of the sealing ring. Check and make sure that there is no deformation on the sealing ring rack. Close the lid.

Ensure that the steam release valve, float valve, and anti-block shield are dust-free and debris-free. After putting a lid on, ensure that the float valve drops down. Do not put the lid on if you use a Sauté cooking function.

Initial Test:
Add three cups of water into the inner pot. Close the lid.

After that, turn the steam release handle to the sealing position. Then, press the "steam" button onto the control panel. Adjust the time for two minutes. It will take ten seconds to preheat. The display shows "ON" on the screen. The steam will release until the float valve pops up. The steam cooking function will start when pressure is reached. The instant pot will beep when cooking time is completed and turn to the "Keep Warm" button.

Introduction to Pressure Cooking:
Pressure cooking is a versatile method to cook any meal. It is an efficient way to cook food quickly. You can cook your favorite meals using pressure cooking.

The pressure cooker has three stages when pressure cooking:

Preheating and Pressurization:
Select desired cooking program in pressure cooking. The main unit will take ten seconds to ensure you have selected the cooking function. The display shows "ON" onto the screen to signify it has started preheating. When the Instant pot is preheated, the liquid is vaporized in the inner pot to build steam. When the steam has built up, the float valve pops up. It would be best if you locked the lid for safe cooking.

When the float valve pops up, the silicone cap attached to the bottom of the float valve seals the steam inner side of the cooking chamber. Allow the pressure to rise. If pressure is high, then it means that the cooking temperature is high.

High pressure = High temperature

Cooking:
When the float valve pops up, the main unit needs a few minutes to build pressure. When desired pressure level is reached, cooking starts. The display shows "ON" onto the screen in HH: MM (hours: mins)

Smart program settings – pressure level (HI or Lo), Temperature, Cooking time, and Keeping warm will automatically be on or off. You can adjust at any time during cooking.

Depressurization:
When pressure cooking is completed, read the recipe instructions for depressurization of the main unit. If automatic keep warm is on, the display shows counting automatically. If not, adjust the cooking time. When cooking time is completed, the display shows "END."

There are two methods for the venting process:

Natural Release Method:
Some recipes call the natural release method to release steam or pressure. Leave the steam releases to handle in the sealing position. If the cooking temperature is dropped, the unit depressurizes naturally. The depressurization time increases vary based on the quantity of food and liquid. When the cooker has depressurized, the float valve drops in the lid of the main unit.

Quick-Release Method:
Some recipes call the quick release method to release steam or pressure. Turn the steam releases handle from the sealing position to the venting position. Use the natural release method to vent the remaining pressure/steam.

10-minute Natural Release:
Leave the steam releases to handle in the sealing position for ten minutes after cooking is completed, then turn the steam release handle to the venting position.

Main Functions of Instant Pot

There are two programs in the Instant Pot cooking appliance: Pressure cooking and Non-pressure cooking.

Pressure cooking has the following cooking functions:
• Pressure cook, Soup/Broth, Meat/Stew, Bean/Chili, Rice, Porridge, and Steam, etc

The non-pressure cooking has the following cooking functions:
• Slow cook, Sauté, Yogurt, and Keep warm, etc.

Pressure Cooking Programs

1. Pressure Cook:
Pressure cooking is the most used cooking function. It cooks food under high pressure. It takes 30 minutes to prepare a meal.

Cooking Method of Using Pressure Cook:
• Place steam rack in the bottom of the inner pot.
• Add liquid to the inner pot. Place ingredients onto the steam rack.
• Insert the inner pot in the cooker base. Close lid.
• Select "Pressure Cook" cooking function.

- Select "High" or "Low" pressure level. Press "Keep warm" to turn the automatic "Keep Warm" setting on or off.
- Press the start button to begin cooking.
- Follow the direction of the recipe to choose the exact venting method.

Cooking function	Setting	Suggested use	Imp note
Pressure cook	Less/normal/more	Manual programming	Press pressure level to toggle between high and low pressure Press +/- button to select cooking time Adjust according to the recipe instruction

Note: You can use the following liquids using the pressure cooking method: Stock, soup, broth, juice, water, filter water, etc.

2. Steam:

The steam cooking method is mostly used for vegetables. You can steam any vegetable. Insert steam rack in the bottom of the inner pot.
Cooking Method of Using Steam:
- Place steam rack in the bottom of the inner pot.
- Add liquid/broth/water/stock in the inner pot. Place ingredients onto the steam rack.
- Insert the inner pot in the cooker base. Close lid.
- Select "Steam" cooking function.
- Select "High" or "Low" pressure level. Press "Keep Warm" to turn automatic keep the warm setting on or off.
- Press the start button to begin cooking.
- Follow the direction of the recipe to choose the exact venting method.

Cooking function	Setting	Suggested use	Imp note
Steam	Less/normal/more	Vegetables/Fish and Seafood/ Meat	Insert steam rack in the bottom of the inner pot to elevate food from cooking liquid Use quick-release method to prevent food from burning/overcooking

3. Rice:

You can cook white rice, basmati rice, short-grain, and jasmine rice using the rice cooking method. It prefers high pressure to cook rice.
Cooking Method of Using Rice:
- Add liquid/broth/water/stock in the inner pot. Place rice into the pot.
- Insert the inner pot in the cooker base. Close lid.
- Select "Rice" cooking function.
- Select "High" or "Low" pressure level. Press "Keep Warm" to turn automatic keep the warm setting on or off.
- Press the start button to begin cooking.
- Follow the direction of the recipe to choose the exact venting method.

Cooking function	Setting	Suggested use	Imp note
Rice	Less/Normal/More	Tender/Normal texture/Soft texture	Automated cooking smart program. Depending upon the quantity of rice, adjust the cooking time – the cooking range is 8-15 minutes. When cooking time is done, wait for ten minutes. Use quick method to release pressure or release remaining pressure using natural release method

4. Bean/Chili:

Using the bean/chili cooking method, you can cook various beans, including black-eyed peas, kidney beans, and white beans. It prefers high pressure to cook bean/chili.

Cooking Method of Using Bean/Chili:
- Add liquid/broth/water/stock in the inner pot. Place bean/chili into the pot.
- Insert the inner pot in the cooker base. Close lid.
- Select the "Bean/Chili" cooking function.
- Select "High" or "Low" pressure level. Press "Keep Warm" to turn the automatic "Keep Warm" setting on or off.
- Press the start button to begin cooking.
- Follow the direction of the recipe to choose the exact venting method.

Cooking function	Setting	Suggested use	Imp note
Bean/chili	Less/Normal/More	Firm texture/Soft texture/Very soft texture	Insert steam rack in the bottom of the inner pot to elevate food from cooking liquid Use a quick-release method to prevent food from burning/overcooking

5. Soup/Broth:

Using the soup/broth cooking method, you can prepare soup, stock, or broth. You need to select the "Soup" cooking function.

Cooking Method of Using Soup/Broth:
- Add liquid to the inner pot. Place ingredients into the pot.
- Insert the inner pot in the cooker base. Close lid.
- Select "Soup/Broth" cooking function.
- Select "High" or "Low" pressure level. Press "Keep Warm" to turn the automatic "Keep Warm" setting on or off.
- Press the start button to begin cooking.
- Follow the direction of the recipe to choose the exact venting method.

Cooking function	Setting	Suggested use	Imp note
Soup/Broth	Less/Normal/More	Soup without meat/soup with meat/bone broth	The Liquid remains clear because there is less boiling motion Use natural release method always when coup has a high starch content

6. Porridge:

Using the porridge cooking method, you can cook different kinds of grains. This cooking method prefers high pressure.

Cooking Method of Using Porridge:
- Add liquid to the inner pot. Place ingredients into the pot.
- Insert the inner pot in the cooker base. Close lid.
- Select "porridge" cooking function.
- Select "High" or "Low" pressure level. Press "Keep Warm" to turn the automatic "Keep Warm" setting on or off.
- Press the start button to begin cooking.
- Follow the direction of the recipe to choose the exact venting method.

Cooking function	Setting	Suggested use	Imp note
Porridge	Less/Normal/More	Rice porridge/ White rice, porridge/Oatmeal, rolled, steel-cut	Adjust cooking time according to the recipe's instructions. Use natural release method to release pressure when foods expand

7. Meat/Stew:

Using the meat/stew cooking method, you can cook chicken, beef, lamb, pork, and seafood and make different stews, including chicken stews, beef stew, vegetable stew, lamb stew, and sausage stew, and fish stew, etc.

Cooking Method of Using Meat/Stews:
- Add liquid to the inner pot. Place ingredients into the pot.
- Insert the inner pot in the cooker base. Close lid.
- Select the "meat/stews" cooking function.
- Select "High" or "Low" pressure level. Press "Keep Warm" to turn the automatic "Keep Warm" setting on or off.
- Press the start button to begin cooking.
- Follow the direction of the recipe to choose the exact venting method.

Cooking function	Setting	Suggested use	Imp note
Meat/stew	Less/Normal/More	Soft texture/Very soft texture/Fall off bone	Choose a setting on meat texture as you want. Adjust cooking time manually Let rest the meat for 5 to 30 minutes until tender or succulent

Non-Pressure Cooking Programs

1. Slow Cook:

Slow cook is a non-pressure cooking method. It takes a lot of time to cook food but gives tender and delicious meals. This cooking method is best for meats including chicken, beef, lamb, seafood, pork, etc.

Cooking Method of Using Slow Cook:
- Remove inner pot from cooker base.
- Place liquid and ingredients into the inner pot. Insert it into the cooker base. Close the lid or use a glass lid with a venting hole.
- After that, turn the steam release handle to the venting position.
- Select the "slow cook" cooking function.
- Press the cooking function again to adjust the temperature according to the recipe's instructions.
- Press +/- button to adjust the cooking time according to the recipe's instructions.
- Press "Keep Warm" to toggle the keep warm setting on or off.
- The display shows time in counting while cooking.
- When cooking time is completed, the display shows "END" onto the screen.

Cooking function	Setting	Suggested use	Imp note
Slow cook	Less/Normal/More	Low setting/Medium setting/High setting	Follow the recipe's instructions for slow cooking Cooking time should be set for a minimum of ten hours for best results

2. Sauté:

Sauté cooking method is used for sautéing meats, vegetables, and many more. You don't need to use water for this setting. Pour oil into the inner pot.

Cooking Method of Using Sauté:
- Insert the inner pot into the cooker base. But, don't put the lid.
- Select "sauté" cooking function.
- Press sauté mode again to adjust the cooking temperature.
- Wait for ten seconds; then display shows "ON" to indicate that it has started preheating.
- Place food in the inner pot when the display shows "HOT" onto the screen.
- When cooking time is completed, the display shows "END" onto the screen.

Cooking function	Setting	Suggested use	Imp note
Sauté	Less/Normal/More	Simmering/sautéing or searing/ stir-frying	The display shows "Hot" to "ON" indicates the main unit is maintaining the cooking temp 30 minutes is perfect cooking time for safety

Deglaze the Inner Pot (Turn Pressure Cooking to Sauté Mode):
You should sauté the meat and vegetables before pressure cooking because it is the perfect way to boost the flavor. If you are using sauté cooking mode after pressure cooking, deglaze the inner pot to ensure meal ingredients do not burn. Remove the ingredients from the inner pot and add water to the hot bottom surface to deglaze.

3. Yogurt:
Using yogurt function, you can make yogurt at home. You can add it to different dishes.
Cooking Method of Using Yogurt:
- Select "yogurt" cooking function.
- Press yogurt cooking mode again to select cooking time.
- Press +/- button to select the fermentation time if you want.
- Wait for ten seconds the unit begins preheating.
- The display shows cooking time in counting.
- When fermentation is completed, the unit beeps, and the display shows "END."

Cooking function	Setting	Suggested use	Imp note
Yogurt	Less/Normal/More	For low temperature fermentation/Fermenting milk after cultured has been included/Pasteurizing milk	Fermentation time is 24 hours Adjust the fermentation time according to the recipe's instructions. Pasteurizing time cannot be preset. When yogurt program is running, the display shows "BOIL." If you want extra thick yogurt, do pasteurize two times.

Buttons and User Guide of Instant Pot

The Instant Pot series has user-friendly operating buttons.

Pressure cooking temperature:
Select the cooking function and press "Pressure level" to toggle between HI and Lo pressure levels.
Pressure Cooking Time:
Select the cooking function, and then press the smart program button again to adjust the Less, Normal, and More cooking time options. Press +/- button to increase or decrease the time if you want.
Non-Pressure Cooking Temperature:
Select the non-pressure cooking functions, and then presses the smart program button again to Less, Normal and More cooking temperature levels if you want.
Non-Pressure Cooking Time:
Select the non-pressure cooking functions, and then presses +/- button to adjust the cooking time. The cooking time can be changed during cooking.
Cancel and Standby Mode:
When the unit is plugged in, the display shows "OFF" to indicate "Standby mode."
Press the "Cancel" button to stop the cooking function at any time. The main unit returns to standby mode.
Turn Sound ON/OFF:

15

Sound ON: When the main unit is in standby mode, press the + button until the displays show "ON" onto the screen.

Sound OFF: When the main unit is in standby mode, press and hold – button until the display shows "OFF" onto the screen.

Keep Warm:
The "Keep Warm" mode automatically turns on all cooking functions except Yogurt and Sauté.

Reset:
When the main unit is in standby mode, press the "cancel" button to reset cooking functions, temperature, pressure level, cooking time, etc.

Cooking Lid:
When the display shows "lid", it indicates that the pressure lid is not adequately secured or missing.

Preheat:
When the display shows "ON", it indicates that the main unit is preheating.

Display Timer:
The display shows "Time" onto the screen in the following:
• When the cooking function is running, the display timer is a countdown to indicate the cooking time remaining in the cooking function.
• The display timer countdown until the cooking function begins when the delay starts.
• When keep warm is running, the display timer counts to indicate how long food has been warming.

Auto:
The display shows "Auto" to indicate that the rice cooking function is running.

Boil:
The display shows "Boil" to indicate that the Yogurt function is pasteurizing.

Hot:
The display shows "Hot" to indicate that food should be placed in the inner pot – (In sauté cooking function).

End:
The display shows "End" to indicate that cooking time is completed.

Food Burn:
The display shows "Food burn" to indicate overheating in the cooking chamber.

Accessories of Instant Pot

The Instant Pot comes with different accessories.

1. Pressure Cooking Lid:
The pressure cooking lid is made with stainless steel. The pressure cooking lid is used in many cooking methods.
Open and remove the pressure lid:
• Grip the upper lid handle, turn it counterclockwise, and lift it.
Close the pressure lid:
• Turn the lid clockwise until the symbol present on the lid aligns with the symbol of the cooker base.

2. Steam Release Handle:
Turn the steam release handle from sealing to venting and vice versa, open and close the valve, venting, sealing the cooker as you want. When the unit releases pressure, steam is removed from the top of the steam release handle. It is the main accessory for your safety and pressure cooking. It must be installed before cooking.
Remove the steam release valve:
• Lift the steam release valve and wait until all steam is removed.
• Install the steam release handle
• Put steam release handle on steam release pipe and press down tightly.

3. Anti-Block Shield:
The anti-block shield should be installed because it is necessary to prevent food particles from the steam release pipe. It is an essential accessory for your safety.
Remove the anti-block shield:
• Lift the lid tightly and press firmly against the side of the anti-block shield with your thumbs.
• Install the anti-block shield:
• Put anti-block shield over prongs and press it down.

4. Sealing Ring:
You should install a sealing ring to create a tight sealing between the lid and cooker base. You should install a sealing ring before cooking. It should be cleaned after every use. You should install 1 sealing ring while using the unit.
Remove the sealing ring:

- Lift the edges of the silicone rubber and pull the sealing ring out. When the sealing ring is removed, check the rack to ensure it is secured.
Install the sealing rings:
- Put sealing ring over the sealing ring rack and press it firmly.

5. Float Valve:
The float valve shows that pressure is built up within the inner pot and appears in two positions.
Pressurized:
- The float valve is appeared and pops up with the lid.
Depressurized:
- The float valve is pinched into the lid.

6. Inner Pot:
The inner pot is an essential accessory in the Instant Pot appliance. Place food in the inner pot. Close the lid.

7. Cooker Base:
The cooker base is present at the bottom of the main unit. The inner pot is inserted into the cooker base. Don't place food directly in the cooker base.

Cleaning and Maintenance of Instant Pot

The cleaning process of Instant Pot is super easy. You should clean it after every use.

- Remove all accessories from the main unit, including the cooker base.
- Don't use chemical detergents, scouring pads or powdered on accessories.
- Rinse condensation collector after every use.
- Rinse sealing ring, anti-block shield, silicone cap, steam release valve, and float valve under hot and soapy water. You can put them in the dishwasher.
- Remove all small parts from the lid before cleaning.
- When the steam release valve is removed, clean the inner part of the steam release pipe to prevent clogging.
- Hold it vertically and turn it 360 degrees to remove water from the lid.
- If there is tough food residue stuck at the bottom, soak it in hot water for a few hours.
- If there is an odor present in the pot, combine 1 cup of white vinegar and 1 cup of water, run pressure cook for 5 to 10 minutes, and then use a quick method to release pressure.
- When all parts get dried, return to the main unit.
- Don't put the main unit in the dishwasher. Wipe the main unit with a soft cloth.
- Wipe the exterior part of the main unit with a moist and soft cloth.

Troubleshooting

Problem – 1
If you face difficulty in closing the lid
Possible reason
The sealing ring is not installed correctly.
May be contents in the Instant pot is still hot.
Solution
Again install the sealing ring properly
Turn the steam release handle to the venting position and slowly lower the lid on the cooker base.
Problem – 2
If you face difficulty in opening the lid
Possible reason
Pressure is present inside the unit
Solution
Release pressure according to the recipe's instructions.
Problem – 3
Steam is leaked from the side of the pressure lid
Possible reason
The lid is closed properly
The sealing ring is not installed
The sealing ring is damaged
Solution
Install the sealing ring
Replace the sealing ring
Open and then close the lid
Clean the sealing ring thoroughly

Vegetable:

FOOD	COOKING TIME
Sweet potato – cubed	2-4 minutes
Sweet potato – whole	12-15 minutes
Corn	3-5 minutes
Carrots	6-8 minutes
Butternut squash	4-6 minutes
Cauliflower	2-3 minutes
Brussels sprouts	2-3 minutes
Cabbage	2-3 minutes
Asparagus	1-2 minutes
Broccoli	1-2 minutes

Meats and Eggs:

FOOD	COOKING TIME
Eggs	5 minutes
Pork ribs	15-20 minutes
Lamb leg	15 minutes
Chicken breast	6-8 minutes
Chicken stock	40-45 minutes
Beef stew	20 minutes
Beef ribs	20-25 minutes
Whole chicken	8 minutes

Beans and Lentils:

FOOD	COOKING TIME
Soybeans (Soaked)	18-20 minutes
Lima beans (Soaked)	6-10 minutes
Yellow lentils (Dry)	1-2 minutes
Green lentils (Dry)	8-10 minutes
Kidney beans (Soaked)	6-9 minutes
Chickpeas (Soaked)	10-15 minutes
Black-eyed peas (Soaked)	4-5 minutes
Black beans (Soaked)	6-8 minutes

Seafood and Fish:

FOOD	COOKING TIME
Fish stock	7-8 minutes
Shrimp or prawn	1-3 minutes
Mussels	1-2 minutes
Whole fish	4-5 minutes

Ham and Hash

Prep time: 10 minutes| **Cook time:** 25 minutes| **Serves:** 1

2 large eggs
½ tablespoon butter, melted
¼ cup frozen hash browns or potatoes
2 tablespoons diced ham
½ tablespoon chopped pickled jalapeño peppers
2 tablespoons shredded Cheddar cheese
⅛ teaspoon salt
1 cup water
1 tablespoon salsa

Grease an 8-oz. ramekin. Set aside.
In a small bowl, whisk together eggs and butter.
Add potatoes, ham, jalapeños, Cheddar cheese, and salt. Combine completely.
Pour mixture into prepared ramekin and cover with foil.
Pour water into Inner Pot and add the Steam Rack. Place ramekin on Steam Rack.
Put on the pressure cooker's lid and turn the steam valve to "Sealing" position.
Press the "Pressure Cook" button two times to select "Less" option.
Use the Pressure Level button to adjust the pressure to "Low Pressure".
Once the cooking cycle is completed, allow the steam to release naturally.
When all the steam is released, remove the pressure lid from the top carefully.
Carefully remove ramekin from the Inner Pot and remove foil.
Serve topped with salsa.

Per Serving: Calories 334; Fat 10.9g; Sodium 354mg; Carbs 20.5g; Fiber 4.1g; Sugar 8.2g; Protein 06g

Cheddar Egg Puff

Prep time: 10 minutes| **Cook time:** 20 minutes| **Serves:** 1

2 large eggs
½ tablespoon butter, melted
2 tablespoons cottage cheese
1 tablespoon chopped green chilies
2 tablespoons shredded Cheddar cheese
½ tablespoon all-purpose flour
⅛ teaspoon salt
1/16 teaspoon black pepper
1/16 teaspoon garlic powder
1/16 teaspoon ground cayenne pepper
1 cup water

Grease an 8-oz. ramekin. Set aside.
In a small bowl, whisk together eggs and butter.
Add cottage cheese, chilies, Cheddar cheese, flour, salt, black pepper, garlic powder, and cayenne pepper.

Combine completely. Pour mixture into prepared ramekin and cover with foil.
Pour water into Inner Pot and add the Steam Rack. Place ramekin on Steam Rack.
Put on the pressure cooker's lid and turn the steam valve to "Sealing" position.
Press the "Pressure Cook" button two times to select "Less" option.
Use the "+/-" keys on the control panel to set the cooking time to 15 minutes.
Use the Pressure Level button to adjust the pressure to "Low Pressure".
Once the cooking cycle is completed, allow the steam to release naturally.
When all the steam is released, remove the pressure lid from the top carefully.
Carefully remove ramekin from Inner Pot and remove foil. Serve immediately.

Per Serving: Calories 284; Fat 9g; Sodium 441mg; Carbs 7g; Fiber 4.6g; Sugar 5g; Protein 19g

Avocado Toast with Boiled Egg

Prep time: 10 minutes| **Cook time:** 5 minutes| **Serves:** 1

1 cup water
1 large egg
½ medium avocado, peeled, pitted, and sliced
1 (1-oz.) slice sourdough bread, toasted
⅛ teaspoon salt
⅛ teaspoon black pepper
⅛ teaspoon crushed red pepper flakes
½ tablespoon roasted pepitas
½ teaspoon olive oil

Pour water into Inner Pot and add the Steam Rack. Place egg on Steam Rack.
Put on the pressure cooker's lid and turn the steam valve to "Sealing" position.
Press the "Pressure Cook" button two times to select "Less" option.
Use the Pressure Level button to adjust the pressure to "Low Pressure".
Use the "+/-" keys on the control panel to set the cooking time to 5 minutes.
Once the cooking cycle is completed, quickly and carefully turn the steam release handle from Sealing position to the Venting position.
When all the steam is released, remove the pressure lid from the top carefully.
Spread avocado slices evenly over toast.
Carefully peel soft-boiled egg and place it on top of avocado.
Sprinkle salt, black pepper, red pepper flakes, pepitas, and oil over avocado.
Break open egg with fork and serve immediately.

Per Serving: Calories 219; Fat 10g; Sodium 891mg; Carbs 22.9g; Fiber 4g; Sugar 4g; Protein 13g

Feta Frittata

Prep time: 10 minutes| **Cook time:** 10 minutes| **Serves:** 1

2 large eggs
½ tablespoon heavy cream
2 tablespoons chopped spinach
2 tablespoons crumbled feta cheese
½ tablespoon chopped kalamata olives
1 cup water
¼ teaspoon balsamic glaze
⅛ teaspoon salt

Grease an 8-oz. ramekin. Set aside.
In a small bowl, whisk together eggs and cream. Add spinach, feta, and olives. Combine completely.
Pour mixture into prepared ramekin and cover with foil.
Pour water into Inner Pot and add the Steam Rack. Place ramekin on Steam Rack.
Put on the pressure cooker's lid and turn the steam valve to "Sealing" position.
Press the "Pressure Cook" button two times to select "Less" option.
Use the "+/-" keys on the control panel to set the cooking time to 10 minutes.
Use the Pressure Level button to adjust the pressure to "Low Pressure".
Once the cooking cycle is completed, allow the steam to release naturally.
When all the steam is released, remove the pressure lid from the top carefully.
Drizzle with balsamic glaze and salt.
Serve immediately.

Per Serving: Calories 382; Fat 12.9g; Sodium 414mg; Carbs 11g; Fiber 5g; Sugar 9g; Protein 21g

Bacon-Cheddar Egg Bites

Prep time: 10 minutes| **Cook time:** 8 minutes| **Serves:** 1

5 large eggs
¼ cup cottage cheese
⅛ teaspoon salt
1 tablespoon butter, melted
7 teaspoons crumbled bacon bits
7 tablespoons shredded Cheddar cheese
1 cup water

In a blender, combine eggs, cottage cheese, salt, and butter, and blend until smooth.
Spray a silicone egg bites mold with cooking spray.
Into each cup of the mold, add 1 teaspoon bacon bits.
Pour egg mixture into the mold, dividing mixture evenly among cups.
Top each egg bite with 1 tablespoon Cheddar, then cover the mold with foil.
Pour water into Inner Pot and add the Steam Rack. Place mold on Steam Rack.
Put on the pressure cooker's lid and turn the steam valve to "Sealing" position.
Press the "Pressure Cook" button one time to select "Less" option.

Use the "+/-" keys on the control panel to set the cooking time to 8 minutes.
Use the Pressure Level button to adjust the pressure to "High Pressure".
Once the cooking cycle is completed, allow the steam to release naturally.
When all the steam is released, remove the pressure lid from the top carefully.
Invert mold onto a plate and squeeze egg bites out.
Serve immediately.

Per Serving: Calories 372; Fat 20g; Sodium 891mg; Carbs 29g; Fiber 3g; Sugar 8g; Protein 17g

Maple Steel-Cut Oats

Prep time: 5 minutes| **Cook time:** 15 minutes| **Serves:** 1

⅓ cup steel-cut oats
1 cup water
3 tablespoons maple syrup
3 tablespoons vanilla almond milk

In the Inner Pot, combine oats and water.
Put on the pressure cooker's lid and turn the steam valve to "Sealing" position.
Press the "Pressure Cook" button two times to select "Less" option.
Use the "+/-" keys on the control panel to set the cooking time to 15 minutes.
Use the Pressure Level button to adjust the pressure to "Low Pressure".
Once the cooking cycle is completed, allow the steam to release naturally.
When all the steam is released, remove the pressure lid from the top carefully.
Stir oats and add maple syrup and almond milk. Ladle into a bowl and serve immediately.

Per Serving: Calories 354; Fat 10.9g; Sodium 454mg; Carbs 10g; Fiber 3.1g; Sugar 5.2g; Protein 10g

Brown Sugar Quinoa

Prep time: 10 minutes| **Cook time:** 2 minutes| **Serves:** 1

½ cup uncooked quinoa, rinsed
1 cup vanilla almond milk
1 tablespoon butter
1/16 teaspoon salt
2 tablespoons brown sugar
½ cup whole milk
¼ cup heavy cream

To the Inner Pot, add quinoa, almond milk, butter, and salt.
Put on the pressure cooker's lid and turn the steam valve to "Sealing" position.
Press the "Pressure Cook" button two times to select "Less" option.
Use the "+/-" keys on the control panel to set the cooking time to 2 minutes.
Use the Pressure Level button to adjust the pressure to "Low Pressure".

Once the cooking cycle is completed, allow the steam to release naturally.
When all the steam is released, remove the pressure lid from the top carefully.
Stir in brown sugar and milk and scoop into a bowl.
Serve topped with cream.

Per Serving: Calories 389; Fat 11g; Sodium 501mg; Carbs 28.9g; Fiber 4.6g; Sugar 8g; Protein 6g

Creamy Oatmeal

Prep time: 10 minutes| **Cook time:** 2 minutes| **Serves:** 1

½ cup rolled oats
1 cup water
1/16 teaspoon salt
½ tablespoon butter
3 teaspoons brown sugar
⅛ teaspoon vanilla extract
⅛ teaspoon ground cinnamon
½ tablespoon heavy cream

In the Inner Pot, combine oats, water, and salt.
Put on the pressure cooker's lid and turn the steam valve to "Sealing" position.
Press the "Pressure Cook" button two times to select "Less" option.
Use the "+/-" keys on the control panel to set the cooking time to 2 minutes.
Use the Pressure Level button to adjust the pressure to "Low Pressure".
Once the cooking cycle is completed, quickly and carefully turn the steam release handle from Sealing position to the Venting position.
When all the steam is released, remove the pressure lid from the top carefully.
Stir oats, then add butter, brown sugar, vanilla, cinnamon, and cream.
Scoop into a bowl and serve immediately.

Per Serving: Calories 284; Fat 9g; Sodium 441mg; Carbs 7g; Fiber 4.6g; Sugar 5g; Protein 19g

Coconut Oatmeal

Prep time: 10 minutes| **Cook time:** 15 minutes| **Serves:** 1

½ cup rolled oats
1 cup water
1/16 teaspoon salt
3 tablespoons cream of coconut
2 tablespoons whole milk
¼ cup raspberries
2 tablespoons toasted coconut

In the Inner Pot, combine oats, water, and salt.
Put on the pressure cooker's lid and turn the steam valve to "Sealing" position.
Press the "Pressure Cook" button two times to select "Less" option.
Use the "+/-" keys on the control panel to set the cooking time to 2 minutes.

Use the Pressure Level button to adjust the pressure to "Low Pressure".
Once the cooking cycle is completed, quickly and carefully turn the steam release handle from Sealing position to the Venting position.
When all the steam is released, remove the pressure lid from the top carefully.
Stir oats, then add cream of coconut and milk.
Scoop into a bowl and top with raspberries and toasted coconut.
Serve immediately.

Per Serving: Calories 349; Fat 2.9g; Sodium 511mg; Carbs 12g; Fiber 3g; Sugar 8g; Protein 17g

Blueberry- Oatmeal

Prep time: 10 minutes| **Cook time:** 2 minutes| **Serves:** 1

½ cup rolled oats
½ cup water
½ cup vanilla almond milk
1/16 teaspoon salt
3 tablespoons blueberries
3 teaspoons brown sugar
⅛ teaspoon almond extract
¼ teaspoon ground cinnamon
1 tablespoon heavy cream
1 tablespoon granola
2 teaspoons sliced almonds

In the Inner Pot, combine oats, water, almond milk, salt, and blueberries.
Put on the pressure cooker's lid and turn the steam valve to "Sealing" position.
Press the "Pressure Cook" button two times to select "Less" option.
Use the "+/-" keys on the control panel to set the cooking time to 2 minutes.
Use the Pressure Level button to adjust the pressure to "Low Pressure".
Once the cooking cycle is completed, quickly and carefully turn the steam release handle from Sealing position to the Venting position.
When all the steam is released, remove the pressure lid from the top carefully.
Stir oats, then add brown sugar, almond extract, and cinnamon.
Stir to combine and scoop into a bowl.
Top with cream, granola, and almonds.
Serve immediately.

Per Serving: Calories 372; Fat 20g; Sodium 891mg; Carbs 29g; Fiber 3g; Sugar 8g; Protein 17g

Breakfast Biscuits and Gravy

Prep time: 10 minutes| **Cook time:** 15 minutes| **Serves:** 1

1 slice uncooked thick-cut bacon, minced
¼ cup ground breakfast sausage
1 tablespoon all-purpose flour
1/16 teaspoon ground cayenne pepper
⅛ teaspoon salt
⅛ teaspoon black pepper

½ cup whole milk
2 cooked buttermilk biscuits, halved

Press the "Sauté" button two times to select "More" option.
Without the lid, add bacon and cook about 4 minutes until crispy.
Using a slotted spoon, remove bacon and set aside, leaving the bacon grease in the pot.
Add sausage and sauté about 5 minutes until browned and cooked through.
Sprinkle sausage with flour, cayenne pepper, salt, and black pepper.
Mix to fully coat sausage and cook 1 minute.
Whisk in milk. Cook gravy, whisking continuously, about 3–5 minutes until thickened.
Press Cancel button to turn off the heat and add bacon bits.
Lay biscuit halves on a serving plate and top with sausage mixture.
Serve immediately.

Per Serving: Calories 334; Fat 7.9g; Sodium 704mg; Carbs 6g; Fiber 3.6g; Sugar 6g; Protein 18g

Breakfast Grits

Prep time: 10 minutes| **Cook time:** 10 minutes| **Serves:** 1

¼ cup grits
½ cup whole milk
1 ½ cups water
1 tablespoon butter
3 tablespoons brown sugar
2 tablespoons heavy cream

In a suitable cake pan, add grits, milk, and ½ cup water, and mix to combine.
Pour remaining 1 cup water into Inner Pot and add the Steam Rack. Place pan on Steam Rack.
Put on the pressure cooker's lid and turn the steam valve to "Sealing" position.
Press the "Pressure Cook" button two times to select "Less" option.
Use the "+/-" keys on the control panel to set the cooking time to 10 minutes.
Use the Pressure Level button to adjust the pressure to "Low Pressure".
Once the cooking cycle is completed, quickly and carefully turn the steam release handle from Sealing position to the Venting position.
When all the steam is released, remove the pressure lid from the top carefully.
Carefully remove cake pan from Inner Pot and mix in butter, brown sugar, and cream.
Scoop into a bowl and serve, or enjoy immediately from the pan.

Per Serving: Calories 289; Fat 14g; Sodium 791mg; Carbs 8.9g; Fiber 4.6g; Sugar 8g; Protein 16g

Vegetable Egg White

Prep time: 10 minutes| **Cook time:** 15 minutes| **Serves:** 1

3 large egg whites
½ tablespoon butter, melted
2 tablespoons cottage cheese
1 tablespoon chopped and sautéed mushrooms
1 tablespoon chopped and sautéed red bell pepper
1 tablespoon chopped and sautéed yellow onion
2 tablespoons chopped and sautéed spinach
2 tablespoons shredded Cheddar cheese
½ tablespoon all-purpose flour
⅛ teaspoon salt
1/16 teaspoon black pepper
1/16 teaspoon garlic powder
1/16 teaspoon ground cayenne pepper
1 cup water

Grease an 8-oz. ramekin. Set aside.
In a small bowl, whisk together egg whites and butter.
Add cottage cheese, mushrooms, bell pepper, onion, spinach, Cheddar, flour, salt, black pepper, garlic powder, and cayenne pepper. Combine completely.
Pour mixture into prepared ramekin and cover with foil.
Pour water into the Inner Pot and then place the Steam Rack. Place ramekin on Steam Rack.
Put on the pressure cooker's lid and turn the steam valve to "Sealing" position.
Press the "Pressure Cook" button two times to select "Less" option.
Use the "+/-" keys on the control panel to set the cooking time to 15 minutes.
Use the Pressure Level button to adjust the pressure to "Low Pressure".
Once the cooking cycle is completed, allow the steam to release naturally.
When all the steam is released, remove the pressure lid from the top carefully.
Carefully remove ramekin from Inner Pot and remove foil.
Serve immediately.

Per Serving: Calories 282; Fat 19g; Sodium 354mg; Carbs 15g; Fiber 5.1g; Sugar 8.2g; Protein 12g

Vanilla Bean Yogurt

Prep time: 10 minutes| **Cook time:** 6 hours | **Serves:** 1

¾ cup ultra-pasteurized whole milk
¼ teaspoon yogurt starter, such as store-bought plain yogurt
1 tablespoon sweetened condensed milk
¼ teaspoon vanilla extract
¼ teaspoon vanilla bean paste
1 cup water

In an 8-oz. Mason jar or ramekin, mix all ingredients except water very thoroughly.
Cover with plastic wrap or foil.

Pour water into Inner Pot and add the Steam Rack. Place jar on Steam Rack.
Press the "Yogurt" button one time to select "Normal" option.
Use the "+/-" keys on the control panel to set the cooking time to 6 hours.
Cover the jar with plastic wrap or the jar lid and then transfer to the refrigerator.
Chill overnight, then serve.

Per Serving: Calories 382; Fat 10.9g; Sodium 354mg; Carbs 20.5g; Fiber 4.1g; Sugar 8.2g; Protein 06g

Creamy Pumpkin Yogurt

Prep time: 10 minutes| **Cook time:** 6 hours | **Serves:** 2
¾ cup ultra-pasteurized whole milk
¼ teaspoon yogurt starter, such as store-bought plain yogurt
1 tablespoon sugar
⅛ teaspoon vanilla extract
1 ½ tablespoons pumpkin puree
1/16 teaspoon pumpkin pie spice
1 cup water

In an 8-oz. Mason jar or ramekin, mix all ingredients except water very thoroughly.
Cover with plastic wrap or foil.
Pour water into Inner Pot and add the Steam Rack. Place jar on Steam Rack.
Press the "Yogurt" button two times to select "Normal" option.
Use the "+/-" keys on the control panel to set the cooking time to 6 hours.
Chill overnight in the refrigerator, then serve.

Per Serving: Calories 221; Fat 7.9g; Sodium 704mg; Carbs 6g; Fiber 3.6g; Sugar 6g; Protein 18g

Blueberry French Toast Bake

Prep time: 10 minutes| **Cook time:** 35 minutes| **Serves:** 1
French Toast
1 large egg
¾ cup whole milk
2 tablespoons granulated sugar
¼ teaspoon vanilla extract
¼ teaspoon almond extract
4 slices stale Texas Toast bread, cubed into 1" pieces
¼ cup blueberries
¼ teaspoon ground cinnamon
½ tablespoon brown sugar
1 cup water
Cream Cheese Glaze
3 tablespoons confectioners' sugar
1 ½ tablespoons cream cheese, softened
⅛ teaspoon vanilla extract
¼ teaspoon whole milk

Grease a suitable cake pan. Set aside for later use.
In a small bowl, whisk together egg, milk, granulated sugar, vanilla, and almond extract.

Arrange bread cubes in prepared cake pan, then pour milk mixture over the top and let soak 5 minutes.
Sprinkle top with blueberries, cinnamon, and brown sugar.
Cover pan tightly with foil.
Pour water into Inner Pot and add the Steam Rack. Place pan on Steam Rack.
Put on the pressure cooker's lid and turn the steam valve to "Sealing" position.
Press the "Pressure Cook" button two times to select "Normal" option.
Use the Pressure Level button to adjust the pressure to "Low Pressure".
Once the cooking cycle is completed, quickly and carefully turn the steam release handle from Sealing position to the Venting position.
When all the steam is released, remove the pressure lid from the top carefully.
Carefully remove pan from the Inner Pot, remove foil, and cool 5 minutes.
Spread glaze evenly on bread and enjoy immediately.

Per Serving: Calories 289; Fat 14g; Sodium 791mg; Carbs 8.9g; Fiber 4.6g; Sugar 8g; Protein 16g

Banana Oatmeal

Prep time: 10 minutes| **Cook time:** 7 minutes| **Serves:** 6
3 cups old fashioned rolled oats
¼ teaspoon salt
2 large bananas, mashed (1 heaping cup)
2 large eggs, lightly beaten
⅓ cup xylitol

In a medium bowl, place the oats, salt, bananas, eggs, and xylitol and stir to combine well.
Lightly spray a suitable cake pan with cooking spray. Transfer the oat mixture to the pan.
Pour 1½ cups water into the Inner Pot. Place a Steam Rack in the Inner Pot and place the pan on the steam rack.
Put on the pressure cooker's lid and turn the steam valve to "Sealing" position.
Press the "Pressure Cook" button two times to select "Less" option.
Use the "+/-" keys on the control panel to set the cooking time to 7 minutes.
Use the Pressure Level button to adjust the pressure to "Low Pressure".
Once the cooking cycle is completed, allow the steam to release naturally.
When all the steam is released, remove the pressure lid from the top carefully.
Allow the oatmeal to cool 5 minutes before serving.

Per Serving: Calories 334; Fat 10.9g; Sodium 454mg; Carbs 10g; Fiber 3.1g; Sugar 5.2g; Protein 10g

Sausage Pancake Bites

Prep time: 10 minutes| **Cook time:** 15 minutes| **Serves:** 1

1 cup pancake mix
¼ cup whole milk
1 ½ cups water
3 tablespoons maple syrup
3 ½ fully cooked frozen sausage links, split in half

Grease a silicone egg bites mold. Set aside.
In a small bowl, mix together pancake mix, milk, ½ cup water, and maple syrup.
Spoon 1 ½ tablespoons batter into each cup of prepared mold.
Place half of a sausage link in the middle of the batter in each cup, pressing down slightly.
Top each sausage link with an additional ½ tablespoon batter.
Cover the mold with a paper towel, then cover tightly with foil.
Pour remaining 1 cup water into Inner Pot and add the Steam Rack. Place mold on Steam Rack.
Put on the pressure cooker's lid and turn the steam valve to "Sealing" position.
Press the "Pressure Cook" button two times to select "Less" option.
Use the "+/-" keys on the control panel to set the cooking time to 15 minutes.
Use the Pressure Level button to adjust the pressure to "Low Pressure".
Once the cooking cycle is completed, allow the steam to release naturally.
When all the steam is released, remove the pressure lid from the top carefully.
Carefully remove mold from Inner Pot, then invert pancake bites onto a plate.
Serve immediately.

Per Serving: Calories 372; Fat 7.9g; Sodium 704mg; Carbs 6g; Fiber 3.6g; Sugar 6g; Protein 18g

Denver Omelet

Prep time: 10 minutes| **Cook time:** 15 minutes| **Serves:** 1

2 large eggs
½ tablespoon butter, melted
2 tablespoons cottage cheese
2 tablespoons diced ham
1 tablespoon diced and sautéed red onion
1 tablespoon diced green bell pepper
2 tablespoons shredded Cheddar cheese
⅛ teaspoon salt
1 cup water

Grease an 8-oz. ramekin. Set aside for later use.
In a small bowl, whisk together eggs and butter. Add cottage cheese, ham, onion, bell pepper, Cheddar, and salt. Combine completely.
Pour mixture into prepared ramekin and cover with foil.
Pour water into Inner Pot and add the Steam Rack. Place ramekin on Steam Rack.

Put on the pressure cooker's lid and turn the steam valve to "Sealing" position.
Press the "Pressure Cook" button two times to select "Less" option.
Use the "+/-" keys on the control panel to set the cooking time to 15 minutes.
Use the Pressure Level button to adjust the pressure to "Low Pressure".
Once the cooking cycle is completed, allow the steam to release naturally.
When all the steam is released, remove the pressure lid from the top carefully.
Carefully remove ramekin from Inner Pot and remove foil.
Serve immediately.

Per Serving: Calories 219; Fat 10g; Sodium 891mg; Carbs 22.9g; Fiber 4g; Sugar 4g; Protein 13g

Egg Kale Casserole

Prep time: 10 minutes| **Cook time:** 20 minutes| **Serves:** 6

1 tablespoon avocado oil
1 small yellow onion, peeled and chopped
5 large kale leaves, tough stems removed and finely chopped
1 clove garlic, diced
2 tablespoons lemon juice
½ teaspoon salt
9 large eggs
2 tablespoons water
1½ teaspoons dried rosemary
1 teaspoon dried oregano
¼ teaspoon black pepper
½ cup nutritional yeast

Add the oil to the pot, Press the "Sauté" button two time to select "Normal" mode and heat oil for 1 minute.
Add the onion and sauté 2 minutes until just softened.
Add the kale, garlic, lemon juice, and ¼ teaspoon salt. Stir and allow to cook 2 minutes more. Press the Cancel button.
Meanwhile, in a medium bowl, whisk together the eggs, water, rosemary, oregano, ¼ teaspoon salt, pepper, and nutritional yeast.
Add the onion and kale mixture to the egg mixture and stir to combine.
Rinse the Inner Pot, add 2 cups water, and place a steam rack inside.
Spray a 7" spring form pan with cooking spray. Transfer the egg mixture to the spring form pan.
Place the pan on the steam rack and secure the lid.
Put on the pressure cooker's lid and turn the steam valve to "Sealing" position.
Press the "Pressure Cook" button two times to select "Less" option.
Use the "+/-" keys on the control panel to set the cooking time to 12 minutes.
Use the Pressure Level button to adjust the pressure to "Low Pressure".
Once the cooking cycle is completed, quickly and carefully turn the steam release handle from Sealing position to the Venting position.

When all the steam is released, remove the pressure lid from the top carefully.
Remove the pan from pot and allow to cool 5 minutes before slicing and serving.

Per Serving: Calories 334; Fat 12.9g; Sodium 414mg; Carbs 11g; Fiber 5g; Sugar 9g; Protein 11g

Raspberry Steel Cut Oatmeal Bars

Prep time: 10 minutes| **Cook time:** 15 minutes| **Serves:** 6

3 cups steel cut oats
3 large eggs
2 cups unsweetened vanilla almond milk
⅓ cup Erythritol
1 teaspoon pure vanilla extract
¼ teaspoon salt
1 cup frozen raspberries

In a medium bowl, mix together all ingredients except the raspberries.
Once the ingredients are well combined, fold in the raspberries.
Spray a 6" cake pan with cooking oil.
Transfer the oat mixture to the pan and cover the pan with aluminum foil.
Pour 1 cup water into the Inner Pot and place the Steam Rack inside.
Place the pan with the oat mixture on top of the rack.
Put on the pressure cooker's lid and turn the steam valve to "Sealing" position.
Press the "Pressure Cook" button two times to select "Less" option.
Use the "+/-" keys on the control panel to set the cooking time to 15 minutes.
Use the Pressure Level button to adjust the pressure to "Low Pressure".
Once the cooking cycle is completed, quickly and carefully turn the steam release handle from Sealing position to the Venting position.
When all the steam is released, remove the pressure lid from the top carefully.
Carefully remove the pan from the Inner Pot and remove the foil.
Allow to cool completely before cutting into bars and serving.

Per Serving: Calories 284; Fat 9g; Sodium 441mg; Carbs 7g; Fiber 4.6g; Sugar 5g; Protein 19g

Blueberry Quinoa Porridge

Prep time: 10 minutes| **Cook time:** 1 minutes| **Serves:** 6

1½ cups dry quinoa
3 cups water
1 cup frozen wild blueberries
½ teaspoon pure stevia powder
1 teaspoon pure vanilla extract

Using a fine-mesh strainer, rinse the quinoa very well until the water runs clear.
Add the quinoa, water, blueberries, stevia, and vanilla to the Inner Pot. Stir to combine.

Put on the pressure cooker's lid and turn the steam valve to "Sealing" position.
Press the "Pressure Cook" button two times to select "Less" option.
Use the "+/-" keys on the control panel to set the cooking time to 1 minute.
Use the Pressure Level button to adjust the pressure to "Low Pressure".
Once the cooking cycle is completed, quickly and carefully turn the steam release handle from Sealing position to the Venting position.
When all the steam is released, remove the pressure lid from the top carefully.
Allow the quinoa to cool slightly before spooning into bowls to serve.

Per Serving: Calories 221; Fat 7.9g; Sodium 704mg; Carbs 6g; Fiber 3.6g; Sugar 6g; Protein 18g

Buckwheat Granola

Prep time: 10 minutes| **Cook time:** 10 minutes| **Serves:** 8

1½ cups raw buckwheat groats
1½ cups old fashioned rolled oats
⅓ cup walnuts, chopped
⅓ cup unsweetened shredded coconut
¼ cup coconut oil, melted
1" piece fresh ginger, peeled and grated
3 tablespoons date syrup
1 teaspoon ground cinnamon
¼ teaspoon salt

In a medium bowl, mix together the buckwheat groats, oats, walnuts, and shredded coconut until well combined.
Add the coconut oil, ginger, date syrup, cinnamon, and salt and stir to combine.
Transfer this mixture to a 6" cake pan.
Pour 1 cup water into the Inner Pot and place a Steam Rack inside. Place the pan on the rack.
Put on the pressure cooker's lid and turn the steam valve to "Sealing" position.
Press the "Pressure Cook" button two times to select "Less" option.
Use the "+/-" keys on the control panel to set the cooking time to 10 minutes.
Use the Pressure Level button to adjust the pressure to "Low Pressure".
Once the cooking cycle is completed, quickly and carefully turn the steam release handle from Sealing position to the Venting position.
When all the steam is released, remove the pressure lid from the top carefully.
Spread the granola onto a large sheet pan and allow it to cool, undisturbed, for 1 hour. It will crisp as it cools.

Per Serving: Calories 282; Fat 19g; Sodium 354mg; Carbs 15g; Fiber 5.1g; Sugar 8.2g; Protein 12g

Cinnamon Oatmeal Muffins

Prep time: 10 minutes| **Cook time:** 15 minutes| **Serves:** 6

3 cups old fashioned rolled oats
1 teaspoon baking powder
¼ teaspoon salt
1 teaspoon ground cinnamon
¼ cup unsweetened vanilla almond milk
¼ cup fresh orange juice
3⅓ cups mashed bananas
1 large egg
¼ cup Erythritol

In a medium bowl, mix all of the ingredients together, stirring until well combined.
Place six silicone muffin cups inside of a suitable cake pan.
Spoon the oatmeal mixture into the muffin cups. Cover the pan with aluminum foil.
Pour 1 cup water into the Inner Pot and place the Steam Rack inside.
Place the cake pan with the muffins on the rack.
Put on the pressure cooker's lid and turn the steam valve to "Sealing" position.
Press the "Pressure Cook" button two times to select "Less" option.
Use the "+/-" keys on the control panel to set the cooking time to 15 minutes.
Use the Pressure Level button to adjust the pressure to "Low Pressure".
Once the cooking cycle is completed, quickly and carefully turn the steam release handle from Sealing position to the Venting position.
When all the steam is released, remove the pressure lid from the top carefully.
Carefully remove the pan from the Inner Pot and remove the foil from the top.
Serve.

Per Serving: Calories 372; Fat 20g; Sodium 891mg; Carbs 29g; Fiber 3g; Sugar 8g; Protein 7g

Chocolate Oatmeal

Prep time: 10 minutes| **Cook time:** 6 minutes| **Serves:** 4

1 cup steel cut oats
1 (125-oz.) can full-fat unsweetened coconut milk
2 cups water
½ cup cacao powder
½ cup Erythritol
⅛ teaspoon sea salt

Place the oats, coconut milk, water, cacao powder, Erythritol, and salt in the Inner Pot and stir to combine.
Put on the pressure cooker's lid and turn the steam valve to "Sealing" position.
Press the "Pressure Cook" button two times to select "Less" option.
Use the "+/-" keys on the control panel to set the cooking time to 6 minutes.
Use the Pressure Level button to adjust the pressure to "Low Pressure".

Once the cooking cycle is completed, quickly and carefully turn the steam release handle from Sealing position to the Venting position. When all the steam is released, remove the pressure lid from the top carefully.
Allow the oatmeal to cool slightly before spooning into bowls to serve.

Per Serving: Calories 361; Fat 7.9g; Sodium 704mg; Carbs 6g; Fiber 3.6g; Sugar 6g; Protein 18g

Banana Date Porridge

Prep time: 10 minutes| **Cook time:** 4 minutes| **Serves:** 4

1 cup buckwheat groats
1½ cups unsweetened vanilla almond milk
1 cup water
1 large banana, mashed
5 pitted dates, chopped
¾ teaspoon ground cinnamon
¾ teaspoon pure vanilla extract

Place the buckwheat groats, almond milk, water, banana, dates, cinnamon, and vanilla in the Inner Pot and stir.
Put on the pressure cooker's lid and turn the steam valve to "Sealing" position.
Press the "Pressure Cook" button two times to select "Less" option.
Use the "+/-" keys on the control panel to set the cooking time to 4 minutes.
Use the Pressure Level button to adjust the pressure to "Low Pressure".
Once the cooking cycle is completed, quickly and carefully turn the steam release handle from Sealing position to the Venting position.
When all the steam is released, remove the pressure lid from the top carefully.
Allow the porridge to cool slightly before spooning into bowls to serve.

Per Serving: Calories 349; Fat 2.9g; Sodium 511mg; Carbs 12g; Fiber 3g; Sugar 8g; Protein 7g

Banana Walnut Oats

Prep time: 10 minutes| **Cook time:** 4 minutes| **Serves:** 4

2 cups steel cut oats
2½ cups water
2½ cups unsweetened vanilla almond milk
3 medium bananas, thinly sliced
1½ teaspoons ground cinnamon
1 teaspoon pure vanilla extract
¼ teaspoon salt
4 tablespoons walnut pieces

Add the steel cut oats, water, almond milk, banana slices, cinnamon, vanilla, and salt to the Inner Pot and stir to combine.
Put on the pressure cooker's lid and turn the steam valve to "Sealing" position.
Press the "Pressure Cook" button two times to select "Less" option.

Use the "+/-" keys on the control panel to set the cooking time to 4 minutes.
Use the Pressure Level button to adjust the pressure to "Low Pressure".
Once the cooking cycle is completed, allow the steam to release naturally for 10 minutes, turn the steam release handle to the Venting position.
When all the steam is released, remove the pressure lid from the top carefully.
Serve the oatmeal in a bowl topped with 1 tablespoon walnut pieces for each serving.

Per Serving: Calories 284; Fat 9g; Sodium 441mg; Carbs 7g; Fiber 4.6g; Sugar 5g; Protein 19g

Artichoke Egg Casserole

Prep time: 10 minutes| **Cook time:** 18 minutes| **Serves:** 8
12 large eggs
¼ cup water
4 cups baby spinach, roughly chopped
1 (14-oz.) can baby artichoke hearts, drained and roughly chopped
1 tablespoon chopped fresh chives
1 tablespoon fresh lemon juice
¾ teaspoon table salt
½ teaspoon black pepper
¼ teaspoon garlic salt

Spray a suitable round pan or 7-cup round glass bowl with cooking spray.
In a medium bowl, whisk together the eggs and water.
Stir in the spinach, artichokes, chives, lemon juice, table salt, pepper, and garlic salt.
Transfer the mixture to the prepared pan.
Place 2 cups water in the Inner Pot and place the Steam Rack inside. Place the pan on top of the Steam Rack.
Put on the pressure cooker's lid and turn the steam valve to "Sealing" position.
Press the "Pressure Cook" button two times to select "Less" option.
Use the "+/-" keys on the control panel to set the cooking time to 18 minutes.
Use the Pressure Level button to adjust the pressure to "Low Pressure".
Once the cooking cycle is completed, quickly and carefully turn the steam release handle from Sealing position to the Venting position.
When all the steam is released, remove the pressure lid from the top carefully.
Remove egg casserole from pot and allow to cool 5 minutes before slicing and serving.

Per Serving: Calories 219; Fat 10g; Sodium 891mg; Carbs 22.9g; Fiber 4g; Sugar 4g; Protein 13g

Almond Granola

Prep time: 10 minutes| **Cook time:** 7 minutes| **Serves:** 8
1½ cups old fashioned rolled oats
½ cup unsweetened shredded coconut

¼ cup monk fruit sweetener
⅛ teaspoon salt
¾ cup almond butter
¼ cup coconut oil

In a medium bowl, mix together the oats, coconut, sweetener, and salt.
Add the almond butter and oil and mix until well combined.
Spray a 6" cake pan with nonstick cooking oil.
Transfer the oat mixture to the pan.
Add 1 cup water to the Inner Pot of your Instant Pot.
Place the steam rack inside, and place the pan on top of the steam rack.
Put on the pressure cooker's lid and turn the steam valve to "Sealing" position.
Press the "Pressure Cook" button two times to select "Less" option.
Use the "+/-" keys on the control panel to set the cooking time to 7 minutes.
Use the Pressure Level button to adjust the pressure to "Low Pressure".
Once the cooking cycle is completed, quickly and carefully turn the steam release handle from Sealing position to the Venting position.
When all the steam is released, remove the pressure lid from the top carefully.
Remove the pan from the Inner Pot and transfer the granola to a baking sheet to cool completely.
Serve.

Per Serving: Calories 382; Fat 10.9g; Sodium 354mg; Carbs 20.5g; Fiber 4.1g; Sugar 8.2g; Protein 06g

Pumpkin Quinoa

Prep time: 10 minutes| **Cook time:** 1 minutes| **Serves:** 4
¾ cup dry quinoa
2 cups water
¾ cup pumpkin purée
¼ cup monk fruit sweetener
1½ teaspoons pumpkin pie spice
1 teaspoon pure vanilla extract
¼ teaspoon salt

Using a fine-mesh strainer, rinse the quinoa very well until the water runs clear.
Add the quinoa, water, pumpkin purée, sweetener, pumpkin pie spice, vanilla, and salt to the Inner Pot.
Stir to combine.
Put on the pressure cooker's lid and turn the steam valve to "Sealing" position.
Press the "Pressure Cook" button two times to select "Less" option.
Use the "+/-" keys on the control panel to set the cooking time to 1 minute.
Use the Pressure Level button to adjust the pressure to "Low Pressure".
Once the cooking cycle is completed, quickly and carefully turn the steam release handle from Sealing position to the Venting position.
When all the steam is released, remove the pressure lid from the top carefully.

Allow the quinoa to cool slightly before spooning into bowls to serve.

Per Serving: Calories 351; Fat 7.9g; Sodium 704mg; Carbs 6g; Fiber 3.6g; Sugar 6g; Protein 18g

Poppy Seed Oatmeal Cups

Prep time: 10 minutes| **Cook time:** 5 minutes| **Serves:** 4

2 cups old fashioned rolled oats
1 teaspoon baking powder
2 tablespoons Erythritol
1 tablespoon poppy seeds
¼ teaspoon salt
1 large egg
Juice and zest from 1 Meyer lemon
1 cup unsweetened vanilla almond milk

Lightly grease four (8-oz.) ramekin dishes. Set aside.
In a medium bowl, mix together the oats, baking powder, Erythritol, poppy seeds, and salt.
Add the egg, juice and zest from the lemon, and the almond milk and stir to combine.
Divide the oatmeal mixture into the four dishes.
Pour ½ cup water into the Inner Pot of the Instant Pot.
Place the Steam Rack inside the Inner Pot and place the ramekins on top of the rack.
Put on the pressure cooker's lid and turn the steam valve to "Sealing" position.
Press the "Pressure Cook" button two times to select "Less" option.
Use the "+/-" keys on the control panel to set the cooking time to 5 minutes.
Use the Pressure Level button to adjust the pressure to "Low Pressure".
Once the cooking cycle is completed, quickly and carefully turn the steam release handle from Sealing position to the Venting position.
When all the steam is released, remove the pressure lid from the top carefully.
Serve.

Per Serving: Calories 289; Fat 14g; Sodium 791mg; Carbs 8.9g; Fiber 4.6g; Sugar 8g; Protein 16g

Apple Steel Cut Oats

Prep time: 10 minutes| **Cook time:** 4 minutes| **Serves:** 6

2 cups steel cut oats
3 cups unsweetened vanilla almond milk
3 cups water
3 small apples, peeled, cored, and cut into 1"-thick chunks
2 teaspoons ground cinnamon
¼ cup date syrup
¼ teaspoon salt

Add the steel cut oats, almond milk, water, apple chunks, cinnamon, date syrup, and salt to the Inner Pot and stir to combine.

Put on the pressure cooker's lid and turn the steam valve to "Sealing" position.
Press the "Pressure Cook" button two times to select "Less" option.
Use the "+/-" keys on the control panel to set the cooking time to 4 minutes.
Use the Pressure Level button to adjust the pressure to "Low Pressure".
Once the cooking cycle is completed, quickly and carefully turn the steam release handle from Sealing position to the Venting position.
When all the steam is released, remove the pressure lid from the top carefully.
Serve warm.

Per Serving: Calories 372; Fat 12.9g; Sodium 414mg; Carbs 11g; Fiber 5g; Sugar 9g; Protein 11g

Berry Steel Cut Oats

Prep time: 10 minutes| **Cook time:** 4 minutes| **Serves:** 6

2 cups steel cut oats
3 cups unsweetened almond milk
3 cups water
1 teaspoon pure vanilla extract
⅓ cup monk fruit sweetener
¼ teaspoon salt
1½ cups frozen berry blend with strawberries, blackberries, and raspberries

Add the steel cut oats, almond milk, water, vanilla, sweetener, and salt to the Inner Pot and stir to combine. Place the frozen berries on top.
Put on the pressure cooker's lid and turn the steam valve to "Sealing" position.
Press the "Pressure Cook" button two times to select "Less" option.
Use the "+/-" keys on the control panel to set the cooking time to 4 minutes.
Use the Pressure Level button to adjust the pressure to "Low Pressure".
Once the cooking cycle is completed, allow the steam to release naturally for 10 minutes, then turn the steam release handle to the Venting position.
When all the steam is released, remove the pressure lid from the top carefully.
Serve warm.

Per Serving: Calories 282; Fat 19g; Sodium 354mg; Carbs 15g; Fiber 5.1g; Sugar 8.2g; Protein 12g

Banana Bites

Prep time: 10 minutes| **Cook time:** 6 minutes| **Serves:** 3

1¾ cups old fashioned rolled oats
3 small ripe bananas
3 large eggs
2 tablespoons Erythritol
1 teaspoon ground cinnamon
1 teaspoon pure vanilla extract
1 teaspoon baking powder

Place the oats, bananas, eggs, Erythritol, cinnamon, vanilla, and baking powder in a large, powerful blender and blend until very smooth, about 1 minute.
Pour the mixture into a silicone mold with seven wells.
Place a paper towel on top and then top with aluminum foil.
Tighten the edges to prevent extra moisture getting inside.
Place the mold on top of your steam rack with handles.
Pour 1 cup water into the Inner Pot. Place the Steam Rack and mold inside.
Put on the pressure cooker's lid and turn the steam valve to "Sealing" position.
Press the "Pressure Cook" button two times to select "Less" option.
Use the "+/-" keys on the control panel to set the cooking time to 6 minutes.
Use the Pressure Level button to adjust the pressure to "Low Pressure".
Once the cooking cycle is completed, quickly and carefully turn the steam release handle from Sealing position to the Venting position.
When all the steam is released, remove the pressure lid from the top carefully.
Pull the steam rack and mold out of the Inner Pot and remove the aluminum foil and paper towel.
Allow the pancake bites to cool completely, and then use a knife to pull the edges of the bites away from the mold.
Press on the bottom of the mold and the pancake bites will pop right out.

Per Serving: Calories 284; Fat 9g; Sodium 441mg; Carbs 7g; Fiber 4.6g; Sugar 5g; Protein 19g

Cinnamon Breakfast Loaf

Prep time: 10 minutes| **Cook time:** 30 minutes| **Serves:** 6
½ cup ground golden flaxseed meal
½ cup almond flour
1 tablespoon ground cinnamon
2 teaspoons baking powder
½ teaspoon salt
⅔ cup xylitol
4 large eggs
½ cup coconut oil, melted and cooled

In a medium bowl, whisk together the flaxseed meal, flour, cinnamon, baking powder, salt, and xylitol.
In a separate medium bowl, whisk together the eggs and cooled coconut oil.
Pour the wet ingredients into the dry ingredients and stir to combine.
Grease a suitable cake pan well and pour the mixture into the pan and cover with aluminum foil.
Pour 1½ cups water into the Inner Pot and place the Steam Rack with handles in the pot.
Place the cake pan on top of the Steam Rack.
Put on the pressure cooker's lid and turn the steam valve to "Sealing" position.

Press the "Pressure Cook" button two times to select "Normal" option.
Use the "+/-" keys on the control panel to set the cooking time to 30 minutes.
Use the Pressure Level button to adjust the pressure to "Low Pressure".
Once the cooking cycle is completed, quickly and carefully turn the steam release handle from Sealing position to the Venting position.
When all the steam is released, remove the pressure lid from the top carefully.
Slice and serve.

Per Serving: Calories 351; Fat 7.9g; Sodium 704mg; Carbs 6g; Fiber 3.6g; Sugar 6g; Protein 18g

Vegetable Breakfast Bowls

Prep time: 10 minutes| **Cook time:** 20 minutes| **Serves:** 2
2 tablespoons avocado oil
3 leeks, white and light green portion thinly sliced
8 oz. sliced baby bella mushrooms
½ teaspoon salt
¼ teaspoon black pepper
2 large carrots, peeled and sliced
5 kale leaves, tough stems removed and finely chopped
Juice from ½ medium lemon

Add the oil to the Inner Pot and press the Sauté button tow times to choose "Normal.".
Allow the oil to heat 2 minutes and then add the leeks, mushrooms, salt, and pepper.
Sauté the leeks and mushrooms 10 minutes.
Press the Cancel button.
Add the carrots, kale, and lemon juice and stir to combine.
Put on the pressure cooker's lid and turn the steam valve to "Sealing" position.
Press the "Pressure Cook" button two times to select "Less" option.
Use the "+/-" keys on the control panel to set the cooking time to 4 minutes.
Use the Pressure Level button to adjust the pressure to "Low Pressure".
Once the cooking cycle is completed, quickly and carefully turn the steam release handle from Sealing position to the Venting position.
When all the steam is released, remove the pressure lid from the top carefully.
Serve immediately.

Per Serving: Calories 221; Fat 7.9g; Sodium 704mg; Carbs 6g; Fiber 3.6g; Sugar 6g; Protein 18g

Root Vegetable Casserole

Prep time: 10 minutes| **Cook time:** 30 minutes| **Serves:** 4
1 tablespoon avocado oil
1 small yellow onion, peeled and diced
1 small turnip, peeled and diced
1 medium parsnip, peeled and diced
2 small carrots, peeled and diced

1 teaspoon kosher salt
8 large eggs
1 tablespoon lemon juice
1 tablespoon fresh thyme leaves

Add the oil to the Inner Pot and press the Sauté button tow times to choose "Normal." Allow the oil to heat 1 minute and then add the onion, turnip, parsnip, carrots, and salt. Cook for 10 minutes until the vegetables are softened. Press the Cancel button.
In a medium bowl, whisk together the eggs and lemon juice.
Add the thyme and vegetable mixture and stir to combine.
Spray the inside of a 7-cup glass bowl with cooking spray. Transfer the egg mixture to the bowl.
Add 1 cup water to the Inner Pot and place the steam rack inside.
Place the bowl on top of the steam rack.
Put on the pressure cooker's lid and turn the steam valve to "Sealing" position.
Press the "Pressure Cook" button two times to select "Less" option.
Use the "+/-" keys on the control panel to set the cooking time to 18 minutes.
Use the Pressure Level button to adjust the pressure to "Low Pressure".
Once the cooking cycle is completed, quickly and carefully turn the steam release handle from Sealing position to the Venting position.
When all the steam is released, remove the pressure lid from the top carefully.
Remove bowl from pot and allow to cool 5 minutes before slicing and serving.

Per Serving: Calories 334; Fat 7.9g; Sodium 704mg; Carbs 6g; Fiber 3.6g; Sugar 6g; Protein 18g

Strawberries Quinoa Porridge

Prep time: 10 minutes| **Cook time:** 1 minutes| **Serves:** 6
1½ cups dry quinoa
1½ cups water
1 (166-oz.) can unsweetened full-fat coconut milk
½ teaspoon pure stevia powder
1 teaspoon pure vanilla extract
1 cup sliced strawberries
⅓ cup unsweetened shredded coconut

Using a fine-mesh strainer, rinse the quinoa very well until the water runs clear.
Add the quinoa, water, coconut milk, stevia, and vanilla to the Inner Pot. Stir to combine.
Put on the pressure cooker's lid and turn the steam valve to "Sealing" position.
Press the "Pressure Cook" button two times to select "Less" option.
Use the "+/-" keys on the control panel to set the cooking time to 1 minute.
Use the Pressure Level button to adjust the pressure to "Low Pressure".
Once the cooking cycle is completed, quickly and carefully turn the steam release handle from Sealing position to the Venting position.

When all the steam is released, remove the pressure lid from the top carefully.
Stir in strawberries. Allow the quinoa to cool slightly before spooning into bowls to serve. Top each bowl with a portion of the coconut.

Per Serving: Calories 372; Fat 20g; Sodium 891mg; Carbs 29g; Fiber 3g; Sugar 8g; Protein 7g

Eggs with Asparagus

Prep time: 10 minutes| **Cook time:** 3 minutes| **Serves:** 1
2 large eggs
5 large asparagus spears, woody ends removed

Place the whole eggs and asparagus into the steamer basket.
Pour 1 cup water into the Inner Pot and place the Steam Rack inside.
Place the steamer basket with the eggs and asparagus on the rack.
Put on the pressure cooker's lid and turn the steam valve to "Sealing" position.
Press the "Pressure Cook" button two times to select "Less" option.
Use the "+/-" keys on the control panel to set the cooking time to 3 minutes.
Use the Pressure Level button to adjust the pressure to "Low Pressure".
Once the cooking cycle is completed, quickly and carefully turn the steam release handle from Sealing position to the Venting position.
When all the steam is released, remove the pressure lid from the top carefully.
Prepare an ice bath by filling a large bowl with cold water and ice.
Carefully remove the steamer basket from the Inner Pot.
Place the eggs into the ice bath until they have cooled enough to handle.
Peel the eggs and serve with the asparagus.

Per Serving: Calories 312; Fat 7.9g; Sodium 704mg; Carbs 6g; Fiber 3.6g; Sugar 6g; Protein 18g

5-Ingredient Oatmeal

Prep time: 10 minutes| **Cook time:** 6 minutes| **Serves:** 2
2 cups water
1 cup old-fashioned oats
¾ cup milk
2 tablespoons brown sugar
½ teaspoon ground cinnamon

Pour 1 cup of water into the pressure cooker pot and place a steamer rack Steam Rack in the bottom.
In a heat-safe bowl, stir together the remaining 1 cup of water, oats, milk, brown sugar, and cinnamon.
Place the bowl on the Steam Rack.
Put on the pressure cooker's lid and turn the steam valve to "Sealing" position.

Press the "Pressure Cook" button one time to select "Less" option.
Use the "+/-" keys on the control panel to set the cooking time to 6 minutes.
Use the Pressure Level button to adjust the pressure to "High Pressure".
Once the cooking cycle is completed, allow the steam to release naturally for 10 minutes, then turn the steam release handle to the Venting position.
When all the steam is released, remove the pressure lid from the top carefully.
Remove the bowl from the pressure cooker and stir.
Serve.

Per Serving: Calories 349; Fat 2.9g; Sodium 511mg; Carbs 12g; Fiber 3g; Sugar 8g; Protein 7g

Loaded Bacon Grits

Prep time: 10 minutes| **Cook time:** 15 minutes| **Serves:** 4

3 cups water
1½ cups milk
1 cup quick grits (not instant grits)
¼ teaspoon salt
½ cup shredded cheddar cheese
¼ cup real bacon bits
2 tablespoons unsalted butter, at room temperature
1 tablespoon chopped fresh chives

Pour 1 cup of water into the pressure cooker pot and place a steamer rack Steam Rack in the bottom.
In a heat-safe bowl, stir together the remaining 2 cups of water, milk, grits, and salt.
Place the bowl on the Steam Rack.
Put on the pressure cooker's lid and turn the steam valve to "Sealing" position.
Press the "Pressure Cook" button one time to select "Less" option.
Use the "+/-" keys on the control panel to set the cooking time to 15 minutes.
Use the Pressure Level button to adjust the pressure to "High Pressure".
Once the cooking cycle is completed, allow the steam to release naturally.
When all the steam is released, remove the pressure lid from the top carefully.
Remove the bowl from the pressure cooker and stir. The grits will thicken as they cool.
Stir in the cheese, bacon bits, butter, and chives.

Per Serving: Calories 282; Fat 7.9g; Sodium 704mg; Carbs 6g; Fiber 3.6g; Sugar 6g; Protein 18g

Ham Cheese Egg Bites

Prep time: 10 minutes| **Cook time:** 11 minutes| **Serves:** 7

Nonstick cooking spray
1 cup water

4 large eggs
½ cup chopped ham
½ cup shredded cheddar cheese
¼ cup cottage cheese
½ tablespoon chopped fresh parsley
¼ teaspoon garlic powder
¼ teaspoon salt
¼ teaspoon black pepper

Spray the cups of a silicone egg mold with nonstick cooking spray.
Pour the water into the pressure cooker pot and place a steamer rack Steam Rack in the bottom.
In a medium bowl, whisk the eggs.
Stir in the ham, cheddar cheese, cottage cheese, parsley, garlic powder, salt, and pepper until well mixed.
Divide the egg mixture evenly into the seven egg-bite mold cups. Place the egg-bite mold on the Steam Rack.
Put on the pressure cooker's lid and turn the steam valve to "Sealing" position.
Press the "Pressure Cook" button one time to select "Less" option.
Use the "+/-" keys on the control panel to set the cooking time to 11 minutes.
Use the Pressure Level button to adjust the pressure to "High Pressure".
Once the cooking cycle is completed, allow the steam to release naturally.
When all the steam is released, remove the pressure lid from the top carefully.
Remove the mold from the pressure cooker and cool on a wire rack before using a spoon or butter knife to remove the egg bites from the mold.

Per Serving: Calories 219; Fat 10g; Sodium 891mg; Carbs 22.9g; Fiber 4g; Sugar 4g; Protein 13g

Sausage Spinach Quiche

Prep time: 10 minutes| **Cook time:** 30 minutes| **Serves:** 4

8 oz. ground sausage
¼ cup finely chopped onion
6 large eggs
½ cup heavy cream
1½ cups chopped spinach
¼ cup Parmesan cheese
¼ teaspoon garlic powder
¼ teaspoon salt
¼ teaspoon black pepper
½ cup chopped tomato
1 cup water
Nonstick cooking spray

Press the "Sauté" button two time on the Instant Pot to select "Normal" settings.
When the pot is hot, add the ground sausage and chopped onion and sauté until the sausage is browned.
Press cancel or turn off the burner.
Transfer the sausage and onion mixture to a paper towel–lined plate and set aside to drain.
Wipe out the inside of the pressure cooker pot when it is cool enough to handle.

In a medium bowl, whisk together the eggs and heavy cream.
Stir in the spinach, Parmesan cheese, garlic powder, salt, and pepper until well blended.
Add the sausage and onion mixture to the egg mixture, along with the tomato, and stir well.
Pour the water into the pressure cooker pot and place a steamer rack Steam Rack in the bottom.
Spray a soufflé dish with nonstick cooking spray.
Pour the egg mixture into the prepared soufflé dish and cover loosely with aluminum foil.
Place the dish on the Steam Rack inside the pot.
Put on the pressure cooker's lid and turn the steam valve to "Sealing" position.
Press the "Pressure Cook" button one time to select "Normal" option.
Use the "+/-" keys on the control panel to set the cooking time to 30 minutes.
Use the Pressure Level button to adjust the pressure to "High Pressure".
Once the cooking cycle is completed, allow the steam to release naturally.
When all the steam is released, remove the pressure lid from the top carefully.

Per Serving: Calories 284; Fat 9g; Sodium 441mg; Carbs 7g; Fiber 4.6g; Sugar 5g; Protein 19g

Blueberry Coffee Cake

Prep time: 10 minutes| **Cook time:** 35 minutes| **Serves:** 8

Nonstick cooking spray
2¼ cups all-purpose flour
1 teaspoon baking powder
1 teaspoon baking soda
¼ teaspoon salt
1 cup granulated sugar
1 cup plain unsweetened Greek yogurt
8 tablespoons (1 stick) unsalted butter
1 large egg
1 cup blueberries
1 cup water
¼ cup brown sugar
¼ teaspoon ground cinnamon
½ cup purchased cream cheese frosting, melted

Spray a 6-cup Bundt pan with nonstick cooking spray.
In a medium bowl, whisk together 2 cups of flour, the baking powder, baking soda, and salt.
In a large bowl, beat together the granulated sugar, yogurt, 8 tablespoons room-temperature butter, and egg with a hand mixer until smooth.
Add the dry ingredients to the wet ingredients and mix with the hand mixer until completely combined. Fold in the blueberries.
Pour the batter into the prepared Bundt pan.
Lay a paper towel over the top of the pan, then cover the paper towel and pan loosely with aluminum foil.

Pour the water into the pressure cooker pot and place a steamer rack Steam Rack in the bottom.
Place the foil-covered Bundt pan on the Steam Rack.
Put on the pressure cooker's lid and turn the steam valve to "Sealing" position.
Press the "Pressure Cook" button one time to select "Normal" option.
Use the Pressure Level button to adjust the pressure to "High Pressure".
Once the cooking cycle is completed, allow the steam to release naturally.
When all the steam is released, remove the pressure lid from the top carefully.
Meanwhile, mix the brown sugar, remaining ¼ cup flour, 2 tablespoons melted butter, and cinnamon together in a small bowl until it forms a crumbly texture. Set aside.
Carefully remove the Bundt pan from the pot and cool on a wire rack.
When cool enough to handle, invert the pan over a serving plate.
Drizzle the cake with the melted cream cheese frosting and top with the crumble mixture.

Per Serving: Calories 382; Fat 10.9g; Sodium 354mg; Carbs 20.5g; Fiber 4.1g; Sugar 8.2g; Protein 06g

Chocolate Chip Banana Bread

Prep time: 10 minutes| **Cook time:** 55 minutes| **Serves:** 8

Nonstick cooking spray
¾ cup brown sugar
8 tablespoons (1 stick) unsalted butter
2 large eggs, at room temperature
2 cups mashed overripe bananas
2 cups all-purpose flour
1½ teaspoons baking soda
¼ teaspoon salt
¾ cup chocolate chips
1½ cups water

Spray a 6-cup Bundt pan with nonstick cooking spray and lightly dust it with flour.
In a medium bowl, beat together the brown sugar, butter, and eggs with a hand mixer until creamy.
Beat in the mashed bananas until evenly incorporated.
Add the flour, baking soda, and salt and beat until well mixed; be careful not to overmix.
Fold in the chocolate chips.
Pour the batter into the prepared Bundt pan.
Lay a paper towel over the top of the pan, then cover the paper towel and pan loosely with aluminum foil.
Pour the water into the pressure cooker pot and place a steamer rack Steam Rack in the bottom.
Place the foil-covered Bundt pan on the Steam Rack.
Put on the pressure cooker's lid and turn the steam valve to "Sealing" position.
Press the "Pressure Cook" button one time to select "More" option.

Use the "+/-" keys on the control panel to set the cooking time to 55 minutes.
Use the Pressure Level button to adjust the pressure to "High Pressure".
Once the cooking cycle is completed, allow the steam to release naturally for 10 minutes, then turn the steam release handle to the Venting position.
When all the steam is released, remove the pressure lid from the top carefully.
Carefully remove the Bundt pan from the pot. If the bread still seems doughy, replace the paper towel and foil and return it to the pot to pressure cook for an additional 5 minutes.
Allow the banana bread to cool completely on a wire rack before removing the bread from the pan.

Per Serving: Calories 251; Fat 19g; Sodium 354mg; Carbs 15g; Fiber 5.1g; Sugar 8.2g; Protein 12g

Vanilla Yogurt with Granola

Prep time: 10 minutes| **Cook time:** 8 hours | **Serves:** 16

8 cups whole milk
2 tablespoons yogurt with active cultures
4 cups granola
1 cup honey

Add the milk with active cultures and whisk together until the yogurt is completely blended into the milk.
Press the "Yogurt" button one time to select "More" option. The display indicates "boiL."
Heat the milk until it reaches 180 degrees F, about one and half an hour.
When done, leave the milk in the pot until it cools to 115 degrees F, about 1 hour.
Gently skim off this layer with a skimmer or slotted spoon and discard the thin film.
Add the prepared yogurt with active cultures and whisk together until the yogurt is completely blended into the milk.
Press the "Yogurt" button one time to select "Normal" option. The display indicates 08:00. Cook for 8 hours.
After 8 hours, the yogurt should be thickened and ready to serve or store in containers in the refrigerator.
Serve in ½-cup portions, each topped with ¼ cup granola and 1 tablespoon honey.

Per Serving: Calories 214; Fat 10.9g; Sodium 454mg; Carbs 10g; Fiber 3.1g; Sugar 5.2g; Protein 10g

Biscuit Dumplings and Gravy

Prep time: 10 minutes| **Cook time:** 15 minutes| **Serves:** 4

1 tablespoon unsalted butter
1-pound pork sausage
¼ cup all-purpose flour
2⅓ cups whole milk
2 teaspoons dried thyme
1 teaspoon salt
1½ teaspoons black pepper
¾ cup Bisquick or other baking mix

Melt the butter using the Sauté function at Normal cooking temperature.
When melted, add the sausage and cook until browned, about 8 minutes.
Break up the sausage as it cooks, leaving some bigger pieces for better texture.
Do not drain the pot. Add the flour and stir well.
Continue to cook the flour and sausage mixture until brown, 2 to 3 minutes. Make sure to stir often.
When the mixture starts to brown, slowly add 2 cups of milk and mix; then add the thyme, salt, and ½ teaspoon of pepper.
Scrape the bottom of the pot well to release any browned bits.
Turn the pot off and allow it to cool for 3 to 4 minutes.
In a medium bowl, mix together the Bisquick, remaining ⅓ cup of milk, and remaining 1 teaspoon of pepper. Stir until the dough just comes together.
Drop dollops of the dough into the sausage gravy.
Put on the pressure cooker's lid and turn the steam valve to "Sealing" position.
Press the "Pressure Cook" button one time to select "Less" option.
Use the "+/-" keys on the control panel to set the cooking time to 5 minutes.
Use the Pressure Level button to adjust the pressure to "High Pressure".
Once the cooking cycle is completed, quickly and carefully turn the steam release handle from Sealing position to the Venting position.
When all the steam is released, remove the pressure lid from the top carefully.
Serve

Per Serving: Calories 282; Fat 7.9g; Sodium 704mg; Carbs 6g; Fiber 3.6g; Sugar 6g; Protein 18g

Ham Cheese Omelet

Prep time: 10 minutes| **Cook time:** 6 minutes| **Serves:** 4

Nonstick cooking spray
5 large eggs
2 tablespoons whole milk
½ cup chopped deli ham
½ cup shredded cheddar cheese
¼ cup sliced or cubed red bell pepper
1 cup roughly chopped fresh baby spinach
¼ cup chopped fresh flat-leaf parsley
¼ teaspoon garlic powder
¼ teaspoon red pepper flakes
Salt
Black pepper

Grease a 7-inch Bundt pan with cooking spray.
In a medium bowl, whisk together the eggs and milk.
Add all the remaining ingredients, season with salt and pepper, and stir to combine.

Pour the mixture into the prepared pan. Do not cover the pan.
Set the Steam Rack in the Inner Pot and pour in 1 cup of water.
Place the Bundt pan on the Steam Rack and lock the lid on the pressure cooker.
Put on the pressure cooker's lid and turn the steam valve to "Sealing" position.
Press the "Pressure Cook" button.
Use the "+/-" keys on the control panel to set the cooking time to 6 minutes.
Use the Pressure Level button to adjust the pressure to "High Pressure".
Once the cooking cycle is completed, quickly and carefully turn the steam release handle from Sealing position to the Venting position.
When all the steam is released, remove the pressure lid from the top carefully.

Per Serving: Calories 284; Fat 9g; Sodium 441mg; Carbs 7g; Fiber 4.6g; Sugar 5g; Protein 19g

Egg Bites

Prep time: 10 minutes| **Cook time:** 12 minutes| **Serves:** 3

Nonstick cooking spray
4 large eggs
¼ cup cottage cheese
½ cup shredded cheddar cheese
4 cooked bacon slices, crumbled

Spray a 7-cup silicone egg bite mold with cooking spray.
In a medium bowl, whisk the eggs until they're fluffy.
Beat in the cottage cheese until it is fully incorporated.
Stir in the cheddar cheese and bacon.
Divide the egg mixture among the cups of the prepared egg mold, filling each cup about three-quarters full.
Cover the mold with the lid or with foil.
Set the Steam Rack in the Inner Pot and pour in 1 cup of water.
Place the egg bite mold on the Steam Rack and lock the lid on the pressure cooker.
Put on the pressure cooker's lid and turn the steam valve to "Sealing" position.
Press the "Pressure Cook" button.
Use the Pressure Level button to adjust the pressure to "Low Pressure".
Use the "+/-" keys on the control panel to set the cooking time to 12 minutes.
Once the cooking cycle is completed, allow the steam to release naturally.
When all the steam is released, remove the pressure lid from the top carefully.
Remove the lid and let the egg bites cool for a minute or two before inverting them onto a plate.

Per Serving: Calories 289; Fat 14g; Sodium 791mg; Carbs 8.9g; Fiber 4.6g; Sugar 8g; Protein 16g

Unsweetened Applesauce

Prep time: 10 minutes| **Cook time:** 8 minutes| **Serves:** 6

6 apples (about 1½ lbs.)
¼ cup water
¼ teaspoon ground cinnamon

Peel and core the apples. Cut each apple into roughly eight large chunks.
In the Inner Pot, combine the apples, water, and cinnamon.
Put on the pressure cooker's lid and turn the steam valve to "Sealing" position.
Press the "Pressure Cook" button.
Use the "+/-" keys on the control panel to set the cooking time to 8 minutes.
Use the Pressure Level button to adjust the pressure to "High Pressure".
Once the cooking cycle is completed, allow the steam to release naturally for 10 minutes, then turn the steam release handle to the Venting position.
When all the steam is released, remove the pressure lid from the top carefully.
use a potato masher or heavy wooden spoon to gently mash the apples into applesauce.
Serve warm or refrigerate in an airtight container for up to 10 days.

Per Serving: Calories 289; Fat 14g; Sodium 791mg; Carbs 8.9g; Fiber 4.6g; Sugar 8g; Protein 6g

Classic Hummus

Prep time: 10 minutes| **Cook time:** 60 minutes| **Serves:** ½ cups

¾ cup dried chickpeas
1½ cups water
4 garlic cloves
½ teaspoon baking soda
2 tablespoons tahini
1 tablespoon lemon juice
¼ teaspoon kosher salt
¼ teaspoon ground cumin

In the Inner Pot, combine the chickpeas, water, garlic, and baking soda.
Put on the pressure cooker's lid and turn the steam valve to "Sealing" position.
Press the "Pressure Cook" button.
Use the "+/-" keys on the control panel to set the cooking time to 60 minutes.
Use the Pressure Level button to adjust the pressure to "High Pressure".
Once the cooking cycle is completed, quickly and carefully turn the steam release handle from Sealing position to the Venting position.
When all the steam is released, remove the pressure lid from the top carefully.
stir in the tahini and lemon juice.
Use an immersion blender to puree the hummus into a smooth paste.
Season with salt and cumin.

Serve warm or chilled.

Per Serving: Calories 284; Fat 9g; Sodium 441mg; Carbs 7g; Fiber 4.6g; Sugar 5g; Protein 19g

Refried Beans

Prep time: 10 minutes| **Cook time:** 60 minutes| **Serves:** 6

6 cups Chicken Stock or store-bought chicken stock
3 cups dried pinto beans
1 yellow onion, diced
1 tablespoon apple cider vinegar
2 teaspoons ground cumin
½ teaspoon kosher salt

In the Inner Pot, combine the stock, beans, onion, vinegar, cumin, and salt.
Put on the pressure cooker's lid and turn the steam valve to "Sealing" position.
Press the "Pressure Cook" button.
Use the "+/-" keys on the control panel to set the cooking time to 60 minutes.
Use the Pressure Level button to adjust the pressure to "High Pressure".
Once the cooking cycle is completed, allow the steam to release naturally for 10 minutes, then turn the steam release handle to the Venting position.
When all the steam is released, remove the pressure lid from the top carefully.
Carefully remove the lid.
Reserve ½ cup of the bean cooking liquid, then drain the beans.
Return the beans to the pot and use an immersion blender to blend them to your desired consistency.
Serve.

Per Serving: Calories 224; Fat 7.9g; Sodium 704mg; Carbs 6g; Fiber 3.6g; Sugar 6g; Protein 18g

Classic Black Beans

Prep time: 10 minutes| **Cook time:** 40 minutes| **Serves:** 4

2 tablespoons olive oil
1 yellow onion, diced
1 green bell pepper, seeded and diced
1 jalapeño pepper, seeded and minced
2 garlic cloves, minced
1 teaspoon dried oregano
1 teaspoon ground cumin
1 cup dried black beans
1 tablespoon apple cider vinegar
½ teaspoon kosher salt
1½ cups water

Press the "Sauté" button two times to select "Normal" mode on the Inner Pot and pour in the oil.

When the oil is hot, add the onion, bell pepper, jalapeño, and garlic.
Cook, stirring frequently, for 3 to 5 minutes, until softened. Press Cancel.
Stir in the oregano and cumin, then add the beans, vinegar, salt, and water.
Put on the pressure cooker's lid and turn the steam valve to "Sealing" position.
Press the "Pressure Cook" button one time to select "Normal" option.
Use the "+/-" keys on the control panel to set the cooking time to 40 minutes.
Use the Pressure Level button to adjust the pressure to "High Pressure".
Once the cooking cycle is completed, allow the steam to release naturally for 10 minutes, then turn the steam release handle to the Venting position.
When all the steam is released, remove the pressure lid from the top carefully.
Serve.

Per Serving: Calories 184; Fat 5g; Sodium 441mg; Carbs 17g; Fiber 4.6g; Sugar 5g; Protein 9g

Cilantro-Lime Brown Rice

Prep time: 10 minutes| **Cook time:** 15 minutes| **Serves:** 4

1 cup long-grain brown rice, rinsed
1¼ cups water
Zest and juice of 1 lime
¼ cup freshly chopped cilantro
1 teaspoon kosher salt

In the Inner Pot, combine the rice and water. Stir well.
Put on the pressure cooker's lid and turn the steam valve to "Sealing" position.
Press the "Pressure Cook" button one time to select "Less" option.
Use the "+/-" keys on the control panel to set the cooking time to 15 minutes.
Use the Pressure Level button to adjust the pressure to "High Pressure".
Once the cooking cycle is completed, allow the steam to release naturally for 10 minutes, then turn the steam release handle to the Venting position.
When all the steam is released, remove the pressure lid from the top carefully.
stir in the lime zest, lime juice, cilantro, and salt before serving.

Per Serving: Calories 334; Fat 7.9g; Sodium 704mg; Carbs 6g; Fiber 3.6g; Sugar 6g; Protein 18g

Coconut Brown Rice

Prep time: 10 minutes| **Cook time:** 15 minutes| **Serves:** 6

2 tablespoons unsweetened shredded coconut
1½ cups long-grain brown rice, rinsed
1 (14-oz.) can light coconut milk
½ cup water
¼ teaspoon kosher salt

Press the "Sauté" button two times to select "Normal" mode.
Stir in the shredded coconut. Cook, stirring frequently, for 2 to 3 minutes or until toasted and golden brown.
Press Cancel button to stop this cooking program.
Transfer the toasted coconut to a small dish and set aside.
In the Inner Pot, combine the rice, coconut milk, water, and salt. Stir well to combine.
Put on the pressure cooker's lid and turn the steam valve to "Sealing" position.
Press the "Pressure Cook" button one time to select "Less" option.
Use the "+/-" keys on the control panel to set the cooking time to 15 minutes.
Use the Pressure Level button to adjust the pressure to "High Pressure".
Once the cooking cycle is completed, allow the steam to release naturally for 10 minutes, then turn the steam release handle to the Venting position.
When all the steam is released, remove the pressure lid from the top carefully.
stir in the toasted coconut before serving.

Per Serving: Calories 372; Fat 20g; Sodium 891mg; Carbs 29g; Fiber 3g; Sugar 8g; Protein 7g

Feta Chickpea Salad

Prep time: 10 minutes| **Cook time:** 15 minutes| **Serves:** 4

2 tablespoons olive oil, plus ¼ cup
1 red onion, diced
1 red bell pepper, seeded and diced
1 zucchini, diced
1 cup dried chickpeas, soaked overnight
3 cups water
1 cup baby spinach
3 tablespoons lemon juice
¼ teaspoon kosher salt
¼ teaspoon black pepper
¼ cup crumbled feta cheese
1 teaspoon dried oregano

Press the "Sauté" button two times to select "Normal" mode.
Pour in 2 tablespoons of olive oil. When the oil is hot, add the onion, bell pepper, and zucchini.
Cook, stirring frequently, for 4 to 5 minutes, or until softened.
Press Cancel.
Add the chickpeas and water.
Put on the pressure cooker's lid and turn the steam valve to "Sealing" position.
Press the "Pressure Cook" button one time to select "Less" option.
Use the "+/-" keys on the control panel to set the cooking time to 15 minutes.
Use the Pressure Level button to adjust the pressure to "High Pressure".
Once the cooking cycle is completed, allow the steam to release naturally for 10 minutes,

then turn the steam release handle to the Venting position.
When all the steam is released, remove the pressure lid from the top carefully.
stir in the remaining ¼ cup of olive oil, the spinach, lemon juice, salt, and black pepper.
Top with the feta and oregano and serve.

Per Serving: Calories 221; Fat 7.9g; Sodium 704mg; Carbs 6g; Fiber 3.6g; Sugar 6g; Protein 18g

Potato Pea Salad

Prep time: 10 minutes| **Cook time:** 4 minutes| **Serves:** 6

1½ lbs. (4 or 5) yellow potatoes
1 shallot, finely chopped
¼ cup apple cider vinegar
¼ cup olive oil
1 teaspoon Dijon mustard
½ teaspoon kosher salt
4 oz. sugar snap peas, halved lengthwise

Cut each potato into 12 pieces by cutting it in half lengthwise, cutting each half lengthwise again, then cutting each of those pieces crosswise into thirds.
In a large bowl, whisk together the shallot, vinegar, oil, mustard, and salt. Set the dressing aside.
Pour 2 cups of water into the Inner Pot and insert the Steam Rack or a steamer basket. Add the potatoes.
Put on the pressure cooker's lid and turn the steam valve to "Sealing" position.
Press the "Pressure Cook" button one time to select "Less" option.
Use the "+/-" keys on the control panel to set the cooking time to 4 minutes.
Use the Pressure Level button to adjust the pressure to "High Pressure".
Once the cooking cycle is completed, quickly and carefully turn the steam release handle from Sealing position to the Venting position.
When all the steam is released, remove the pressure lid from the top carefully.
transfer the cooked potatoes to the bowl of dressing.
Stir in the peas.
Serve this salad warm or chilled.

Per Serving: Calories 312; Fat 12.9g; Sodium 414mg; Carbs 11g; Fiber 5g; Sugar 9g; Protein 11g

Cider Collard Greens

Prep time: 10 minutes| **Cook time:** 12 minutes| **Serves:** 6

6 no-sugar-added uncured bacon slices, diced
1 yellow onion, diced
16 oz. frozen chopped collard greens
1 tablespoon apple cider vinegar
¼ teaspoon kosher salt
¼ teaspoon garlic powder

Press the "Sauté" button two times to select "Normal" mode and add the bacon.
Cook for 3 minutes, stirring frequently, until the fat renders.
Stir in the onion and cook for 3 minutes, stirring frequently, until soft.
Press Cancel.
Stir in the collard greens, vinegar, salt, and garlic powder.
Use your spoon to scrape up anything that's stuck to the bottom of the pot.
Put on the pressure cooker's lid and turn the steam valve to "Sealing" position.
Press the "Pressure Cook" button one time to select "Less" option.
Use the "+/-" keys on the control panel to set the cooking time to 12 minutes.
Use the Pressure Level button to adjust the pressure to "High Pressure".
Once the cooking cycle is completed, quickly and carefully turn the steam release handle from Sealing position to the Venting position.
When all the steam is released, remove the pressure lid from the top carefully.
Carefully remove the lid, stir, and serve.

Per Serving: Calories 282; Fat 10.9g; Sodium 354mg; Carbs 20.5g; Fiber 4.1g; Sugar 8.2g; Protein 06g

Garlicky Brussels Sprouts

Prep time: 10 minutes| **Cook time:** 2 minutes| **Serves:** 6

1 tablespoon olive oil
1 pound Brussels sprouts, bottoms trimmed
½ cup Vegetable Broth or store-bought low-sodium vegetable broth
5 garlic cloves, minced
¼ teaspoon kosher salt
¼ teaspoon black pepper

Press the "Sauté" button two times to select "Normal" mode and pour in the oil.
When the oil is hot, add the Brussels sprouts.
Cook undisturbed for 3 to 4 minutes, until lightly browned.
Press Cancel.
Add the broth and garlic.
Put on the pressure cooker's lid and turn the steam valve to "Sealing" position.
Press the "Pressure Cook" button one time to select "Less" option.
Use the "+/-" keys on the control panel to set the cooking time to 2 minutes.
Use the Pressure Level button to adjust the pressure to "High Pressure".
Once the cooking cycle is completed, quickly and carefully turn the steam release handle from Sealing position to the Venting position.
When all the steam is released, remove the pressure lid from the top carefully.
Serve.

Per Serving: Calories 289; Fat 14g; Sodium 791mg; Carbs 8.9g; Fiber 4.6g; Sugar 8g; Protein 6g

Cinnamon Acorn Squash

Prep time: 10 minutes| **Cook time:** 5 minutes| **Serves:** 4

2 acorn squash
4 teaspoons coconut oil
4 teaspoons pure maple syrup
¼ teaspoon ground cinnamon
¼ teaspoon kosher salt

Cut the squash in half through the root, then scoop out and discard the seeds.
Divide the coconut oil, maple syrup, cinnamon, and salt evenly between the centers of each squash half.
Pour 1 cup of water into the Inner Pot and insert the Steam Rack.
Stack the squash, cut-side up, on top of the Steam Rack.
Put on the pressure cooker's lid and turn the steam valve to "Sealing" position.
Press the "Pressure Cook" button three times to select "Less" option.
Use the "+/-" keys on the control panel to set the cooking time to 5 minutes.
Use the Pressure Level button to adjust the pressure to "High Pressure".
Once the cooking cycle is completed, allow the steam to release naturally for 10 minutes, then turn the steam release handle to the Venting position.
When all the steam is released, remove the pressure lid from the top carefully.
Serve.

Per Serving: Calories 184; Fat 5g; Sodium 441mg; Carbs 17g; Fiber 4.6g; Sugar 5g; Protein 9g

Mashed Potato and Cauliflower

Prep time: 10 minutes| **Cook time:** 8 minutes| **Serves:** 6

1 pound potatoes, peeled and cubed
2 cups fresh or frozen cauliflower florets
4 garlic cloves
¼ cup unsweetened nondairy milk, such as almond or coconut
¼ teaspoon kosher salt

½ teaspoon black pepper

Pour 2 cups of water into the Inner Pot and place the Steam Rack or a steamer basket.
Add the potatoes, cauliflower, and garlic.
Put on the pressure cooker's lid and turn the steam valve to "Sealing" position.
Press the "Pressure Cook" button one time to select "Less" option.
Use the "+/-" keys on the control panel to set the cooking time to 8 minutes.
Use the Pressure Level button to adjust the pressure to "High Pressure".
Once the cooking cycle is completed, quickly and carefully turn the steam release handle from Sealing position to the Venting position.
When all the steam is released, remove the pressure lid from the top carefully.

Drain the water. Return the vegetables to the pot and add the milk, salt, and pepper.
Use a potato masher to mash the potatoes and cauliflower to your desired consistency, and then serve.

Per Serving: Calories 289; Fat 14g; Sodium 791mg; Carbs 18.9g; Fiber 4.6g; Sugar 8g; Protein 6g

Honey Sweet Potatoes

Prep time: 15 minutes| **Cook time:** 7 minutes| **Serves:** 4

1 pound sweet potatoes (about 2 medium potatoes), cut into ½-inch rounds
2 teaspoons coconut oil
1 teaspoon honey
1 teaspoon chili powder
¼ teaspoon smoked paprika
¼ teaspoon kosher salt

Pour ½ cup of water into the Inner Pot, then add the potato slices.
Put on the pressure cooker's lid and turn the steam valve to "Sealing" position.
Press the "Pressure Cook" button two times to select "Less" option.
Use the "+/-" keys on the control panel to set the cooking time to 4 minutes.
Use the Pressure Level button to adjust the pressure to "High Pressure".
Once the cooking cycle is completed, quickly and carefully turn the steam release handle from Sealing position to the Venting position.
When all the steam is released, remove the pressure lid from the top carefully.
Press Cancel to stop this cooking program.
Stir in the coconut oil, honey, chili powder, paprika, and salt.
Press the "Sauté" button two times to select "Normal" mode and cook for 2 to 3 minutes, until the potatoes are coated with a thick glaze.
Serve.

Per Serving: Calories 334; Fat 7.9g; Sodium 704mg; Carbs 6g; Fiber 3.6g; Sugar 6g; Protein 18g

Cinnamon Raisin Granola Bars

Prep time: 15 minutes| **Cook time:** 10 minutes| **Serves:** 10

2 cups quick-cooking oats
⅓ cup date syrup
⅓ cup avocado oil
⅓ cup monk fruit sweetener
⅓ cup almond butter
⅓ cup raisins
½ teaspoon ground cinnamon

In a medium bowl, combine the oats, date syrup, oil, sweetener, almond butter, raisins, and cinnamon.
Spray a 5" baking dish with cooking spray.
Press the oat mixture firmly into the pan.

Add 1 cup water to the Inner Pot and place the Steam Rack inside.
Place the baking dish on top of the Steam Rack.
Put on the pressure cooker's lid and turn the steam valve to "Sealing" position.
Press the "Pressure Cook" button one time to select "Less" option.
Use the "+/-" keys on the control panel to set the cooking time to 10 minutes.
Use the Pressure Level button to adjust the pressure to "High Pressure".
Once the cooking cycle is completed, quickly and carefully turn the steam release handle from Sealing position to the Venting position.
When all the steam is released, remove the pressure lid from the top carefully.
Once completely cooled, turn the pan upside down onto a cutting board to remove the granola from the pan.
Cut into ten bars and serve.

Per Serving: Calories 361; Fat 7.9g; Sodium 704mg; Carbs 6g; Fiber 3.6g; Sugar 6g; Protein 18g

Almond Butter Chocolate Chip Granola Bars

Prep time: 15 minutes| **Cook time:** 10 minutes| **Serves:** 10
2 cups quick-cooking oats
⅔ cup almond butter
⅓ cup avocado oil
⅓ cup monk fruit sweetener
⅓ cup stevia-sweetened dark chocolate chips
¼ teaspoon salt

In a medium bowl, combine the oats, almond butter, oil, sweetener, chocolate chips, and salt.
Spray a 5" baking dish with cooking spray.
Press the oat mixture firmly into the pan.
Add 1 cup water to the Inner Pot and place the steam rack inside.
Place the baking dish on top of the steam rack.
Put on the pressure cooker's lid and turn the steam valve to "Sealing" position.
Press the "Pressure Cook" button one time to select "Less" option.
Use the "+/-" keys on the control panel to set the cooking time to 10 minutes.
Use the Pressure Level button to adjust the pressure to "Low Pressure".
Once the cooking cycle is completed, quickly and carefully turn the steam release handle from Sealing position to the Venting position.
When all the steam is released, remove the pressure lid from the top carefully.
Carefully remove the pan from the Inner Pot and place it on a baking rack to cool completely.
Once completely cooled, turn the pan upside down onto a cutting board to remove the granola from the pan.
Cut into ten bars and serve.

Per Serving: Calories 219; Fat 10g; Sodium 891mg; Carbs 22.9g; Fiber 4g; Sugar 4g; Protein 13g

Hot Cauliflower Bites

Prep time: 15 minutes| **Cook time:** 2 minutes| **Serves:** 4
1 large head cauliflower, cut into large pieces
½ cup buffalo hot sauce

Pour 1 cup water into the Inner Pot and place the Steam Rack inside.
Place the cauliflower in a 7-cup glass bowl and add the buffalo hot sauce.
Toss to evenly coat. Place the bowl on top of the steam rack.
Put on the pressure cooker's lid and turn the steam valve to "Sealing" position.
Press the "Pressure Cook" button one time to select "Less" option.
Use the "+/-" keys on the control panel to set the cooking time to 2 minutes.
Use the Pressure Level button to adjust the pressure to "High Pressure".
Once the cooking cycle is completed, quickly and carefully turn the steam release handle from Sealing position to the Venting position.
When all the steam is released, remove the pressure lid from the top carefully.
Transfer to a plate and serve with toothpicks.

Per Serving: Calories 234; Fat 19g; Sodium 354mg; Carbs 15g; Fiber 5.1g; Sugar 8.2g; Protein 12g

Nacho Cheese Sauce

Prep time: 5 minutes| **Cook time:** 10 minutes| **Serves:** 4
1¼ cups vegetable broth
1 cup plain nondairy yogurt
3 tablespoons oat flour
¼ teaspoon salt
¼ teaspoon garlic salt
½ teaspoon cumin
1 teaspoon chili powder
¼ teaspoon paprika
⅛ teaspoon cayenne powder

Press the "Sauté" button two time to select "Normal" mode.
Add the broth to the Inner Pot and let it come to a boil.
Meanwhile, in a small bowl, mix together the yogurt and flour. Stir until well combined.
Press the "Sauté" button twice to select "Normal" option.
Add the yogurt mixture, salt, and spices to the pot and cook and stir until thick and bubbly, about 5 minutes.
Transfer to a bowl and serve.

Per Serving: Calories 184; Fat 5g; Sodium 441mg; Carbs 17g; Fiber 4.6g; Sugar 5g; Protein 9g

Buffalo Chicken Dip

Prep time: 10 minutes| **Cook time:** 7 minutes| **Serves:** 10

2 cups cooked, shredded chicken
1 cup vegan nondairy blue cheese-style dressing
8 oz. nondairy cream cheese
½ cup buffalo hot sauce

In a 7" glass bowl, add the chicken, blue cheese dressing, cream cheese, and hot sauce. Mix.
Add 1 cup water to the Inner Pot and place the steam rack inside. Place the bowl on top of the steam rack.
Put on the pressure cooker's lid and turn the steam valve to "Sealing" position.
Press the "Pressure Cook" button one time to select "Less" option.
Use the "+/-" keys on the control panel to set the cooking time to 7 minutes.
Use the Pressure Level button to adjust the pressure to "High Pressure".
Once the cooking cycle is completed, allow the steam to release naturally.
When all the steam is released, remove the pressure lid from the top carefully.
Stir the dip and then serve warm.

Per Serving: Calories 382; Fat 10.9g; Sodium 354mg; Carbs 20.5g; Fiber 4.1g; Sugar 8.2g; Protein 06g

Spinach Artichoke Dip

Prep time: 10 minutes| **Cook time:** 6 minutes| **Serves:** 10

½ cup vegetable stock
1 (10-oz.) package frozen, cut spinach
1 (14-oz.) can artichoke quarters, drained
8 oz. nondairy cream cheese
¾ cup nondairy Greek yogurt
¼ cup vegan mayonnaise
1 teaspoon onion powder
¼ teaspoon garlic salt
¼ teaspoon black pepper
1 cup nutritional yeast

Add all of the ingredients to the Inner Pot of the Inner Pot.
Put on the pressure cooker's lid and turn the steam valve to "Sealing" position.
Press the "Pressure Cook" button one time to select "Less" option.
Use the "+/-" keys on the control panel to set the cooking time to 6 minutes.
Use the Pressure Level button to adjust the pressure to "High Pressure".
Once the cooking cycle is completed, quickly and carefully turn the steam release handle from Sealing position to the Venting position.
When all the steam is released, remove the pressure lid from the top carefully.
Stir well and then transfer the dip to a serving bowl. The dip will thicken as it sits.

Per Serving: Calories 372; Fat 20g; Sodium 891mg; Carbs 29g; Fiber 3g; Sugar 8g; Protein 7g

Sweet Potato Hummus

Prep time: 10 minutes| **Cook time:** 8 minutes| **Serves:** 10

2 tablespoons avocado oil
1 large sweet potato, peeled and cut into cubes
½ teaspoon salt
3 cloves garlic, minced
Juice from 1 large lemon
1 (15-oz.) can cooked chickpeas
¼ cup tahini
1 teaspoon ground cumin

Press the "Sauté" button two time to select "Normal" mode and pour the oil into the Inner Pot.
Allow it to heat 2 minutes.
Add the sweet potato and salt and sauté 2 minutes. Add the garlic and sauté an additional 30 seconds.
Press the Cancel button. Add the lemon juice.
Put on the pressure cooker's lid and turn the steam valve to "Sealing" position.
Press the "Pressure Cook" button one time to select "Less" option.
Use the "+/-" keys on the control panel to set the cooking time to 2 minutes.
Use the Pressure Level button to adjust the pressure to "High Pressure".
Once the cooking cycle is completed, quickly and carefully turn the steam release handle from Sealing position to the Venting position.
When all the steam is released, remove the pressure lid from the top carefully.
Transfer the contents of the Inner Pot to a large food processor.
Add the chickpeas, tahini, and cumin and process until you have a smooth mixture.
Allow the hummus to chill in the refrigerator at least 30 minutes before serving.

Per Serving: Calories 282; Fat 7.9g; Sodium 704mg; Carbs 6g; Fiber 3.6g; Sugar 6g; Protein 18g

Cauliflower Hummus

Prep time: 15 minutes| **Cook time:** 15 minutes| **Serves:** 10

1 tablespoon avocado oil
1 small yellow onion, chopped
3 cloves garlic, minced
1 small head cauliflower, cut into florets
¾ cup water
½ teaspoon salt
Juice from 1 large lemon
1 (15-oz.) can cooked chickpeas
¼ cup tahini
1 teaspoon ground cumin

Press the "Sauté" button two time to select "Normal" mode and pour the oil into the Inner Pot.

Allow it to heat 1 minute.
Add the onion and sauté 7 minutes until the onion is soft and starting to brown.
Add the garlic and sauté an additional 30 seconds. Press the Cancel button.
Add the cauliflower and water.
Put on the pressure cooker's lid and turn the steam valve to "Sealing" position.
Press the "Pressure Cook" button one time to select "Less" option.
Use the "+/-" keys on the control panel to set the cooking time to 5 minutes.
Use the Pressure Level button to adjust the pressure to "Low Pressure".
Once the cooking cycle is completed, quickly and carefully turn the steam release handle from Sealing position to the Venting position.
When all the steam is released, remove the pressure lid from the top carefully.
Transfer the contents of the Inner Pot to a large food processor, except the liquid.
Add the salt, lemon juice, chickpeas, tahini, and cumin and process until you have a smooth mixture.
If the mixture is too thick, add some of the liquid from the Inner Pot until it is the consistency you prefer.
Allow the hummus to chill in the refrigerator at least 30 minutes before serving.

Per Serving: Calories 234; Fat 12.9g; Sodium 414mg; Carbs 11g; Fiber 5g; Sugar 9g; Protein 11g

Black Bean Dip

Prep time: 10 minutes| **Cook time:** 7 minutes| **Serves:** 10
1 tablespoon avocado oil
1 medium yellow onion, peeled and chopped
2 (15-oz.) cans black beans, drained
1 teaspoon ground cumin
½ teaspoon chili powder
½ teaspoon smoked paprika
½ teaspoon salt
Juice from ½ medium lime
¼ cup nutritional yeast

Press the "Sauté" button two time to select "Normal" mode and add the oil to the Inner Pot.
Let it heat 1 minute and then add the onion.
Sauté the onion, stirring occasionally until softened, about 3 minutes. Press the Cancel button.
Add the beans, cumin, chili powder, paprika, and salt.
Put on the pressure cooker's lid and turn the steam valve to "Sealing" position.
Press the "Pressure Cook" button one time to select "Less" option.
Use the "+/-" keys on the control panel to set the cooking time to 3 minutes.
Use the Pressure Level button to adjust the pressure to "Low Pressure".
Once the cooking cycle is completed, quickly and carefully turn the steam release handle from Sealing position to the Venting position.

When all the steam is released, remove the pressure lid from the top carefully.
Add the lime juice and nutritional yeast and use an immersion blender to blend the dip.
Serve warm.

Per Serving: Calories 270; Fat 10.9g; Sodium 454mg; Carbs 10g; Fiber 3.1g; Sugar 5.2g; Protein 10g

White Bean Dip

Prep time: 5 minutes| **Cook time:** 8 minutes| **Serves:** 10
1 tablespoon avocado oil
1 medium yellow onion, peeled and chopped
2 cloves garlic, minced
2 (15-oz.) cans cannellini beans, drained
1 (15-oz.) can diced tomatoes, drained
½ teaspoon salt
¼ teaspoon black pepper
½ cup chopped fresh basil
1 tablespoon fresh lemon juice

Press the "Sauté" button two time to select "Normal" mode and add the oil to the Inner Pot.
Let it heat 1 minute and then add the onion.
Sauté the onion, stirring occasionally until softened, about 3 minutes.
Add the garlic and sauté an additional 30 seconds. Press the Cancel button.
Add the beans, tomatoes, salt, and pepper and stir to combine.
Put on the pressure cooker's lid and turn the steam valve to "Sealing" position.
Press the "Pressure Cook" button one time to select "Less" option.
Use the "+/-" keys on the control panel to set the cooking time to 3 minutes.
Use the Pressure Level button to adjust the pressure to "High Pressure".
Once the cooking cycle is completed, quickly and carefully turn the steam release handle from Sealing position to the Venting position.
When all the steam is released, remove the pressure lid from the top carefully.
Stir in the basil and lemon juice and then use an immersion blender to blend to a chunky consistency.
Serve warm or cold.

Per Serving: Calories 349; Fat 2.9g; Sodium 511mg; Carbs 12g; Fiber 3g; Sugar 8g; Protein 7g

Tamari Edamame

Prep time: 5 minutes| **Cook time:** 1 minutes| **Serves:** 4
1 (10-oz.) bag frozen edamame in pods
2 tablespoons reduced sodium tamari
¼ teaspoon kosher salt

Place 1 cup water in the Inner Pot and place a Steam Rack in the pot.
Place the edamame in a steamer basket and place basket on top of the steam rack.

Put on the pressure cooker's lid and turn the steam valve to "Sealing" position.
Press the "Steam" button one time to select "Less" option.
Use the "+/-" keys on the control panel to set the cooking time to 1 minutes.
Use the Pressure Level button to adjust the pressure to "Low Pressure".
Once the cooking cycle is completed, quickly and carefully turn the steam release handle from Sealing position to the Venting position.
When all the steam is released, remove the pressure lid from the top carefully.
Transfer the edamame to a medium bowl and top with the tamari and salt and serve.

Per Serving: Calories 281; Fat 7.9g; Sodium 704mg; Carbs 6g; Fiber 3.6g; Sugar 6g; Protein 18g

Cinnamon Almonds

Prep time: 5 minutes| **Cook time:** 2 minutes| **Serves:** 8
2 cups raw unsalted almonds
1 teaspoon ground cinnamon
2 tablespoons water
40 drops pure liquid stevia
½ teaspoon pure vanilla extract
¼ teaspoon coarse salt

Place all the ingredients into a 7-cup glass bowl and toss to combine.
Pour ½ cup hot water into the Inner Pot and place the steam rack inside.
Place the bowl with the almonds on top of the rack.
Put on the pressure cooker's lid and turn the steam valve to "Sealing" position.
Press the "Pressure Cook" button one time to select "Less" option.
Use the "+/-" keys on the control panel to set the cooking time to 2 minutes.
Use the Pressure Level button to adjust the pressure to "High Pressure".
Once the cooking cycle is completed, quickly and carefully turn the steam release handle from Sealing position to the Venting position.
When all the steam is released, remove the pressure lid from the top carefully.
Serve warm.

Per Serving: Calories 289; Fat 14g; Sodium 791mg; Carbs 18.9g; Fiber 4.6g; Sugar 8g; Protein 6g

Lentil Balls

Prep time: 40 minutes| **Cook time:** 15 minutes| **Serves:** 4
For the Lentil Balls
⅓ cup cooked black beans, drained
½ cup old fashioned rolled oats
1¼ cups cooked lentils
¼ cup unsweetened almond milk
¼ teaspoon coarse salt
¼ teaspoon ground ginger
⅛ teaspoon garlic powder

⅛ teaspoon black pepper
2 tablespoons avocado oil
2 tablespoons oat flour
For the Sauce
¾ cup tomato sauce
1 tablespoon tomato paste
¼ cup maple syrup
2 tablespoons cup coconut aminos
1 tablespoon apple cider vinegar
½ teaspoon ground ginger
¼ teaspoon crushed red pepper flakes

In a medium bowl, partially mash the black beans to make the Lentil Balls.
In a food processor pulse the oats a few times. Add the lentils and pulse again.
Add the milk, salt, ginger, garlic powder, and pepper and pulse. Do not over mix.
Combine the lentil mixture and black beans, stirring well.
Form into tablespoon-sized balls and refrigerate 30 minutes.
Mix all of the sauce ingredients together in a medium bowl to make the sauce.
Press the Sauté button twice to choose More.
Add the avocado oil to the Inner Pot. Allow it to heat 2 minutes.
Place the oat flour in a shallow bowl and dredge each lentil ball in the flour to coat it.
Add the lentil balls to the oil and carefully move them around to brown, about 1 minute per side.
Remove the balls and place them inside a suitable cake pan.
Cover with the sauce and a paper towel, then cover tightly with foil.
Add ½ cup water to Inner Pot and scrape up any brown bits from the bottom.
Place the steam rack in the pot and the pan of lentil balls on top of it.
Put on the pressure cooker's lid and turn the steam valve to "Sealing" position.
Press the "Pressure Cook" button one time to select "Less" option.
Use the "+/-" keys on the control panel to set the cooking time to 5 minutes.
Use the Pressure Level button to adjust the pressure to "Low Pressure".
Once the cooking cycle is completed, quickly and carefully turn the steam release handle from Sealing position to the Venting position.
When all the steam is released, remove the pressure lid from the top carefully.
Serve.

Per Serving: Calories 334; Fat 7.9g; Sodium 704mg; Carbs 6g; Fiber 3.6g; Sugar 6g; Protein 18g

Quinoa Energy Balls

Prep time: 15 minutes| **Cook time:** 5 minutes| **Serves:** 5
½ cup quinoa
1 cup water
¼ cup almond butter
2 teaspoons raw honey
½ teaspoon ground cinnamon
½ teaspoon blackstrap molasses

⅛ teaspoon fine sea salt

Place the quinoa in a fine-mesh strainer and rinse under water until the water runs clear.
Add the quinoa and water to the Inner Pot.
Put on the pressure cooker's lid and turn the steam valve to "Sealing" position.
Press the "Pressure Cook" button one time to select "Less" option.
Use the "+/-" keys on the control panel to set the cooking time to 5 minutes.
Use the Pressure Level button to adjust the pressure to "High Pressure".
Once the cooking cycle is completed, quickly and carefully turn the steam release handle from Sealing position to the Venting position.
When all the steam is released, remove the pressure lid from the top carefully.
Transfer the cooked quinoa to a medium bowl and allow it to cool.
Once it is cooled, add the rest of the ingredients to the bowl and stir to combine.
Form the mixture into 1" balls and place them onto a tray or plate.
Place them in the freezer about 30 minutes to firm.
Keep stored in the refrigerator.

Per Serving: Calories 372; Fat 20g; Sodium 891mg; Carbs 29g; Fiber 3g; Sugar 8g; Protein 7g

Broccoli Bites

Prep time: 10 minutes| **Cook time:** 1 minutes| **Serves:** 4

1 large crown broccoli, cut into large pieces
2 tablespoons toasted sesame oil
½ teaspoon salt
¼ teaspoon ground ginger
⅛ teaspoon garlic powder
2 tablespoons sesame seeds

Place the broccoli pieces into a suitable cake pan.
In a small bowl, whisk together the oil, salt, ginger, and garlic powder.
Add it to the broccoli and toss to coat.
Pour 1 cup water into the Inner Pot and place the Steam Rack inside.
Place the pan with broccoli on top of the steam rack.
Put on the pressure cooker's lid and turn the steam valve to "Sealing" position.
Press the "Pressure Cook" button one time to select "Less" option.
Use the "+/-" keys on the control panel to set the cooking time to 1 minute.
Use the Pressure Level button to adjust the pressure to "High Pressure".
Once the cooking cycle is completed, quickly and carefully turn the steam release handle from Sealing position to the Venting position.
When all the steam is released, remove the pressure lid from the top carefully.
Carefully remove the pan from the Inner Pot.
Add the sesame seeds to the broccoli and toss to coat. Transfer to a plate and serve with toothpicks.

Per Serving: Calories 312; Fat 19g; Sodium 354mg; Carbs 15g; Fiber 5.1g; Sugar 8.2g; Protein 12g

Hard-Boiled Eggs

Prep time: 5 minutes| **Cook time:** 10 minutes| **Serves:** 6

6 large eggs

Pour 1 cup water into the Inner Pot of your Inner Pot and place the Steam Rack inside.
Carefully place the eggs directly onto the steam rack.
Put on the pressure cooker's lid and turn the steam valve to "Sealing" position.
Press the "Steam" button one time to select "Normal" option.
Use the "+/-" keys on the control panel to set the cooking time to 7 minutes.
Use the Pressure Level button to adjust the pressure to "High Pressure".
Once the cooking cycle is completed, quickly and carefully turn the steam release handle from Sealing position to the Venting position.
When all the steam is released, remove the pressure lid from the top carefully.
Immediately transfer the eggs to a bowl filled with iced water and let them sit 15 minutes.
Remove the eggs from the water and peel the shells away from the eggs.
Store in the refrigerator.

Per Serving: Calories 382; Fat 7.9g; Sodium 704mg; Carbs 6g; Fiber 3.6g; Sugar 6g; Protein 38g

Avocado Hummus

Prep time: 15 minutes| **Cook time:** 10 minutes| **Serves:** 8

¾ cup dry chickpeas
3 cups water
1 teaspoon salt
1 large avocado, peeled, pitted, and sliced
2 tablespoons olive oil plus ⅛ teaspoon for drizzling
2 tablespoons fresh lemon juice
½ teaspoon crushed red pepper flakes

Put the chickpeas in a bowl and cover with 3" water.
Allow to soak 4–8 hours and then drain.
Add the soaked chickpeas, 3 cups water, and salt to the Inner Pot.
Put on the pressure cooker's lid and turn the steam valve to "Sealing" position.
Press the "Pressure Cook" button one time to select "Less" option.
Use the "+/-" keys on the control panel to set the cooking time to 10 minutes.
Use the Pressure Level button to adjust the pressure to "High Pressure".
Once the cooking cycle is completed, allow the steam to release naturally for 10 minutes, then turn the steam release handle to the Venting position.

When all the steam is released, remove the pressure lid from the top carefully.
Transfer the chickpeas to your food processor and add the avocado, oil, and lemon juice.
Process until the mixture is super smooth.
If the mixture is too thick, add water, 1 teaspoon at a time until desired consistency is reached.
Refrigerate until completely cooled and then sprinkle with crushed red pepper flakes and drizzle with the remaining ⅛ teaspoon olive oil before serving.

Per Serving: Calories 184; Fat 5g; Sodium 441mg; Carbs 17g; Fiber 4.6g; Sugar 5g; Protein 9g

Avocado Deviled Eggs

Prep time: 15 minutes| **Cook time:** 7 minutes| **Serves:** 12
6 large eggs
1 medium avocado, peeled, pitted, and diced
2½ tablespoons mayonnaise
2 teaspoons lime juice
1 clove garlic, crushed
⅛ teaspoon cayenne pepper
⅛ teaspoon salt
1 medium jalapeño pepper, sliced
12 dashes hot sauce

Pour 1 cup water into the Inner Pot and place the Steam Rack inside.
Carefully place the eggs directly onto the steam rack.
Put on the pressure cooker's lid and turn the steam valve to "Sealing" position.
Press the "Steam" button one time to select "Normal" option.
Use the "+/-" keys on the control panel to set the cooking time to 7 minutes.
Use the Pressure Level button to adjust the pressure to "Low Pressure".
Once the cooking cycle is completed, quickly and carefully turn the steam release handle from Sealing position to the Venting position.
When all the steam is released, remove the pressure lid from the top carefully.
Immediately transfer the eggs to a bowl filled with iced water and let them sit 15 minutes.
Remove the eggs from the water and peel the shells away from the eggs.
Slice the eggs in half.
Scoop egg yolks into a medium bowl and add the avocado, mayonnaise, lime juice, garlic, cayenne pepper, and salt.
Mash the egg yolk mixture until filling is evenly combined.
Spoon the filling into a piping bag and pipe filling into each egg white.
Top each with a jalapeño slice and a dash of hot sauce.

Per Serving: Calories 219; Fat 10g; Sodium 891mg; Carbs 22.9g; Fiber 4g; Sugar 4g; Protein 13g

Cauliflower Queso with Bell Pepper

Prep time: 5 minutes| **Cook time:** 5 minutes| **Serves:** 5
1 head cauliflower, cut into about 4 cups florets
2 cups water
1½ cups carrots, chopped into ½-inch-thick round pieces
½ cup raw cashews
1 (15-oz.) can no-salt-added diced tomatoes
½ cup nutritional yeast
1 tablespoon white miso paste
2 teaspoons gluten-free chili powder
1 red bell pepper, diced
4 scallions, white and green parts, diced

In your Inner Pot, combine the cauliflower, water, carrots, and cashews.
Put on the pressure cooker's lid and turn the steam valve to "Sealing" position.
Press the "Pressure Cook" button one time to select "Less" option.
Use the "+/-" keys on the control panel to set the cooking time to 5 minutes.
Use the Pressure Level button to adjust the pressure to "High Pressure".
Once the cooking cycle is completed, quickly and carefully turn the steam release handle from Sealing position to the Venting position.
When all the steam is released, remove the pressure lid from the top carefully.
Drain the water, then transfer the mixture to a blender or food processor.
Add the liquid from the can of tomatoes and set the drained tomatoes aside.
Add the nutritional yeast, miso, and chili powder and blend until very smooth.
Transfer to a medium bowl and stir in the drained tomatoes, bell pepper, and scallions.
Serve immediately.

Per Serving: Calories 282; Fat 7.9g; Sodium 704mg; Carbs 6g; Fiber 3.6g; Sugar 6g; Protein 18g

Lemon Eggplant in Vegetable Broth

Prep time: 5 minutes| **Cook time:** 15 minutes| **Serves:** 2
¼ to ½ cup Vegetable Broth
1 medium eggplant, peeled and sliced
1 cup water
3 garlic cloves, unpeeled
2 tablespoons lemon juice
2 tablespoons tahini
1 tablespoon white miso paste
½ teaspoon ground cumin, plus more for garnish

Press the Sauté button twice to select the cooking mode and the Normal cooking temperature.
Pour in 2 tablespoons of the broth.
Arrange as many slices of eggplant as possible in one layer on the bottom of the pot.
Sauté for 2 minutes, then flip, adding more of the broth as needed.

After another 2 minutes, pile the first batch of eggplant on one side of the Inner Pot and add the remaining eggplant.
Sauté on each side for 2 minutes, adding broth as needed. Add the water and garlic.
Put on the pressure cooker's lid and turn the steam valve to "Sealing" position.
Press the "Pressure Cook" button one time to select "Less" option.
Use the "+/-" keys on the control panel to set the cooking time to 3 minutes.
Use the Pressure Level button to adjust the pressure to "High Pressure".
Once the cooking cycle is completed, quickly and carefully turn the steam release handle from Sealing position to the Venting position.
When all the steam is released, remove the pressure lid from the top carefully.
Using a pair of tongs, remove the garlic and take off the outer peel.
In a blender, combine the garlic, eggplant, lemon juice, tahini, miso, and cumin.
Blend until smooth. Serve warm or cover, refrigerate, and serve cold.

Per Serving: Calories 221; Fat 12.9g; Sodium 414mg; Carbs 11g; Fiber 5g; Sugar 9g; Protein 11g

Garlic Collard Greens in Vegetable Broth

Prep time: 10 minutes| **Cook time:** 10 minutes| **Serves:** 4-6
1½ lbs. collard greens, stems removed, leaves chopped
1½ cups Easy Vegetable Broth or no-salt-added vegetable broth
3 tablespoons rice vinegar
3 garlic cloves, minced
1 (2-inch) knob fresh ginger, grated

In your Inner Pot, combine the collard greens, broth, vinegar, garlic, and ginger.
Put on the pressure cooker's lid and turn the steam valve to "Sealing" position.
Press the "Pressure Cook" button one time to select "Less" option.
Use the "+/-" keys on the control panel to set the cooking time to 10 minutes.
Use the Pressure Level button to adjust the pressure to "High Pressure".
Once the cooking cycle is completed, quickly and carefully turn the steam release handle from Sealing position to the Venting position.
When all the steam is released, remove the pressure lid from the top carefully.
Serve and enjoy.

Per Serving: Calories 289; Fat 14g; Sodium 791mg; Carbs 18.9g; Fiber 4.6g; Sugar 8g; Protein 6g

Sweet Potatoes with Maple Syrup

Prep time: 10 minutes| **Cook time:** 9 minutes| **Serves:**4-6
4 sweet potatoes (about 2 lbs.), peeled and cut into 1-inch chunks

1 cup orange juice
2 garlic cloves, minced
1 (1-inch) knob fresh ginger, peeled and grated, or 1 teaspoon ground ginger
1 (1-inch) knob fresh turmeric, peeled and grated, or 1 teaspoon ground turmeric
½ teaspoon ground cinnamon
1 tablespoon maple syrup

In your Inner Pot, combine the sweet potatoes, orange juice, garlic, ginger, turmeric, and cinnamon.
Put on the pressure cooker's lid and turn the steam valve to "Sealing" position.
Press the "Pressure Cook" button one time to select "Less" option.
Use the "+/-" keys on the control panel to set the cooking time to 9 minutes.
Use the Pressure Level button to adjust the pressure to "High Pressure".
Once the cooking cycle is completed, quickly and carefully turn the steam release handle from Sealing position to the Venting position.
When all the steam is released, remove the pressure lid from the top carefully.
Add the maple syrup and mash the potatoes with a handheld potato masher or a large fork.
Stir to blend and serve immediately.

Per Serving: Calories 184; Fat 5g; Sodium 441mg; Carbs 17g; Fiber 4.6g; Sugar 5g; Protein 9g

Dijon Brussels Sprouts

Prep time: 10 minutes| **Cook time:** 1 minutes| **Serves:** 4-6
1 pound fresh Brussels sprouts
1 cup water
2 garlic cloves, smashed
3 tablespoons apple cider vinegar
2 tablespoons Dijon mustard
1 tablespoon maple syrup
Black pepper

In your Inner Pot, combine the Brussels sprouts, water, and garlic.
Put on the pressure cooker's lid and turn the steam valve to "Sealing" position.
Press the "Pressure Cook" button one time to select "Less" option.
Use the "+/-" keys on the control panel to set the cooking time to 1 minute.
Use the Pressure Level button to adjust the pressure to "High Pressure".
Once the cooking cycle is completed, quickly and carefully turn the steam release handle from Sealing position to the Venting position.
When all the steam is released, remove the pressure lid from the top carefully.
In a small bowl, whisk together the vinegar, mustard, and maple syrup.
When the cook time is complete, quick-release the pressure and carefully remove the lid.
Drain the water and mince the garlic. Add the dressing to the sprouts and garlic and toss to coat.

Season with pepper and serve immediately.

Per Serving: Calories 122; Fat 7.9g; Sodium 704mg; Carbs 6g; Fiber 3.6g; Sugar 6g; Protein 18g

Jalapeño Peppers with Cashews

Prep time: 10 minutes| **Cook time:** 30 minutes| **Serves:** 4-6

2 jalapeño peppers
½ pound dried great northern beans, rinsed and sorted
½ medium onion, roughly chopped
4 cups water
½ cup cashews
¼ cup unsweetened plant-based milk
2 garlic cloves, crushed
2 tablespoons nutritional yeast
1 tablespoon chickpea miso paste
1 tablespoon apple cider vinegar

Slice 1 of the jalapeños pepper in half lengthwise and remove the seeds.
In your Inner Pot, combine the halved pepper, beans, onion, and 3 cups of the water.
Put on the pressure cooker's lid and turn the steam valve to "Sealing" position.
Press the "Pressure Cook" button one time to select "Normal" option.
Use the "+/-" keys on the control panel to set the cooking time to 30 minutes.
Use the Pressure Level button to adjust the pressure to "High Pressure".
While cooking, boil the remaining 1 cup of water and, using a large bowl, pour it over the cashews; let soak for at least 30 minutes.
Drain and discard the soaking liquid before using the cashews.
Once the cooking cycle is completed, allow the steam to release naturally for 10 minutes, then turn the steam release handle to the Venting position.
When all the steam is released, remove the pressure lid from the top carefully.
Remove the jalapeño pepper from the pot and finely chop it.
Finely chop the remaining raw jalapeño, removing the seeds if you prefer a milder dish.
Set both peppers aside.
Drain the beans and onion, then combine them in a blender with the cashews, milk, garlic, nutritional yeast, miso, and vinegar. Blend until creamy. Spoon into a medium mixing bowl and stir in the jalapeños.
Serve immediately.

Per Serving: Calories 295; Fat 10.9g; Sodium 354mg; Carbs 20.5g; Fiber 4.1g; Sugar 8.2g; Protein 06g

Simple Lentil-Walnut Dip

Prep time: 10 minutes| **Cook time:** 10 minutes| **Serves:** 4-6

¾ cup walnuts
2 cups water

1 cup green or brown lentils
½ medium onion, roughly chopped
1 bay leaf
2 garlic cloves, minced
2 tablespoons lemon juice
1 tablespoon white miso paste
1 tablespoon apple cider vinegar
Black pepper

Press the "Sauté" button two times to select "Normal" settings and allow it to heat for 2 minutes.
Pour in the walnuts and sauté for 3 to 5 minutes, stirring occasionally, until slightly darker in color and the oils begin to release.
Remove from the Inner Pot and set aside.
In your Inner Pot, combine the water, lentils, onion, and bay leaf.
Put on the pressure cooker's lid and turn the steam valve to "Sealing" position.
Press the "Pressure Cook" button one time to select "Less" option.
Use the "+/-" keys on the control panel to set the cooking time to 10 minutes.
Use the Pressure Level button to adjust the pressure to "High Pressure".
Once the cooking cycle is completed, allow the steam to release naturally for 10 minutes, then turn the steam release handle to the Venting position.
When all the steam is released, remove the pressure lid from the top carefully.
Remove and discard the bay leaf.
In a blender, combine the lentils, onion, garlic, lemon juice, miso, vinegar, and pepper to taste. Blend until creamy.
Serve either immediately as a warm dip or chill.

Per Serving: Calories 282; Fat 7.9g; Sodium 704mg; Carbs 6g; Fiber 3.6g; Sugar 6g; Protein 18g

Spiced Potatoes Dip

Prep time: 15 minutes| **Cook time:** 27 minutes| **Serves:** 4-6

1 cup unsweetened plant-based milk
½ cup vegetable broth
2 scallions, white and green parts, chopped
2 tablespoons nutritional yeast
1 tablespoon arrowroot powder
1 teaspoon garlic powder
1 teaspoon minced fresh rosemary
1 teaspoon mustard powder
Black pepper
Salt
1½ lbs. russet potatoes (4 or 5 medium), peeled
1 cup water

In a large mixing bowl, whisk together the milk, broth, scallions, nutritional yeast, arrowroot powder, garlic powder, rosemary, and mustard powder.
Season to taste with pepper and salt.
Using a Mandoline, the slicing blade on a food processor, or the slicing side of a box grater, slice the potatoes very thinly.

In a 7-inch-round ovenproof baking dish, arrange a 1-inch layer of potatoes, followed by enough of the sauce to just cover the potatoes.
Continue layering until all the potatoes are submerged under the sauce in the dish.
Pour the water into your Inner Pot and insert the Steam Rack. Place the dish on the Steam Rack.
Put on the pressure cooker's lid and turn the steam valve to "Sealing" position.
Press the "Pressure Cook" button one time to select "Normal" option.
Use the "+/-" keys on the control panel to set the cooking time to 27 minutes.
Use the Pressure Level button to adjust the pressure to "High Pressure".
Once the cooking cycle is completed, quickly and carefully turn the steam release handle from Sealing position to the Venting position.
When all the steam is released, remove the pressure lid from the top carefully.
Serve immediately.

Per Serving: Calories 361; Fat 10.9g; Sodium 454mg; Carbs 10g; Fiber 3.1g; Sugar 5.2g; Protein 10g

Corn with Tofu Crema

Prep time: 10 minutes| **Cook time:** 6 minutes| **Serves:** 4-6

1 cup water
4 to 6 frozen mini corncobs
1 (14-oz.) package silken tofu, drained
1 tablespoon lemon juice
1 tablespoon apple cider vinegar
1 teaspoon ground cumin
Salt
1 lime, cut into wedges
1 tablespoon no-salt-added gluten-free chili powder

Pour the water into the Inner Pot and place the Steam Rack inside. Set the corn on the Steam Rack.
Put on the pressure cooker's lid and turn the steam valve to "Sealing" position.
Press the "Pressure Cook" button one time to select "Less" option.
Use the "+/-" keys on the control panel to set the cooking time to 6 minutes.
Use the Pressure Level button to adjust the pressure to "High Pressure".
Once the cooking cycle is completed, quickly and carefully turn the steam release handle from Sealing position to the Venting position.
When all the steam is released, remove the pressure lid from the top carefully.
In a blender or food processor, combine the tofu, lemon juice, vinegar, cumin, and salt to taste. Blend well and set aside.
Rub each cob with a lime wedge and then slather it with a generous amount of crema.
Sprinkle ¼ to ½ teaspoon chili powder on each.
Serve immediately.

Per Serving: Calories 334; Fat 7.9g; Sodium 704mg; Carbs 6g; Fiber 3.6g; Sugar 6g; Protein 18g

Beet Hummus

Prep time: 10 minutes| **Cook time:** 45 minutes| **Serves:** 4-6

3 cups water
1 cup dried chickpeas, rinsed and sorted
1 medium beet, peeled and quartered
½ cup tahini
2 tablespoons lemon juice
4 garlic cloves, crushed
Salt

In your Inner Pot, combine the water, chickpeas, and beets.
Put on the pressure cooker's lid and turn the steam valve to "Sealing" position.
Press the "Pressure Cook" button one time to select "More" option.
Use the "+/-" keys on the control panel to set the cooking time to 45 minutes.
Use the Pressure Level button to adjust the pressure to "High Pressure".
Once the cooking cycle is completed, allow the steam to release naturally for 10 minutes, then turn the steam release handle to the Venting position.
When all the steam is released, remove the pressure lid from the top carefully.
In a blender or food processor, combine the tahini, lemon juice, garlic, and salt to taste.
Using a slotted spoon, remove the chickpeas and beets from the pot and add them to the other ingredients.
Blend well to combine, adding a tablespoon at a time of the remaining liquid in the Inner Pot.
Serve.

Per Serving: Calories 382; Fat 7.9g; Sodium 704mg; Carbs 6g; Fiber 3.6g; Sugar 6g; Protein 18g

Garlic Baby Potatoes

Prep time: 10 minutes| **Cook time:** 7 minutes| **Serves:** 4-6

2 lbs. baby red-skinned potatoes
1 cup water
3 tablespoons plant-based butter, melted, or olive oil
1 teaspoon garlic powder
1 teaspoon dried thyme
1 teaspoon dried rosemary, crushed
1 teaspoon salt
Black pepper

Pierce the potatoes with a fork and slice any larger potatoes in half.
In your Inner Pot, combine the potatoes and water.
Put on the pressure cooker's lid and turn the steam valve to "Sealing" position.
Press the "Pressure Cook" button one time to select "Less" option.

Use the "+/-" keys on the control panel to set the cooking time to 7 minutes.
Use the Pressure Level button to adjust the pressure to "High Pressure".
Once the cooking cycle is completed, quickly and carefully turn the steam release handle from Sealing position to the Venting position.
When all the steam is released, remove the pressure lid from the top carefully.
Drain the water and select the Sauté function. Add the butter or olive oil, garlic powder, thyme, rosemary, salt, and pepper to taste.
Stir to combine and allow the potatoes to brown slightly for 3 to 4 minutes.

Per Serving: Calories 184; Fat 5g; Sodium 441mg; Carbs 17g; Fiber 4.6g; Sugar 5g; Protein 9g

Creamed Spinach with Cashews

Prep time: 10 minutes| **Cook time:** 12 minutes| **Serves:** 4-6
½ medium onion, diced
4 garlic cloves, minced
1 (16-oz.) package frozen chopped spinach
1¾ cups unsweetened plant-based milk
1 cup water
¾ cup raw cashews
1 tablespoon lemon juice
1 teaspoon chickpea miso paste
½ teaspoon ground or freshly grated nutmeg
Black pepper

Press the "Sauté" button two time to select "Normal" settings and allow it to heat for 2 minutes.
Sauté the onion until translucent, 3 to 5 minutes, adding water as needed to prevent sticking.
Add the garlic and sauté for 30 seconds.
Cancel the Sauté function, then add the spinach and 1¼ cups of the milk.
Put on the pressure cooker's lid and turn the steam valve to "Sealing" position.
Press the "Pressure Cook" button one time to select "Less" option.
Use the "+/-" keys on the control panel to set the cooking time to 5 minutes.
Use the Pressure Level button to adjust the pressure to "High Pressure".
Once the cooking cycle is completed, allow the steam to release naturally.
When all the steam is released, remove the pressure lid from the top carefully.
Boil the water and, pour it over the cashews; let soak for at least 30 minutes before draining.
In a blender, combine the drained cashews, the remaining ½ cup of milk, the lemon juice, miso, nutmeg, and pepper to taste. Blend until smooth.
Combine the sauce with the spinach.
Serve immediately.

Per Serving: Calories 372; Fat 20g; Sodium 891mg; Carbs 29g; Fiber 3g; Sugar 8g; Protein 7g

Polenta with Mushroom Ragù

Prep time: 10 minutes| **Cook time:** 30 minutes| **Serves:** 4-6
1 medium onion, diced
1⅓ cups Easy Vegetable Broth
2 garlic cloves, minced
8 oz. white button mushrooms, sliced
8 oz. cremini mushrooms, sliced
3 tablespoons tomato paste
2 teaspoons dried thyme
1 teaspoon balsamic vinegar
Black pepper
3 cups water
1 cup polenta or ground cornmeal
1 cup unsweetened plant-based milk

Press the "Sauté" button two times to select "Normal" settings and allow it to heat for 2 minutes.
Sauté the onion until translucent, 3 to 5 minutes, adding broth as needed to prevent it from sticking.
Add the garlic and cook for 30 seconds. Add the mushrooms and sauté about 5 minutes, until softened.
Stir in the tomato paste, thyme, vinegar, and pepper to taste.
Add ⅓ cup of the broth and scrape up any browned bits from the bottom of the pot.
Bring to a simmer and cook for 3 minutes.
Cancel the Sauté function and remove the mushroom mixture to a small bowl.
Rinse and dry the Inner Pot.
Press the "Sauté" button two times to select "Normal" settings.
Then combine the water, polenta, milk, and the remaining 1 cup of broth, whisking continuously, for 5 minutes.
Press Cancel button to stop this cooking program.
Put on the pressure cooker's lid and turn the steam valve to "Sealing" position.
Press the "Pressure Cook" button one time to select "Less" option.
Use the "+/-" keys on the control panel to set the cooking time to 10 minutes.
Use the Pressure Level button to adjust the pressure to "High Pressure".
Once the cooking cycle is completed, allow the steam to release naturally.
When all the steam is released, remove the pressure lid from the top carefully.
Stir, then transfer to a serving bowl and top with the mushroom ragù.
Serve immediately.

Per Serving: Calories 295; Fat 12.9g; Sodium 414mg; Carbs 11g; Fiber 5g; Sugar 9g; Protein 11g

Chickpea Mushrooms

Prep time: 15 minutes| **Cook time:** 40 minutes| **Serves:** 8

2 cups dried chickpeas, soaked overnight and drained
½ teaspoon salt
9 cups water
½ pound fresh green beans, trimmed and cut into 1" pieces
4 oz. sliced button mushrooms
½ red bell pepper, seeded, thinly sliced, and cut into 1" pieces
½ medium red onion, peeled and diced
¼ cup chopped fresh flat-leaf parsley
2 tablespoons chopped fresh chives
2 tablespoons chopped fresh tarragon
¼ cup olive oil
2 tablespoons red wine vinegar
1 teaspoon Dijon mustard
1 teaspoon honey
½ teaspoon black pepper
¼ teaspoon salt
¼ cup grated Parmesan cheese

Add chickpeas, salt, and 8 cups water to the Inner Pot.
Put on the pressure cooker's lid and turn the steam valve to "Sealing" position.
Press the "Pressure Cook" button one time to select "More" option.
Use the "+/-" keys on the control panel to set the cooking time to 40 minutes.
Use the Pressure Level button to adjust the pressure to "Low Pressure".
Once the cooking cycle is completed, allow the steam to release naturally for 10 minutes, then turn the steam release handle to the Venting position.
When all the steam is released, remove the pressure lid from the top carefully.
Drain chickpeas. transfer to a large bowl and cool to room temperature.
Add remaining 1 cup water to the Inner Pot.
Add rack to pot, top with steamer basket, and add green beans.
Put on the pressure cooker's lid and turn the steam valve to "Sealing" position.
Press the "Pressure Cook" button one time to select "Less" option.
Use the "+/-" keys on the control panel to set the cooking time to 10 minutes.
Use the Pressure Level button to adjust the pressure to "High Pressure".
Once the cooking cycle is completed, allow the steam to release naturally.
When all the steam is released, remove the pressure lid from the top carefully.
Rinse the green beans with cool water and add to bowl with the chickpeas.
Add green bean to the mushrooms along bell pepper, red onion, parsley, chives, and tarragon, mix well.
In a small bowl, combine olive oil, vinegar, mustard, honey, black pepper, and salt.

Whisk to combine, then pour over chickpea and green bean mixture, and toss to coat.
Top with cheese and serve immediately.

Per Serving: Calories 122; Fat 7.9g; Sodium 704mg; Carbs 6g; Fiber 3.6g; Sugar 6g; Protein 18g

Chickpea Salad

Prep time: 15 minutes| **Cook time:** 20 minutes| **Serves:** 12

1 pound dried chickpeas
1½ tablespoons plus ¼ cup olive oil
4 cups water
¾ teaspoon salt
4 scallions, sliced
1 medium red onion, peeled and diced
1 small green bell pepper, seeded and diced
1 small red bell pepper, seeded and diced
½ cup minced fresh parsley
1 large carrot, peeled and grated
2 teaspoons lemon juice
2 teaspoons white wine vinegar
1 tablespoon olive oil mayonnaise
1 clove garlic, peeled and minced
⅛ teaspoon ground white pepper
½ teaspoon dried oregano
¼ cup grated Parmesan cheese

Place chickpeas in the Inner Pot along with 1½ tablespoons oil, 4 cups of water, and salt.
Put on the pressure cooker's lid and turn the steam valve to "Sealing" position.
Press the "Pressure Cook" button one time to select "Less" option.
Use the Pressure Level button to adjust the pressure to "Low Pressure".
Once the cooking cycle is completed, allow the steam to release naturally.
When all the steam is released, remove the pressure lid from the top carefully.
Add scallions, onion, bell peppers, parsley, and carrot to chickpeas and toss to combine.
In a small bowl, combine remaining ¼ cup of oil, lemon juice, vinegar, mayonnaise, garlic, white pepper, and oregano, and whisk to mix.
Pour dressing over chickpea mixture and stir to combine. Sprinkle cheese on top.
Close lid and allow to stand on the Keep Warm setting for 10 minutes before serving.

Per Serving: Calories 221; Fat 19g; Sodium 354mg; Carbs 15g; Fiber 5.1g; Sugar 8.2g; Protein 12g

Homemade Three-Bean Salad

Prep time: 15 minutes| **Cook time:** 30 minutes| **Serves:** 8

¼ pound dried pinto beans, soaked overnight and drained
¼ pound dried black beans, soaked overnight and drained

¼ pound dried red beans, soaked overnight and drained
8 cups water
1 tablespoon light olive oil
1 stalk celery, chopped
½ medium red onion, peeled and chopped
½ medium green bell pepper, seeded and chopped
¼ cup minced fresh cilantro
¼ cup minced fresh flat-leaf parsley
3 tablespoons olive oil
3 tablespoons red wine vinegar
1 tablespoon honey
½ teaspoon black pepper
½ teaspoon sea salt

Place beans, water, and light olive oil in the Inner Pot.
Put on the pressure cooker's lid and turn the steam valve to "Sealing" position.
Press the "Bean/Chili" button twice to select "Normal" option.
Use the Pressure Level button to adjust the pressure to "Low Pressure".
Once the cooking cycle is completed, allow the steam to release naturally.
When all the steam is released, remove the pressure lid from the top carefully and drain the beans, set aside to cool to room temperature.
Transfer cooled beans to a large bowl. Add celery, onion, bell pepper, cilantro, and parsley.
Mix well. In a small bowl, whisk together olive oil, vinegar, honey, black pepper, and salt.
Pour dressing over bean mixture and toss to coat. Refrigerate for 4 hours before serving.

Per Serving: Calories 219; Fat 10g; Sodium 891mg; Carbs 22.9g; Fiber 4g; Sugar 4g; Protein 13g

Cannellini Bean Salads

Prep time: 15 minutes| **Cook time:** 40 minutes| **Serves:** 6
1 cup dried cannellini beans, soaked overnight and drained
4 cups water
4 cups vegetable stock
1 tablespoon olive oil
1 teaspoon salt
2 cloves garlic, peeled and minced
½ cup diced tomato
½ teaspoon dried sage
½ teaspoon black pepper

Add beans and water to the Inner Pot.
Put on the pressure cooker's lid and turn the steam valve to "Sealing" position.
Press the "Bean/Chili" button twice to select "Normal" option.
Use the Pressure Level button to adjust the pressure to "High Pressure".
Once the cooking cycle is completed, quickly and carefully turn the steam release handle from Sealing position to the Venting position.
When all the steam is released, remove the pressure lid from the top carefully.

Drain and rinse beans, and return to pot along with stock. Soak for 1 hour.
Add olive oil, salt, garlic, tomato, sage, and pepper to beans.
Put on the pressure cooker's lid and turn the steam valve to "Sealing" position.
Press the "Pressure Cook" button one time to select "Less" option.
Use the "+/-" keys on the control panel to set the cooking time to 10 minutes.
Use the Pressure Level button to adjust the pressure to "Low Pressure".
Once the cooking cycle is completed, quickly and carefully turn the steam release handle from Sealing position to the Venting position.
When all the steam is released, remove the pressure lid from the top carefully.
Serve hot.

Per Serving: Calories 289; Fat 14g; Sodium 791mg; Carbs 18.9g; Fiber 4.6g; Sugar 8g; Protein 6g

Salty Edamame

Prep time: 10 minutes| **Cook time:** 25 minutes| **Serves:** 4
1 cup shelled edamame
8 cups water
1 tablespoon vegetable oil
1 teaspoon coarse sea salt
2 tablespoons soy sauce

Add edamame and 4 cups of water to the Inner Pot.
Put on the pressure cooker's lid and turn the steam valve to "Sealing" position.
Press the "Pressure Cook" button one time to select "Less" option.
Use the "+/-" keys on the control panel to set the cooking time to 1 minutes.
Use the Pressure Level button to adjust the pressure to "High Pressure".
Once the cooking cycle is completed, quickly and carefully turn the steam release handle from Sealing position to the Venting position.
When all the steam is released, remove the pressure lid from the top carefully.
Add the remaining 4 cups of water and resuming cooking on Pressure Cook mode for 11 minutes at High Pressure.
Once the cooking cycle is completed, allow the pressure release naturally.
When done, drain edamame and transfer to a serving bowl.
Sprinkle with salt and serve with soy sauce on the side for dipping.

Per Serving: Calories 334; Fat 7.9g; Sodium 704mg; Carbs 6g; Fiber 3.6g; Sugar 6g; Protein 18g

Garlicky Black-Eyed Pea Soup

Prep time: 10 minutes| **Cook time:** 30 minutes| **Serves:** 8
2 tablespoons light olive oil
2 stalks celery, chopped

1 medium white onion, peeled and chopped
2 cloves garlic, peeled and minced
2 tablespoons chopped fresh oregano
1 teaspoon fresh thyme leaves
1 pound dried black-eyed peas, soaked overnight and drained
¼ teaspoon salt
1 teaspoon black pepper
4 cups water
1 (15-oz.) can diced tomatoes

Press the "Sauté" button two time to select "Normal" and then heat oil.
Add celery and onion, and cook for 5 minutes or until just tender.
Add garlic, oregano, and thyme, and cook until fragrant, about 30 seconds.
Press the Cancel button.
Add black-eyed peas, salt, pepper, water, and tomatoes to the Inner Pot and stir well.
Put on the pressure cooker's lid and turn the steam valve to "Sealing" position.
Press the "Pressure Cook" button one time to select "Less" option.
Use the Pressure Level button to adjust the pressure to "Low Pressure".
Once the cooking cycle is completed, allow the steam to release naturally.
When all the steam is released, remove the pressure lid from the top carefully.
Stir well. Serve hot.

Per Serving: Calories 310; Fat 7.9g; Sodium 704mg; Carbs 6g; Fiber 3.6g; Sugar 6g; Protein 18g

Dill Black-Eyed Peas

Prep time: 10 minutes| **Cook time:** 20 minutes| **Serves:** 8

¼ cup olive oil
4 sprigs oregano, leaves minced and stems reserved
2 sprigs thyme, leaves stripped and stems reserved
4 sprigs dill, fronds chopped and stems reserved
1 pound dried black-eyed peas, soaked overnight and drained
¼ teaspoon salt
1 teaspoon black pepper
4 cups water

In a small bowl, combine oil, oregano leaves, thyme leaves, and dill fronds, and mix to combine.
Cover and set aside. Tie herb stems together with butcher's twine.
Add to the Inner Pot along with black-eyed peas, salt, pepper, and water.
Put on the pressure cooker's lid and turn the steam valve to "Sealing" position.
Press the "Pressure Cook" button one time to select "Less" option.
Use the Pressure Level button to adjust the pressure to "Low Pressure".
Once the cooking cycle is completed, allow the steam to release naturally.

When all the steam is released, remove the pressure lid from the top carefully.
Remove and discard herb stem bundle, and drain off any excess liquid.
Stir in olive oil mixture.
Serve hot.

Per Serving: Calories 184; Fat 5g; Sodium 441mg; Carbs 17g; Fiber 4.6g; Sugar 5g; Protein 9g

Black Bean Sliders

Prep time: 10 minutes| **Cook time:** 55 minutes| **Serves:** 8

1 tablespoon olive oil
1 slice bacon
1 small red bell pepper, seeded and diced
2 cups vegetable broth
1 cup dried black beans, soaked overnight and drained
½ teaspoon garlic powder
¼ teaspoon coriander
½ teaspoon chili powder
½ teaspoon ground cumin
½ teaspoon sea salt
¼ cup chopped fresh cilantro
1 large egg
1 cup panko bread crumbs
16 slider buns

Press the "Sauté" button twice to select "Normal" and then heat oil.
Add bacon and bell pepper. Cook until bacon is cooked through, about 5 minutes.
Add broth and scrape bottom of pot to release browned bits.
Add beans, garlic powder, coriander, chili powder, cumin, salt, and cilantro.
Stir well, then press the Cancel button.
Put on the pressure cooker's lid and turn the steam valve to "Sealing" position.
Press the "Pressure Cook" button one time to select "Normal" option.
Use the "+/-" keys on the control panel to set the cooking time to 30 minutes.
Use the Pressure Level button to adjust the pressure to "Low Pressure".
Once the cooking cycle is completed, allow the steam to release naturally.
When all the steam is released, remove the pressure lid from the top carefully.
Remove and discard bacon.
Without the lid, press the Sauté button, press again to change the heat to Less, and simmer bean mixture for 10 minutes to thicken.
Transfer mixture to a large bowl. Once cool enough to handle, quickly mix in egg and bread crumbs.
Form into 16 equal-sized small patties.
Cook on stovetop in a skillet over medium heat for approximately 2–3 minutes per side until browned.
Remove from heat and add each patty to a bun.
Serve warm.

Per Serving: Calories 314; Fat 7.9g; Sodium 704mg; Carbs 6g; Fiber 3.6g; Sugar 6g; Protein 18g

Beans with Tomato and Parsley

Prep time: 10 minutes| **Cook time:** 60 minutes| **Serves:** 4

2 tablespoons light olive oil
1 medium white onion, peeled and chopped
2 cloves garlic, peeled and minced
1 pound dried giant beans, soaked overnight and drained
2 thyme sprigs
1 bay leaf
5 cups water
1 (15-oz.) can diced tomatoes, drained
1 (8-oz.) can tomato sauce
¼ cup chopped fresh flat-leaf parsley
2 tablespoons chopped fresh oregano
1 tablespoon chopped fresh dill
½ cup crumbled feta cheese
1 small lemon, cut into 8 wedges

Press the "Sauté" button twice to select the cooking mode and "Normal" cooking temperature, then add and heat oil.
Add onion and cook until tender, about 3 minutes.
Add garlic and cook until fragrant, about 30 seconds. Press the Cancel button.
Add beans, thyme, bay leaf, and water to the Inner Pot.
Put on the pressure cooker's lid and turn the steam valve to "Sealing" position.
Press the "Pressure Cook" button one time to select "More" option.
Use the "+/-" keys on the control panel to set the cooking time to 50 minutes.
Use the Pressure Level button to adjust the pressure to "Low Pressure".
Once the cooking cycle is completed, quickly and carefully turn the steam release handle from Sealing position to the Venting position.
When all the steam is released, remove the pressure lid from the top carefully.
Add diced tomatoes and tomato sauce.
Close lid and let stand on the Keep Warm setting for 10 minutes to heat through.
Remove and discard bay leaf. Stir in herbs and ladle into soup bowls.
Garnish with feta and lemon slices, and serve hot.

Per Serving: Calories 382; Fat 10.9g; Sodium 354mg; Carbs 20.5g; Fiber 4.1g; Sugar 8.2g; Protein 06g

Black Beans with Corn and Tomato Relish

Prep time: 10 minutes| **Cook time:** 30 minutes| **Serves:** 6

½ pound dried black beans, soaked overnight and drained
1 medium white onion, peeled and sliced in half
2 cloves garlic, peeled and lightly crushed
8 cups water

1 cup corn kernels
1 large tomato, seeded and chopped
½ medium red onion, peeled and chopped
¼ cup minced fresh cilantro
½ teaspoon ground cumin
¼ teaspoon smoked paprika
¼ teaspoon black pepper
¼ teaspoon salt
3 tablespoons olive oil
3 tablespoons lime juice

Add beans, white onion, garlic, and water to the Inner Pot.
Put on the pressure cooker's lid and turn the steam valve to "Sealing" position.
Press the "Bean/Chili" button twice to select "Normal" option.
Use the Pressure Level button to adjust the pressure to "High Pressure".
Once the cooking cycle is completed, allow the steam to release naturally.
When all the steam is released, remove the pressure lid from the top carefully.
Discard onion and garlic. Drain beans well and transfer to a medium bowl.
Cool to room temperature, about 30 minutes.
In a separate small bowl, combine corn, tomato, red onion, cilantro, cumin, paprika, pepper, and salt.
Toss to combine. Add to black beans and gently fold to mix.
Whisk together olive oil and lime juice in a small bowl and pour over black bean mixture. Gently toss to coat.
Serve at room temperature or refrigerate for at least 2 hours.

Per Serving: Calories 372; Fat 20g; Sodium 891mg; Carbs 29g; Fiber 3g; Sugar 8g; Protein 7g

White Bean Soup

Prep time: 10 minutes| **Cook time:** 30 minutes| **Serves:** 8

4 cups water
1 pound dried white kidney beans, soaked overnight and drained
2 medium carrots, peeled and sliced
2 medium onions, peeled and diced
2 stalks celery, thinly sliced
1 medium parsnip, peeled and thinly sliced
1 cup tomato sauce
1 tablespoon dried rosemary
1 tablespoon dried thyme
3 bay leaves
4 tablespoons minced fresh parsley
¼ cup olive oil
4 cloves garlic, peeled
¾ teaspoon salt
½ teaspoon black pepper

Place water, beans, carrots, onions, celery, parsnip, tomato sauce, rosemary, thyme, bay leaves, parsley, oil, and garlic in the Inner Pot.
Put on the pressure cooker's lid and turn the steam valve to "Sealing" position.

Press the "Bean/Chili" button twice to select "Normal" option.
Use the Pressure Level button to adjust the pressure to "Low Pressure".
Once the cooking cycle is completed, allow the steam to release naturally.
When all the steam is released, remove the pressure lid from the top carefully.
Discard bay leaves, and season with salt and pepper.
Serve hot.

Per Serving: Calories 349; Fat 2.9g; Sodium 511mg; Carbs 12g; Fiber 3g; Sugar 8g; Protein 7g

Creamy White Bean Soup

Prep time: 10 minutes| **Cook time:** 27 minutes| **Serves:** 6

1 tablespoon olive oil
1 medium white onion, peeled and chopped
1 medium carrot, peeled and chopped
1 stalk celery, chopped
2 cloves garlic, peeled and minced
1 cup dried cannellini beans, soaked overnight and drained
4 cups vegetable broth
1 (15-oz.) can diced tomatoes
1 teaspoon minced fresh sage
½ teaspoon black pepper
½ teaspoon sea salt

Press the "Sauté" button two time to select "Normal" and heat oil.
Add onion, carrot, and celery and sauté 5 minutes.
Add garlic and cook 30 seconds. Stir in beans. Press the Cancel button.
Add broth, tomatoes, sage, pepper, and salt and stir.
Put on the pressure cooker's lid and turn the steam valve to "Sealing" position.
Press the "Pressure Cook" button one time to select "Less" option.
Use the Pressure Level button to adjust the pressure to "Low Pressure".
Once the cooking cycle is completed, quickly and carefully turn the steam release handle from Sealing position to the Venting position.
When all the steam is released, remove the pressure lid from the top carefully.
Remove 1 cup beans and mash until smooth. Stir back into pot.
Serve hot.

Per Serving: Calories 372; Fat 20g; Sodium 891mg; Carbs 29g; Fiber 3g; Sugar 8g; Protein 7g

Herbed Lima Beans

Prep time: 10 minutes| **Cook time:** 6 minutes| **Serves:** 6

1 pound frozen baby lima beans, thawed
2 cloves garlic, peeled and minced
2 thyme sprigs
1 bay leaf

2 tablespoons olive oil
3 cups water
1 tablespoon chopped fresh dill
1 tablespoon chopped fresh tarragon
1 tablespoon chopped fresh mint

Add lima beans, garlic, thyme, bay leaf, oil, and water to the Inner Pot.
Put on the pressure cooker's lid and turn the steam valve to "Sealing" position.
Press the "Pressure Cook" button one time to select "Less" option.
Use the "+/-" keys on the control panel to set the cooking time to 6 minutes.
Use the Pressure Level button to adjust the pressure to "High Pressure".
Once the cooking cycle is completed, quickly and carefully turn the steam release handle from Sealing position to the Venting position.
When all the steam is released, remove the pressure lid from the top carefully.
Discard thyme and bay leaf, and stir well.
Stir in dill, tarragon, and mint, and serve.

Per Serving: Calories 219; Fat 10g; Sodium 891mg; Carbs 22.9g; Fiber 4g; Sugar 4g; Protein 13g

Greek Navy Bean Soup

Prep time: 10 minutes| **Cook time:** 30 minutes| **Serves:** 8

1 cup small dried navy beans, soaked overnight and drained
1 large stalk celery, halved lengthwise and sliced into ½" pieces
1 large carrot, peeled, halved, and sliced into ½" pieces
2 medium onions, peeled and chopped
½ cup tomato purée
½ cup olive oil
2 bay leaves
1 medium chili pepper, stemmed and minced
2 teaspoons smoked paprika
8 cups water
½ teaspoon salt

Add beans, celery, carrot, onions, tomato purée, oil, bay leaves, chili pepper, paprika, and water to the Inner Pot.
Put on the pressure cooker's lid and turn the steam valve to "Sealing" position.
Press the "Bean/Chili" button twice to select "Normal" option.
Use the Pressure Level button to adjust the pressure to "High Pressure".
Once the cooking cycle is completed, allow the steam to release naturally.
When all the steam is released, remove the pressure lid from the top carefully.
Season with salt. Remove and discard bay leaves.
Serve hot.

Per Serving: Calories 282; Fat 12.9g; Sodium 414mg; Carbs 11g; Fiber 5g; Sugar 9g; Protein 11g

Three-Bean Chili

Prep time: 10 minutes| **Cook time:** 40 minutes| **Serves:** 12

1 cup dried pinto beans, soaked overnight and drained
1 cup dried red beans, soaked overnight and drained
1 cup dried black beans, soaked overnight and drained
2 medium white onions, peeled and chopped
2 medium red bell peppers, seeded and chopped
2 stalks celery, chopped
1 (28-oz.) can diced tomatoes
1 (15-oz.) can tomato sauce
¼ cup chili powder
2 tablespoons smoked paprika
1 teaspoon ground cumin
1 teaspoon ground coriander
½ teaspoon salt
½ teaspoon black pepper
3 cups vegetable broth
1 cup water

Place all ingredients in the Inner Pot and stir to combine.
Put on the pressure cooker's lid and turn the steam valve to "Sealing" position.
Press the "Bean/Chili" button twice to select "Normal" option.
Use the Pressure Level button to adjust the pressure to "Low Pressure".
Once the cooking cycle is completed, quickly and carefully turn the steam release handle from Sealing position to the Venting position.
When all the steam is released, remove the pressure lid from the top carefully.
Press Cancel button to stop this cooking program.
Press the "Sauté" button twice to select "Less" mode and let chili simmer, uncovered, until desired thickness is reached.
Serve warm.

Per Serving: Calories 289; Fat 14g; Sodium 791mg; Carbs 18.9g; Fiber 4.6g; Sugar 8g; Protein 6g

White Bean Barley Soup

Prep time: 10 minutes| **Cook time:** 37 minutes| **Serves:** 8

2 tablespoons light olive oil
½ medium onion, peeled and chopped
1 medium carrot, peeled and chopped
1 stalk celery, chopped
2 cloves garlic, peeled and minced
2 sprigs fresh thyme
1 bay leaf
½ teaspoon black pepper
1 (14-oz.) can fire-roasted diced tomatoes, undrained
½ cup medium pearl barley, rinsed and drained
4 cups vegetable broth
2 cups water
2 (15-oz.) cans Great Northern beans, drained
½ teaspoon salt

Press the "Sauté" button twice to select "Normal" and heat oil.
Add onion, carrot, and celery. Cook until just tender, about 5 minutes.
Add garlic, thyme, bay leaf, and pepper, and cook until fragrant, about 30 seconds. Press the Cancel button.
Add the tomatoes, barley, broth, and water.
Put on the pressure cooker's lid and turn the steam valve to "Sealing" position.
Press the "Soup" button one time to select "Less" option.
Use the Pressure Level button to adjust the pressure to "Low Pressure".
Once the cooking cycle is completed, allow the steam to release naturally.
When all the steam is released, remove the pressure lid from the top carefully.
Stir soup, then add beans and salt. Close lid and let stand on the Keep Warm setting for 10 minutes.
Remove and discard bay leaf.
Serve hot.

Per Serving: Calories 382; Fat 7.9g; Sodium 704mg; Carbs 6g; Fiber 3.6g; Sugar 6g; Protein 18g

Bean and Lentil Chili

Prep time: 10 minutes| **Cook time:** 25 minutes| **Serves:** 6

2 tablespoons vegetable oil
1 large Spanish onion, peeled and diced
1 small jalapeño pepper, seeded and minced
1 clove garlic, peeled and minced
1 cup dried brown or green lentils, rinsed and drained
1 (15-oz.) can black beans, drained
1 cup pearl barley, rinsed and drained
3 tablespoons chili powder
1 tablespoon sweet paprika
1 teaspoon dried oregano
1 teaspoon ground cumin
1 (28-oz.) can diced tomatoes
1 chipotle pepper in adobo sauce, minced
6 cups vegetable broth
½ teaspoon salt
¼ teaspoon black pepper

Press the "Sauté" button two time to select "Normal" and heat oil.
Add onion and cook until just tender, about 3 minutes. Stir in jalapeño and cook for 1 minute.
Add garlic and cook until fragrant, about 30 seconds.
Stir in lentils, black beans, barley, chili powder, paprika, oregano, cumin, tomatoes, chipotle pepper, and vegetable broth.
Put on the pressure cooker's lid and turn the steam valve to "Sealing" position.
Press the "Pressure Cook" button one time to select "Less" option.
Use the "+/-" keys on the control panel to set the cooking time to 10 minutes.
Use the Pressure Level button to adjust the pressure to "Low Pressure".

Once the cooking cycle is completed, quickly and carefully turn the steam release handle from Sealing position to the Venting position. When all the steam is released, remove the pressure lid from the top carefully.
Press the Cancel button, then press the Sauté button twice to choose "Less".
Bring to a simmer. Season with salt and black pepper, and simmer until slightly thickened, about 10 minutes.
Serve immediately.

Per Serving: Calories 450; Fat 7.9g; Sodium 704mg; Carbs 6g; Fiber 3.6g; Sugar 6g; Protein 18g

Chili-Spiced Beans

Prep time: 10 minutes| **Cook time:** 40 minutes| **Serves:** 8
1 pound dried pinto beans, soaked overnight and drained
1 medium onion, peeled and chopped
¼ cup chopped fresh cilantro
1 (15-oz.) can tomato sauce
¼ cup chili powder
2 tablespoons smoked paprika
1 teaspoon ground cumin
1 teaspoon ground coriander
½ teaspoon black pepper
2 cups vegetable broth
1 cup water

Place all ingredients in the Inner Pot and stir to combine.
Put on the pressure cooker's lid and turn the steam valve to "Sealing" position.
Press the "Bean/Chili" button one time to select "Normal" option.
Use the Pressure Level button to adjust the pressure to "Low Pressure".
Once the cooking cycle is completed, quickly and carefully turn the steam release handle from Sealing position to the Venting position. When all the steam is released, remove the pressure lid from the top carefully.
Press Cancel button to stop this cooking program.
Press the "Sauté" button two time to select "Less" mode and let beans simmer, uncovered, until desired thickness is reached.
Serve warm.

Per Serving: Calories 334; Fat 7.9g; Sodium 704mg; Carbs 6g; Fiber 3.6g; Sugar 6g; Protein 18g

Lima Bean Soup

Prep time: 10 minutes| **Cook time:** 17 minutes| **Serves:** 6
1 tablespoon olive oil
1 small onion, peeled and diced
1 clove garlic, peeled and minced
2 cups vegetable stock
½ cup water
2 cups dried lima beans, soaked overnight and drained

½ teaspoon salt
½ teaspoon black pepper
2 tablespoons thinly sliced chives

Press the "Sauté" button two time to select "Normal" mode on the Inner Pot and heat oil.
Add onion and cook until golden brown, about 10 minutes.
Add garlic and cook until fragrant, about 30 seconds.
Press the Cancel button.
Add stock, water, and lima beans.
Put on the pressure cooker's lid and turn the steam valve to "Sealing" position.
Press the "Pressure Cook" button one time to select "Less" option.
Use the "+/-" keys on the control panel to set the cooking time to 6 minutes.
Use the Pressure Level button to adjust the pressure to "High Pressure".
Once the cooking cycle is completed, allow the steam to release naturally.
When all the steam is released, remove the pressure lid from the top carefully.
Purée soup with an immersion blender or in batches in a blender.
Season with salt and pepper, then sprinkle with chives before serving.

Per Serving: Calories 212; Fat 10.9g; Sodium 454mg; Carbs 10g; Fiber 3.1g; Sugar 5.2g; Protein 10g

Vegetarian Loaf

Prep time: 10 minutes| **Cook time:** 50 minutes| **Serves:** 6
1 cup dried pinto beans, soaked overnight and drained
8 cups water
1 tablespoon vegetable oil
1 teaspoon salt
1 cup diced onion
1 cup chopped walnuts
½ cup rolled oats
1 large egg, beaten
¾ cup ketchup
1 teaspoon garlic powder
1 teaspoon dried basil
1 teaspoon dried parsley
½ teaspoon salt
½ teaspoon black pepper

Add beans and 4 cups of water to the Inner Pot.
Put on the pressure cooker's lid and turn the steam valve to "Sealing" position.
Press the "Pressure Cook" button one time to select "Less" option.
Use the "+/-" keys on the control panel to set the cooking time to 1 minutes.
Use the Pressure Level button to adjust the pressure to "High Pressure".
Once the cooking cycle is completed, quickly and carefully turn the steam release handle from Sealing position to the Venting position. When all the steam is released, remove the pressure lid from the top carefully; drain and rinse the beans and then return to the pot

with the remaining 4 cups of water. Soak for 1 hour.
Still in the pot. Add the oil and salt.
Put on the pressure cooker's lid and turn the steam valve to "Sealing" position.
Press the "Pressure Cook" button one time to select "Less" option.
Use the "+/-" keys on the control panel to set the cooking time to 11 minutes.
Use the Pressure Level button to adjust the pressure to "High Pressure".
Once the cooking cycle is completed, allow the pressure release naturally.
In a suitable bowl, stir in onion, walnuts, oats, egg, ketchup, garlic powder, basil, parsley, salt, and pepper.
Spread the mixture into a loaf pan and bake for 30–35 minutes in the preheated oven at 350 degrees F.
Cool for 20 minutes in pan before slicing and serving.

Per Serving: Calories 221; Fat 7.9g; Sodium 704mg; Carbs 6g; Fiber 3.6g; Sugar 6g; Protein 18g

Chickpea Soup

Prep time: 10 minutes| **Cook time:** 25 minutes| **Serves:** 8
1 pound dried chickpeas
4 cups water
¾ teaspoon salt
½ teaspoon black pepper
10 strands saffron
2 medium onions, peeled and diced
1 cup olive oil
1 teaspoon dried oregano
3 tablespoons lemon juice
2 tablespoons chopped fresh parsley

Add chickpeas, water, salt, pepper, saffron, onions, oil, and oregano to the Inner Pot and stir well.
Put on the pressure cooker's lid and turn the steam valve to "Sealing" position.
Press the "Bean/Chili" button one time to select "Less" option.
Use the Pressure Level button to adjust the pressure to "Low Pressure".
Once the cooking cycle is completed, allow the steam to release naturally.
When all the steam is released, remove the pressure lid from the top carefully.
Serve hot or cold, sprinkled with lemon juice. Garnish with chopped parsley.

Per Serving: Calories 289; Fat 14g; Sodium 791mg; Carbs 18.9g; Fiber 4.6g; Sugar 8g; Protein 6g

White Bean Soup with Kale

Prep time: 10 minutes| **Cook time:** 27 minutes| **Serves:** 8
1 tablespoon light olive oil
2 stalks celery, chopped
1 medium yellow onion, peeled and chopped
2 cloves garlic, peeled and minced
1 tablespoon chopped fresh oregano
4 cups chopped kale
1 pound dried Great Northern beans, soaked overnight and drained
8 cups vegetable broth
¼ cup lemon juice
1 tablespoon olive oil
1 teaspoon black pepper

Press the "Sauté" button two time to select "Normal" mode and heat light olive oil.
Add celery and onion and cook 5 minutes. Add garlic and oregano and sauté 30 seconds.
Add kale and turn to coat, then cook until just starting to wilt, about 1 minute.
Press the Cancel button.
Add beans, broth, lemon juice, olive oil, and pepper to the Inner Pot and stir well.
Put on the pressure cooker's lid and turn the steam valve to "Sealing" position.
Press the "Pressure Cook" button one time to select "Less" option.
Use the Pressure Level button to adjust the pressure to "Low Pressure".
Once the cooking cycle is completed, allow the steam to release naturally.
When all the steam is released, remove the pressure lid from the top carefully.
Serve hot.

Per Serving: Calories 450; Fat 7.9g; Sodium 704mg; Carbs 6g; Fiber 3.6g; Sugar 6g; Protein 18g

White Bean Cassoulet

Prep time: 10 minutes| **Cook time:** 45 minutes| **Serves:** 8
1 tablespoon olive oil
1 medium onion, peeled and diced
2 cups dried cannellini beans, soaked overnight and drained
1 medium parsnip, peeled and diced
2 medium carrots, peeled and diced
2 stalks celery, diced
1 medium zucchini, trimmed and chopped
½ teaspoon fennel seed
¼ teaspoon ground nutmeg
½ teaspoon garlic powder
1 teaspoon sea salt
½ teaspoon black pepper
2 cups vegetable broth
1 (15-oz.) can diced tomatoes, including juice
2 sprigs rosemary

Press the "Sauté" button two time to select "Normal" mode on the Inner Pot and heat oil.
Add onion and cook until translucent, about 5 minutes. Add beans and toss.
Add a layer of parsnip, then a layer of carrots, and next a layer of celery.
Finally, add a layer of zucchini. Sprinkle in fennel seed, nutmeg, garlic powder, salt, and pepper.
Press Cancel button to stop this cooking program.
Gently pour in broth and canned tomatoes.
Top with rosemary.

Put on the pressure cooker's lid and turn the steam valve to "Sealing" position.
Press the "Pressure Cook" button one time to select "Normal" option.
Use the "+/-" keys on the control panel to set the cooking time to 30 minutes.
Use the Pressure Level button to adjust the pressure to "Low Pressure".
Once the cooking cycle is completed, allow the steam to release naturally for 10 minutes, then turn the steam release handle to the Venting position.
When all the steam is released, press Cancel button to stop this cooking program and remove the pressure lid from the top carefully.
Press the Sauté button twice to select the cooking mode and "Less" cooking temperature, and simmer bean mixture uncovered for 10 minutes to thicken.
Transfer to a serving bowl and carefully toss. Remove and discard rosemary and serve.

Per Serving: Calories 220; Fat 10.9g; Sodium 354mg; Carbs 20.5g; Fiber 4.1g; Sugar 8.2g; Protein 06g

Toasted Orzo Salad

Prep time: 10 minutes| **Cook time:** 10 minutes| **Serves:** 6
2 tablespoons light olive oil
1 clove garlic, peeled and crushed
2 cups orzo
3 cups vegetable broth
½ cup sliced black olives
3 scallions, thinly sliced
1 medium Roma tomato, seeded and diced
1 medium red bell pepper, seeded and diced
¼ cup crumbled feta cheese
1 tablespoon olive oil
1 tablespoon red wine vinegar
½ teaspoon black pepper
¼ teaspoon salt

Press the "Sauté" button twice to select "Normal" and heat light olive oil.
Add garlic and orzo and cook, stirring frequently, until orzo is light golden brown, about 5 minutes.
Press Cancel button to stop this cooking program, add the broth and stir.
Put on the pressure cooker's lid and turn the steam valve to "Sealing" position.
Press the "Pressure Cook" button one time to select "Less" option.
Use the "+/-" keys on the control panel to set the cooking time to 3 minutes.
Use the Pressure Level button to adjust the pressure to "Low Pressure".
Once the cooking cycle is completed, quickly and carefully turn the steam release handle from Sealing position to the Venting position.
When all the steam is released, remove the pressure lid from the top carefully.
Transfer orzo to a medium bowl, then set aside to cool to room temperature, about 30 minutes.

Add olives, scallions, tomato, bell pepper, feta, olive oil, vinegar, black pepper, and salt, and stir until combined.
Serve at room temperature or refrigerate for at least 2 hours.

Per Serving: Calories 282; Fat 12.9g; Sodium 414mg; Carbs 11g; Fiber 5g; Sugar 9g; Protein 11g

Beefsteak Tomatoes with Cheese

Prep time: 10 minutes| **Cook time:** 30 minutes| **Serves:** 4
½ cup orzo
4 large beefsteak tomatoes
1 cup shredded mozzarella cheese
2 cloves garlic, peeled and minced
2 tablespoons minced fresh basil
2 tablespoons minced fresh parsley
½ teaspoon salt
¼ teaspoon black pepper
2 tablespoons olive oil

Place orzo in the Inner Pot and add water just to cover.
Put on the pressure cooker's lid and turn the steam valve to "Sealing" position.
Press the "Pressure Cook" button one time to select "Less" option.
Use the "+/-" keys on the control panel to set the cooking time to 3 minutes.
Use the Pressure Level button to adjust the pressure to "Low Pressure".
Once the cooking cycle is completed, quickly and carefully turn the steam release handle from Sealing position to the Venting position.
When all the steam is released, remove the pressure lid from the top carefully.
Drain orzo and set aside. Cut tops off tomatoes and scoop out seeds and pulp.
Place pulp in a medium bowl. Add orzo, cheese, garlic, basil, parsley, salt, and pepper. Stuff tomatoes with orzo mixture and place on a baking sheet.
Drizzle oil over tomatoes and bake for 15–20 minutes at 350 degrees F in your preheated oven.
Serve hot.

Per Serving: Calories 289; Fat 14g; Sodium 791mg; Carbs 18.9g; Fiber 4.6g; Sugar 8g; Protein 6g

Pasta with Marinated Artichokes

Prep time: 10 minutes| **Cook time:** 10 minutes| **Serves:** 6
1-pound whole-wheat spaghetti, broken in half
3½ cups water
4 tablespoons olive oil
¼ teaspoon salt
2 cups baby spinach
1 cup drained marinated artichoke hearts
2 tablespoons chopped fresh oregano
2 tablespoons chopped fresh flat-leaf parsley
1 teaspoon black pepper

½ cup grated Parmesan cheese

Add pasta, water, 2 tablespoons oil, and salt to the Inner Pot.
Put on the pressure cooker's lid and turn the steam valve to "Sealing" position.
Press the "Pressure Cook" button one time to select "Less" option.
Use the "+/-" keys on the control panel to set the cooking time to 5 minutes.
Use the Pressure Level button to adjust the pressure to "High Pressure".
Once the cooking cycle is completed, allow the steam to release naturally.
When all the steam is released, press Cancel button and remove the pressure lid from the top carefully.
Press the "Sauté" Button, two times to select "Normal" settings.
Stir in remaining 2 tablespoons oil and spinach. Toss until spinach is wilted.
Stir in artichokes, oregano, and parsley until well mixed.
Sprinkle with pepper and cheese, and serve immediately.

Per Serving: Calories 302; Fat 19g; Sodium 354mg; Carbs 15g; Fiber 5.1g; Sugar 8.2g; Protein 12g

Couscous with Tomatoes

Prep time: 10 minutes| **Cook time:** 3 minutes| **Serves:** 4

1 tablespoon tomato paste
2 cups vegetable broth
1 cup couscous
1 cup halved cherry tomatoes
½ cup halved mixed olives
¼ cup minced fresh flat-leaf parsley
2 tablespoons minced fresh oregano
2 tablespoons minced fresh chives
1 tablespoon olive oil
1 tablespoon red wine vinegar
½ teaspoon black pepper

Pour tomato paste and broth into the Inner Pot and stir until completely dissolved. Stir in couscous.
Put on the pressure cooker's lid and turn the steam valve to "Sealing" position.
Press the "Pressure Cook" button one time to select "Less" option.
Use the "+/-" keys on the control panel to set the cooking time to 3 minutes.
Use the Pressure Level button to adjust the pressure to "High Pressure".
Once the cooking cycle is completed, allow the steam to release naturally for 10 minutes, then turn the steam release handle to the Venting position.
When all the steam is released, remove the pressure lid from the top carefully.
Fluff couscous with a fork.
Add tomatoes, olives, parsley, oregano, chives, oil, vinegar, and pepper, and stir until combined.
Serve warm or at room temperature.

Per Serving: Calories 334; Fat 7.9g; Sodium 704mg; Carbs 6g; Fiber 3.6g; Sugar 6g; Protein 18g

Couscous with Crab

Prep time: 10 minutes| **Cook time:** 7 minutes| **Serves:** 4

1 cup couscous
1 clove garlic, peeled and minced
2 cups water
3 tablespoons olive oil
¼ cup minced fresh flat-leaf parsley
1 tablespoon minced fresh dill
8 oz. jumbo lump crabmeat
3 tablespoons lemon juice
½ teaspoon black pepper
¼ cup grated Parmesan cheese

Place couscous, garlic, water, and 1 tablespoon oil in the Inner Pot and stir well.
Put on the pressure cooker's lid and turn the steam valve to "Sealing" position.
Press the "Pressure Cook" button one time to select "Less" option.
Use the "+/-" keys on the control panel to set the cooking time to 7 minutes.
Use the Pressure Level button to adjust the pressure to "Low Pressure".
Once the cooking cycle is completed, allow the steam to release naturally for 10 minutes, then turn the steam release handle to the Venting position.
When all the steam is released, remove the pressure lid from the top carefully.
Fluff couscous with a fork.
Add parsley, dill, crabmeat, lemon juice, pepper, and remaining 2 tablespoons oil, and stir until combined.
Top with cheese and serve immediately.

Per Serving: Calories 184; Fat 5g; Sodium 441mg; Carbs 17g; Fiber 4.6g; Sugar 5g; Protein 9g

Pepper Couscous Salad

Prep time: 10 minutes| **Cook time:** 7 minutes| **Serves:** 4

1 cup couscous
2 cups water
½ cup chopped Kalamata olives
1 medium red bell pepper, seeded and diced
1 clove garlic, peeled and minced
1 teaspoon olive oil
1 teaspoon red wine vinegar
½ teaspoon salt

Stir couscous and water together in the Inner Pot.
Put on the pressure cooker's lid and turn the steam valve to "Sealing" position.
Press the "Pressure Cook" button one time to select "Less" option.
Use the "+/-" keys on the control panel to set the cooking time to 7 minutes.
Use the Pressure Level button to adjust the pressure to "High Pressure".

Once the cooking cycle is completed, allow the steam to release naturally.
When all the steam is released, remove the pressure lid from the top carefully for 10 minutes, then turn the steam release handle to the Venting position.
Fluff couscous with a fork. Stir in olives, bell pepper, garlic, oil, vinegar, and salt.
Cover and refrigerate for 2 hours before serving.

Per Serving: Calories 382; Fat 7.9g; Sodium 704mg; Carbs 6g; Fiber 3.6g; Sugar 6g; Protein 18g

Pasta Primavera

Prep time: 10 minutes| **Cook time:** 20 minutes| **Serves:** 8
1-pound bowtie pasta
4 cups water
2 tablespoons olive oil
1½ cups chopped summer squash
1½ cups chopped zucchini
3 cups chopped broccoli
½ cup sun-dried tomatoes
2 cloves garlic, peeled and chopped
1 cup white wine
2 tablespoons cold unsalted butter
½ teaspoon salt
¾ teaspoon black pepper
¼ cup chopped fresh basil

Place pasta, water, and 1 tablespoon oil in the Inner Pot.
Put on the pressure cooker's lid and turn the steam valve to "Sealing" position.
Press the "Pressure Cook" button one time to select "Less" option.
Use the "+/-" keys on the control panel to set the cooking time to 4 minutes.
Use the Pressure Level button to adjust the pressure to "Low Pressure".
Once the cooking cycle is completed, quickly and carefully turn the steam release handle from Sealing position to the Venting position.
When all the steam is released, press Cancel button and remove the pressure lid from the top carefully.
Press the "Sauté" Button, two times to select "Normal" settings.
Heat remaining 1 tablespoon oil.
Add squash, zucchini, broccoli, and sun-dried tomatoes, and cook until very tender, about 10 minutes.
Add garlic and wine. Allow wine to reduce for about 2–3 minutes.
Add butter to pot, stirring constantly to create an emulsion. Season with salt and pepper.
Pour sauce and vegetables over pasta, and stir to coat.
Top with basil and enjoy.

Per Serving: Calories 361; Fat 7.9g; Sodium 704mg; Carbs 6g; Fiber 3.6g; Sugar 6g; Protein 18g

Rotini with Red Wine Marinara

Prep time: 10 minutes| **Cook time:** 25 minutes| **Serves:** 6
1-pound rotini
4 cups water
1 tablespoon olive oil
½ medium yellow onion, peeled and diced
3 cloves garlic, peeled and minced
1 (15-oz.) can crushed tomatoes
½ cup red wine
1 teaspoon sugar
2 tablespoons chopped fresh basil
½ teaspoon salt
¼ teaspoon black pepper

Add pasta and water to the Inner Pot.
Put on the pressure cooker's lid and turn the steam valve to "Sealing" position.
Press the "Pressure Cook" button one time to select "Less" option.
Use the "+/-" keys on the control panel to set the cooking time to 4 minutes.
Use the Pressure Level button to adjust the pressure to "Low Pressure".
Once the cooking cycle is completed, quickly and carefully turn the steam release handle from Sealing position to the Venting position.
When all the steam is released, press the Cancel button and remove the pressure lid from the top carefully.
Press the "Sauté" Button two times to select "Normal" settings and heat oil.
Add onion and cook until it begins to caramelize, about 10 minutes. Add garlic and cook 30 seconds.
Add tomatoes, red wine, and sugar, and simmer for 10 minutes.
Add basil, salt, pepper, and pasta.
Serve immediately.

Per Serving: Calories 212; Fat 7.9g; Sodium 704mg; Carbs 6g; Fiber 3.6g; Sugar 6g; Protein 18g

Couscous with Olives

Prep time: 10 minutes| **Cook time:** 7 minutes| **Serves:** 4
1 tablespoon tomato paste
2 cups vegetable broth
1 cup couscous
1 cup sliced cherry tomatoes
½ large English cucumber, chopped
½ cup pitted and chopped mixed olives
¼ cup minced fresh flat-leaf parsley
2 tablespoons minced fresh oregano
2 tablespoons minced fresh chives
1 tablespoon olive oil
1 tablespoon red wine vinegar
½ teaspoon black pepper

Stir together tomato paste and broth until completely dissolved.
Add to the Inner Pot with couscous and stir well.
Put on the pressure cooker's lid and turn the steam valve to "Sealing" position.

Press the "Pressure Cook" button one time to select "Less" option.
Use the "+/-" keys on the control panel to set the cooking time to 7 minutes.
Use the Pressure Level button to adjust the pressure to "High Pressure".
Once the cooking cycle is completed, allow the steam to release naturally for 10 minutes, then turn the steam release handle to the Venting position.
When all the steam is released, remove the pressure lid from the top carefully.
Fluff couscous with a fork. Add all remaining ingredients and stir until combined.
Serve warm or at room temperature.

Per Serving: Calories 372; Fat 20g; Sodium 891mg; Carbs 29g; Fiber 3g; Sugar 8g; Protein 7g

Bowtie Pesto Pasta Salad

Prep time: 10 minutes| **Cook time:** 5 minutes| **Serves:** 8
1-pound whole-wheat bowtie pasta
4 cups water
1 tablespoon olive oil
2 cups halved cherry tomatoes
2 cups baby spinach
½ cup chopped fresh basil
½ cup prepared pesto
½ teaspoon black pepper
½ cup grated Parmesan cheese

Add pasta, water, and olive oil to the Inner Pot.
Put on the pressure cooker's lid and turn the steam valve to "Sealing" position.
Press the "Pressure Cook" button one time to select "Less" option.
Use the "+/-" keys on the control panel to set the cooking time to 4 minutes.
Use the Pressure Level button to adjust the pressure to "Low Pressure".
Once the cooking cycle is completed, quickly and carefully turn the steam release handle from Sealing position to the Venting position.
When all the steam is released, remove the pressure lid from the top carefully.
Drain off any excess liquid. Allow pasta to cool to room temperature, about 30 minutes.
Stir in tomatoes, spinach, basil, pesto, pepper, and cheese.
Refrigerate for 2 hours. Stir well before serving.

Per Serving: Calories 221; Fat 7.9g; Sodium 704mg; Carbs 6g; Fiber 3.6g; Sugar 6g; Protein 18g

Israeli Pasta Salad

Prep time: 10 minutes| **Cook time:** 5 minutes| **Serves:** 6
½ pound whole-wheat penne pasta
4 cups water
1 tablespoon plus ¼ cup olive oil
1 cup quartered cherry tomatoes

½ English cucumber, chopped
½ medium orange bell pepper, seeded and chopped
½ medium red onion, peeled and chopped
½ cup crumbled feta cheese
1 teaspoon fresh thyme leaves
1 teaspoon chopped fresh oregano
½ teaspoon black pepper
¼ cup lemon juice

Add pasta, water, and 1 tablespoon oil to the Inner Pot.
Put on the pressure cooker's lid and turn the steam valve to "Sealing" position.
Press the "Pressure Cook" button one time to select "Less" option.
Use the "+/-" keys on the control panel to set the cooking time to 4 minutes.
Use the Pressure Level button to adjust the pressure to "High Pressure".
Once the cooking cycle is completed, quickly and carefully turn the steam release handle from Sealing position to the Venting position.
When all the steam is released, remove the pressure lid from the top carefully.
Drain and set aside to cool for 30 minutes.
Stir in tomatoes, cucumber, bell pepper, onion, feta, thyme, oregano, black pepper, lemon juice, and remaining ¼ cup oil.
Serve.

Per Serving: Calories 334; Fat 7.9g; Sodium 704mg; Carbs 6g; Fiber 3.6g; Sugar 6g; Protein 18g

Rotini with Walnut Pesto

Prep time: 10 minutes| **Cook time:** 4 minutes| **Serves:** 8
1 cup packed fresh basil leaves
⅓ cup chopped walnuts
¼ cup grated Parmesan cheese
¼ cup plus 1 tablespoon olive oil
1 clove garlic, peeled
1 tablespoon lemon juice
¼ teaspoon salt
1-pound whole-wheat rotini pasta
4 cups water
1-pint cherry tomatoes
1 cup fresh or frozen green peas
½ teaspoon black pepper

In a food processor, add basil and walnuts.
Pulse until finely chopped, about 12 pulses.
Add cheese, ¼ cup oil, garlic, lemon juice, and salt, and pulse until a rough paste forms, about 10 pulses.
Refrigerate until ready to use.
Add pasta, water, and remaining 1 tablespoon oil to the Inner Pot.
Put on the pressure cooker's lid and turn the steam valve to "Sealing" position.
Press the "Pressure Cook" button one time to select "Less" option.
Use the "+/-" keys on the control panel to set the cooking time to 4 minutes.
Use the Pressure Level button to adjust the pressure to "High Pressure".

Once the cooking cycle is completed, quickly and carefully turn the steam release handle from Sealing position to the Venting position. When all the steam is released, remove the pressure lid from the top carefully.
Drain off any excess liquid. Allow pasta to cool to room temperature, about 30 minutes.
Stir in basil mixture until pasta is well coated. Add tomatoes, peas, and pepper and toss to coat.
Refrigerate for 2 hours. Stir well before serving.

Per Serving: Calories 237; Fat 7.9g; Sodium 704mg; Carbs 6g; Fiber 3.6g; Sugar 6g; Protein 18g

Tomato, Arugula and Feta Pasta Salad

Prep time: 10 minutes| **Cook time:** 5 minutes| **Serves:** 8

1-pound rotini
4 cups water
3 tablespoons olive oil
2 medium Roma tomatoes, diced
2 cloves garlic, peeled and minced
1 medium red bell pepper, seeded and diced
2 tablespoons white wine vinegar
5 oz. baby arugula
1 cup crumbled feta cheese
½ teaspoon salt
½ teaspoon black pepper

Add pasta, water, and 1 tablespoon oil to the Inner Pot.
Put on the pressure cooker's lid and turn the steam valve to "Sealing" position.
Press the "Pressure Cook" button one time to select "Less" option.
Use the "+/-" keys on the control panel to set the cooking time to 4 minutes.
Use the Pressure Level button to adjust the pressure to "High Pressure".
Once the cooking cycle is completed, quickly and carefully turn the steam release handle from Sealing position to the Venting position. When all the steam is released, remove the pressure lid from the top carefully.
Drain pasta, then rinse with cold water. Set aside.
In a large bowl, mix remaining 2 tablespoons oil, tomatoes, garlic, bell pepper, vinegar, arugula, and cheese.
Stir in pasta and season with salt and pepper. Cover and refrigerate for 2 hours before serving.

Per Serving: Calories 289; Fat 14g; Sodium 791mg; Carbs 18.9g; Fiber 4.6g; Sugar 8g; Protein 6g

Mixed Vegetable Couscous

Prep time: 10 minutes| **Cook time:** 10 minutes| **Serves:** 8

1 tablespoon light olive oil
1 medium zucchini, trimmed and chopped
1 medium yellow squash, chopped
1 large red bell pepper, seeded and chopped
1 large orange bell pepper, seeded and chopped
2 tablespoons chopped fresh oregano
2 cups Israeli couscous
3 cups vegetable broth
½ cup crumbled feta cheese
¼ cup red wine vinegar
¼ cup olive oil
½ teaspoon black pepper
¼ cup chopped fresh basil

Press the "Sauté" Button two times to select "Normal" settings and heat light olive oil.
Add zucchini, squash, bell peppers, and oregano, and sauté 8 minutes.
Press the Cancel button. Transfer to a serving bowl and set aside to cool.
Add couscous and broth to the Inner Pot and stir well.
Put on the pressure cooker's lid and turn the steam valve to "Sealing" position.
Press the "Pressure Cook" button one time to select "Less" option.
Use the "+/-" keys on the control panel to set the cooking time to 2 minutes.
Use the Pressure Level button to adjust the pressure to "High Pressure".
Once the cooking cycle is completed, allow the steam to release naturally.
When all the steam is released, remove the pressure lid from the top carefully.
Fluff with a fork and stir in cooked vegetables, cheese, vinegar, olive oil, black pepper, and basil.
Serve warm.

Per Serving: Calories 226; Fat 10.9g; Sodium 354mg; Carbs 20.5g; Fiber 4.1g; Sugar 8.2g; Protein 06g

Toasted Couscous with Feta

Prep time: 10 minutes| **Cook time:** 10 minutes| **Serves:** 8

1 tablespoon plus ¼ cup light olive oil
2 cups Israeli couscous
3 cups vegetable broth
2 large tomatoes, seeded and diced
1 large English cucumber, diced
1 medium red onion, peeled and chopped
½ cup crumbled feta cheese
¼ cup red wine vinegar
½ teaspoon black pepper
¼ cup chopped flat-leaf parsley
¼ cup chopped fresh basil

Press the "Sauté" Button two times to select "normal" settings and heat 1 tablespoon oil.
Add couscous and cook, stirring frequently, until couscous is light golden brown, about 7 minutes.
Press the Cancel button. Add broth and stir.
Put on the pressure cooker's lid and turn the steam valve to "Sealing" position.
Press the "Pressure Cook" button one time to select "Less" option.
Use the "+/-" keys on the control panel to set the cooking time to 2 minutes.

Use the Pressure Level button to adjust the pressure to "Low Pressure".
Once the cooking cycle is completed, allow the steam to release naturally.
When all the steam is released, remove the pressure lid from the top carefully.
Fluff couscous with a fork, then transfer to a medium bowl and set aside to cool.
Add remaining ¼ cup oil, tomatoes, cucumber, onion, feta, vinegar, pepper, parsley, and basil, and stir until combined. Serve.

Per Serving: Calories 302; Fat 12.9g; Sodium 414mg; Carbs 11g; Fiber 5g; Sugar 9g; Protein 11g

Pasta with Chickpeas and Cabbage

Prep time: 10 minutes| **Cook time:** 30 minutes| **Serves:** 8
1-pound rotini pasta
8 cups water
2 tablespoons olive oil
1 stalk celery, thinly sliced
1 medium red onion, peeled and sliced
1 small head savoy cabbage, cored and shredded
⅔ cup dried chickpeas, soaked overnight and drained
8 oz. button mushrooms, sliced
½ teaspoon salt
¾ teaspoon black pepper
½ cup grated Pecorino Romano cheese

Add pasta, 4 cups water, and 1 tablespoon oil to the Inner Pot.
Put on the pressure cooker's lid and turn the steam valve to "Sealing" position.
Press the "Pressure Cook" button one time to select "Less" option.
Use the "+/-" keys on the control panel to set the cooking time to 4 minutes.
Use the Pressure Level button to adjust the pressure to "Low Pressure".
Once the cooking cycle is completed, quickly and carefully turn the steam release handle from Sealing position to the Venting position.
When all the steam is released, press the Cancel button and remove the pressure lid from the top carefully.
Press the "Sauté" Button, two times to select "normal" settings and heat remaining 1 tablespoon oil.
Add celery and onion, and cook until just tender, about 4 minutes.
Stir in cabbage and cook until wilted, about 2 minutes.
Add chickpeas, mushrooms, and remaining 4 cups water. Stir well, then press the Cancel button.
Put on the pressure cooker's lid and turn the steam valve to "Sealing" position.
Press the "Pressure Cook" button one time to select "Less" option.
Use the Pressure Level button to adjust the pressure to "Low Pressure".
Once the cooking cycle is completed, allow the steam to release naturally.

When all the steam is released, remove the pressure lid from the top carefully.
Season with salt and pepper. Use a fork to mash some of the chickpeas to thicken sauce. Pour sauce over pasta and top with cheese. Serve hot.

Per Serving: Calories 184; Fat 5g; Sodium 441mg; Carbs 17g; Fiber 4.6g; Sugar 5g; Protein 9g

Dill Pasta Salad

Prep time: 10 minutes| **Cook time:** 5 minutes| **Serves:** 8
½ cup low-fat plain Greek yogurt
1 tablespoon apple cider vinegar
2 tablespoons chopped fresh dill
1 teaspoon honey
1-pound whole-wheat elbow macaroni
4 cups water
1 tablespoon olive oil
1 medium red bell pepper, seeded and chopped
1 medium sweet onion, peeled and diced
1 stalk celery, diced
½ teaspoon black pepper

In a small bowl, combine yogurt and vinegar. Add dill and honey, and mix well. Refrigerate until ready to use.
Place pasta, water, and olive oil to the Inner Pot.
Put on the pressure cooker's lid and turn the steam valve to "Sealing" position.
Press the "Pressure Cook" button one time to select "Less" option.
Use the "+/-" keys on the control panel to set the cooking time to 4 minutes.
Use the Pressure Level button to adjust the pressure to "Low Pressure".
Once the cooking cycle is completed, quickly and carefully turn the steam release handle from Sealing position to the Venting position.
When all the steam is released, remove the pressure lid from the top carefully.
Drain off any excess liquid. Cool pasta to room temperature, about 30 minutes.
Add prepared dressing and toss until pasta is well coated.
Add bell pepper, onion, celery, and black pepper, and toss to coat.
Refrigerate for 2 hours. Stir well before serving.

Per Serving: Calories 382; Fat 7.9g; Sodium 704mg; Carbs 6g; Fiber 3.6g; Sugar 6g; Protein 18g

Angel Hair Pasta with Spinach and White Wine

Prep time: 10 minutes| **Cook time:** 15 minutes| **Serves:** 6
1-pound angel hair pasta
4¼ cups water
2 tablespoons olive oil
¼ medium yellow onion, peeled and diced

2 cloves garlic, peeled and minced
½ cup white wine
1 tablespoon unsalted butter
1 tablespoon all-purpose flour
½ teaspoon salt
¼ teaspoon black pepper
1 cup steamed spinach

Place pasta, 4 cups water, and 1 tablespoon oil in the Inner Pot.
Put on the pressure cooker's lid and turn the steam valve to "Sealing" position.
Press the "Pressure Cook" button one time to select "Less" option.
Use the "+/-" keys on the control panel to set the cooking time to 4 minutes.
Use the Pressure Level button to adjust the pressure to "High Pressure".
Once the cooking cycle is completed, quickly and carefully turn the steam release handle from Sealing position to the Venting position.
When all the steam is released, press Cancel button and remove the pressure lid from the top carefully.
Press the "Sauté" Button two times to select "Normal" settings and heat remaining 1 tablespoon oil.
Add onion and garlic. Cook until onion is soft, about 5 minutes.
Add white wine and remaining ¼ cup water, then bring to a low simmer for about 10 minutes.
Add butter and flour, stirring until completely combined and sauce begins to thicken.
Season with salt and pepper.
In a large mixing bowl, combine spinach, pasta, and white wine sauce, then toss until the pasta is completely coated.
Serve immediately.

Per Serving: Calories 219; Fat 10g; Sodium 891mg; Carbs 22.9g; Fiber 4g; Sugar 4g; Protein 13g

Tahini Soup

Prep time: 10 minutes| **Cook time:** 5 minutes| **Serves:** 6
2 cups orzo
8 cups water
1 tablespoon olive oil
1 teaspoon salt
½ teaspoon black pepper
½ cup tahini
¼ cup lemon juice

Add pasta, water, oil, salt, and pepper to the Inner Pot.
Put on the pressure cooker's lid and turn the steam valve to "Sealing" position.
Press the "Pressure Cook" button one time to select "Less" option.
Use the "+/-" keys on the control panel to set the cooking time to 4 minutes.
Use the Pressure Level button to adjust the pressure to "High Pressure".
Once the cooking cycle is completed, quickly and carefully turn the steam release handle from Sealing position to the Venting position.

When all the steam is released, remove the pressure lid from the top carefully.
Add tahini to a small mixing bowl and slowly add lemon juice while whisking constantly.
Once lemon juice has been incorporated, take about ½ cup hot broth from the pot and slowly add to tahini mixture while whisking, until creamy smooth.
Pour mixture into the soup and mix well.
Serve immediately.

Per Serving: Calories 320; Fat 19g; Sodium 354mg; Carbs 15g; Fiber 5.1g; Sugar 8.2g; Protein 12g

Marinara Spaghetti with Mozzarella Cheese

Prep time: 10 minutes| **Cook time:** 5 minutes| **Serves:** 8
1-pound spaghetti
4 cups water
1 tablespoon olive oil
4 cups cooked pinto beans
4 cups marinara sauce
1 cup shredded mozzarella cheese
2 tablespoons chopped fresh basil

Add pasta, water, and olive oil to the Inner Pot.
Put on the pressure cooker's lid and turn the steam valve to "Sealing" position.
Press the "Pressure Cook" button one time to select "Less" option.
Use the "+/-" keys on the control panel to set the cooking time to 4 minutes.
Use the Pressure Level button to adjust the pressure to "High Pressure".
Once the cooking cycle is completed, quickly and carefully turn the steam release handle from Sealing position to the Venting position.
When all the steam is released, remove the pressure lid from the top carefully.
Add beans and marinara sauce, and stir well.
Top with cheese and basil and serve hot.

Per Serving: Calories 334; Fat 7.9g; Sodium 704mg; Carbs 6g; Fiber 3.6g; Sugar 6g; Protein 18g

Spaghetti with Meat Sauce

Prep time: 10 minutes| **Cook time:** 20 minutes| **Serves:** 6
1-pound spaghetti
4 cups water
3 tablespoons olive oil
1 medium white onion, peeled and diced
½ pound lean ground veal
½ teaspoon salt
¼ teaspoon black pepper
¼ cup white wine
½ cup tomato sauce
1 (3") cinnamon stick
2 bay leaves
1 clove garlic, peeled
¼ cup grated aged mizithra or Parmesan cheese

Add pasta, water, and 1 tablespoon oil to the Inner Pot.

Put on the pressure cooker's lid and turn the steam valve to "Sealing" position.

Press the "Pressure Cook" button one time to select "Less" option.

Use the "+/-" keys on the control panel to set the cooking time to 4 minutes.

Use the Pressure Level button to adjust the pressure to "High Pressure".

Once the cooking cycle is completed, quickly and carefully turn the steam release handle from Sealing position to the Venting position.

When all the steam is released, press Cancel button and remove the pressure lid from the top carefully.

Press the "Sauté" Button, two times to select "normal" settings and heat remaining 2 tablespoons oil.

Add onion and cook until soft, about 3 minutes.

Add veal and crumble well. Keep stirring until meat is browned, about 5 minutes.

Add salt, pepper, wine, and tomato sauce, and mix well.

3 Stir in cinnamon stick, bay leaves, and garlic. Press the Cancel button.

Put on the pressure cooker's lid and turn the steam valve to "Sealing" position.

Press the "Pressure Cook" button one time to select "Less" option.

Use the "+/-" keys on the control panel to set the cooking time to 5 minutes.

Use the Pressure Level button to adjust the pressure to "Low Pressure".

Once the cooking cycle is completed, quickly and carefully turn the steam release handle from Sealing position to the Venting position.

When all the steam is released, remove the pressure lid from the top carefully.

Remove and discard cinnamon stick and bay leaves.

Place pasta in a large bowl. Sprinkle with cheese and spoon meat sauce over top. Serve immediately.

Per Serving: Calories 357; Fat 7.9g; Sodium 704mg; Carbs 6g; Fiber 3.6g; Sugar 6g; Protein 18g

Avgolemono

Prep time: 10 minutes| **Cook time:** 13 minutes| **Serves:** 6

6 cups chicken stock
½ cup orzo
1 tablespoon olive oil
12 oz. cooked chicken breast, shredded
½ teaspoon salt
½ teaspoon black pepper
¼ cup lemon juice
2 large eggs

2 tablespoons chopped fresh dill
1 tablespoon chopped fresh flat-leaf parsley

Add stock, orzo, and olive oil to the Inner Pot.
Put on the pressure cooker's lid and turn the steam valve to "Sealing" position.
Press the "Pressure Cook" button one time to select "Less" option.
Use the "+/-" keys on the control panel to set the cooking time to 3 minutes.
Use the Pressure Level button to adjust the pressure to "High Pressure".
Once the cooking cycle is completed, quickly and carefully turn the steam release handle from Sealing position to the Venting position.
When all the steam is released, remove the pressure lid from the top carefully.
Stir in chicken, salt, and pepper.
In a medium bowl, combine lemon juice and eggs, then slowly whisk in hot cooking liquid. Immediately add egg mixture to soup and stir well.
Let stand on the Keep Warm setting, stirring occasionally, for 10 minutes.
Add dill and parsley. Serve immediately.

Per Serving: Calories 349; Fat 2.9g; Sodium 511mg; Carbs 12g; Fiber 3g; Sugar 8g; Protein 7g

Zesty Couscous

Prep time: 10 minutes| **Cook time:** 5 minutes| **Serves:** 6

2 cups couscous
2½ cups water
1 cup low-sodium chicken broth
1 teaspoon salt
1 tablespoon unsalted butter
1 teaspoon grated lemon zest

Place all ingredients in the Inner Pot and stir to combine.
Put on the pressure cooker's lid and turn the steam valve to "Sealing" position.
Press the "Pressure Cook" button one time to select "Less" option.
Use the "+/-" keys on the control panel to set the cooking time to 4 minutes.
Use the Pressure Level button to adjust the pressure to "High Pressure".
Once the cooking cycle is completed, quickly and carefully turn the steam release handle from Sealing position to the Venting position.
When all the steam is released, remove the pressure lid from the top carefully.
Stir well. Serve immediately.

Per Serving: Calories 351; Fat 10.9g; Sodium 454mg; Carbs 10g; Fiber 3.1g; Sugar 5.2g; Protein 10g

Chicken Enchiladas

Prep time: 10 minutes| **Cook time:** 35 minutes| **Serves:** 4

3 medium boneless, skinless chicken breasts
Kosher salt
Black pepper
1 cup chicken broth or water
2 garlic cloves, minced
½ onion, sliced
2 (10-oz.) cans green enchilada sauce
½ cup sour cream, plus more for serving
10 to 12 corn tortillas
2 cups Monterey Jack cheese

Season the chicken with salt and pepper and place it in the Inner Pot, along with the broth, garlic, and onion.
Put on the pressure cooker's lid and turn the steam valve to "Sealing" position.
Press the "Pressure Cook" button two times to select "Less" option.
Use the "+/-" keys on the control panel to set the cooking time to 7 minutes.
Use the Pressure Level button to adjust the pressure to "High Pressure".
Once the cooking cycle is completed, allow the steam to release naturally.
When all the steam is released, remove the pressure lid from the top carefully.
Heat your oven to 375 degrees F in advance.
Remove the chicken, shred it, and combine in a large bowl with ½ cup of enchilada sauce and the sour cream. Season with salt and pepper.
Spread another ½ cup of enchilada sauce into a 9-by-13-inch baking dish.
Warm the tortillas slightly in the oven, on the stove, or in the microwave to make them pliable.
Fill each with 2 to 3 tablespoons of the chicken mixture and a sprinkle of cheese.
Roll into cigar shapes and place, side-by-side and seam-side down, into the baking dish.
Top with the remaining sauce and cheese.
Cover with foil.
Bake for 15 minutes. Remove the foil and bake for 5 to 10 minutes more, until the cheese is melted.
Serve hot.

Per Serving: Calories 382; Fat 7.9g; Sodium 704mg; Carbs 6g; Fiber 3.6g; Sugar 6g; Protein 18g

Chicken Pot Pie

Prep time: 10 minutes| **Cook time:** 25 minutes| **Serves:** 4-5

1 frozen puff pastry sheet
1 tablespoon olive oil
1 small onion, chopped
2 medium carrots, peeled and chopped
2 celery stalks, chopped
2 medium potatoes, cut into ¾-inch cubes

3 medium bone-in, skin-on chicken breasts
1½ cups chicken broth
1 teaspoon kosher salt
2 tablespoons all-purpose flour
2 tablespoons cold butter
½ cup heavy cream or whole milk
1 cup frozen peas
Black pepper

Thaw the puff pastry sheet on the counter for 30 minutes.
Press the "Sauté" Button, two times to select "Normal" settings and add the oil.
Add the onion, carrots, and celery. Stir and cook for 3 minutes.
Add the potatoes, chicken, broth, and salt.
Put on the pressure cooker's lid and turn the steam valve to "Sealing" position.
Press the "Pressure Cook" button two times to select "Less" option.
Use the "+/-" keys on the control panel to set the cooking time to 7 minutes.
Use the Pressure Level button to adjust the pressure to "High Pressure".
Meanwhile, once the pastry sheet is pliable but still cold, lay it out on a baking sheet and cut into 4 even squares or rectangles. Bake for 15 minutes.
Remove the chicken and, once cool enough to handle, pull off the meat and discard the skin and bones.
Cut the meat into cubes.
Once the cooking cycle of Instant Pot is completed, allow the steam to release naturally.
When all the steam is released, press Cancel button and remove the pressure lid from the top carefully.
Press the "Sauté" Button, two times to select "Normal" settings
In a small bowl, combine the flour and butter into a smooth paste.
Add the paste to the simmering broth along with the cream or milk and peas.
Cook, stirring, until the paste has dissolved, 3 to 5 minutes. Add the chicken and season with salt and pepper.
To serve, spoon the stew into bowls and top with the puff pastry.

Per Serving: Calories 489; Fat 11g; Sodium 501mg; Carbs 8.9g; Fiber 4.6g; Sugar 8g; Protein 26g

Chicken with Potatoes and Peas

Prep time: 10 minutes| **Cook time:** 15 minutes| **Serves:** 4

4 small or 3 large bone-in, skin-on chicken breasts
Kosher salt
Black pepper
4 tablespoons olive oil, plus extra for garnish
3 garlic cloves, minced
1 fresh rosemary sprig, chopped (leaves only)
1 teaspoon dried oregano

Pinch red pepper flakes
1-pound large fingerling potatoes, washed and
pricked with a knife
2 cups chicken broth
1 cup frozen peas
1 lemon
½ cup olives

Season the chicken with salt and pepper.
In a large bowl, coat the chicken with 2
tablespoons of olive oil, the garlic, rosemary,
oregano, and red pepper flakes.
Marinate for at least 30 minutes in the
refrigerator.
Press the "Sauté" Button, two times to select
"More" settings.
Add the remaining 2 tablespoons of olive oil
and coat the bottom of the pot.
Add the chicken, skin-side down (reserving
any marinade), and cook without moving for
about 5 minutes, until the skin is crispy.
Remove the chicken and select Cancel. Add
the potatoes and broth.
Place the chicken on top, skin-side up, and
pour the reserved marinade on top. Season
with salt and pepper.
Put on the pressure cooker's lid and turn the
steam valve to "Sealing" position.
Press the "Pressure Cook" button two times to
select "Less" option.
Use the "+/-" keys on the control panel to set
the cooking time to 7 minutes.
Use the Pressure Level button to adjust the
pressure to "High Pressure".
Once the cooking cycle is completed, allow the
steam to release naturally for 10 minutes,
then turn the steam release handle to the
Venting position.
When all the steam is released, remove the
pressure lid from the top carefully.
Remove the chicken. Stir in the peas and cook
until warmed.
Serve the potatoes and peas topped with the
chicken.
Just before serving, add a squeeze of lemon,
a drizzle of olive oil, and the olives.

Per Serving: Calories 221; Fat 7.9g; Sodium
704mg; Carbs 6g; Fiber 3.6g; Sugar 6g;
Protein 18g

Chicken Wings

Prep time: 10 minutes| **Cook time:** 20
minutes| **Serves:** 4-5
3 lbs. chicken wings
1 cup water
Kosher salt
2 cups wing sauce

Add the chicken wings and water to the Inner
Pot and season with salt.
Put on the pressure cooker's lid and turn the
steam valve to "Sealing" position.
Press the "Pressure Cook" button two times to
select "Less" option.
Use the "+/-" keys on the control panel to set
the cooking time to 10 minutes.

Use the Pressure Level button to adjust the
pressure to "High Pressure".
Once the cooking cycle is completed, allow the
steam to release naturally for 10 minutes,
then turn the steam release handle to the
Venting position.
When all the steam is released, remove the
pressure lid from the top carefully.
Remove the wings to a cooling rack to drain.
In a large bowl, toss the wings in the sauce.
Place on a baking sheet and broil for about 5
minutes in your preheated oven, until crispy.
Flip the wings and repeat.
Place the cooling rack with the wings on a
baking sheet and refrigerate for 1 hour.
Heat the oil to 385 degrees F in your oven.
Once hot, carefully lower 7 or 8 wings into the
oil and fry for 3 minutes until crispy. Remove
and place back on the rack. Repeat with the
remaining wings.
Toss the wings in the sauce and serve
immediately.

Per Serving: Calories 372; Fat 20g; Sodium
891mg; Carbs 29g; Fiber 3g; Sugar 8g;
Protein 7g

Chicken Dumplings

Prep time: 10 minutes| **Cook time:** 30
minutes| **Serves:** 8
For the chicken and broth
4 tablespoons butter
8 medium bone-in, skin-on chicken thighs
Kosher salt
Black pepper
½ cup all-purpose flour
4 celery stalks, chopped
3 carrots, peeled and chopped
2 onions, chopped
3½ cups chicken broth, preferably homemade
(try the recipe here)
½ cup whole milk or half-and-half
2 tablespoons cornstarch
For the dumplings
1¾ cups all-purpose flour
¼ cup cornmeal
1 tablespoon baking powder
½ teaspoon kosher salt
¼ teaspoon black pepper
1 cup whole milk or half-and-half
3 tablespoons melted butter

Press the "Sauté" Button, two times to select
"More" settings.
Add the butter. Season the chicken with salt
and pepper and dredge in the flour, shaking
off the excess.
Once the butter is sizzling and the pot is hot,
add half of the chicken in one layer.
Brown on one side for 3 or 4 minutes, without
moving, and flip and brown on the other side.
Remove and repeat with the remaining
chicken. Set aside.
Add the celery, carrots, and onions to the pot.
Sauté for 3 minutes, scraping the bottom of
the pot.
Press Cancel button to stop this cooking
program.

Add the chicken and broth. Season with salt and pepper.

Put on the pressure cooker's lid and turn the steam valve to "Sealing" position.

Press the "Pressure Cook" button two times to select "Less" option.

Use the "+/-" keys on the control panel to set the cooking time to 11 minutes.

Use the Pressure Level button to adjust the pressure to "High Pressure".

Once the cooking cycle is completed, allow the steam to release naturally.

When all the steam is released, remove the pressure lid from the top carefully.

While the chicken is cooking, make the dumplings.

Mix together the flour, cornmeal, baking powder, salt, and pepper in a medium bowl.

Add the milk or half-and-half and melted butter, and stir just until incorporated (don't over-mix). Set aside.

Once cooking is complete, use a quick release. Remove the chicken and set aside.

Add the milk to the broth in the pot, mix, and season with salt and pepper.

In a small bowl, combine ½ cup of hot broth with the cornstarch and whisk well to combine.

Add back to the pot and stir.

Press the "Sauté" Button, two times to select "normal" settings.

Once simmering, scoop heaping tablespoons of the dumpling mixture and drop them into the pot.

Reduce Sauté heat to low and cook for 12 to 15 minutes, loosely covered with the top without locking it, until the dumplings have doubled in size.

Meanwhile, bone the chicken, remove and discard the skin, and shred the meat.

Add back to the pot and serve in bowls.

Per Serving: Calories 334; Fat 7.9g; Sodium 704mg; Carbs 6g; Fiber 3.6g; Sugar 6g; Protein 18g

Mushroom and Chicken Sausage Risotto

Prep time: 10 minutes| **Cook time:** 25 minutes| **Serves:** 4

2 tablespoons canola oil
12 oz. fully cooked chicken sausage, cut into ¼-inch slices
3 tablespoons butter
1 pound mushrooms (cremini, shiitake, oyster, or a mix), thinly sliced
1 medium yellow onion, chopped
3 garlic cloves, minced
3 thyme sprigs, leaves only, plus more leaves for garnish
Kosher salt
Black pepper
1 tablespoon soy sauce
½ cup dry white wine or red wine
4 cups good-quality chicken broth, preferably homemade (try the recipe here)
2 cups Arborio or Calrose rice
¼ cup finely grated Parmesan cheese

Press the "Sauté" Button, two times to select "More" settings. Add the oil.

Once hot, add the sausage and cook, stirring, for 5 minutes, until browned. Remove the sausage.

Reduce the heat to Normal. Melt the butter, then add the mushrooms and onion.

Cook, stirring, for 6 minutes until the onion is translucent and the mushrooms are cooked.

Add the garlic and cook for 1 minute more.

Add the thyme and season with salt and pepper.

Add the soy sauce and wine. Cook, scraping up any brown bits off the bottom of the pot, for about 3 minutes, or until the alcohol smell has gone.

Add the broth and rice and stir. Press Cancel to stop this cooking program.

Put on the pressure cooker's lid and turn the steam valve to "Sealing" position.

Press the "Pressure Cook" button two times to select "Less" option.

Use the "+/-" keys on the control panel to set the cooking time to 6 minutes.

Use the Pressure Level button to adjust the pressure to "High Pressure".

Once the cooking cycle is completed, quickly and carefully turn the steam release handle from Sealing position to the Venting position.

When all the steam is released, remove the pressure lid from the top carefully and stir.

If the risotto is too soupy, press the "Sauté" button two times to select "Normal" mode and cook, uncovered, for a few minutes.

Add the sausage and Parmesan.

Serve topped with thyme leaves.

Per Serving: Calories 289; Fat 14g; Sodium 791mg; Carbs 18.9g; Fiber 4.6g; Sugar 8g; Protein 6g

Chicken Tikka Masala

Prep time: 10 minutes| **Cook time:** 20 minutes| **Serves:** 4

2 tablespoons butter
1 small onion, chopped
3 garlic cloves, minced
1 (1-inch) piece ginger, peeled and grated
2 teaspoons ground cumin
2 teaspoons paprika
1 teaspoon ground turmeric
Big pinch cayenne
1 tablespoon sugar
1 (15-oz.) can diced or crushed tomatoes with juice
4 medium boneless, skinless chicken breasts
½ cup chicken broth
Kosher salt
Black pepper
¼ cup heavy cream
Juice of 1 lemon

Press the "Sauté" Button, two times to select "More" settings. Add the butter.

When the butter sizzles, add the onion, garlic, and ginger and stir. Cook for 3 to 4 minutes, stirring, until the onion is translucent.

Select Cancel and add the cumin, paprika, turmeric, and cayenne and stir, scraping the bottom.

Add the sugar and tomatoes with juice, stir, then add the chicken and broth.

Nestle the chicken in the mixture and season with salt and pepper.

Put on the pressure cooker's lid and turn the steam valve to "Sealing" position.

Press the "Pressure Cook" button two times to select "Less" option.

Use the "+/-" keys on the control panel to set the cooking time to 7 minutes.

Use the Pressure Level button to adjust the pressure to "High Pressure".

Once the cooking cycle is completed, quickly and carefully turn the steam release handle from Sealing position to the Venting position.

When all the steam is released, remove the pressure lid from the top carefully.

Carefully remove the chicken and chop.

Press Cancel button.

Press the "Sauté" Button two times to select "normal" settings and simmer for 4 to 5 minutes until the liquid is reduced.

While simmering, add the cream and return the chicken to the pot.

Add the lemon juice and stir. Season as needed.

Serve and enjoy.

Per Serving: Calories 372; Fat 20g; Sodium 891mg; Carbs 29g; Fiber 3g; Sugar 8g; Protein 27g

Spiced Coconut Chicken

Prep time: 10 minutes| **Cook time:** 20 minutes| **Serves:** 4-5

1 tablespoon olive oil
1 onion, cut into ¼-inch slices
1 (1-inch) piece ginger, peeled and cut into ¼-inch slices
3 medium garlic cloves, minced
1 tablespoon curry powder
1 teaspoon ground turmeric
2 lbs. bone-in, skin-on chicken thighs
Kosher salt
Black pepper
1 (14-oz.) can light coconut milk
½ cup water
1⅓ cups jasmine rice, rinsed
2 tablespoons cilantro leaves plus stems, stems and leaves divided
1½ teaspoons sugar
1 lime, halved (one half cut into wedges, for serving)

Press the "Sauté" button two times to select "Normal" mode and add the oil.

Once hot, add the onion and ginger and sauté for 2 minutes.

Add the garlic, curry powder, and turmeric and cook, stirring, for 1 minute.

Press Cancel button.

Add the chicken and season with salt and pepper. Add the coconut milk and water.

Put on the pressure cooker's lid and turn the steam valve to "Sealing" position.

Press the "Pressure Cook" button two times to select "Normal" option.

Use the "+/-" keys on the control panel to set the cooking time to 13 minutes.

Use the Pressure Level button to adjust the pressure to "High Pressure".

Once the cooking cycle is completed, allow the steam to release naturally for 10 minutes, then turn the steam release handle to the Venting position.

When all the steam is released, remove the pressure lid from the top carefully.

Transfer the chicken to a platter. Add the rice, chopped cilantro stems, and sugar.

Select "Pressure Cook" and cook on High Pressure for 4 minutes.

Meanwhile, remove the skin and bones from the chicken and discard.

Select Cancel and let naturally release for 10 minutes. Release any remaining steam.

Add the chicken back to the pot and add the juice of half the lime.

Stir and season with salt and pepper.

Serve in bowls topped with cilantro leaves and lime wedges.

Per Serving: Calories 184; Fat 5g; Sodium 441mg; Carbs 17g; Fiber 4.6g; Sugar 5g; Protein 9g

Roasted Chicken with Tomatoes

Prep time: 10 minutes| **Cook time:** 25 minutes| **Serves:** 4

3 bacon slices, cut into ½-inch pieces
1 (3- to 4-pound) chicken, cut into 8 pieces
Kosher salt
Black pepper
1 tablespoon olive oil
1 onion, cut into ⅛-inch slices
4 garlic cloves, minced
8 oz. cremini mushrooms, chopped
¾ cup dry red wine
1 (15-oz.) can diced or crushed tomatoes with juice
1 bay leaf

Press the "Sauté" button two times to select "Normal" mode.

Once hot, add the bacon. Cook until lightly crisp, flipping as needed, and drain on a paper towel.

Season the chicken with salt and pepper. Turn the heat to More and add the olive oil.

Add the chicken, skin-side down, and cook for 5 minutes, or until browned. Transfer to a plate.

Add the onion and garlic and cook, stirring, for 2 minutes.

Add the mushrooms and cook, stirring, for 3 minutes more.

Add the wine and scrape the bottom of the pan to deglaze. Cook for 3 to 5 minutes.

Stir in the tomatoes with juice, bay leaf, and bacon.

Return the chicken to the pot, with the dark meat on the bottom and breasts on the top, skin-side up.

Put on the pressure cooker's lid and turn the steam valve to "Sealing" position.
Press the "Pressure Cook" button two times to select "Normal" option.
Use the "+/-" keys on the control panel to set the cooking time to 10 minutes.
Use the Pressure Level button to adjust the pressure to "High Pressure".
Once the cooking cycle is completed, quickly and carefully turn the steam release handle from Sealing position to the Venting position.
When all the steam is released, remove the pressure lid from the top carefully.
Remove the bay leaf and serve.

Per Serving: Calories 489; Fat 11g; Sodium 501mg; Carbs 8.9g; Fiber 4.6g; Sugar 8g; Protein 26g

Stuffed Turkey Breast

Prep time: 10 minutes| **Cook time:** 55 minutes| **Serves:** 6-8

5 tablespoons butter
1 large onion, chopped
2 celery stalks, chopped
¾ cup chopped mushrooms
2 garlic cloves, minced
2 tablespoons chopped fresh sage
1 heaping tablespoon chopped fresh parsley
¾ teaspoon kosher salt, plus more for seasoning
¼ teaspoon black pepper, plus more for seasoning
2 cups plain breadcrumbs
3 cups chicken broth
1 (2- to 3-pound) boneless, skinless turkey breast, butterflied to an even thickness

Press the "Sauté" button two times to select "Normal" mode.
Once hot, add 3 tablespoons of butter. Once the butter is melted, add the onion and celery. Stir and cook for 3 minutes until the onion is translucent.
Add the mushrooms and garlic. Stir and cook for 3 minutes more, or until the mushrooms are soft.
Press the Cancel button.
Transfer the vegetables and butter to a large bowl.
Add the sage, parsley, salt, pepper, and breadcrumbs and mix.
Add the broth, a bit at a time, and mix until you get a moist but crumbly texture, using ¾ to 1 cup of broth.
Lay the turkey breast top-side down on your work surface.
If it isn't an even thickness, pound the thick parts until it's mostly even.
Sprinkle with salt and pepper. Spread the stuffing mixture on the breast, making it about as thick as the turkey breast itself, and leaving at least 1 inch on each side.
Roll up tightly and secure with kitchen twine.
Season the outside of the breast with salt and pepper.
Press the "Sauté" button two times to select "More" mode.

Once hot, add the remaining 2 tablespoons of butter.
Once melted, brown the stuffed turkey on all sides, about 3 minutes per side.
Finish with it lying seam-side down in the pot.
Press the Cancel button to stop this cooking program.
Add the remaining 2 cups of chicken broth and close the lid in right way.
Put on the pressure cooker's lid and turn the steam valve to "Sealing" position.
Press the "Pressure Cook" button two times to select "Less" option.
Use the "+/-" keys on the control panel to set the cooking time to 25 minutes.
Use the Pressure Level button to adjust the pressure to "High Pressure".
Once the cooking cycle is completed, allow the steam to release naturally.
When all the steam is released, remove the pressure lid from the top carefully.
Remove the turkey and let it rest, tented with foil.
Press the "Sauté" button two times to select "More" mode. Reduce the cooking liquid for 10 to 15 minutes until concentrated.
Remove the kitchen twine from the turkey and spoon the gravy over the top.
Slice and serve.

Per Serving: Calories 237; Fat 10.9g; Sodium 354mg; Carbs 20.5g; Fiber 4.1g; Sugar 8.2g; Protein 06g

Penne and Turkey Meatballs

Prep time: 10 minutes| **Cook time:** 6 minutes| **Serves:** 4

1-pound lean ground turkey
½ cup plain or panko breadcrumbs
3 tablespoons grated Parmesan cheese, plus extra for garnish
¼ yellow onion, finely chopped
2 garlic cloves, minced
1 tablespoon finely chopped fresh basil, plus more for garnish
1 egg, beaten
½ teaspoon kosher salt
¼ teaspoon black pepper
3 tablespoons olive oil
1 (15-oz.) can diced tomatoes with juice
1 (14- to 15-oz.) can tomato purée or sauce
½ cup water
8 oz. uncooked penne pasta

In a medium bowl, combine the turkey, breadcrumbs, Parmesan, onion, garlic, basil, egg, salt, and pepper. Mix well.
Form 1½-inch meatballs and place on a plate.
Press the "Sauté" button two times to select "More" mode.
Once hot, coat the bottom of the pot with the oil.
Add the meatballs, one at a time, in close proximity and, if possible, in one layer. Cook for 1 minute.
Add the tomatoes with juice, tomato purée or sauce, water, and pasta.

Carefully push the pasta down so that it's mostly submerged in the sauce.
Put on the pressure cooker's lid and turn the steam valve to "Sealing" position.
Press the "Pressure Cook" button two times to select "Less" option.
Use the "+/-" keys on the control panel to set the cooking time to 5 minutes.
Use the Pressure Level button to adjust the pressure to "High Pressure".
Once the cooking cycle is completed, quickly and carefully turn the steam release handle from Sealing position to the Venting position.
When all the steam is released, remove the pressure lid from the top carefully.
Serve topped with more Parmesan and basil.

Per Serving: Calories 219; Fat 10g; Sodium 891mg; Carbs 22.9g; Fiber 4g; Sugar 4g; Protein 13g

Duck with Vegetables

Prep time: 10 minutes| **Cook time:** 30 minutes| **Serves:** 4
2 tablespoons canola oil
4 duck legs
Kosher salt
pepper
8 oz. small Cipollini or pearl onions
8 oz. sliced mushrooms
4 garlic cloves, minced
½ cup dry red wine
1 cup chicken broth

Press the "Sauté" button two times to select "More" mode and add the oil.
Dry the duck well and season with salt and pepper.
Place skin-side down in the pot and cook for about 5 minutes, or until nicely browned. Remove.
Turn the heat down to medium. Carefully discard all but 2 tablespoons of the fat and oil in the pot.
Add the onions and sauté until lightly browned, about 3 minutes. Add the mushrooms and garlic.
Cook, stirring, for 3 minutes more.
Add the wine and scrape up any brown bits off the bottom of the pot, cooking for 1 minute.
Add the broth and duck.
Put on the pressure cooker's lid and turn the steam valve to "Sealing" position.
Press the "Pressure Cook" button two times to select "Normal" option.
Use the "+/-" keys on the control panel to set the cooking time to 20 minutes.
Use the Pressure Level button to adjust the pressure to "High Pressure".
Once the cooking cycle is completed, quickly and carefully turn the steam release handle from Sealing position to the Venting position.
When all the steam is released, remove the pressure lid from the top carefully.
Serve the duck with the onions and mushrooms and spoon over some of the cooking liquid.

Per Serving: Calories 478; Fat 12.9g; Sodium 414mg; Carbs 11g; Fiber 5g; Sugar 9g; Protein 11g

Teriyaki Wing

Prep time: 10 minutes| **Cook time:** 15 minutes| **Serves:** 6
3 lbs. "party" chicken wings (separated at the joints)
½ cup plus 2 tablespoons low-sodium soy sauce
Salt and black pepper
⅓ cup packed brown sugar
2 tablespoons cider vinegar or rice vinegar
4 teaspoons finely chopped fresh ginger
4 medium garlic cloves, finely chopped
1 tablespoon cornstarch

Pour 1½ cups water into the pot and place a Steam Rack or steamer basket inside.
In a large bowl, toss the wings with 2 tablespoons of the soy sauce and season with salt and pepper.
Place the wings on the Steam Rack or steamer basket.
Put on the pressure cooker's lid and turn the steam valve to "Sealing" position.
Press the "Pressure Cook" button three times to select "Less" option.
Use the "+/-" keys on the control panel to set the cooking time to 5 minutes.
Use the Pressure Level button to adjust the pressure to "High Pressure".
Once the cooking cycle is completed, allow the steam to release naturally.
When all the steam is released, remove the pressure lid from the top carefully.
Preheat the broiler and move an oven rack so that it is 4 inches below the broiler element.
Line a baking sheet with foil and spray it with cooking spray.
Transfer the wings to the prepared baking sheet.
Discard the cooking liquid and remove the Steam Rack or steaming basket from the pot.
Add the remaining ½ cup soy sauce, the brown sugar, vinegar, ginger, and garlic to the pot.
Press the "Sauté" button two times to select "Normal" mode.
Bring to a simmer and cook, stirring frequently, until the sugar has dissolved, 3 minutes.
In a small bowl, mix the cornstarch with 1 tablespoon water.
Add the cornstarch mixture to the pot and cook, stirring constantly, until the sauce has thickened, 1 minute.
Spoon the sauce over the wings, turning them so both sides are covered.
Broil the wings until browned and crispy on the edges, 3 minutes.
When done, serve and enjoy.

Per Serving: Calories 184; Fat 5g; Sodium 441mg; Carbs 17g; Fiber 4.6g; Sugar 5g; Protein 9g

Chicken–Stuffed Sweet Potatoes

Prep time: 15 minutes| **Cook time:** 18 minutes| **Serves:** 4

1 cup thin barbecue sauce
1 pound boneless, skinless chicken thighs, fat trimmed
4 small (8-oz.) sweet potatoes, pricked with a fork
Salt and black pepper
1 cup sour cream
2 green onions, thinly sliced

Combine the barbecue sauce and chicken in the pot.
Place a tall Steam Rack over the chicken and arrange the sweet potatoes on top.
Put on the pressure cooker's lid and turn the steam valve to "Sealing" position.
Press the "Pressure Cook" button two times to select "Less" option.
Use the "+/-" keys on the control panel to set the cooking time to 18 minutes.
Use the Pressure Level button to adjust the pressure to "High Pressure".
Once the cooking cycle is completed, allow the steam to release naturally for 10 minutes, then turn the steam release handle to the Venting position.
When all the steam is released, remove the pressure lid from the top carefully.
Split the sweet potatoes open lengthwise, season with salt and pepper, and set aside.
Remove the Steam Rack from the pot. Pull the chicken into shreds with two forks, return it to the sauce, and stir to combine.
Divide the chicken among the sweet potatoes; you may not need all of the sauce.
Top with dollops of sour cream and a sprinkle of the green onions and serve.

Per Serving: Calories 334; Fat 12.9g; Sodium 414mg; Carbs 11g; Fiber 5g; Sugar 9g; Protein 31g

Makhani Chicken

Prep time: 15 minutes| **Cook time:** 15 minutes| **Serves:** 4

3 tablespoons butter or ghee, at room temperature
1 medium yellow onion, halved and sliced through the root end
1 (10-oz.) can Ro-Tel tomatoes with green chilies, with juice
2 tablespoons mild Indian curry paste (such as Patek's)
1½ lbs. boneless, skinless chicken thighs, fat trimmed, cut into 2- to 3-inch pieces
2 tablespoons all-purpose flour
Salt and black pepper

Put 1 tablespoon of the butter or ghee to the Instant pot
Press the "Sauté" button two times to select "Normal" mode.
Add the onion and cook, stirring frequently, until browned, 6 minutes. Press Cancel button.

Add the tomatoes to the pot, stir, and scrape up any browned bits on the bottom of the pot.
Add the curry paste and stir to combine.
Nestle the chicken into the sauce.
Put on the pressure cooker's lid and turn the steam valve to "Sealing" position.
Press the "Pressure Cook" button two times to select "Normal" option.
Use the "+/-" keys on the control panel to set the cooking time to 8 minutes.
Use the Pressure Level button to adjust the pressure to "High Pressure".
Once the cooking cycle is completed, quickly and carefully turn the steam release handle from Sealing position to the Venting position.
When all the steam is released, remove the pressure lid from the top carefully.
Press the "Sauté" button two times to select "Normal" mode.
And add the flour mixture to the pot and cook until the sauce is thickened, 1 minute.
Season with salt and pepper and serve.

Per Serving: Calories 489; Fat 11g; Sodium 501mg; Carbs 8.9g; Fiber 4.6g; Sugar 8g; Protein 26g

Stuffed Chicken Parmesan

Prep time: 15 minutes| **Cook time:** 15 minutes| **Serves:** 4

1 slice sturdy sandwich bread, finely chopped
1 small (5-oz.) zucchini, grated
½ cup grated Italian cheese blend
1 teaspoon Italian seasoning
Salt and black pepper
4 medium (8-oz.) boneless, skinless chicken breasts
1 (24-oz.) jar thin marinara sauce (such as Rao's)

In a medium bowl, combine the breadcrumbs, zucchini, cheese, and Italian seasoning.
Season with salt and pepper. Cut a horizontal slit into each chicken breast to form a 5- to 6-inch-long pocket.
Stuff the chicken breasts with the breadcrumb mixture. Season the chicken with salt and pepper.
Pour the sauce into the pot. Add ¼ cup water to the marinara jar, screw on the lid, and shake.
Add the tomato-y water to the pot. Set a handled Steam Rack in the pot and place the chicken breasts on the Steam Rack.
Put on the pressure cooker's lid and turn the steam valve to "Sealing" position.
Press the "Pressure Cook" button two times to select "Normal" option.
Use the "+/-" keys on the control panel to set the cooking time to 8 minutes.
Use the Pressure Level button to adjust the pressure to "Low Pressure".
Once the cooking cycle is completed, allow the steam to release naturally.
When all the steam is released, remove the pressure lid from the top carefully.
Press the "Sauté" button two times to select "Less" mode.

Remove the Steam Rack, nestle the chicken into the sauce, and simmer a few minutes more.
Serve the chicken with the sauce.

Per Serving: Calories 584; Fat 15g; Sodium 441mg; Carbs 17g; Fiber 4.6g; Sugar 5g; Protein 29g

Mustard–Braised Chicken

Prep time: 15 minutes| **Cook time:** 35 minutes| **Serves:** 4

2 slices thick-cut bacon, chopped
8 bone-in chicken thighs, skin removed and fat trimmed
Salt and black pepper
4 cups quartered cremini mushrooms (8 oz.)
2 large shallots, thinly sliced (¾ cup)
1½ cups bottled hard apple cider (12 oz.)
2 tablespoons grainy mustard

Press the "Sauté" button two times to select "Normal" mode.
Add the bacon and cook, stirring occasionally, until the bacon is browned, 3 to 4 minutes.
Transfer to a bowl with a slotted spoon; leave the drippings in the pot.
Season the chicken all over with salt and pepper.
Add half the chicken to the pot and cook until browned on one side, 3 minutes. Transfer to a plate.
Add the mushrooms and shallots to the pot and sauté until the shallots are tender, 3 minutes.
Add the cider and mustard and bring to a simmer.
Add all the chicken, any accumulated juices, and the bacon to the pot.
Put on the pressure cooker's lid and turn the steam valve to "Sealing" position.
Press the "Pressure Cook" button two times to select "Less" option.
Use the Pressure Level button to adjust the pressure to "High Pressure".
Once the cooking cycle is completed, quickly and carefully turn the steam release handle from Sealing position to the Venting position.
When all the steam is released, remove the pressure lid from the top carefully.
Transfer the chicken and vegetables to a serving dish with a slotted spoon. Cover with foil and set aside.
Press the "Sauté" button two times to select "More" mode, and bring to a simmer.
Using a ladle, skim any liquid fat that pools on top of the sauce and discard.
Cook until the sauce is reduced by half, 5 minutes. Press Cancel button.
Pour the sauce over the chicken and serve.

Per Serving: Calories 483; Fat 7.9g; Sodium 704mg; Carbs 6g; Fiber 3.6g; Sugar 6g; Protein 18g

Chicken Penne Puttanesca

Prep time: 15 minutes| **Cook time:** 11 minutes| **Serves:** 4

2 small (6- to 7-oz.) boneless, skinless chicken breasts
Salt and black pepper
2 tablespoons olive oil
12 oz. dry penne pasta
2½ cups store-bought chicken or vegetable broth, or homemade
1 (15-oz.) can diced tomatoes with Italian herbs, with juices
½ cup oil-cured black or Kalamata olives
4 oil-packed rolled anchovies with capers, plus 1 tablespoon oil from the jar
Pinch of red pepper flakes

Pat the chicken dry with paper towels. Season the chicken all over with salt and several grinds of pepper.
Put the oil to the Instant pot.
Press the "Sauté" button two times to select "Normal" mode.
Add the chicken and cook until golden brown on one side, 3 minutes.
Add the penne, broth, tomatoes, olives, anchovies and oil, red pepper flakes, and several grinds of pepper.
Stir everything together and place the chicken breasts on top of the pasta mixture.
Put on the pressure cooker's lid and turn the steam valve to "Sealing" position.
Press the "Pressure Cook" button two times to select "Less" option.
Use the "+/-" keys on the control panel to set the cooking time to 6 minutes.
Use the Pressure Level button to adjust the pressure to "Low Pressure".
Once the cooking cycle is completed, quickly and carefully turn the steam release handle from Sealing position to the Venting position.
When all the steam is released, remove the pressure lid from the top carefully.
Transfer the chicken to a cutting board and chop it into bite-size pieces.
Return the chicken to the pot and stir to combine.
Serve.

Per Serving: Calories 302; Fat 7.9g; Sodium 704mg; Carbs 6g; Fiber 3.6g; Sugar 6g; Protein 18g

Italian Sausage Ragu with Polenta

Prep time: 10 minutes| **Cook time:** 15 minutes| **Serves:** 4

2 tablespoons olive oil
8 oz. bulk spicy Italian sausage
1 medium yellow onion, chopped
1 red or green bell pepper, chopped
1 tablespoon balsamic vinegar
1 cup thin marinara sauce (such as Rao's or Trader Joe's Organic Marinara)
¼ cup store-bought chicken broth, or homemade
12 oz. boneless, skinless chicken thighs, fat trimmed, cut into 2-inch pieces

Salt and black pepper
¾ cup polenta (not quick-cooking)
OPTIONAL GARNISH
½ cup shaved Parmesan cheese curls

Put 1 tablespoon of the oil in the Instant pot.
Press the "Sauté" button two times to select "Normal" mode.
Add the sausage and cook, stirring occasionally, until browned, 3 minutes.
Add the onion and bell pepper and cook until tender, 4 minutes. Press Cancel.
Add the vinegar and scrape up the browned bits on the bottom of the pan.
Add the marinara sauce and broth and stir to combine. Season the chicken all over with salt and pepper.
Add it to the pot and stir to combine.
Place a tall Steam Rack in the pot over the chicken.
Place 2⅔ cups warm water, the remaining 1 tablespoon oil, and ½ teaspoon salt in a 7-inch round metal baking pan.
Gradually whisk in the polenta. Cover tightly with foil and place on the Steam Rack.
Put on the pressure cooker's lid and turn the steam valve to "Sealing" position.
Press the "Pressure Cook" button two times to select "Less" option.
Use the "+/-" keys on the control panel to set the cooking time to 8 minutes.
Use the Pressure Level button to adjust the pressure to "High Pressure".
Once the cooking cycle is completed, allow the steam to release naturally for 10 minutes, then turn the steam release handle to the Venting position.
When all the steam is released, remove the pressure lid from the top carefully.
Remove the Steam Rack from the pot.
Serve the polenta in shallow bowls, topped with the chicken ragu and garnished with the cheese curls.

Per Serving: Calories 483; Fat 7.9g; Sodium 704mg; Carbs 6g; Fiber 3.6g; Sugar 6g; Protein 18g

Chicken Burrito Bowls

Prep time: 10 minutes| **Cook time:** 18 minutes| **Serves:** 4
2 teaspoons taco seasoning
6 to 8 boneless, skinless chicken thighs, fat trimmed
2 tablespoons olive oil
¾ cup fresh refrigerated tomato salsa
1 cup plus 1 tablespoon store-bought chicken
¾ cup red quinoa, rinsed
1 (15-oz.) can black beans, drained
Salt and black pepper
1 cup prepared guacamole

Rub the taco seasoning into the chicken.
Put the oil in the instant pot. Press the "Sauté" button two times to select "More" mode.

When the oil is hot, brown the chicken in batches on one side only until golden brown, 3 minutes per batch.
Drain off the fat in the pot and return the pot to the appliance.
Add ½ cup of the salsa and ¼ cup of the broth to the pot.
Add the chicken and any accumulated juices to the pot.
Spoon the remaining ¼ cup salsa over the chicken.
Place a tall Steam Rack in the pot over the chicken.
In a 7-inch metal baking pan, combine the quinoa and remaining ¾ cup plus 1 tablespoon broth.
Spoon the beans over the quinoa mixture, but don't stir them in.
Place the uncovered baking pan on the Steam Rack.
Put on the pressure cooker's lid and turn the steam valve to "Sealing" position.
Press the "Pressure Cook" button two times to select "Less" option.
Use the "+/-" keys on the control panel to set the cooking time to 12 minutes.
Use the Pressure Level button to adjust the pressure to "High Pressure".
Once the cooking cycle is completed, allow the steam to release naturally.
When all the steam is released, remove the pressure lid from the top carefully.
Remove the baking pan and Steam Rack from the pot.
Fluff the quinoa-bean mixture with a fork and season with salt and pepper.
Divide the quinoa among bowls and top with the chicken and some of the cooking liquid from the pot.
Top with the guacamole. Sprinkle with the optional toppings, if using, and serve.

Per Serving: Calories 489; Fat 11g; Sodium 501mg; Carbs 8.9g; Fiber 4.6g; Sugar 8g; Protein 26g

Faux-Tesserae Chicken Dinner

Prep time: 10 minutes| **Cook time:** 45 minutes| **Serves:** 4-6
1 (4-pound) whole roasting chicken, neck and giblets in cavity removed and reserved
1 pound red potatoes, cut into 1¼-inch chunks
2 large carrots, peeled and cut into 1-inch pieces
2 tablespoons olive oil
4 teaspoons lemon pepper seasoning
OPTIONAL GRAVY
1½ tablespoons all-purpose flour
1½ tablespoons butter, at room temperature
Salt and black pepper

Place the Steam Rack with handles in the Instant pot and add 1 cup water.
Place the neck and giblets, if you have them, in the water.

Toss the vegetables with 1 tablespoon of the oil and 1 teaspoon of the lemon pepper seasoning.

Stuff about half the potatoes and carrots into the chicken cavity.

Tuck the wings behind the chicken's back and tie the drumsticks together with butcher's twine.

Season the outside of the chicken with the remaining lemon pepper seasoning.

Place the chicken breast-side up on the Steam Rack.

Place the remaining carrots and potatoes around the chicken. Drizzle with the remaining 1 tablespoon oil.

Put on the pressure cooker's lid and turn the steam valve to "Sealing" position.

Press the "Pressure Cook" button two times to select "Normal" option.

Use the "+/-" keys on the control panel to set the cooking time to 28 minutes.

Use the Pressure Level button to adjust the pressure to "High Pressure".

Once the cooking cycle is completed, quickly and carefully turn the steam release handle from Sealing position to the Venting position.

When all the steam is released, remove the pressure lid from the top carefully.

Press the "Sauté" button two times to select "Normal" mode for 5 minutes.

For crispy skin, preheat your oven and adjust the oven rack so that it is 8 inches below the broiler element.

Transfer the chicken on the Steam Rack to a foil-lined baking sheet.

Place the loose vegetables in a serving bowl and cover with foil.

Broil the chicken, rotating the pan once, until the skin on top is browned, about 6 minutes.

Carve the chicken and serve with the vegetables and a little of the cooking liquid.

If you want to make gravy and there is still cooking liquid in the pot, select Sauté and adjust to More.

When the liquid boils, the liquid fat will collect on the sides of the pot.

Skim fat with a spoon and then discard.

In a small bowl, whisk together butter and flour until smooth. Stir flour mixture into cooking liquid and simmer until thickened, 2 minutes. Press Cancel.

Serve with chicken.

Per Serving: Calories 334; Fat 19g; Sodium 354mg; Carbs 15g; Fiber 5.1g; Sugar 8.2g; Protein 12g

Quinoa–Stuffed Peppers

Prep time: 10 minutes| **Cook time:** 20 minutes| **Serves:** 4
⅔ cup dry quinoa, rinsed and drained
1¾ cups store-bought chicken broth, or homemade
Salt and black pepper
1-pound raw Italian chicken or turkey sausages, casings removed
½ cup chopped fresh basil
4 medium bell peppers, top ¼ inch of stem end removed, seeds discarded
1 cup thin jarred marinara sauce (such as Rao's)
1 cup grated mozzarella cheese

Place the quinoa, 1 cup of the broth, a pinch of salt, and a few grinds of pepper in the pot.

Put on the pressure cooker's lid and turn the steam valve to "Sealing" position.

Press the "Pressure Cook" button two times to select "Less" option.

Use the "+/-" keys on the control panel to set the cooking time to 1 minutes.

Use the Pressure Level button to adjust the pressure to "High Pressure".

Once the cooking cycle is completed, allow the steam to release naturally for 10 minutes, then turn the steam release handle to the Venting position.

When all the steam is released, remove the pressure lid from the top carefully.

Add the sausage and basil to the quinoa and mix well to combine. Stuff the quinoa mixture into the peppers.

In a small bowl, combine the remaining ¾ cup broth with the marinara sauce.

Pour 1¼ cups of the mixture into the pot.

Place a Steam Rack with handles in the pot and set the peppers on top. Spoon the remaining sauce over the peppers and sprinkle with the cheese.

Put on the pressure cooker's lid and turn the steam valve to "Sealing" position.

Press the "Pressure Cook" button two times to select "Less" option.

Use the "+/-" keys on the control panel to set the cooking time to 15 minutes.

Use the Pressure Level button to adjust the pressure to "High Pressure".

Once the cooking cycle is completed, allow the steam to release naturally.

When all the steam is released, remove the pressure lid from the top carefully.

Carefully lift the Steam Rack from the pot and transfer the peppers to dinner plates.

Spoon the sauce over the peppers.

Per Serving: Calories 382; Fat 12.9g; Sodium 414mg; Carbs 11g; Fiber 5g; Sugar 9g; Protein 31g

Chicken with Black Bean Garlic Sauce

Prep time: 10 minutes| **Cook time:** 10 minutes| **Serves:** 4
1½ lbs. boneless, skinless chicken thighs, fat trimmed, cut into 2-inch pieces
½ cup store-bought chicken broth, or homemade
3 tablespoons black bean garlic sauce (such as Lee Kum Kee brand)
1½ tablespoons julienned fresh ginger
1 tablespoon soy sauce
1 teaspoon balsamic vinegar
Black pepper
1½ cups long-grain white rice, rinsed
4 cups 1½-inch broccoli florets (10 oz.)
2 teaspoons cornstarch

Combine the chicken, broth, black bean garlic sauce, ginger, soy sauce, and vinegar in the Inner Pot.

Add several grinds of pepper.

Combine the rice with 1½ cups cold water in a 7 × 3-inch round metal baking pan.

Place the baking pan, uncovered, on a tall Steam Rack set over the chicken mixture.

Put on the pressure cooker's lid and turn the steam valve to "Sealing" position.

Press the "Pressure Cook" button three times to select "Less" option.

Use the "+/-" keys on the control panel to set the cooking time to 5 minutes.

Use the Pressure Level button to adjust the pressure to "High Pressure".

Once the cooking cycle is completed, quickly and carefully turn the steam release handle from Sealing position to the Venting position.

When all the steam is released, remove the pressure lid from the top carefully.

Remove the rice in the baking pan and the Steam Rack, if you used them, and set aside.

Add the broccoli to the pot, stir gently to combine, and place a regular pot lid on the Inner Pot.

Press the "Sauté" button two times to select "Normal" mode, and simmer for 3 minutes.

While the mixture is cooking, mix the cornstarch with 2 teaspoons of cold water.

Add to the pot, stir, and continue to cook until the sauce is thickened, 30 seconds.

Serve immediately with the rice.

Per Serving: Calories 372; Fat 20g; Sodium 891mg; Carbs 29g; Fiber 3g; Sugar 8g; Protein 27g

Game Hens with Garlic

Prep time: 10 minutes| **Cook time:** 20 minutes| **Serves:** 4

2 (24-oz.) Cornish game hens
1 tablespoon olive oil
2 teaspoons Herbes de Provence
Salt and black pepper
40 medium garlic cloves (about ¾ cup), peeled
¼ cup dry white wine
½ cup store-bought chicken broth, or homemade
1½ tablespoons all-purpose flour
1 tablespoon butter, at room temperature

Place the hens breast-side down on a clean cutting board.

Using kitchen shears, cut down the backbone of each bird.

Cut lengthwise through the breastbone to cleave the birds in half.

Add the oil to the Instant pot, Press the "Sauté" button two times to select "More" mode.

Rub the hens all over with the Herbes de Provence, salt, and pepper.

Brown the poultry skin-side down in batches until golden brown on one side, 4 minutes per batch.

Transfer to a plate. Adjust the cooking temperature to "Normal".

Add the garlic and cook, stirring frequently, until fragrant and browned in places, 1 minute.

Add the wine, scrape up any browned bits on the bottom of the pot, and simmer for 1 minute.

Add the broth and stir to combine. Place a Steam Rack with handles in the pot.

Place the hen halves skin-side up on the rack. You may have to stack them a bit, which is fine.

Put on the pressure cooker's lid and turn the steam valve to "Sealing" position.

Press the "Poultry" button three times to select "Less" option.

Use the "+/-" keys on the control panel to set the cooking time to 8 minutes.

Use the Pressure Level button to adjust the pressure to "High Pressure".

Once the cooking cycle is completed, allow the steam to release naturally for 10 minutes, then turn the steam release handle to the Venting position.

When all the steam is released, remove the pressure lid from the top carefully.

Transfer the hens to a serving plate, and cover loosely with foil.

In a small bowl, mix the flour and butter until smooth.

Press the "Sauté" button two times to select "Normal" mode.

Whisk the flour mixture into the liquid in the pot and simmer until the sauce has thickened, 1 minute.

Season the sauce with salt and pepper, spoon over the hens, and serve immediately.

Per Serving: Calories 471; Fat 7.9g; Sodium 704mg; Carbs 6g; Fiber 3.6g; Sugar 6g; Protein 18g

Wine Glazed Whole Chicken

Prep time: 10 minutes| **Cook time:** 18 minutes| **Serves:** 8

1 medium-sized, whole chicken (3 lbs.)
2 tablespoon sugar
2 teaspoons kosher salt
1 tablespoon onion powder
1 tablespoon garlic powder
1 tablespoon paprika
2 teaspoons black pepper
½ teaspoon cayenne pepper
1 cup water or chicken broth
1 tablespoon red wine
2 teaspoons soy sauce
1 minced green onion

In a medium bowl, combine the sugar, salt, onion powder, garlic powder, paprika, black pepper, and cayenne pepper.

Prepare the Inner Pot by adding the water to the pot and placing the steam rack in it.

Pour the wine and soy sauce into the pot.

Rub all sides of the chicken with the spice mix.

Place the chicken on the steam rack and

Put on the pressure cooker's lid and turn the steam valve to "Sealing" position.
Press the "Poultry" button three times to select "Normal" option.
Use the "+/-" keys on the control panel to set the cooking time to 18 minutes.
Use the Pressure Level button to adjust the pressure to "High Pressure".
Once the cooking cycle is completed, allow the steam to release naturally.
When all the steam is released, remove the pressure lid from the top carefully.
Top with minced green onion and serve.

Per Serving: Calories 289; Fat 14g; Sodium 791mg; Carbs 18.9g; Fiber 4.6g; Sugar 8g; Protein 6g

Seasoned Chicken

Prep time: 10 minutes| **Cook time:** 15 minutes| **Serves:** 6-8

5 lbs. chicken thighs
4 cloves garlic, minced
½ cup soy sauce
½ cup white vinegar
½ cup water
1 teaspoon black peppercorns
3 bay leaves
½ teaspoon salt
½ teaspoon black pepper

Add the garlic, soy sauce, vinegar, water, peppercorns, bay leaves, salt and pepper to the Inner Pot and stir well.
Add the chicken thighs. Stir to coat the chicken.
Put on the pressure cooker's lid and turn the steam valve to "Sealing" position.
Press the "Poultry" button three times to select "Less" option.
Use the "+/-" keys on the control panel to set the cooking time to 15 minutes.
Use the Pressure Level button to adjust the pressure to "High Pressure".
Once the cooking cycle is completed, allow the steam to release naturally.
When all the steam is released, remove the pressure lid from the top carefully.
Remove the bay leaves, stir and serve.

Per Serving: Calories 584; Fat 15g; Sodium 441mg; Carbs 17g; Fiber 4.6g; Sugar 5g; Protein 29g

Italian Chicken

Prep time: 10 minutes| **Cook time:** 15 minutes| **Serves:** 6

8 boneless, skinless chicken thighs
1 teaspoon kosher salt
½ teaspoon black pepper
1 tablespoon olive oil
2 medium-sized, chopped carrots
1 cup stemmed and quartered cremini mushrooms
1 chopped onion
3 cloves garlic, smashed

1 tablespoon tomato paste
2 cups cherry tomatoes, cut in half
½ cup pitted green olives
½ cup water
½ cup thinly-sliced fresh basil
¼ cup chopped fresh Italian parsley

Season the chicken thighs with ½ teaspoon salt and pepper.
Press the "Sauté" button two times to select "More" mode.
Wait 1 minute and add the oil to the bottom of the pot.
Add the carrots, mushrooms, onions, and ½ teaspoon salt and sauté for about 5 minutes until soft.
Add the garlic and tomato paste and cook for another 30 seconds.
Add the cherry tomatoes, chicken thighs, water and olives, stir well.
Put on the pressure cooker's lid and turn the steam valve to "Sealing" position.
Press the "Pressure Cook" button two times to select "Less" option.
Use the "+/-" keys on the control panel to set the cooking time to 10 minutes.
Use the Pressure Level button to adjust the pressure to "High Pressure".
Once the cooking cycle is completed, quickly and carefully turn the steam release handle from Sealing position to the Venting position.
When all the steam is released, remove the pressure lid from the top carefully.
Top with fresh basil and parsley.
Serve and enjoy.

Per Serving: Calories 334; Fat 7.9g; Sodium 704mg; Carbs 6g; Fiber 3.6g; Sugar 6g; Protein 18g

Thai Chicken

Prep time: 10 minutes| **Cook time:** 10 minutes| **Serves:** 4

2 lbs. chicken thighs, boneless and skinless
1 cup lime juice
½ cup fish sauce
¼ cup olive oil
2 tablespoon coconut nectar
1 teaspoon ginger, grated
1 teaspoon mint, chopped
2 teaspoons cilantro, finely chopped

In a medium bowl, whisk together lime juice, fish sauce, olive oil, coconut nectar, ginger, mint and cilantro until combined.
Add the chicken thighs to the instant pot.
Pour the marinade on top.
Put on the pressure cooker's lid and turn the steam valve to "Sealing" position.
Press the "Pressure Cook" button two times to select "Less" option.
Use the "+/-" keys on the control panel to set the cooking time to 10 minutes.
Use the Pressure Level button to adjust the pressure to "High Pressure".

Once the cooking cycle is completed, quickly and carefully turn the steam release handle from Sealing position to the Venting position. When all the steam is released, remove the pressure lid from the top carefully.
Serve.

Per Serving: Calories 472; Fat 10.9g; Sodium 354mg; Carbs 10.5g; Fiber 4.1g; Sugar 8.2g; Protein 26g

Spicy Chicken Wings

Prep time: 10 minutes| **Cook time:** 10 minutes| **Serves:** 4

3 lbs. chicken wings
2 tablespoons olive oil
¼ cup light brown sugar
½ teaspoon garlic powder
½ teaspoon cayenne pepper
½ teaspoon black pepper
½ teaspoon paprika
½ teaspoon salt
1½ cups chicken broth or water

Rinse and dry the chicken wings with a paper towel. Put in the large bowl.
In a medium bowl, combine the olive oil, sugar, garlic powder, cayenne pepper, black pepper, paprika, and salt. Mix well.
Rub all sides of the chicken with the spice mix.
Pour the chicken broth into the Inner Pot and add the wings.
Put on the pressure cooker's lid and turn the steam valve to "Sealing" position.
Press the "Pressure Cook" button two times to select "Less" option.
Use the "+/-" keys on the control panel to set the cooking time to 10 minutes.
Use the Pressure Level button to adjust the pressure to "High Pressure".
Once the cooking cycle is completed, quickly and carefully turn the steam release handle from Sealing position to the Venting position. When all the steam is released, remove the pressure lid from the top carefully.
Serve.

Per Serving: Calories 489; Fat 11g; Sodium 501mg; Carbs 8.9g; Fiber 4.6g; Sugar 8g; Protein 26g

Hot Wings

Prep time: 10 minutes| **Cook time:** 20 minutes| **Serves:** 6

4 lbs. chicken wings, sectioned, frozen or fresh
½ cup cayenne pepper hot sauce
1 tablespoon Worcestershire sauce
½ cup butter
½ teaspoon kosher salt
1-2 tablespoon sugar, light brown
1½ cups water

Mix the hot sauce with the Worcestershire sauce, butter, salt, and brown sugar;

microwave for 20 seconds or until the butter is melted.
Pour the water into the Inner Pot and place the Steam Rack.
Place chicken wings on the steam rack and lock the lid in right way.
Put on the pressure cooker's lid and turn the steam valve to "Sealing" position.
Press the "Pressure Cook" button two times to select "Less" option.
Use the "+/-" keys on the control panel to set the cooking time to 10 minutes.
Use the Pressure Level button to adjust the pressure to "High Pressure".
Once the cooking cycle is completed, quickly and carefully turn the steam release handle from Sealing position to the Venting position. When all the steam is released, remove the pressure lid from the top carefully.
Preheat the oven.
Carefully transfer the chicken wings to a baking sheet.
Brush the tops of the chicken wings with the sauce.
Place under the broiler for 4 to 5 minutes until browned.
Brush the other side with the remaining sauce and broil for another 4-5 minutes.
Serve.

Per Serving: Calories 521; Fat 7.9g; Sodium 704mg; Carbs 6g; Fiber 3.6g; Sugar 6g; Protein 18g

Lime Chicken Wings

Prep time: 10 minutes| **Cook time:** 20 minutes| **Serves:** 4

2 lbs. chicken wings
3 tablespoon honey
2 tablespoon soy sauce
1 small lime, juiced
½ teaspoon sea salt
½ cup water

In a bowl, combine the soy sauce, lime juice, honey and salt.
Rinse and dry the chicken wings with a paper towel.
Add the chicken wings and honey mixture to a Ziploc bag and shake a couple of times.
Then refrigerate for 60 minutes.
Pour the water into the Inner Pot and add the chicken wings with marinade.
Put on the pressure cooker's lid and turn the steam valve to "Sealing" position.
Press the "Pressure Cook" button two times to select "Less" option.
Use the "+/-" keys on the control panel to set the cooking time to 15 minutes.
Use the Pressure Level button to adjust the pressure to "High Pressure".
Once the cooking cycle is completed, allow the steam to release naturally for 10 minutes, then turn the steam release handle to the Venting position.
When all the steam is released, remove the pressure lid from the top carefully.

Press the "Sauté" button two times to select "Normal" mode and continue to cook until the sauce thickens.
Serve.

Per Serving: Calories 219; Fat 10g; Sodium 891mg; Carbs 22.9g; Fiber 4g; Sugar 4g; Protein 13g

Sesame Chicken

Prep time: 10 minutes| **Cook time:** 15 minutes| **Serves:** 6

6 boneless chicken thigh fillets
5 tablespoons sweet chili sauce
5 tablespoon hoisin sauce
1 chunk peeled, grated fresh ginger
4 peeled and crushed cloves garlic
1 tablespoon rice vinegar
1½ tablespoon sesame seeds
1 tablespoon soy sauce
½ cup chicken stock

In a medium bowl, whisk together the chili sauce, hoisin sauce, ginger, garlic, vinegar, sesame seeds, soy sauce, and chicken stock until combined.
Add the chicken thigh fillets to the Inner Pot and pour over the sauce mixture.
Put on the pressure cooker's lid and turn the steam valve to "Sealing" position.
Press the "Pressure Cook" button two times to select "Less" option.
Use the "+/-" keys on the control panel to set the cooking time to 15 minutes.
Use the Pressure Level button to adjust the pressure to "High Pressure".
Once the cooking cycle is completed, allow the steam to release naturally for 10 minutes, then turn the steam release handle to the Venting position.
When all the steam is released, remove the pressure lid from the top carefully.
Serve with cooked rice, mashed potato or any other garnish.

Per Serving: Calories 219; Fat 10g; Sodium 891mg; Carbs 22.9g; Fiber 4g; Sugar 4g; Protein 23g

Salsa Verde Chicken

Prep time: 10 minutes| **Cook time:** 20 minutes| **Serves:** 6

2½ lbs. boneless chicken breasts
1 teaspoon smoked paprika
1 teaspoon cumin
1 teaspoon salt
2 cup (16 oz.) salsa Verde

Add the chicken breasts, paprika, cumin, and salt to the Inner Pot.
Pour the salsa Verde on top.
Put on the pressure cooker's lid and turn the steam valve to "Sealing" position.
Press the "Pressure Cook" button two times to select "Less" option.

Use the Pressure Level button to adjust the pressure to "High Pressure".
Once the cooking cycle is completed, quickly and carefully turn the steam release handle from Sealing position to the Venting position.
When all the steam is released, remove the pressure lid from the top carefully.
Shred the meat, serve and enjoy.

Per Serving: Calories 382; Fat 7.9g; Sodium 704mg; Carbs 6g; Fiber 3.6g; Sugar 6g; Protein 18g

Sriracha Chicken

Prep time: 10 minutes| **Cook time:** 15 minutes| **Serves:** 4

4 diced chicken breasts
5 tablespoon soy sauce
2-3 tablespoon honey
¼ cup sugar
4 tablespoons cold water
1 tablespoon minced garlic
2-3 tablespoon sriracha
2 tablespoon cornstarch

In the Inner Pot, whisk together soy sauce, honey, sugar, 2 tablespoons of water, garlic, and sriracha until combined.
Toss the chicken breasts in the mixture.
Put on the pressure cooker's lid and turn the steam valve to "Sealing" position.
Press the "Pressure Cook" button two times to select "Less" option.
Use the "+/-" keys on the control panel to set the cooking time to 9 minutes.
Use the Pressure Level button to adjust the pressure to "High Pressure".
Once the cooking cycle is completed, quickly and carefully turn the steam release handle from Sealing position to the Venting position.
When all the steam is released, remove the pressure lid from the top carefully.
Meanwhile, in a small bowl combine 2 tablespoons of water and cornstarch.
Pour the cornstarch mixture into the pot.
Press the "Sauté" button two times to select "Less" mode, simmer and stir occasionally until the sauce begins to thicken.
Serve.

Per Serving: Calories 372; Fat 20g; Sodium 891mg; Carbs 29g; Fiber 3g; Sugar 8g; Protein 27g

8-Ingredient Chicken

Prep time: 10 minutes| **Cook time:** 25 minutes| **Serves:** 4

2 lbs. boneless chicken thighs
¼ cup soy sauce
3 tablespoons organic ketchup
¼ cup coconut oil
¼ cup honey
2 teaspoons garlic powder
½ teaspoon black pepper
1½ teaspoon sea salt

Combine the soy sauce, ketchup, coconut oil, honey, garlic powder, pepper, and salt in the Inner Pot.
Toss the chicken thighs in the mixture.
Put on the pressure cooker's lid and turn the steam valve to "Sealing" position.
Press the "Pressure Cook" button two times to select "Less" option.
Use the "+/-" keys on the control panel to set the cooking time to 18 minutes.
Use the Pressure Level button to adjust the pressure to "High Pressure".
Once the cooking cycle is completed, quickly and carefully turn the steam release handle from Sealing position to the Venting position.
When all the steam is released, remove the pressure lid from the top carefully.
Press the "Sauté" button two times to select "Less" mode and simmer for 5 minutes.
Serve with vegetables.

Per Serving: Calories 361; Fat 7.9g; Sodium 704mg; Carbs 6g; Fiber 3.6g; Sugar 6g; Protein 18g

Chicken Coconut Curry

Prep time: 15 minutes| **Cook time:** 15 minutes| **Serves:** 4
2 lbs. chicken breast or thighs
16 oz. canned coconut milk
16 oz. canned tomato sauce
6 oz. can tomato paste
2 cloves garlic, minced
1 cup onion, chopped or ¼ cup dry minced onion
2 tablespoon curry powder
3 tablespoon honey
1 teaspoon salt

Mix all of the ingredients in the Inner Pot and stir to combine.
Put on the pressure cooker's lid and turn the steam valve to "Sealing" position.
Press the "Pressure Cook" button two times to select "Less" option.
Use the "+/-" keys on the control panel to set the cooking time to 15 minutes.
Use the Pressure Level button to adjust the pressure to "High Pressure".
Once the cooking cycle is completed, allow the steam to release naturally for 10 minutes, then turn the steam release handle to the Venting position.
When all the steam is released, remove the pressure lid from the top carefully.
Serve with cooked rice, potato or peas.

Per Serving: Calories 471; Fat 19g; Sodium 354mg; Carbs 15g; Fiber 5.1g; Sugar 8.2g; Protein 12g

Chicken Curry

Prep time: 15 minutes| **Cook time:** 15 minutes| **Serves:** 2
1 lb. chicken breast, chopped
1 tablespoon olive oil

1 yellow onion, thinly sliced
1 bag (1 oz.) chicken curry base
5 oz. canned coconut cream
6 potatoes, cut into halves
½ cup water
½ bunch coriander, chopped

Press the "Sauté" button two times to select "Normal" mode. and heat the oil.
Add the chicken and sauté for 2 minutes, until the chicken starts to brown.
Add onion, stir and cook for 1 more minute.
Press Cancel button to stop this cooking program.
In a medium bowl, combine the chicken curry base and coconut cream, stir well.
Pour into the pot, add potatoes and stir. Add water.
Put on the pressure cooker's lid and turn the steam valve to "Sealing" position.
Press the "Pressure Cook" button two times to select "Less" option.
Use the "+/-" keys on the control panel to set the cooking time to 15 minutes.
Use the Pressure Level button to adjust the pressure to "High Pressure".
Once the cooking cycle is completed, quickly and carefully turn the steam release handle from Sealing position to the Venting position.
When all the steam is released, remove the pressure lid from the top carefully.
Top with coriander and serve.

Per Serving: Calories 334; Fat 12.9g; Sodium 414mg; Carbs 11g; Fiber 5g; Sugar 9g; Protein 31g

Chicken Cacciatore

Prep time: 15 minutes| **Cook time:** 30 minutes| **Serves:** 4
4 chicken thighs, with the bone, skin removed
2 tablespoons olive oil
1 teaspoon kosher salt
1 teaspoon black pepper
½ cup diced green bell pepper
¼ cup diced red bell pepper
½ cup diced onion
½ (14 oz.) can crushed tomatoes
2 tablespoon chopped parsley or basil
½ teaspoon dried oregano
1 bay leaf

Press the "Sauté" button two times to select "More" mode.
Wait 1 minute and add 1 tablespoon of oil to the bottom of the pot.
Season the meat with salt and pepper.
Brown the meat for a few minutes on each side. Remove the chicken from the pot and set aside.
Pour another 1 tablespoon of oil into the pot.
Add bell peppers and onion and sauté for about 5 minutes or until soft and golden.
Put the chicken thighs in the Instant pot. Pour over the tomatoes.
Add the parsley, oregano and bay leaf, stir well.

Press the Cancel button to stop this cooking program and lock the lid in right way.
Put on the pressure cooker's lid and turn the steam valve to "Sealing" position.
Press the "Pressure Cook" button two times to select "Normal" option.
Use the "+/-" keys on the control panel to set the cooking time to 25 minutes.
Use the Pressure Level button to adjust the pressure to "High Pressure".
Once the cooking cycle is completed, allow the steam to release naturally.
When all the steam is released, remove the pressure lid from the top carefully.
Serve.

Per Serving: Calories 584; Fat 15g; Sodium 441mg; Carbs 17g; Fiber 4.6g; Sugar 5g; Protein 29g

Chicken Nachos

Prep time: 15 minutes| **Cook time:** 20 minutes| **Serves:** 6
2 lbs. chicken thighs, boneless, skinless
1 tablespoon olive oil
1 package (1 oz.) taco seasoning mix
⅔ cup mild red salsa
⅓ cup mild Herdez salsa Verde
½ cup water

Press the "Sauté" button two times to select "Normal" mode. and heat the oil.
Add the chicken thighs and brown the meat nicely for a few minutes on each side.
In a medium bowl, combine the taco seasoning and salsa.
Pour the mixture in the pot, add water and stir well.
Press the Cancel button to stop this cooking program and lock the lid in right way.
Put on the pressure cooker's lid and turn the steam valve to "Sealing" position.
Press the "Pressure Cook" button two times to select "Less" option.
Use the "+/-" keys on the control panel to set the cooking time to 15 minutes.
Use the Pressure Level button to adjust the pressure to "High Pressure".
Once the cooking cycle is completed, allow the steam to release naturally for 10 minutes, then turn the steam release handle to the Venting position.
When all the steam is released, remove the pressure lid from the top carefully.
Shred the meat and serve with tortilla chips.

Per Serving: Calories 412; Fat 20g; Sodium 491mg; Carbs 9g; Fiber 3g; Sugar 8g; Protein 31g

Chicken Piccata

Prep time: 15 minutes| **Cook time:** 15 minutes| **Serves:** 4
4 chicken breasts skinless, boneless, 1½ to 1¾ lbs.
1 tablespoon olive oil

¼ teaspoon black pepper
½ teaspoon salt
1 cup chicken broth
¼ cup fresh lemon juice
2 tablespoon butter
2 tablespoon brined capers, drained
2 tablespoon flat-leaf fresh parsley, chopped
Cooked rice or pasta

Press the "Sauté" button two times to select "Normal" mode.
Wait 2 minutes and add the oil to the bottom of the Inner Pot.
Season the chicken with salt and pepper.
Add to the pot and brown the meat for 3 minutes on each side. Add the broth.
Put on the pressure cooker's lid and turn the steam valve to "Sealing" position.
Press the "Pressure Cook" button two times to select "Less" option.
Use the "+/-" keys on the control panel to set the cooking time to 5 minutes.
Use the Pressure Level button to adjust the pressure to "High Pressure".
Once the cooking cycle is completed, quickly and carefully turn the steam release handle from Sealing position to the Venting position.
When all the steam is released, remove the pressure lid from the top carefully.
Remove the chicken from the pot to a serving bowl.
Press the "Sauté" button two times to select "Normal" mode and simmer for 5 minutes.
Add fresh lemon juice.
Add the butter. Once the butter is melted, add parsley and capers, stir.
Pour the sauce over chicken breasts.
Serve with rice or pasta.

Per Serving: Calories 349; Fat 2.9g; Sodium 511mg; Carbs 12g; Fiber 3g; Sugar 8g; Protein 7g

Chicken Adobo

Prep time: 15 minutes| **Cook time:** 30 minutes| **Serves:** 4
4 chicken drumsticks
½ teaspoon kosher salt
1 teaspoon black pepper
2 tablespoons olive oil
¼ cup white vinegar
⅓ cup soy sauce
¼ cup sugar
1 onion, chopped
5 cloves garlic, crushed
2 bay leaves

Press the "Sauté" button two times to select "More" mode.
Wait 1 minute and add the oil to the bottom of the pot.
Season the legs with salt and ½ teaspoon pepper.
Add the chicken drumsticks to the Inner Pot and brown for 4 minutes on each side.
Add the vinegar, soy sauce, sugar, onion, garlic, bay leaves and ½ teaspoon pepper.

Put on the pressure cooker's lid and turn the steam valve to "Sealing" position.
Press the "Pressure Cook" button two times to select "Less" option.
Use the "+/-" keys on the control panel to set the cooking time to 10 minutes.
Use the Pressure Level button to adjust the pressure to "High Pressure".
Once the cooking cycle is completed, quickly and carefully turn the steam release handle from Sealing position to the Venting position.
When all the steam is released, remove the pressure lid from the top carefully.
Press the "Sauté" button two times to select "Less" mode and simmer for 10 minutes.
Remove the bay leaves.
Serve and enjoy.

Per Serving: Calories 489; Fat 11g; Sodium 501mg; Carbs 8.9g; Fiber 4.6g; Sugar 8g; Protein 26g

Chicken Congee

Prep time: 15 minutes| **Cook time:** 35 minutes| **Serves:** 6

6 chicken drumsticks
6 cups water
1 cup Jasmine rice
1 tablespoon fresh ginger
2 cloves garlic, crushed
Salt to taste
½ cup scallions, chopped
2 teaspoons sesame oil, optional

Add the chicken, rice, water, ginger and garlic to the Inner Pot. Stir well.
Put on the pressure cooker's lid and turn the steam valve to "Sealing" position.
Press the "Pressure Cook" button two times to select "Less" option.
Use the "+/-" keys on the control panel to set the cooking time to 25 minutes.
Use the Pressure Level button to adjust the pressure to "High Pressure".
Once the cooking cycle is completed, allow the steam to release naturally for 10 minutes, then turn the steam release handle to the Venting position.
When all the steam is released, remove the pressure lid from the top carefully.
Take the chicken out from the pot, shred the meat and discard the bones.
Return the chicken meat to the pot.
Press the "Sauté" button two times to select "Normal" mode and cook for about 10 minutes.
Top with scallions and sesame oil.
Serve and enjoy.

Per Serving: Calories 478; Fat 19g; Sodium 354mg; Carbs 15g; Fiber 5.1g; Sugar 8.2g; Protein 32g

Chicken Puttanesca

Prep time: 15 minutes| **Cook time:** 25 minutes| **Serves:** 6

6 chicken thighs, skin on
2 tablespoons olive oil
1 cup water
14 oz. canned chopped tomatoes
2 cloves garlic, crushed
½ teaspoon red chili flakes or to taste
6 oz. pitted black olives
1 tablespoon capers, rinsed and drained
1 tablespoon fresh basil, chopped
1 teaspoon kosher salt
1 teaspoon black pepper

Press the "Sauté" button two times to select "Normal" mode. and heat the oil.
Add the chicken thighs skin side down and Brown the meat for 4-6 minutes.
Transfer the meat to a bowl.
Add the water, tomatoes, garlic, chili flakes, black olives, capers, fresh basil, salt and pepper to the Inner Pot. Stir well and bring to a simmer.
Return the chicken to the pot.
Put on the pressure cooker's lid and turn the steam valve to "Sealing" position.
Press the "Pressure Cook" button two times to select "Less" option.
Use the "+/-" keys on the control panel to set the cooking time to 16 minutes.
Use the Pressure Level button to adjust the pressure to "High Pressure".
Once the cooking cycle is completed, allow the steam to release naturally for 10 minutes, then turn the steam release handle to the Venting position.
When all the steam is released, remove the pressure lid from the top carefully.
Serve.

Per Serving: Calories 475; Fat 10.9g; Sodium 354mg; Carbs 10.5g; Fiber 4.1g; Sugar 8.2g; Protein 26g

Chicken with Potatoes

Prep time: 15 minutes| **Cook time:** 21 minutes| **Serves:** 4

2 lbs. chicken thighs, skinless and boneless
2 tablespoons olive oil
¾ cup chicken stock
3 tablespoon Dijon mustard
¼ cup lemon juice
2 tablespoon Italian seasoning
2 lbs. red potatoes, peeled and cut into quarters
1 teaspoon salt
1 teaspoon black pepper

Press the "Sauté" button two times to select "Normal" mode. and heat the oil.
Season the chicken thighs with ½ teaspoon salt and ½ teaspoon pepper.
Add the chicken to the Inner Pot and brown the meat for 3 minutes on each side.
In a medium bowl, combine the stock, mustard, lemon juice and Italian seasoning.
Pour the mixture over the chicken.
Add the potatoes, ½ teaspoon salt and ½ teaspoon pepper. Stir.

Put on the pressure cooker's lid and turn the steam valve to "Sealing" position.
Press the "Pressure Cook" button two times to select "Less" option.
Use the "+/-" keys on the control panel to set the cooking time to 15 minutes.
Use the Pressure Level button to adjust the pressure to "High Pressure".
Once the cooking cycle is completed, allow the steam to release naturally.
When all the steam is released, remove the pressure lid from the top carefully.
Serve.

Per Serving: Calories 382; Fat 7.9g; Sodium 704mg; Carbs 6g; Fiber 3.6g; Sugar 6g; Protein 18g

Chicken Drumsticks

Prep time: 15 minutes| **Cook time:** 20 minutes| **Serves:** 6

6 chicken drumsticks
1 tablespoon olive oil
1 onion, chopped
1 teaspoon garlic, minced
½ cup + 2 tablespoon water
½ cup sugar-free barbecue sauce
1½ tablespoon arrowroot

Press the "Sauté" button two times to select "Normal" mode and then heat the oil.
Add the onion and sauté for about 3 minutes, until softened.
Add the garlic and cook for another 30 seconds.
Add ½ cup of water and barbecue sauce, stir well.
Add the chicken drumsticks to the pot.
Put on the pressure cooker's lid and turn the steam valve to "Sealing" position.
Press the "Pressure Cook" button two times to select "Less" option.
Use the "+/-" keys on the control panel to set the cooking time to 10 minutes.
Use the Pressure Level button to adjust the pressure to "High Pressure".
Once the cooking cycle is completed, quickly and carefully turn the steam release handle from Sealing position to the Venting position.
When all the steam is released, remove the pressure lid from the top carefully.
In a cup, whisk together the remaining water and arrowroot until combined. Add to the pot.
Press the "Sauté" button two times to select "More" mode and cook for 5 minutes.
Serve the drumsticks with the sauce.

Per Serving: Calories 412; Fat 20g; Sodium 491mg; Carbs 9g; Fiber 3g; Sugar 8g; Protein 31g

Chicken Tomato Drumsticks

Prep time: 15 minutes| **Cook time:** 40 minutes| **Serves:** 6

6 chicken drumsticks (24 oz.), skin removed, on the bone

1 tablespoon apple cider vinegar
1 teaspoon oregano, dried
½ teaspoon salt
½ teaspoon black pepper
1 teaspoon olive oil
1½ cups tomato sauce
1 jalapeno, seeded, cut in halves
¼ cup cilantro, chopped

In a medium bowl, combine the apple cider vinegar, oregano, salt and pepper.
Add the chicken to the bowl and coat it well with the marinade.
Press the "Sauté" button two times to select "Normal" mode, add the oil and heat it up.
Lower the chicken into the pot and sear for 5-8 minutes on each side, until nicely browned.
Add the tomato sauce, a half of the jalapeno and cilantro.
Put on the pressure cooker's lid and turn the steam valve to "Sealing" position.
Press the "Pressure Cook" button two times to select "Less" option.
Use the Pressure Level button to adjust the pressure to "High Pressure".
Once the cooking cycle is completed, quickly and carefully turn the steam release handle from Sealing position to the Venting position.
When all the steam is released, remove the pressure lid from the top carefully.
Serve with the remaining cilantro and jalapeno.

Per Serving: Calories 334; Fat 7.9g; Sodium 704mg; Carbs 6g; Fiber 3.6g; Sugar 6g; Protein 18g

Teriyaki Chicken

Prep time: 15 minutes| **Cook time:** 15 minutes| **Serves:** 4

2 lbs. chicken breasts, skinless and boneless
⅔ cup teriyaki sauce
1 tablespoon honey
½ cup chicken stock
½ teaspoon salt
½ teaspoon black pepper
A handful green onions, chopped

Press the "Sauté" button two times to select "More" mode
Add the teriyaki sauce and honey, stir and simmer for 1 minute.
Add the chicken, stock, salt and pepper. Stir well.
Put on the pressure cooker's lid and turn the steam valve to "Sealing" position.
Press the "Pressure Cook" button two times to select "Less" option.
Use the "+/-" keys on the control panel to set the cooking time to 12 minutes.
Use the Pressure Level button to adjust the pressure to "High Pressure".
Once the cooking cycle is completed, allow the steam to release naturally.
When all the steam is released, remove the pressure lid from the top carefully.
Transfer the chicken to a plate and shred the meat.

Remove ½ cup of cooking liquid and return shredded chicken to the pot.
Stir with the green onions and serve.

Per Serving: Calories 289; Fat 14g; Sodium 791mg; Carbs 18.9g; Fiber 4.6g; Sugar 8g; Protein 6g

Buffalo Chicken

Prep time: 15 minutes| **Cook time:** 12 minutes| **Serves:** 4

2 lbs. chicken breasts, skinless, boneless and cut into thin strips
1 small yellow onion, chopped
½ cup celery, chopped
½ cup buffalo sauce
½ cup chicken stock
¼ cup bleu cheese, crumbled

Add the chicken breasts, onion, celery, buffalo sauce and stock to the Inner Pot.
Put on the pressure cooker's lid and turn the steam valve to "Sealing" position.
Press the "Pressure Cook" button two times to select "Less" option.
Use the "+/-" keys on the control panel to set the cooking time to 12 minutes.
Use the Pressure Level button to adjust the pressure to "High Pressure".
Once the cooking cycle is completed, allow the steam to release naturally.
When all the steam is released, remove the pressure lid from the top carefully.
Remove ⅔ cup of cooking liquid. Add crumbled blue cheese to the pot and stir well.
Serve.

Per Serving: Calories 419; Fat 14g; Sodium 791mg; Carbs 8.9g; Fiber 4.6g; Sugar 8g; Protein 31g

Crack Chicken

Prep time: 10 minutes| **Cook time:** 30 minutes| **Serves:** 4

2 lbs. chicken breast, boneless
8 oz. cream cheese
1 (1 oz.) packet ranch seasoning
1 cup water
3 tablespoon cornstarch
4 oz. cheddar cheese, shredded
6-8 bacon slices, cooked

Add the chicken breasts and cream cheese to the Inner Pot.
Season with the ranch seasoning. Add 1 cup of water.
Put on the pressure cooker's lid and turn the steam valve to "Sealing" position.
Press the "Pressure Cook" button two times to select "Normal" option.
Use the "+/-" keys on the control panel to set the cooking time to 25 minutes.
Use the Pressure Level button to adjust the pressure to "High Pressure".

Once the cooking cycle is completed, quickly and carefully turn the steam release handle from Sealing position to the Venting position.
When all the steam is released, remove the pressure lid from the top carefully.
Transfer the chicken to a plate and shred the meat.
Press the Cancel button to stop this cooking program.
Press the "Sauté" button two times to select "Normal" mode and add the cornstarch. Stir well.
Add shredded chicken, cheese and bacon to the pot, stir. Sauté for 3 minutes.
Serve.

Per Serving: Calories 489; Fat 11g; Sodium 501mg; Carbs 8.9g; Fiber 4.6g; Sugar 8g; Protein 26g

Pina Colada Chicken

Prep time: 10 minutes| **Cook time:** 20 minutes| **Serves:** 4

2 lbs. chicken thighs cut into 1-inch pieces
½ cup coconut cream, full fat
2 tablespoon soy sauce
1 can (20 oz.) pineapple chunks
1 teaspoon cinnamon
⅛ teaspoon salt
½ cup green onion, chopped
1 teaspoon arrowroot starch
1 tablespoon water

Combine all of the ingredients, except arrowroot starch, water and green onion, in the Inner Pot and stir to combine.
Put on the pressure cooker's lid and turn the steam valve to "Sealing" position.
Press the "Poultry" button three times to select "Normal" option.
Use the Pressure Level button to adjust the pressure to "High Pressure".
Once the cooking cycle is completed, allow the steam to release naturally for 10 minutes, then turn the steam release handle to the Venting position.
When all the steam is released, remove the pressure lid from the top carefully.
Transfer the chicken to a serving bowl.
In a cup, combine the arrowroot starch and water. Mix well.
Add the mixture to the instant pot.
Press the "Sauté" button two times to select "Normal" mode and continue to cook, stirring occasionally, until the sauce begins to thicken.
Serve the chicken with green onion and sauce.

Per Serving: Calories 412; Fat 20g; Sodium 491mg; Carbs 9g; Fiber 3g; Sugar 8g; Protein 31g

Orange Chicken

Prep time: 10 minutes| **Cook time:** 15 minutes| **Serves:** 4

4 chicken breasts

¼ cup water
¾ cup orange juice
¾ cup barbecue sauce
2 tablespoon soy sauce
1 tablespoon cornstarch + 2 tablespoons water
2 tablespoon green onions, chopped

Add the chicken breasts, ¼ cup of water, orange juice, barbecue sauce, and soy sauce to the Inner Pot. Stir well.
Put on the pressure cooker's lid and turn the steam valve to "Sealing" position.
Press the "Poultry" button three times to select "Normal" option.
Use the Pressure Level button to adjust the pressure to "High Pressure".
Once the cooking cycle is completed, quickly and carefully turn the steam release handle from Sealing position to the Venting position.
When all the steam is released, remove the pressure lid from the top carefully.
In a cup, combine the cornstarch and 2 tablespoons of water.
Press the "Sauté" button two times to select "Normal" mode and add the cornstarch slurry to the pot.
Simmer for 5 minutes or until the sauce has thickened.
Add green onions and serve.

Per Serving: Calories 458; Fat 12.9g; Sodium 414mg; Carbs 11g; Fiber 5g; Sugar 9g; Protein 31g

Apricot Chicken

Prep time: 10 minutes| **Cook time:** 20 minutes| **Serves:** 4-6
2½ lbs. chicken thighs, skinless
1 tablespoon vegetable oil
1 teaspoon kosher salt
1 teaspoon black pepper
3 cloves garlic, minced
1 large onion, chopped
⅛ teaspoon allspice powder
½ cup chicken broth
8 oz. canned apricots
1 lb. canned tomatoes, diced
1 tablespoon fresh ginger, grated
½ teaspoon cinnamon, ground
Fresh parsley, chopped

Press the "Sauté" button two times to select "Normal" mode, add the oil and heat it up.
Season the chicken thighs with salt and pepper.
Add the chicken, garlic, and onion to the Instant pot.
Sprinkle with the allspice powder and cook for 5 minutes or until nicely browned.
Pour the broth. Add the apricots, tomatoes, fresh ginger, and cinnamon to the pot. Stir well.
Press the "Pressure Cook" button two times to select "Less" option.
Use the "+/-" keys on the control panel to set the cooking time to 12 minutes.

Use the Pressure Level button to adjust the pressure to "High Pressure".
Once the cooking cycle is completed, quickly and carefully turn the steam release handle from Sealing position to the Venting position.
When all the steam is released, remove the pressure lid from the top carefully.
Transfer the dish to a serving bowl, top with parsley and serve.

Per Serving: Calories 219; Fat 10g; Sodium 891mg; Carbs 22.9g; Fiber 4g; Sugar 4g; Protein 23g

Shredded Chicken Breast

Prep time: 10 minutes| **Cook time:** 8 minutes| **Serves:** 4
5-2 lbs. boneless chicken breasts
½ teaspoon black pepper
½ teaspoon garlic salt
½ cup chicken broth

Season all sides of the chicken with the black pepper and salt.
Add the chicken breasts to the Inner Pot and pour the chicken broth.
Put on the pressure cooker's lid and turn the steam valve to "Sealing" position.
Press the "Pressure Cook" button two times to select "Less" option.
Use the "+/-" keys on the control panel to set the cooking time to 8 minutes.
Use the Pressure Level button to adjust the pressure to "High Pressure".
Once the cooking cycle is completed, allow the steam to release naturally for 10 minutes, then turn the steam release handle to the Venting position.
When all the steam is released, remove the pressure lid from the top carefully.
Remove the chicken from the pot and shred it with 2 forks.
Serve and enjoy.

Per Serving: Calories 584; Fat 15g; Sodium 441mg; Carbs 17g; Fiber 4.6g; Sugar 5g; Protein 29g

Shredded Chicken with Marinara

Prep time: 20 minutes| **Cook time:** 25 minutes| **Serves:** 6
4 lbs. chicken breasts
½ cup chicken broth
½ teaspoon black pepper
1 teaspoon salt
2 cups marinara sauce

Add the chicken breasts, broth, pepper, and salt to the Inner Pot, stir well.
Put on the pressure cooker's lid and turn the steam valve to "Sealing" position.
Press the "Pressure Cook" button two times to select "Less" option.
Use the Pressure Level button to adjust the pressure to "High Pressure".

Once the cooking cycle is completed, quickly and carefully turn the steam release handle from Sealing position to the Venting position. When all the steam is released, remove the pressure lid from the top carefully.
Shred the chicken in the pot.
Press the "Sauté" button two times to select "Normal" mode.
Add the marinara sauce and simmer for 5 minutes.
Serve with cooked rice, potato, peas or green salad.

Per Serving: Calories 419; Fat 14g; Sodium 791mg; Carbs 8.9g; Fiber 4.6g; Sugar 8g; Protein 31g

Lemon Mustard Chicken with Potatoes

Prep time: 20 minutes| **Cook time:** 20 minutes| **Serves:** 6
2 lbs. chicken thighs
2 tablespoons olive oil
3 lbs. red potatoes, peeled and quartered
2 tablespoon Italian seasoning
3 tablespoon Dijon mustard
1 cup chicken broth
¼ cup lemon juice
1 teaspoon salt
1 teaspoon black pepper

Press the "Sauté" button two times to select "Normal" mode. and heat the oil.
Add the chicken thighs to the pot and sauté for 2-3 minutes, until starting to brown.
Add the potatoes, Italian seasoning, and Dijon mustard. Cook for 2 minutes, stir occasionally.
Pour the broth and lemon juice into the pot, stir. Season with salt and pepper.
Put on the pressure cooker's lid and turn the steam valve to "Sealing" position.
Press the "Poultry" button three times to select "Normal" option.
Use the Pressure Level button to adjust the pressure to "High Pressure".
Once the cooking cycle is completed, allow the steam to release naturally for 10 minutes, then turn the steam release handle to the Venting position.
When all the steam is released, remove the pressure lid from the top carefully.
Serve.

Per Serving: Calories 472; Fat 7.9g; Sodium 704mg; Carbs 6g; Fiber 3.6g; Sugar 6g; Protein 18g

BBQ Chicken with Potatoes

Prep time: 20 minutes| **Cook time:** 15 minutes| **Serves:** 4
2 lbs. chicken (breasts or thighs)
1 cup water
3 large potatoes, unpeeled and quartered
1 cup BBQ sauce
1 tablespoon Italian seasoning
1 tablespoon minced garlic
1 large onion, sliced

Add the chicken, water, potatoes, BBQ sauce, Italian seasoning, garlic and onion to the Inner Pot.
Put on the pressure cooker's lid and turn the steam valve to "Sealing" position.
Press the "Pressure Cook" button two times to select "Less" option.
Use the "+/-" keys on the control panel to set the cooking time to 15 minutes.
Use the Pressure Level button to adjust the pressure to "High Pressure".
Once the cooking cycle is completed, quickly and carefully turn the steam release handle from Sealing position to the Venting position. When all the steam is released, remove the pressure lid from the top carefully.
Transfer the chicken to a plate and shred it.
Return shredded chicken to the pot.
Stir well until fully coated with the sauce.
Serve and enjoy.

Per Serving: Calories 334; Fat 10.9g; Sodium 354mg; Carbs 10.5g; Fiber 4.1g; Sugar 8.2g; Protein 26g

Creamy Chicken with Bacon

Prep time: 20 minutes| **Cook time:** 20 minutes| **Serves:** 4
2 lbs. chicken breasts, skinless and boneless
2 slices bacon, chopped
1 cup chicken stock
1 oz. ranch seasoning
4 oz. cream cheese
Green onions, chopped for serving

Press the "Sauté" button two times to select "Normal" mode.
Add the button and sauté the bacon for 4-5 minutes.
Add the chicken, stock, and ranch seasoning. Stir well.
Put on the pressure cooker's lid and turn the steam valve to "Sealing" position.
Press the "Pressure Cook" button two times to select "Less" option.
Use the "+/-" keys on the control panel to set the cooking time to 12 minutes.
Use the Pressure Level button to adjust the pressure to "High Pressure".
Once the cooking cycle is completed, allow the steam to release naturally.
When all the steam is released, remove the pressure lid from the top carefully.
Transfer the chicken to a plate and shred the meat.
Remove ⅔ cup of cooking liquid from the pot.
Add the cheese, Press the "Sauté" button two time to select "Normal" mode and continue to cook for 3 minutes.
Return chicken to pot and stir.
Press Cancel button to stop the cooking program.
Add green onions, stir and serve.

Per Serving: Calories 490; Fat 19g; Sodium 354mg; Carbs 15g; Fiber 5.1g; Sugar 8.2g; Protein 32g

Cajun Chicken with Rice

Prep time: 20 minutes| **Cook time:** 20 minutes| **Serves:** 4

1 tablespoon olive oil
1 onion, diced
3 cloves garlic, minced
1 lb. chicken breasts, sliced
2 cups chicken broth
1 tablespoon tomato paste
1½ cups white rice, rinsed
1 bell pepper, chopped
Cajun spices:
¼ teaspoon cayenne pepper
2 teaspoons dried thyme
1 tablespoon paprika

Press the "Sauté" button two times to select "Normal" mode. and heat the oil.
Add the onion and garlic and cook until fragrant.
Add the chicken breasts and Cajun spices, stir well. Sauté for another 3 minutes.
Pour the broth and tomato paste into the pot. Stir to dissolve the tomato paste.
Add the rice and bell pepper, stir.
Put on the pressure cooker's lid and turn the steam valve to "Sealing" position.
Press the "Pressure Cook" button two times to select "Less" option.
Use the Pressure Level button to adjust the pressure to "High Pressure".
Once the cooking cycle is completed, allow the steam to release naturally for 10 minutes, then turn the steam release handle to the Venting position.
When all the steam is released, remove the pressure lid from the top carefully.
Serve.

Per Serving: Calories 489; Fat 11g; Sodium 501mg; Carbs 8.9g; Fiber 4.6g; Sugar 8g; Protein 26g

Mojo Chicken Tacos

Prep time: 20 minutes| **Cook time:** 30 minutes| **Serves:** 4

4 skinless, boneless chicken breasts
For the Mojo:
¼ cup olive oil
⅔ cup fresh lime juice
⅔ cup orange juice
8 cloves garlic, minced
1 tablespoon grated orange peel
1 tablespoon dried oregano
2 teaspoons ground cumin
2 teaspoons Kosher salt
¼ teaspoon black pepper
¼ cup chopped fresh cilantro + more for garnishing
To serve:
8 – 12 organic corn tortillas
½ cup red onion, finely diced
1 avocado, sliced

Add the chicken breasts to the Inner Pot.
In a bowl, whisk together all mojo ingredients until combined.

Add this mixture to the pot.
Put on the pressure cooker's lid and turn the steam valve to "Sealing" position.
Press the "Poultry" button three times to select "Normal" option.
Use the "+/-" keys on the control panel to set the cooking time to 20 minutes.
Use the Pressure Level button to adjust the pressure to "High Pressure".
Once the cooking cycle is completed, allow the steam to release naturally.
When all the steam is released, remove the pressure lid from the top carefully.
Transfer the chicken to a plate and shred it.
Return the meat to the pot and stir.
Preheat the oven to broil. Transfer shredded chicken with the sauce to a baking sheet.
Place under the broiler for 5 to 8 minutes, or until the edges of the chicken are brown and crispy.
Top with cilantro. Serve in tacos with chopped onion and sliced avocado.

Per Serving: Calories 412; Fat 10.9g; Sodium 454mg; Carbs 10g; Fiber 3.1g; Sugar 5.2g; Protein 10g

Roasted Tandoori Chicken

Prep time: 20 minutes| **Cook time:** 15 minutes| **Serves:** 6

6 chicken thighs, bone in
½ cup plain yogurt
1-2 tablespoon tandoori paste
1 tablespoon lemon juice
1 teaspoon kosher salt
1 teaspoon black pepper
½ cup water

In a large bowl, combine the yogurt, lemon juice, and tandoori paste.
Add the chicken to the bowl and coat it well with the marinade.
Marinate for at least 6 hours in the refrigerator.
Sprinkle the chicken with salt and pepper.
Place the chicken, marinade and water in the Inner Pot.
Put on the pressure cooker's lid and turn the steam valve to "Sealing" position.
Press the "Pressure Cook" button two times to select "Less" option.
Use the "+/-" keys on the control panel to set the cooking time to 10 minutes.
Use the Pressure Level button to adjust the pressure to "High Pressure".
Once the cooking cycle is completed, allow the steam to release naturally.
When all the steam is released, remove the pressure lid from the top carefully.
Preheat the oven to broil. Place under the broiler for 3 to 5 minutes until browned.
When done, serve and enjoy.

Per Serving: Calories 412; Fat 20g; Sodium 491mg; Carbs 9g; Fiber 3g; Sugar 8g; Protein 31g

Salsa Chicken

Prep time: 20 minutes| **Cook time:** 25 minutes| **Serves:** 4

2 lbs. chicken breasts, skinless and boneless
1 teaspoon kosher salt
1 teaspoon black pepper
A pinch of oregano
2 teaspoons cumin
2 cups chunky salsa, or your preference
½ cup water

Add the chicken breasts to the Inner Pot and season with salt and pepper.
Add the oregano, cumin, salsa and water, stir well.
Put on the pressure cooker's lid and turn the steam valve to "Sealing" position.
Press the "Poultry" button three times to select "More" option.
Use the "+/-" keys on the control panel to set the cooking time to 25 minutes.
Use the Pressure Level button to adjust the pressure to "High Pressure".
Once the cooking cycle is completed, quickly and carefully turn the steam release handle from Sealing position to the Venting position.
When all the steam is released, remove the pressure lid from the top carefully.
Remove the chicken and shred it.
Serve shredded chicken in the casseroles or add to corn tortillas with some avocado, cilantro.

Per Serving: Calories 419; Fat 14g; Sodium 791mg; Carbs 8.9g; Fiber 4.6g; Sugar 8g; Protein 31g

Cream Cheese Chicken

Prep time: 20 minutes| **Cook time:** 20 minutes| **Serves:** 2

1 lb. chicken breasts, boneless and skinless
1 can (10 oz.) Rotel tomato, undrained
1 can (15 oz.) corn, undrained
1 can (15 oz.) black beans, drained
1 package (1 oz.) dry ranch seasoning
1½ teaspoon chili powder
1½ teaspoon cumin
8 oz. cream cheese
¼ cup parsley

Combine all of the ingredients, except cheese, in the Inner Pot.
Put on the pressure cooker's lid and turn the steam valve to "Sealing" position.
Press the "Pressure Cook" button two times to select "Normal" option.
Use the "+/-" keys on the control panel to set the cooking time to 20 minutes.
Use the Pressure Level button to adjust the pressure to "High Pressure".
Once the cooking cycle is completed, allow the steam to release naturally for 10 minutes, then turn the steam release handle to the Venting position.
When all the steam is released, remove the pressure lid from the top carefully.

Transfer the chicken to a plate and shred the meat.
Add the cheese to the pot and stir well. Close the lid and let sit for 5 minutes, until cheese is melted.
Open the lid and return the chicken to the pot. Stir to combine.
Top with parsley and serve.

Per Serving: Calories 501; Fat 7.9g; Sodium 704mg; Carbs 6g; Fiber 3.6g; Sugar 6g; Protein 18g

Coca Cola Chicken

Prep time: 20 minutes| **Cook time:** 25 minutes| **Serves:** 4

4 chicken drumsticks
2 tablespoons olive oil
Salt and black pepper to taste
1 large finely onion, chopped
1 small chopped chili
1 tablespoon balsamic vinegar
500 ml Coca Cola

Press the "Sauté" button two times to select "Normal" mode.
Wait 1 minute and add the oil to the bottom of the pot.
Season the chicken drumsticks with salt and pepper to taste.
Add the drumsticks to the Inner Pot and sear for 4 minutes on each side, until nicely browned.
Remove the chicken from the pot. Add the onions and sauté for about 3-5 minutes, until softened.
Then add the chili, balsamic vinegar and Coca-Cola, stir.
Return the drumsticks to the pot.
Put on the pressure cooker's lid and turn the steam valve to "Sealing" position.
Press the "Pressure Cook" button two times to select "Less" option.
Use the "+/-" keys on the control panel to set the cooking time to 10 minutes.
Use the Pressure Level button to adjust the pressure to "High Pressure".
Once the cooking cycle is completed, allow the steam to release naturally for 10 minutes, then turn the steam release handle to the Venting position.
When all the steam is released, remove the pressure lid from the top carefully.
Serve.

Per Serving: Calories 521; Fat 12.9g; Sodium 414mg; Carbs 11g; Fiber 5g; Sugar 9g; Protein 31g

Hunter Chicken

Prep time: 20 minutes| **Cook time:** 25 minutes| **Serves:** 4

8 chicken drumsticks, bone in
1 yellow onion, chopped
1 cup chicken stock
1 teaspoon garlic powder

28 oz. canned tomatoes and juice, crushed
1 teaspoon oregano, dried
1 bay leaf
1 teaspoon kosher salt
½ cup black olives, pitted and sliced

Press the "Sauté" button two times to select "Normal" mode
Add the onion and cook for 6 to 7 minutes, until the onion is translucent.
Add the stock, garlic powder, tomatoes, oregano, bay leaf and salt, stir well.
Put the chicken in the pot and stir.
Put on the pressure cooker's lid and turn the steam valve to "Sealing" position.
Press the "Pressure Cook" button two times to select "Less" option.
Use the "+/-" keys on the control panel to set the cooking time to 15 minutes.
Use the Pressure Level button to adjust the pressure to "High Pressure".
Once the cooking cycle is completed, allow the steam to release naturally for 10 minutes, then turn the steam release handle to the Venting position.
When all the steam is released, remove the pressure lid from the top carefully.
Remove the bay leaf. Divide the dish among plates, top with olives and serve.

Per Serving: Calories 382; Fat 10.9g; Sodium 454mg; Carbs 10g; Fiber 3.1g; Sugar 5.2g; Protein 20g

Olive Chicken

Prep time: 20 minutes| **Cook time:** 20 minutes| **Serves:** 4
4 chicken breasts, skinless and boneless
½ cup butter
½ teaspoon cumin
1 teaspoon salt
½ teaspoon black pepper
Juice of 1 lemon
1 cup chicken broth
1 can pitted green olives

Press the "Sauté" button two times to select "Normal" mode.
Once hot, add the butter and melt it.
Season the chicken breasts with cumin, salt, and pepper.
Put the breasts into the pot and sauté for 3-5 minutes on each side, until nicely browned.
Add the lemon juice, broth and olives, stir well.
Put on the pressure cooker's lid and turn the steam valve to "Sealing" position.
Press the "Pressure Cook" button two times to select "Less" option.
Use the "+/-" keys on the control panel to set the cooking time to 10 minutes.
Use the Pressure Level button to adjust the pressure to "High Pressure".
Once the cooking cycle is completed, allow the steam to release naturally.
When all the steam is released, remove the pressure lid from the top carefully.
Serve.

Per Serving: Calories 584; Fat 15g; Sodium 441mg; Carbs 17g; Fiber 4.6g; Sugar 5g; Protein 29g

Chili Lime Chicken

Prep time: 20 minutes| **Cook time:** 10 minutes| **Serves:** 4
2 lbs. chicken breasts, bones removed
¾ cup chicken broth or water
Juice of 2 medium limes
1½ teaspoon chili powder
1 teaspoon cumin
1 teaspoon onion powder
6 cloves garlic, minced
½ teaspoon liquid smoke
1 teaspoon kosher salt
1 teaspoon black pepper

Dump all of the ingredients into the Inner Pot and give it a little stir to mix everything evenly.
Put on the pressure cooker's lid and turn the steam valve to "Sealing" position.
Press the "Pressure Cook" button two times to select "Less" option.
Use the "+/-" keys on the control panel to set the cooking time to 10 minutes.
Use the Pressure Level button to adjust the pressure to "High Pressure".
Once the cooking cycle is completed, allow the steam to release naturally for 10 minutes, then turn the steam release handle to the Venting position.
When all the steam is released, remove the pressure lid from the top carefully.
Remove the chicken and shred it.
Serve with the remaining juice from the Inner Pot.

Per Serving: Calories 489; Fat 11g; Sodium 501mg; Carbs 8.9g; Fiber 4.6g; Sugar 8g; Protein 26g

Ginger Chicken

Prep time: 20 minutes| **Cook time:** 15 minutes| **Serves:** 4-6

1 chicken cut into pieces
2 tablespoons olive oil
¼ cup soy sauce
1 large onion, finely diced
1-inch ginger, finely grated
¼ cup dry sherry
¼ cup water
Salt and black pepper to taste.

Press the "Sauté" button two times to select "Normal" mode.
Add and heat the oil.
Put the chicken in the Inner Pot and sauté until the chicken has turned light brown.
Add the soy sauce, onion, ginger, sherry, and water. Mix just until combined.

Put on the pressure cooker's lid and turn the steam valve to "Sealing" position.
Press the "Pressure Cook" button two times to select "Less" option.
Use the "+/-" keys on the control panel to set the cooking time to 10 minutes.
Use the Pressure Level button to adjust the pressure to "High Pressure".
Once the cooking cycle is completed, allow the steam to release naturally.
When all the steam is released, remove the pressure lid from the top carefully.
Season with salt and pepper to taste.
Serve and enjoy.

Per Serving: Calories 478; Fat 7.9g; Sodium 704mg; Carbs 6g; Fiber 3.6g; Sugar 6g; Protein 18g

Fish and Seafood

Calamari with Pimentos

Prep time: 20 minutes| **Cook time:** 25 minutes| **Serves:** 4

3 Pimentos, stem and core removed
2 tablespoons olive oil
½ cup leeks, chopped
2 cloves garlic chopped
1 ½ cups stock, preferably homemade
2 tablespoons fish sauce
⅓ cup dry sherry
Seas salt and black pepper, to taste
½ teaspoons red pepper flakes, crushed
1 teaspoon dried rosemary, chopped
1 teaspoon dried thyme, chopped
1 ½ lbs. frozen calamari, thawed and drained
2 tablespoons fresh chives, chopped

Split your Pimentos into halves and place them over the flame.
Cook, turning a couple of times, until the skin is blistering and blackened.
Allow them to stand for 30 minutes; peel your Pimentos and chop them.
Press the "Sauté" button two times to select "Normal" settings to heat up your Inner Pot; add olive oil.
Once hot, cook the leeks until tender and fragrant, about 4 minutes.
Now, stir in the garlic and cook an additional 30 seconds or until just browned and aromatic.
Add the stock, fish sauce, dry sherry, salt, pepper, red pepper flakes, rosemary, and thyme.
Add the roasted Pimentos. Lastly, place the calamari on top. Pour in 3 cups of water.
Put on the pressure cooker's lid and turn the steam valve to "Sealing" position.
Press the "Pressure Cook" button two times to select "Less" option.
Use the "+/-" keys on the control panel to set the cooking time to 20 minutes.
Use the Pressure Level button to adjust the pressure to "High Pressure".
Once the cooking cycle is completed, quickly and carefully turn the steam release handle from Sealing position to the Venting position.
When all the steam is released, remove the pressure lid from the top carefully.
Serve warm garnished with fresh chopped chives. Enjoy!

Per Serving: Calories 412; Fat 20g; Sodium 491mg; Carbs 9g; Fiber 3g; Sugar 8g; Protein 31g

Curried Halibut Steaks

Prep time: 20 minutes| **Cook time:** 10 minutes| **Serves:** 4

1 tablespoon olive oil
1 cup scallions, chopped
½ cup beef bone broth
1-pound halibut steaks, rinsed and cubed
1 cup tomato purée
1 jalapeño pepper, seeded and minced
1 teaspoon ginger garlic paste
1 tablespoon red curry paste
½ teaspoons ground cumin
1 cup coconut milk, unsweetened
Salt and black pepper, to taste

Press the "Sauté" button two times to select "Normal" settings
Now, heat the olive oil; cook the scallions until tender and fragrant.
Then, use the broth to deglaze the bottom of the Inner Pot. Stir in the remaining ingredients.
Put on the pressure cooker's lid and turn the steam valve to "Sealing" position.
Press the "Pressure Cook" button two times to select "Less" option.
Use the "+/-" keys on the control panel to set the cooking time to 7 minutes.
Use the Pressure Level button to adjust the pressure to "High Pressure".
Once the cooking cycle is completed, quickly and carefully turn the steam release handle from Sealing position to the Venting position.
When all the steam is released, remove the pressure lid from the top carefully.
Taste, adjust the seasonings and serve right now.

Per Serving: Calories 334; Fat 7.9g; Sodium 704mg; Carbs 6g; Fiber 3.6g; Sugar 6g; Protein 18g

Carp Pilaf

Prep time: 20 minutes| **Cook time:** 6 minutes| **Serves:** 4

1 tablespoon olive oil
1 cup chicken stock
1 cup tomato paste
1 teaspoon dried rosemary, crushed
1 tablespoon dried parsley
½ teaspoons dried marjoram leaves
Sea salt and black pepper, to taste
½ teaspoons dried oregano leaves
1 cup Arborio rice
1-pound carp, chopped

Simply throw all of the above ingredients into your Inner Pot.
Put on the pressure cooker's lid and turn the steam valve to "Sealing" position.
Press the "Pressure Cook" button two times to select "Less" option.
Use the "+/-" keys on the control panel to set the cooking time to 6 minutes.
Use the Pressure Level button to adjust the pressure to "High Pressure".
Once the cooking cycle is completed, quickly and carefully turn the steam release handle from Sealing position to the Venting position.
When all the steam is released, remove the pressure lid from the top carefully.

Serve in individual serving bowls, garnished with fresh lemon slices.

Per Serving: Calories 421; Fat 7.9g; Sodium 704mg; Carbs 6g; Fiber 3.6g; Sugar 6g; Protein 18g

Tilapia Fillets with Mushrooms

Prep time: 20 minutes| **Cook time:** 10 minutes| **Serves:** 3

3 tilapia fillets
½ teaspoons sea salt
Black pepper, to taste
1 teaspoon cayenne pepper
1 cup Cremini mushrooms, thinly sliced
½ cup yellow onions, sliced

2 cloves garlic, peeled and minced
2 sprigs thyme, leaves picked
2 sprigs rosemary, leaves picked
2 tablespoons avocado oil

Season the tilapia fillets with salt, black pepper, and cayenne pepper on all sides.
Place the tilapia fillets in the steaming basket fitted for your Inner Pot.
Place the sliced mushroom and yellow onions on top of the fillets.
Add the garlic, thyme, and rosemary; drizzle avocado oil over everything.
Add 1 ½ cups of water to the base of your Inner Pot. Add the steaming basket to the Inner Pot and
Put on the pressure cooker's lid and turn the steam valve to "Sealing" position.
Press the "Pressure Cook" button two times to select "Less" option.
Use the "+/-" keys on the control panel to set the cooking time to 8 minutes.
Use the Pressure Level button to adjust the pressure to "Low Pressure".
Once the cooking cycle is completed, quickly and carefully turn the steam release handle from Sealing position to the Venting position.
When all the steam is released, remove the pressure lid from the top carefully.
Serve immediately.

Per Serving: Calories 472; Fat 12.9g; Sodium 414mg; Carbs 11g; Fiber 5g; Sugar 9g; Protein 31g

Shrimp in Tomato Sauce

Prep time: 20 minutes| **Cook time:** 5 minutes| **Serves:** 4

1 tablespoon butter, at room temperature
1 cup green onion, chopped
1 teaspoon garlic, minced
1 ½ lbs. shrimp, peeled and deveined
1 tablespoon tamari sauce
1 sprig thyme
1 sprig rosemary
2 ripe tomatoes, chopped

Press the "Sauté" button two times to select "Normal" settings

Melt the butter and cook the green onions until they have softened.
Now, stir in the garlic and cook an additional 30 seconds or until it is aromatic.
Add the rest of the above ingredients.
Put on the pressure cooker's lid and turn the steam valve to "Sealing" position.
Press the "Pressure Cook" button two times to select "Less" option.
Use the "+/-" keys on the control panel to set the cooking time to 3 minutes.
Use the Pressure Level button to adjust the pressure to "Low Pressure".
Once the cooking cycle is completed, allow the steam to release naturally.
When all the steam is released, remove the pressure lid from the top carefully.
Serve over hot jasmine rice and enjoy!

Per Serving: Calories 427; Fat 10.9g; Sodium 454mg; Carbs 10g; Fiber 3.1g; Sugar 5.2g; Protein 20g

Trout Salad

Prep time: 20 minutes| **Cook time:** 15 minutes| **Serves:** 4

2 tablespoons olive oil
1 yellow onion, chopped
2 garlic cloves, minced
1 green chili, seeded and minced
2 pieces' ocean trout fillets, deboned and skinless
1 cup water
½ cup dry vermouth
Sea salt and black pepper, to taste
½ teaspoons sweet paprika
2 ripe Roma tomatoes, diced
8 oz. dry egg noodles
2 Lebanese cucumbers, chopped
½ bunch coriander, leaves picked, roughly chopped
¼ cup lime juice

Press the "Sauté" button two times to select "Normal" settings
Now, heat the olive oil and sauté the onion until translucent.
Stir in the garlic and chili; continue to sauté until they are fragrant.
Add the fish, water, vermouth, salt, black pepper, sweet paprika, tomatoes, and noodles.
Put on the pressure cooker's lid and turn the steam valve to "Sealing" position.
Press the "Pressure Cook" button two times to select "Less" option.
Use the "+/-" keys on the control panel to set the cooking time to 10 minutes.
Use the Pressure Level button to adjust the pressure to "Low Pressure".
Once the cooking cycle is completed, quickly and carefully turn the steam release handle from Sealing position to the Venting position.
When all the steam is released, remove the pressure lid from the top carefully.
Flake the fish and allow the mixture to cool completely. Add the cucumbers and coriander.

Drizzle fresh lime juice over the salad and serve. Bon appétit!

Per Serving: Calories 419; Fat 14g; Sodium 791mg; Carbs 8.9g; Fiber 4.6g; Sugar 8g; Protein 31g

Tuna Fillets with Eschalots

Prep time: 20 minutes| **Cook time:** 5 minutes| **Serves:** 4

2 lemons, 1 whole and 1
1-pound tuna fillets
Sea salt and black pepper, to taste
1 tablespoon dried parsley flakes
2 tablespoons butter, melted
2 eschalots, thinly sliced

Place 1 cup of water and lemon juice in the Inner Pot. Add a steamer basket too.
Place the tuna fillets in the steamer basket. Sprinkle the salt, pepper, and parsley over the fish; drizzle with butter and top with thinly sliced eschalots.
Put on the pressure cooker's lid and turn the steam valve to "Sealing" position.
Press the "Steam" button one time to select "Less" option.
Use the "+/-" keys on the control panel to set the cooking time to 3 minutes.
Use the Pressure Level button to adjust the pressure to "High Pressure".
Once the cooking cycle is completed, quickly and carefully turn the steam release handle from Sealing position to the Venting position. When all the steam is released, remove the pressure lid from the top carefully.
Serve immediately with lemon. Bon appétit!

Per Serving: Calories 219; Fat 10g; Sodium 891mg; Carbs 22.9g; Fiber 4g; Sugar 4g; Protein 23g

Chunky Tilapia Stew

Prep time: 20 minutes| **Cook time:** 10 minutes| **Serves:** 2

2 tablespoons sesame oil
1 cup scallions, chopped
2 garlic cloves, minced
⅓ cup dry vermouth
1 cup shellfish stock
2 cups water
2 ripe plum tomatoes, crushed
Sea salt, to taste
¼ teaspoon black pepper, or more to taste
1 teaspoon hot paprika
1-pound tilapia fillets, boneless, skinless and diced
1 tablespoon fresh lime juice
1 teaspoon dried rosemary
½ teaspoons dried oregano
½ teaspoons dried basil

Press the "Sauté" button two times to select "Normal" settings.
Heat the oil and sauté the scallions and garlic until fragrant.

Add a splash of vermouth to deglaze the bottom of the Inner Pot.
Put on the pressure cooker's lid and turn the steam valve to "Sealing" position.
Press the "Pressure Cook" button two times to select "Less" option.
Use the "+/-" keys on the control panel to set the cooking time to 5 minutes.
Use the Pressure Level button to adjust the pressure to "High Pressure".
Once the cooking cycle is completed, quickly and carefully turn the steam release handle from Sealing position to the Venting position. When all the steam is released, remove the pressure lid from the top carefully.
Serve with some extra lime slices if desired. Bon appétit!

Per Serving: Calories 414; Fat 10.9g; Sodium 354mg; Carbs 10.5g; Fiber 4.1g; Sugar 8.2g; Protein 26g

Haddock Fillets with Black Beans

Prep time: 20 minutes| **Cook time:** 5 minutes| **Serves:** 2

1 cup water
2 haddock fillets
2 teaspoons coconut butter, at room temperature
Salt and black pepper, to taste
2 sprigs thyme, chopped
¼ teaspoon caraway seeds
½ teaspoons tarragon
½ teaspoons paprika
4 tomato slices
2 tablespoons fresh cilantro, roughly chopped
1 can black beans, drained

Add 1 cup of water to the bottom of your Inner Pot. Add a steamer insert.
Brush the haddock fillets with coconut butter. Now, season the haddock fillets with salt and pepper.
Place the haddock fillets on top of the steamer insert.
Add thyme, caraway seeds, tarragon, and paprika. Place 2 tomato slices on top of each fillet.
Put on the pressure cooker's lid and turn the steam valve to "Sealing" position.
Press the "Pressure Cook" button two times to select "Less" option.
Use the "+/-" keys on the control panel to set the cooking time to 3 minutes.
Use the Pressure Level button to adjust the pressure to "Low Pressure".
Once the cooking cycle is completed, allow the steam to release naturally.
When all the steam is released, remove the pressure lid from the top carefully.
Transfer the haddock fillets to serving plates. Scatter chopped cilantro over each fillet and serve garnished with black beans. Bon appétit!

Per Serving: Calories 412; Fat 20g; Sodium 491mg; Carbs 9g; Fiber 3g; Sugar 8g; Protein 31g

Foil-Packet Fish with Aioli

Prep time: 20 minutes| **Cook time:** 15 minutes| **Serves:** 2

2 cod fish fillets
½ teaspoons seasoned salt
¼ teaspoon black pepper, or more to taste
½ teaspoons mustard powder
½ teaspoons ancho chili powder
1 shallot, thinly sliced
1 lemon, cut into slices
For Aioli:
1 egg yolk
A pinch of salt
2 garlic cloves, minced
2 teaspoons fresh lemon juice
¼ cup olive oil

Prepare your Inner Pot by adding 1 ½ cups of water and steamer basket to the Inner Pot.
Place a fish fillet in the center of each piece of foil.
Season with salt, pepper, mustard powder, and chili powder.
Top with shallots and wrap tightly.
Put on the pressure cooker's lid and turn the steam valve to "Sealing" position.
Press the "Pressure Cook" button two times to select "Less" option.
Use the "+/-" keys on the control panel to set the cooking time to 10 minutes.
Use the Pressure Level button to adjust the pressure to "High Pressure".
Once the cooking cycle is completed, allow the steam to release naturally.
When all the steam is released, remove the pressure lid from the top carefully.
In your food processor, mix the egg, salt, garlic, and lemon juice.
With the machine running, gradually and slowly add the olive oil.
Garnish the warm fish fillets with lemon slices; serve with aioli on the side. Bon appétit!

Per Serving: Calories 584; Fat 15g; Sodium 441mg; Carbs 17g; Fiber 4.6g; Sugar 5g; Protein 29g

Baked Fish with Parmesan

Prep time: 20 minutes| **Cook time:** 9 minutes| **Serves:** 2

2 ripe tomatoes, sliced
1 teaspoon dried rosemary
1 teaspoon dried marjoram
½ teaspoons dried thyme
4 mahi-mahi fillets
2 tablespoons butter, at room temperature
Sea salt and black pepper, to taste
8 oz. Parmesan cheese, freshly grated

Add 1 ½ cups of water and a rack to your Inner Pot.
Spritz a casserole dish with a nonstick cooking spray.
Arrange the slices of tomatoes on the bottom of the dish. Add the herbs.

Place the mahi-mahi fillets on the top; drizzle the melted butter over the fish.
Season it with salt and black pepper. Place the baking dish on the rack.
Put on the pressure cooker's lid and turn the steam valve to "Sealing" position.
Press the "Pressure Cook" button two times to select "Less" option.
Use the "+/-" keys on the control panel to set the cooking time to 9 minutes.
Use the Pressure Level button to adjust the pressure to "Low Pressure".
Once the cooking cycle is completed, quickly and carefully turn the steam release handle from Sealing position to the Venting position.
When all the steam is released, remove the pressure lid from the top carefully.
Top with parmesan and seal the lid again; allow the cheese to melt and serve.

Per Serving: Calories 489; Fat 11g; Sodium 501mg; Carbs 8.9g; Fiber 4.6g; Sugar 8g; Protein 26g

Salmon Steaks with Kale Pesto Sauce

Prep time: 20 minutes| **Cook time:** 5 minutes| **Serves:** 4

1-pound salmon steaks
1 shallot, peeled and sliced
½ cup Kalamata olives
2 sprigs rosemary
2 tablespoons olive oil
½ teaspoons whole mixed peppercorns
Sea salt, to taste
Kale Pesto Sauce:
1 avocado
1 teaspoon garlic, crushed
2 tablespoons fresh parsley
1 cup kale
2 tablespoons fresh lemon juice
2 tablespoons olive oil

Prepare your Inner Pot by adding 1 ½ cups of water and a steamer basket to its bottom.
Place the salmon steaks in the steamer basket.
Add the shallots, olives, rosemary, olive oil, peppercorns, and salt.
Put on the pressure cooker's lid and turn the steam valve to "Sealing" position.
Press the "Steam" button two times to select "Less" option.
Use the "+/-" keys on the control panel to set the cooking time to 5 minutes.
Use the Pressure Level button to adjust the pressure to "High Pressure".
Once the cooking cycle is completed, quickly and carefully turn the steam release handle from Sealing position to the Venting position.
When all the steam is released, remove the pressure lid from the top carefully.
Add the avocado, garlic, parsley, kale, and lemon juice to your blender.
Then, mix on high until a loose paste forms.
Add the olive oil a little at a time and continue to blend.
Serve the fish fillets with the pesto on the side. Bon appétit!

Per Serving: Calories 424; Fat 7.9g; Sodium 704mg; Carbs 6g; Fiber 3.6g; Sugar 6g; Protein 18g

Parmesan Cod with Basmati Rice

Prep time: 20 minutes| **Cook time:** 5 minutes| **Serves:** 4

2 cups basmati rice
2 cups water
1 ¼ lbs. cod, slice into small pieces
Salt and black pepper, to taste
1 teaspoon paprika
2 bay leaves
1 teaspoon coriander
1 teaspoon lemon thyme
2 tablespoons lemon juice
½ cup heavy cream
1 cup Parmesan cheese, freshly grated

Put on the pressure cooker's lid and turn the steam valve to "Sealing" position.
Press the "Pressure Cook" button two times to select "Less" option.
Use the "+/-" keys on the control panel to set the cooking time to 4 minutes.
Use the Pressure Level button to adjust the pressure to "High Pressure".
Once the cooking cycle is completed, allow the steam to release naturally.
When all the steam is released, remove the pressure lid from the top carefully.
Press the Cancel button to stop this cooking program.
Press the "Sauté" button two times to select "Normal" settings.
Add the remaining ingredients and cook until the Parmesan has melted.
Serve the fish mixture over the hot basmati rice and enjoy!

Per Serving: Calories 521; Fat 7.9g; Sodium 704mg; Carbs 6g; Fiber 3.6g; Sugar 6g; Protein 18g

Butter Grouper

Prep time: 20 minutes| **Cook time:** 5 minutes| **Serves:** 4

4 grouper fillets
4 tablespoons butter
2 tablespoons fresh lemon juice
2 garlic cloves, smashed
½ teaspoons sweet paprika
½ teaspoons dried basil
Sea salt and black pepper, to taste

Add 1 ½ cups of water and steamer basket to the Inner Pot.
Then, place the fish fillets in the steamer basket.
Add the butter; drizzle with lemon juice; add the garlic, paprika, basil, salt, and black pepper.
Put on the pressure cooker's lid and turn the steam valve to "Sealing" position.

Press the "Pressure Cook" button two times to select "Less" option.
Use the "+/-" keys on the control panel to set the cooking time to 4 minutes.
Use the Pressure Level button to adjust the pressure to "Low Pressure".
Once the cooking cycle is completed, quickly and carefully turn the steam release handle from Sealing position to the Venting position.
When all the steam is released, remove the pressure lid from the top carefully.
Serve immediately.

Per Serving: Calories 361; Fat 7.9g; Sodium 704mg; Carbs 6g; Fiber 3.6g; Sugar 6g; Protein 18g

Tuna, Ham and Pea Chowder

Prep time: 20 minutes| **Cook time:** 6 minutes| **Serves:** 5

2 tablespoons olive oil
4 slices ham, chopped
1 cup shallots, chopped
2 cloves garlic, minced
2 carrots, chopped
5 cups seafood stock
1 ¼ lbs. tuna steak, diced
Sea salt and black pepper, to taste
1 teaspoon cayenne pepper
½ teaspoons ground bay leaf
½ teaspoons mustard powder
1 ½ cups double cream
1 ½ cups frozen green peas

Press the "Sauté" button two times to select "Normal" settings.
Heat the oil and fry the ham until crispy.
Then, add the shallot and garlic; continue to cook an additional 2 minutes or until tender and fragrant.
Add the carrot, stock, tuna, salt, black pepper, cayenne pepper, ground bay leaf, and mustard powder.
Put on the pressure cooker's lid and turn the steam valve to "Sealing" position.
Press the "Pressure Cook" button two times to select "Less" option.
Use the "+/-" keys on the control panel to set the cooking time to 6 minutes.
Use the Pressure Level button to adjust the pressure to "High Pressure".
Once the cooking cycle is completed, allow the steam to release naturally.
When all the steam is released, remove the pressure lid from the top carefully.
Add the double cream and frozen peas.
Press the "Sauté" button two times to select "Normal" settings again and cook for a couple of minutes more or until heated through. Bon appétit!

Per Serving: Calories 422; Fat 12.9g; Sodium 414mg; Carbs 11g; Fiber 5g; Sugar 9g; Protein 31g

Ocean Trout Fillets

Prep time: 20 minutes| **Cook time:** 3 minutes| **Serves:** 4

1-pound ocean trout fillets
Sea salt, to taste
1 teaspoon caraway seeds
½ teaspoons mustard seeds
½ teaspoons paprika
½ cup spring onions, chopped
2 garlic cloves, minced
1 teaspoon mixed peppercorns
2 tablespoons champagne vinegar
1 tablespoon fish sauce
2 ½ cups broth, preferably homemade

Place the steaming basket in your Inner Pot.
Sprinkle the ocean trout fillets with salt,
caraway seeds, mustard seeds, and paprika.
Place the ocean trout fillet in the steaming
basket. Add the other ingredients.
Put on the pressure cooker's lid and turn the
steam valve to "Sealing" position.
Press the "Pressure Cook" button two times to
select "Less" option.
Use the "+/-" keys on the control panel to set
the cooking time to 3 minutes.
Use the Pressure Level button to adjust the
pressure to "Low Pressure".
Once the cooking cycle is completed, quickly
and carefully turn the steam release handle
from Sealing position to the Venting position.
When all the steam is released, remove the
pressure lid from the top carefully.
Serve.

Per Serving: Calories 334; Fat 19g; Sodium
354mg; Carbs 15g; Fiber 5.1g; Sugar 8.2g;
Protein 32g

Red Snapper in Mushroom Sauce

Prep time: 20 minutes| **Cook time:** 6 minutes| **Serves:** 4

½ stick butter, at room temperature
2 shallots, peeled and chopped
2 garlic cloves, minced
1 cup brown mushrooms, thinly sliced
2 tablespoons coriander
1 (11-oz.) can tomatillo, chopped
2 tablespoons tomato ketchup
1 cup chicken stock, preferably homemade
1-pound red snapper, cut into bite-sized
chunks
Salt and black pepper, to taste

Press the "Sauté" button two times to select
"Normal" settings.
Then, melt the butter. Once hot, cook the
shallots with garlic until tender and aromatic.
Stir in the mushrooms; cook an additional 3
minutes or until they have softened.
Stir the remaining ingredients into your Inner
Pot.
Put on the pressure cooker's lid and turn the
steam valve to "Sealing" position.
Press the "Pressure Cook" button two times to
select "Less" option.

Use the "+/-" keys on the control panel to set
the cooking time to 6 minutes.
Use the Pressure Level button to adjust the
pressure to "High Pressure".
Once the cooking cycle is completed, quickly
and carefully turn the steam release handle
from Sealing position to the Venting position.
When all the steam is released, remove the
pressure lid from the top carefully.
Serve over hot basmati rice if desired. Enjoy!

Per Serving: Calories 584; Fat 15g; Sodium
441mg; Carbs 17g; Fiber 4.6g; Sugar 5g;
Protein 29g

Portuguese-Fish Medley

Prep time: 20 minutes| **Cook time:** 8 minutes| **Serves:** 4

1-pound fish, mixed pieces for fish soup, cut
into bite-sized pieces
1 yellow onion, chopped
1 celery with leaves, chopped
2 carrots, chopped
2 cloves garlic, minced
1 green bell pepper, thinly sliced
2 tablespoons peanut oil
1 ½ cups seafood stock
⅓ cup dry vermouth
2 fresh tomatoes, puréed
1 tablespoon loosely packed saffron threads
Sea salt and black pepper, to taste
1 teaspoon Piri Piri
2 bay leaves
¼ cup fresh cilantro, roughly chopped
½ lemon, sliced

Simply throw all of the above ingredients,
except for the cilantro and lemon, into your
Inner Pot.
Put on the pressure cooker's lid and turn the
steam valve to "Sealing" position.
Press the "Pressure Cook" button two times to
select "Less" option.
Use the "+/-" keys on the control panel to set
the cooking time to 8 minutes.
Use the Pressure Level button to adjust the
pressure to "Low Pressure".
Once the cooking cycle is completed, quickly
and carefully turn the steam release handle
from Sealing position to the Venting position.
When all the steam is released, remove the
pressure lid from the top carefully.
Ladle the medley into individual bowls; serve
with fresh cilantro and lemon. Enjoy!

Per Serving: Calories 349; Fat 2.9g; Sodium
511mg; Carbs 12g; Fiber 3g; Sugar 8g;
Protein 7g

Prawns with Basmati Rice

Prep time: 20 minutes| **Cook time:** 5 minutes| **Serves:** 5

2 tablespoons olive oil
1 cup red onions, thinly sliced
2 cloves garlic, pressed
2 bell peppers, seeded and thinly sliced

1 serrano pepper, seeded and thinly sliced
2 cups basmati rice
1 (14-oz.) can tomatoes, diced
2 ½ cups vegetable stock
1 tablespoon tamari sauce
1 pound prawns, peeled and deveined
Sea salt and black pepper, to taste
½ teaspoons sweet paprika
1 teaspoon dried rosemary
½ teaspoons dried oregano
2 tablespoons fresh mint, roughly chopped

Press the "Sauté" button two times to select "Normal" settings.
Then, heat the oil and sauté the onions until tender and translucent.
Stir in the garlic; continue to sauté until aromatic.
Add the rest of the above ingredients, except for the mint, to the Inner Pot.
Put on the pressure cooker's lid and turn the steam valve to "Sealing" position.
Press the "Pressure Cook" button two times to select "Less" option.
Use the "+/-" keys on the control panel to set the cooking time to 3 minutes.
Use the Pressure Level button to adjust the pressure to "Low Pressure".
Once the cooking cycle is completed, allow the steam to release naturally.
When all the steam is released, remove the pressure lid from the top carefully.
Serve garnished with fresh mint leaves. Bon appétit!

Per Serving: Calories 382; Fat 10.9g; Sodium 454mg; Carbs 10g; Fiber 3.1g; Sugar 5.2g; Protein 20g

Tuna Fillets with Onions

Prep time: 20 minutes| **Cook time:** 5 minutes| **Serves:** 2

1 cup water
A few sprigs of tarragon
1 lemon, sliced
1-pound tuna filets
1 tablespoon butter, melted
Sea salt and black pepper, to taste
1 large onion, sliced into rings

Put the water, herbs and lemon slices in the Inner Pot; now, place the steamer rack in the Inner Pot.
Lower the tuna fillets onto the rack. Add butter, salt, and pepper; top with onion slices.
Put on the pressure cooker's lid and turn the steam valve to "Sealing" position.
Press the "Steam" button two times to select "Less" option.
Use the Pressure Level button to adjust the pressure to "Low Pressure".
Once the cooking cycle is completed, quickly and carefully turn the steam release handle from Sealing position to the Venting position.
When all the steam is released, remove the pressure lid from the top carefully.
Serve immediately.

Per Serving: Calories 489; Fat 11g; Sodium 501mg; Carbs 8.9g; Fiber 4.6g; Sugar 8g; Protein 26g

Haddock Fillets with Steamed Green Beans

Prep time: 20 minutes| **Cook time:** 6 minutes| **Serves:** 4

1 lime, cut into wedges
½ cup water
4 haddock fillets
1 rosemary sprig
2 thyme sprigs
1 tablespoon fresh parsley
4 teaspoons ghee
Sea salt and black pepper, to taste
2 cloves garlic, minced
4 cups green beans

Place the lime wedges and water in the Inner Pot. Add a steamer rack.
Lower the haddock fillets onto the rack; place the rosemary, thyme, parsley, and ghee on the haddock fillets.
Season with salt and pepper.
Then, add the garlic and green beans to the Inner Pot.
Put on the pressure cooker's lid and turn the steam valve to "Sealing" position.
Press the "Steam" button one time to select "Less" option.
Use the "+/-" keys on the control panel to set the cooking time to 6 minutes.
Use the Pressure Level button to adjust the pressure to "Low Pressure".
Once the cooking cycle is completed, quickly and carefully turn the steam release handle from Sealing position to the Venting position.
When all the steam is released, remove the pressure lid from the top carefully.
Serve the haddock fillets with green beans on the side.
Bon appétit!

Per Serving: Calories 219; Fat 10g; Sodium 891mg; Carbs 22.9g; Fiber 4g; Sugar 4g; Protein 23g

Greek-Shrimp with Feta Cheese

Prep time: 20 minutes| **Cook time:** 2 minutes| **Serves:** 4

1 pound frozen shrimp
1 ½ tablespoons olive oil
2 gloves garlic, minced
1 teaspoon basil
½ teaspoons dry dill weed
1 teaspoon oregano
1 (26-oz.) canned diced tomatoes
½ cup Kalamata olives
2 oz. feta cheese, crumbled
½ lemon, sliced
Chopped fresh mint leaves, for garnish

Add the shrimp, olive oil, garlic, basil, dill, oregano, and tomatoes to the Inner Pot.

Put on the pressure cooker's lid and turn the steam valve to "Sealing" position.
Press the "Pressure Cook" button two times to select "Less" option.
Use the "+/-" keys on the control panel to set the cooking time to 2 minutes.
Use the Pressure Level button to adjust the pressure to "Low Pressure".
Once the cooking cycle is completed, allow the steam to release naturally.
When all the steam is released, remove the pressure lid from the top carefully.
Top with Kalamata olives and feta cheese.
Serve garnished with lemon and mint leaves. Enjoy!

Per Serving: Calories 419; Fat 14g; Sodium 791mg; Carbs 8.9g; Fiber 4.6g; Sugar 8g; Protein 31g

Indian Kulambu

Prep time: 20 minutes| **Cook time:** 2 minutes| **Serves:** 4
2 tablespoons butter
6 curry leaves
1 onion, chopped
2 cloves garlic, crushed
1 (1-inch) piece fresh ginger, grated
1 dried Kashmiri chili, minced
1 cup canned tomatoes, crushed
½ teaspoons turmeric powder
1 teaspoon ground coriander
½ teaspoons ground cumin
Kosher salt and black pepper, to taste
½ (14-oz.) can coconut milk
1-pound salmon fillets
1 tablespoon lemon juice

Press the "Sauté" button two times to select "Normal" settings and melt the butter.
Once hot, cook the curry leaves for about 30 seconds.
Stir in the onions, garlic, ginger and Kashmiri chili and cook for 2 minutes more or until they are fragrant.
Add the tomatoes, turmeric, coriander, cumin, salt, and black pepper.
Continue to sauté for 30 seconds more. Add the coconut milk and salmon.
Press the Cancel button to stop this cooking program.
Put on the pressure cooker's lid and turn the steam valve to "Sealing" position.
Press the "Pressure Cook" button two times to select "Less" option.
Use the "+/-" keys on the control panel to set the cooking time to 2 minutes.
Use the Pressure Level button to adjust the pressure to "Low Pressure".
Once the cooking cycle is completed, quickly and carefully turn the steam release handle from Sealing position to the Venting position.
When all the steam is released, remove the pressure lid from the top carefully.
Spoon the fish curry into individual bowls.
Drizzle lemon juice over the fish curry and serve.
Enjoy!

Per Serving: Calories 479; Fat 10g; Sodium 891mg; Carbs 22.9g; Fiber 4g; Sugar 4g; Protein 23g

Cod Fish with Goat Cheese

Prep time: 20 minutes| **Cook time:** 5 minutes| **Serves:** 4
1-pound baby potatoes
2 tablespoons coconut oil, at room temperature
Sea salt and pepper, to taste
1 ½ lbs. cod fish fillets
½ teaspoons smoked paprika
2 tablespoons fresh Italian parsley, chopped
½ teaspoons fresh ginger, grated
2 cloves garlic, minced
1 cup goat cheese, crumbled

Place the potatoes in the bottom of the Inner Pot.
Add 1 cup of water; then, add coconut oil, salt and pepper. Place the rack over the potatoes.
Place the cod fish fillets on the rack. Season the fillets with paprika and parsley.
Put on the pressure cooker's lid and turn the steam valve to "Sealing" position.
Press the "Steam" button two times to select "Less" option.
Use the Pressure Level button to adjust the pressure to "Low Pressure".
Once the cooking cycle is completed, quickly and carefully turn the steam release handle from Sealing position to the Venting position.
When all the steam is released, remove the pressure lid from the top carefully.
Continue to cook the potatoes until fork tender; add the ginger and garlic and cook for 2 minutes more.
Top with goat cheese and serve. Bon appétit!

Per Serving: Calories 449; Fat 2.9g; Sodium 511mg; Carbs 12g; Fiber 3g; Sugar 8g; Protein 27g

Crab Dip

Prep time: 15 minutes| **Cook time:** 5 minutes| **Serves:** 10
1-pound lump crab meat
6 oz. Cottage cheese, at room temperature
½ cup Romano cheese, shredded
1 cup sour cream
Kosher salt and black pepper, to taste
1 teaspoon smoked paprika
1 ½ cups Cheddar cheese, shredded
¼ cup fresh chives, chopped
2 tablespoons fresh lime juice

Place 1 cup of water and a metal Steam Rack in the Inner Pot.
Spritz a casserole dish with nonstick cooking spray.
Place the crab meat, Cottage cheese, Romano cheese and sour cream in the casserole dish.
Season with salt, black pepper, and smoked paprika.

Top with the Cheddar cheese. Lower the dish onto the Steam Rack.

Put on the pressure cooker's lid and turn the steam valve to "Sealing" position.

Press the "Steam" button two times to select "Less" option.

Use the Pressure Level button to adjust the pressure to "Low Pressure".

Once the cooking cycle is completed, allow the steam to release naturally.

When all the steam is released, remove the pressure lid from the top carefully.

Scatter the chopped chives over the top and add a few drizzles of lime juice.

Serve warm or at room temperature. Enjoy!

Per Serving: Calories 584; Fat 15g; Sodium 441mg; Carbs 17g; Fiber 4.6g; Sugar 5g; Protein 29g

Creole Gumbo

Prep time: 15 minutes| **Cook time:** 10 minutes| **Serves:** 4

2 tablespoons butter, melted
1 shallot, diced
1 sweet pepper, sliced
1 jalapeno pepper, sliced
1-pound tuna, cut into 2-inch chunks
1 tablespoon Creole seasoning
2 carrots, sliced
2 celery stalks, diced
2 ripe tomatoes, pureed
¼ cup ketchup
1 bay leaf
1 cup beef broth
2 tablespoons Worcestershire sauce
1-pound raw shrimp, deveined
1 teaspoon filé powder
Sea salt and black pepper, to taste

Press the "Sauté" button two times to select "Normal" settings and melt the butter.

Once hot, cook the shallot and peppers for about 3 minutes until just tender and fragrant.

Add the remaining ingredients; gently stir to combine.

Put on the pressure cooker's lid and turn the steam valve to "Sealing" position.

Press the "Pressure Cook" button two times to select "Less" option.

Use the "+/-" keys on the control panel to set the cooking time to 5 minutes.

Use the Pressure Level button to adjust the pressure to "High Pressure".

Once the cooking cycle is completed, quickly and carefully turn the steam release handle from Sealing position to the Venting position.

When all the steam is released, remove the pressure lid from the top carefully.

Serve in individual bowls and enjoy!

Per Serving: Calories 489; Fat 11g; Sodium 501mg; Carbs 8.9g; Fiber 4.6g; Sugar 8g; Protein 26g

Blue Crabs with Wine and Herbs

Prep time: 15 minutes| **Cook time:** 5 minutes| **Serves:** 4

2 lbs. frozen blue crab
½ cup water
½ cup dry white wine
Sea salt and black pepper, to taste
2 sprigs rosemary
2 sprigs thyme
1 lemon, cut into wedges

Add the frozen crab legs, water, wine, salt, black pepper, rosemary, and thyme to the Inner Pot.

Put on the pressure cooker's lid and turn the steam valve to "Sealing" position.

Press the "Pressure Cook" button two times to select "Less" option.

Use the "+/-" keys on the control panel to set the cooking time to 3 minutes.

Use the Pressure Level button to adjust the pressure to "High Pressure".

Once the cooking cycle is completed, quickly and carefully turn the steam release handle from Sealing position to the Venting position.

When all the steam is released, remove the pressure lid from the top carefully.

Serve warm, garnished with fresh lemon wedges. Bon appétit!

Per Serving: Calories 478; Fat 7.9g; Sodium 704mg; Carbs 6g; Fiber 3.6g; Sugar 6g; Protein 18g

Sausage and Prawn Boil

Prep time: 15 minutes| **Cook time:** 10 minutes| **Serves:** 4

½-pound beef sausage, sliced
4 baby potatoes
1 cup fume (fish stock)
¼ cup butter
2 cloves garlic, minced
1 teaspoon Old Bay seasoning
¼ teaspoon Tabasco sauce
Sea salt and white pepper, to taste
1 pound prawns
1 fresh lemon, juiced

Place the sausage and potatoes in the Inner Pot; cover with the fish stock.

Put on the pressure cooker's lid and turn the steam valve to "Sealing" position.

Press the "Pressure Cook" button two times to select "Less" option.

Use the "+/-" keys on the control panel to set the cooking time to 5 minutes.

Use the Pressure Level button to adjust the pressure to "High Pressure".

Once the cooking cycle is completed, allow the steam to release naturally.

When all the steam is released, remove the pressure lid from the top carefully.

Reserve. Clean the Inner Pot.

Press the "Sauté" button two times to select "Normal" settings and melt the butter.

Once hot, sauté the minced garlic until aromatic or about 1 minute.

Stir in the Old Bay seasoning, Tabasco, salt, and white pepper. Lastly, stir in the prawns. Continue to simmer for 1 to 2 minutes or until the shrimp turn pink.
Press the "Cancel" button.
Add the sausages and potatoes, drizzle lemon juice over the top and serve warm.

Per Serving: Calories 422; Fat 12.9g; Sodium 414mg; Carbs 11g; Fiber 5g; Sugar 9g; Protein 31g

Sole Fillets with Vegetables

Prep time: 15 minutes| **Cook time:** 13 minutes| **Serves:** 4

2 tablespoons coconut oil
1 small shallot, quartered
4 cloves garlic, sliced
1 cup beef stock
1 ripe tomato, puréed
Salt and black pepper, to taste
1-pound fennel, quartered
1-pound sole fillets
1 lemon, cut into wedges
2 tablespoons fresh Italian parsley

Press the "Sauté" button two times to select "Normal" settings and heat the coconut oil. Once hot, sauté the shallot and garlic until tender and aromatic.
Add the beef stock, tomato, salt, pepper, and fennel.
Press the Cancel button to stop this cooking program.
Put on the pressure cooker's lid and turn the steam valve to "Sealing" position.
Press the "Pressure Cook" button two times to select "Less" option.
Use the "+/-" keys on the control panel to set the cooking time to 10 minutes.
Use the Pressure Level button to adjust the pressure to "High Pressure".
Once the cooking cycle is completed, quickly and carefully turn the steam release handle from Sealing position to the Venting position. When all the steam is released, remove the pressure lid from the top carefully.
Then, remove all the vegetables with a slotted spoon and reserve, keeping them warm.
Add the sole fillets to the Inner Pot.
Choose the "Steam" mode and cook for 3 minutes at Low Pressure.
Once cooking is complete, quickly and carefully turn the steam release handle from Sealing position to the Venting position ; carefully remove the lid.
Garnish the fish fillets with lemon and parsley. With the reserved vegetables, serve and enjoy!

Per Serving: Calories 334; Fat 7.9g; Sodium 704mg; Carbs 6g; Fiber 3.6g; Sugar 6g; Protein 18g

Louisiana-Seafood Boil

Prep time: 15 minutes| **Cook time:** 10 minutes| **Serves:** 4

1 cup jasmine rice
1 tablespoon butter
1 tablespoon olive oil
½-pound chicken breasts, cubed
1-pound shrimp
2 sweet peppers, deveined and sliced
1 habanero pepper, deveined and sliced
1 onion, chopped
4 cloves garlic, minced
1 cup chicken bone broth
2 bay leaves
1 teaspoon oregano
1 teaspoon sage
1 teaspoon basil
1 teaspoon paprika
1 tablespoon fish sauce
Sea salt and black pepper, to taste
1 tablespoon cornstarch

Combine the rice, butter and 1 ½ cups of water in a pot and bring to a rapid boil. Cover and let it simmer on low for 15 minutes. Fluff with a fork and reserve.
Press the "Sauté" button two times to select "Normal" settings and heat the oil. Once hot, cook the chicken breasts for 3 to 4 minutes.
Add the remaining ingredients, except for the cornstarch.
Put on the pressure cooker's lid and turn the steam valve to "Sealing" position.
Press the "Pressure Cook" button two times to select "Less" option.
Use the "+/-" keys on the control panel to set the cooking time to 3 minutes.
Use the Pressure Level button to adjust the pressure to "Low Pressure".
Once the cooking cycle is completed, quickly and carefully turn the steam release handle from Sealing position to the Venting position. When all the steam is released, remove the pressure lid from the top carefully.
Mix the cornstarch with 2 tablespoons of cold water.
Add the cornstarch slurry to the cooking liquid and stir at "Normal" cooking temperature on the "Sauté" mode until the sauce thickens.
Serve over hot jasmine rice. Bon appétit!

Per Serving: Calories 479; Fat 10g; Sodium 891mg; Carbs 22.9g; Fiber 4g; Sugar 4g; Protein 23g

Southern California Cioppino

Prep time: 15 minutes| **Cook time:** 30 minutes| **Serves:** 6

2 tablespoons coconut oil
1 onion, diced
4 garlic cloves, minced
2 celery stalks, diced
2 carrots, diced
1 sweet pepper, diced
2 (14-oz.) cans of tomatoes, crushed
1 cup clam juice
1 teaspoon oyster sauce

½ teaspoons dried parsley flakes
1 teaspoon dried rosemary
1 teaspoon dried basil
1 teaspoon paprika
1 bay leaf
Sea salt and black pepper, to taste
1-pound halibut steaks, cubed
½-pound sea scallops, rinsed and drained
1-pound shrimp, peeled and deveined
½-pound crab legs
¼ cup dry white wine

Press the "Sauté" button two times to select "Normal" settings to heat the coconut oil.
Once hot, sauté the onion, garlic, celery, carrots, and pepper for about 3 minutes or until they are just tender.
Add the canned tomatoes, clam juice, oyster sauce, parsley, rosemary, basil, paprika, bay leaf, salt, and black pepper to the Inner Pot.
Put on the pressure cooker's lid and turn the steam valve to "Sealing" position.
Press the "Soup/Broth" button one time to select "Normal" option.
Use the "+/-" keys on the control panel to set the cooking time to 30 minutes.
Use the Pressure Level button to adjust the pressure to "High Pressure".
Once the cooking cycle is completed, allow the steam to release naturally.
When all the steam is released, remove the pressure lid from the top carefully.
Add the seafood and wine.
Choose the "Steam" mode and cook for 3 minutes at Low Pressure.
Once cooking is complete, use a quick pressure release; carefully remove the lid.
Serve in individual bowls and enjoy!

Per Serving: Calories 412; Fat 20g; Sodium 491mg; Carbs 9g; Fiber 3g; Sugar 8g; Protein 31g

Fish and Vegetables

Prep time: 15 minutes| **Cook time:** 10 minutes| **Serves:** 4
12 oz. halibut steaks, cut into four pieces
1 red bell pepper, sliced
1 green bell pepper, sliced
1 onion, sliced
2 garlic cloves, minced
1 cup cherry tomatoes, halved
Sea salt and black pepper, to taste
1 teaspoon dried rosemary
1 teaspoon basil
½ teaspoons oregano
½ teaspoons paprika
4 teaspoons olive oil

Place 1 cup of water and a metal Steam Rack in the bottom of the Inner Pot.
Place 4 large sheets of heavy-duty foil on a flat surface.
Divide the ingredients between sheets of foil.
Add a splash of water.
Bring the ends of the foil together; fold in the sides to seal. Place the fish packets on the Steam Rack.

Put on the pressure cooker's lid and turn the steam valve to "Sealing" position.
Press the "Steam" button one time to select "Normal" option.
Use the Pressure Level button to adjust the pressure to "High Pressure".
Once the cooking cycle is completed, quickly and carefully turn the steam release handle from Sealing position to the Venting position.
When all the steam is released, remove the pressure lid from the top carefully.
Bon appétit!

Per Serving: Calories 472; Fat 10.9g; Sodium 354mg; Carbs 10.5g; Fiber 4.1g; Sugar 8.2g; Protein 26g

Japanese Seafood Curry

Prep time: 15 minutes| **Cook time:** 5 minutes| **Serves:** 4
2 tablespoons butter, softened
1 onion, chopped
2 cloves garlic, minced
1 (1-inch) pieces fresh ginger, ground
1 red chili, deseeded and minced
1 pound pollack, cut into large chunks
½ pound shrimps, deveined
2 tablespoons sesame oil
1 tablespoon garam masala
1 teaspoon curry paste
1 (3-inch) kombu (dried kelp)
1 package Japanese curry roux
2 tablespoons Shoyu sauce
2 ripe tomatoes, pureed

Press the "Sauté" button two times to select "Normal" settings and melt the butter.
Cook the onion, garlic, ginger, and red chili until just tender and fragrant.
Add the pollack and shrimp and continue to sauté for a couple of minutes more.
Add the remaining ingredients.
Put on the pressure cooker's lid and turn the steam valve to "Sealing" position.
Press the "Pressure Cook" button two times to select "Less" option.
Use the "+/-" keys on the control panel to set the cooking time to 5 minutes.
Use the Pressure Level button to adjust the pressure to "Low Pressure".
Once the cooking cycle is completed, quickly and carefully turn the steam release handle from Sealing position to the Venting position.
When all the steam is released, remove the pressure lid from the top carefully.
Serve your curry over hot steamed rice.
Enjoy!

Per Serving: Calories 390; Fat 7.9g; Sodium 704mg; Carbs 6g; Fiber 3.6g; Sugar 6g; Protein 18g

Spicy Thai Prawns

Prep time: 15 minutes| **Cook time:** 5 minutes| **Serves:** 4
2 tablespoons coconut oil

1 small white onion, chopped
2 cloves garlic, minced
1 ½ lbs. prawns, deveined
½ teaspoons red chili flakes
1 bell pepper, seeded and sliced
1 cup coconut milk
2 tablespoons fish sauce
2 tablespoons lime juice
1 tablespoon sugar
Kosher salt and white pepper, to your liking
½ teaspoons cayenne pepper
1 teaspoon fresh ginger, ground
2 tablespoons fresh cilantro, chopped

Press the "Sauté" button two times to select "Normal" settings and heat the coconut oil; once hot, sauté the onion and garlic until aromatic.
Add the prawns, red chili flakes, bell pepper, coconut milk, fish sauce, lime juice, sugar, salt, white pepper, cayenne pepper, and ginger.
Put on the pressure cooker's lid and turn the steam valve to "Sealing" position.
Press the "Pressure Cook" button two times to select "Less" option.
Use the "+/-" keys on the control panel to set the cooking time to 3 minutes.
Use the Pressure Level button to adjust the pressure to "Low Pressure".
Once the cooking cycle is completed, quickly and carefully turn the steam release handle from Sealing position to the Venting position. When all the steam is released, remove the pressure lid from the top carefully.
Divide between serving bowls and serve garnished with fresh cilantro. Enjoy!

Per Serving: Calories 390; Fat 10.9g; Sodium 454mg; Carbs 10g; Fiber 3.1g; Sugar 5.2g; Protein 20g

Haddock Curry

Prep time: 15 minutes| **Cook time:** 4 minutes| **Serves:** 2

2 tablespoons peanut oil
1 onion, chopped
2 garlic cloves, minced
1 (1-inch) piece fresh root ginger, peeled and grated
2 long red chilies, deseeded and minced
2 tablespoons tamarind paste
1 teaspoon mustard seeds
1 teaspoon turmeric powder
1 teaspoon ground cumin
Sea salt and black pepper
1 can reduced fat coconut milk
1 cup chicken stock
1-pound haddock

Press the "Sauté" button two times to select "Normal" settings and heat the peanut oil.
once hot, sauté the onion, garlic, ginger, and chilies until aromatic.
Add the remaining ingredients and gently stir to combine.
Put on the pressure cooker's lid and turn the steam valve to "Sealing" position.

Press the "Pressure Cook" button two times to select "Less" option.
Use the "+/-" keys on the control panel to set the cooking time to 4 minutes.
Use the Pressure Level button to adjust the pressure to "Low Pressure".
Once the cooking cycle is completed, quickly and carefully turn the steam release handle from Sealing position to the Venting position. When all the steam is released, remove the pressure lid from the top carefully.
Divide between serving bowls and serve warm. Enjoy!

Per Serving: Calories 584; Fat 15g; Sodium 441mg; Carbs 17g; Fiber 4.6g; Sugar 5g; Protein 29g

Tuna and Asparagus Casserole

Prep time: 15 minutes| **Cook time:** 9 minutes| **Serves:** 4

1-pound tuna fillets
1-pound asparagus, trimmed
2 ripe tomatoes, pureed
Sea salt and black pepper, to taste
1 teaspoon paprika
A pinch of fresh thyme
1 tablespoon dry white wine
1 cup Cheddar cheese, grated

Place the tuna fillets in a lightly greased baking dish.
Add the asparagus, tomatoes, salt, black pepper, paprika, thyme, and wine.
Place a steamer rack inside the Inner Pot; add ½ cup of water.
Cut 1 sheet of heavy-duty foil and brush with cooking spray.
Top with the cheese. Cover with foil and lower the baking dish onto the rack.
Put on the pressure cooker's lid and turn the steam valve to "Sealing" position.
Press the "Pressure Cook" button two times to select "Less" option.
Use the "+/-" keys on the control panel to set the cooking time to 9 minutes.
Use the Pressure Level button to adjust the pressure to "Low Pressure".
Once the cooking cycle is completed, quickly and carefully turn the steam release handle from Sealing position to the Venting position. When all the steam is released, remove the pressure lid from the top carefully.
Place the baking dish on a cooling rack for a couple of minutes before slicing and serving. Bon appétit!

Per Serving: Calories 361; Fat 19g; Sodium 354mg; Carbs 15g; Fiber 5.1g; Sugar 8.2g; Protein 32g

Spinach-Stuffed Salmon

Prep time: 15 minutes| **Cook time:** 5 minutes| **Serves:** 3

3 (6-oz.) salmon fillets
Kosher salt and black pepper, to taste

½ teaspoons cayenne pepper
½ teaspoons celery seed, crushed
½ teaspoons dried basil
½ teaspoons dried marjoram
½ cup sour cream
½ cup mozzarella, shredded
1 cup frozen spinach, defrosted
2 cloves garlic, minced
1 tablespoon olive oil
1 lemon, cut into wedges

Add 1 cup of water and a steamer rack to the bottom of your Inner Pot.
Sprinkle your salmon with all spices. In a mixing bowl, thoroughly combine sour cream, mozzarella, spinach, and garlic.
Cut a pocket in each fillet to within ½-inch of the opposite side.
Stuff the pockets with the spinach/cheese mixture. Drizzle with olive oil.
Wrap the salmon fillets in foil and lower onto the rack.
Put on the pressure cooker's lid and turn the steam valve to "Sealing" position.
Press the "Pressure Cook" button two times to select "Less" option.
Use the "+/-" keys on the control panel to set the cooking time to 4 minutes.
Use the Pressure Level button to adjust the pressure to "Low Pressure".
Once the cooking cycle is completed, quickly and carefully turn the steam release handle from Sealing position to the Venting position.
When all the steam is released, remove the pressure lid from the top carefully.
Garnish with lemon wedges and serve warm.

Per Serving: Calories 489; Fat 11g; Sodium 501mg; Carbs 8.9g; Fiber 4.6g; Sugar 8g; Protein 26g

Steamed Tilapia with Spinach

Prep time: 15 minutes| **Cook time:** 12 minutes| **Serves:** 4
1 cup chicken broth
2 cloves garlic, sliced
1-pound tilapia, cut into 4 pieces
1 tablespoon Worcestershire sauce
Salt and black pepper, to taste
2 tablespoons butter, melted
2 cups fresh spinach

Place the chicken broth and garlic in the Inner Pot. Place the Steam Rack on top.
Place the tilapia fillets on a sheet of foil; add Worcestershire sauce, salt, pepper, and butter.
Bring up all sides of the foil to create a packet around your fish.
Put on the pressure cooker's lid and turn the steam valve to "Sealing" position.
Press the "Steam" button two times to select "Normal" option.
Use the Pressure Level button to adjust the pressure to "Low Pressure".
Once the cooking cycle is completed, quickly and carefully turn the steam release handle from Sealing position to the Venting position.

When all the steam is released, remove the pressure lid from the top carefully.
Add the spinach leaves to the cooking liquid. Press the Cancel button to stop this cooking program.
Press the "Sauté" function and let it simmer at "Less" cooking temperature for 1 to 2 minutes or until wilted.
Place the fish fillets on top of the wilted spinach, adjust the seasonings, and serve immediately.
Bon appétit!

Per Serving: Calories 419; Fat 14g; Sodium 791mg; Carbs 8.9g; Fiber 4.6g; Sugar 8g; Protein 31g

Codfish with Scallions

Prep time: 15 minutes| **Cook time:** 3 minutes| **Serves:** 3
1 lemon, sliced
½ cup water
3 fillets smoked codfish
3 teaspoons butter
3 tablespoons scallions, chopped
Sea salt and black pepper, to taste

Place the lemon and water in the bottom of the Inner Pot. Place the steamer rack on top.
Place the cod fish fillets on the steamer rack.
Add the butter, scallions, salt, and black pepper.
Put on the pressure cooker's lid and turn the steam valve to "Sealing" position.
Press the "Steam" button one time to select "Less" option.
Use the Pressure Level button to adjust the pressure to "Low Pressure".
Once the cooking cycle is completed, quickly and carefully turn the steam release handle from Sealing position to the Venting position.
When all the steam is released, remove the pressure lid from the top carefully.
Serve warm and enjoy!

Per Serving: Calories 461; Fat 7.9g; Sodium 704mg; Carbs 6g; Fiber 3.6g; Sugar 6g; Protein 18g

Teriyaki Fish Steaks

Prep time: 15 minutes| **Cook time:** 10 minutes| **Serves:** 4
2 tablespoons butter, melted
4 (6-oz.) salmon steaks
2 cloves garlic, smashed
1 (1-inch) piece fresh ginger, peeled and grated
⅓ cup soy sauce
½ cup water
2 tablespoons brown sugar
2 teaspoons wine vinegar
1 tablespoon cornstarch

Press the "Sauté" button two times to select "Normal" settings and then melt the butter.

Once hot, cook the salmon steaks for 2 minutes per side.

Add the garlic, ginger, soy sauce, water, sugar, and vinegar.

Put on the pressure cooker's lid and turn the steam valve to "Sealing" position.

Press the "Pressure Cook" button two times to select "Less" option.

Use the "+/-" keys on the control panel to set the cooking time to 5 minutes.

Use the Pressure Level button to adjust the pressure to "Low Pressure".

Once the cooking cycle is completed, quickly and carefully turn the steam release handle from Sealing position to the Venting position.

When all the steam is released, remove the pressure lid from the top carefully.

Reserve the fish steaks.

Mix the cornstarch with 2 tablespoons of cold water.

Add the slurry to the cooking liquid. Let it simmer until the sauce thickens.

Spoon the sauce over the fish steaks.

Bon appétit!

Per Serving: Calories 385; Fat 12.9g; Sodium 414mg; Carbs 11g; Fiber 5g; Sugar 9g; Protein 31g

Fish Tacos

Prep time: 15 minutes| **Cook time:** 7 minutes| **Serves:** 4

1 lemon, sliced
2 tablespoons olive oil
1-pound haddock fillets
½ teaspoons ground cumin
½ teaspoons onion powder
1 teaspoon garlic powder
½ teaspoons paprika
Sea salt and black pepper, to taste
1 teaspoon dried basil
1 tablespoon ancho chili powder
4 (6-inch) flour tortillas
4 tablespoons mayonnaise
4 tablespoons sour cream
2 tablespoons fresh cilantro, chopped
Add ½ cup of water, ½ of lemon slices, and a steamer rack to the bottom of the Inner Pot.

Press the "Sauté" button two times to select "Normal" settings and heat the olive oil until sizzling.

Now, sauté the haddock fillets for 1 to 2 minutes per side.

Season the fish fillets with all the spices and lower them onto the rack.

Put on the pressure cooker's lid and turn the steam valve to "Sealing" position.

Press the "Steam" button two times to select "Less" option.

Use the Pressure Level button to adjust the pressure to "Low Pressure".

Once the cooking cycle is completed, quickly and carefully turn the steam release handle from Sealing position to the Venting position.

When all the steam is released, remove the pressure lid from the top carefully.

Break the fish fillets into large bite-sized pieces and divide them between the tortillas.

Add the mayonnaise, sour cream and cilantro to each tortilla.

Garnish with the remaining lemon slices and enjoy!

Per Serving: Calories 397; Fat 7.9g; Sodium 704mg; Carbs 6g; Fiber 3.6g; Sugar 6g; Protein 18g

Halibut Steaks with Wild Rice

Prep time: 15 minutes| **Cook time:** 60 minutes| **Serves:** 6

1 cup wild rice, rinsed and drained
1 tablespoon butter
½ teaspoons salt flakes
½ teaspoons red pepper flakes, crushed
1 ½ lbs. halibut steaks
2 tablespoons olive oil
Sea salt and ground pepper, to your liking
4 tablespoons cream cheese
4 tablespoons mayonnaise
1 teaspoon stone-ground mustard
2 cloves garlic, minced

In a saucepan, bring 3 cups of water and rice to a boil.

Reduce the heat to simmer; cover and let it simmer for 45 to 55 minutes.

Add the butter, salt, and red pepper; fluff with a fork. Cover and reserve, keeping your rice warm.

Cut 4 sheets of aluminum foil. Place the halibut steak in each sheet of foil.

Add the olive oil, salt, and black pepper to the top of the fish; close each packet and seal the edges.

Add 1 cup of water and a steamer rack to the bottom of your Inner Pot. Lower the packets onto the rack.

Put on the pressure cooker's lid and turn the steam valve to "Sealing" position.

Press the "Steam" button one time to select "Less" option.

Use the Pressure Level button to adjust the pressure to "Low Pressure".

Once the cooking cycle is completed, allow the steam to release naturally.

When all the steam is released, remove the pressure lid from the top carefully.

Meanwhile, mix the cream cheese, mayonnaise, stone-ground mustard, and garlic until well combined.

Serve the steamed fish with the mayo sauce and wild rice on the side. Bon appétit!

Per Serving: Calories 482; Fat 7.9g; Sodium 704mg; Carbs 6g; Fiber 3.6g; Sugar 6g; Protein 18g

Shrimp Scampi with Carrots

Prep time: 15 minutes| **Cook time:** 6 minutes| **Serves:** 4

1 tablespoon olive oil
2 garlic cloves, sliced

1 bunch scallions, chopped
2 carrots, grated
1 ½ lbs. shrimp, deveined and rinsed
½ cup dry white wine see
½ cup cream of celery soup
Sea salt and freshly cracked black pepper, to taste
1 teaspoon cayenne pepper
½ teaspoons dried basil
1 teaspoon dried rosemary
½ teaspoons dried oregano

Press the "Sauté" button two times to select "Normal" settings and then heat the oil.
Once hot, cook the garlic, scallions, and carrots for 2 to 3 minutes.
Add a splash of wine to deglaze the Inner Pot.
Add the remaining ingredients.
Put on the pressure cooker's lid and turn the steam valve to "Sealing" position.
Press the "Pressure Cook" button three times to select "Less" option.
Use the "+/-" keys on the control panel to set the cooking time to 3 minutes.
Use the Pressure Level button to adjust the pressure to "Low Pressure".
Once the cooking cycle is completed, allow the steam to release naturally.
When all the steam is released, remove the pressure lid from the top carefully.
Divide between serving bowls and enjoy!

Per Serving: Calories 412; Fat 20g; Sodium 491mg; Carbs 9g; Fiber 3g; Sugar 8g; Protein 31g

Orange Sea Bass

Prep time: 15 minutes| **Cook time:** 15 minutes| **Serves:** 4
1 tablespoon safflower oil
1-pound sea bass
Sea salt, to taste
¼ teaspoon white pepper
2 tablespoons tamari sauce
2 cloves garlic, minced
½ teaspoons dried dill weed
1 orange, juiced
1 tablespoon honey

Press the "Sauté" button two times to select "Normal" settings and heat the oil.
Now, cook the sea bass for 1 to 2 minutes per side. Season your fish with salt and pepper.
Add 1 cup of water and a steamer rack to the bottom of your Inner Pot. Lower the fish onto the rack.
Put on the pressure cooker's lid and turn the steam valve to "Sealing" position.
Press the "Steam" button three times to select "Normal" option.
Use the Pressure Level button to adjust the pressure to "Low Pressure".
Once the cooking cycle is completed, quickly and carefully turn the steam release handle from Sealing position to the Venting position.
When all the steam is released, remove the pressure lid from the top carefully.

Add the remaining ingredients to the cooking liquid and stir to combine well.
Press the "Sauté" button two times to select "Normal" settings again and let it simmer until the sauce thickens.
Spoon the sauce over the reserved fish. Bon appétit!

Per Serving: Calories 334; Fat 7.9g; Sodium 704mg; Carbs 6g; Fiber 3.6g; Sugar 6g; Protein 18g

Prawn Dipping Sauce

Prep time: 15 minutes| **Cook time:** 3 minutes| **Serves:** 8
2 cups crabmeat, flaked
1 onion, chopped
2 cloves garlic, smashed
½ cup cream cheese, softened
½ cup mayonnaise
½ cup Parmesan cheese, grated
1 ½ tablespoons cornichon, finely chopped
¼ cup tomato paste
2 or so dashes of Tabasco
½ cup fresh breadcrumbs

Place all ingredients, except for the breadcrumbs, in a baking dish.
Stir until everything is well incorporated.
Top with breadcrumbs.
Put on the pressure cooker's lid and turn the steam valve to "Sealing" position.
Press the "Steam" button three times to select "Less" option.
Use the Pressure Level button to adjust the pressure to "Low Pressure".
Once the cooking cycle is completed, quickly and carefully turn the steam release handle from Sealing position to the Venting position.
When all the steam is released, remove the pressure lid from the top carefully.
Serve with raw vegetable sticks if desired.
Bon appétit!

Per Serving: Calories 449; Fat 2.9g; Sodium 511mg; Carbs 12g; Fiber 3g; Sugar 8g; Protein 27g

Tilapia Fillets with Peppers

Prep time: 15 minutes| **Cook time:** 3 minutes| **Serves:** 4
1 lemon, sliced
4 (6-oz.) tilapia fillets, skin on
4 teaspoons olive oil
Sea salt and white pepper, to taste
1 tablespoon fresh parsley, chopped
1 tablespoon fresh tarragon, chopped
1 red onion, sliced into rings
2 sweet peppers, julienned
4 tablespoons dry white wine

Place the lemon slices, 1 cup of water, and a metal Steam Rack in the bottom of the Inner Pot.
Place 4 large sheets of heavy-duty foil on a flat surface.

Divide the ingredients between the sheets of foil.
Bring the ends of the foil together; fold in the sides to seal. Place the fish packets on the Steam Rack.
Put on the pressure cooker's lid and turn the steam valve to "Sealing" position.
Press the "Steam" button one time to select "Less" option.
Use the Pressure Level button to adjust the pressure to "Low Pressure".
Once the cooking cycle is completed, quickly and carefully turn the steam release handle from Sealing position to the Venting position. When all the steam is released, remove the pressure lid from the top carefully.
Bon appétit!

Per Serving: Calories 479; Fat 10g; Sodium 891mg; Carbs 22.9g; Fiber 4g; Sugar 4g; Protein 23g

Greek-Style Fish

Prep time: 15 minutes| **Cook time:** 3 minutes| **Serves:** 4

2 tablespoons olive oil
1 ½ lbs. cod fillets
1 pound tomatoes, chopped
Sea salt and black pepper, to taste
2 sprigs rosemary, chopped
2 sprigs thyme, chopped
1 bay leaf
2 cloves garlic, smashed
½ cup Greek olives, pitted and sliced

Place 1 cup of water and a metal Steam Rack in the bottom of the Inner Pot.
Brush the sides and bottom of a casserole dish with olive oil.
Place the cod fillets in the greased casserole dish.
Add the tomatoes, salt, pepper, rosemary, thyme, bay leaf, and garlic.
Lower the dish onto the Steam Rack.
Put on the pressure cooker's lid and turn the steam valve to "Sealing" position.
Press the "Steam" button one time to select "Less" option.
Use the Pressure Level button to adjust the pressure to "Low Pressure".
Once the cooking cycle is completed, quickly and carefully turn the steam release handle from Sealing position to the Venting position. When all the steam is released, remove the pressure lid from the top carefully.
Serve garnished with Greek olives and enjoy!

Per Serving: Calories 478; Fat 7.9g; Sodium 704mg; Carbs 6g; Fiber 3.6g; Sugar 6g; Protein 18g

French Fish En Papillote

Prep time: 15 minutes| **Cook time:** 3 minutes| **Serves:** 4

2 tablespoons olive oil

4 (7-oz.) rainbow trout fillets
1 tablespoon fresh chives, chopped
1 tablespoon fresh parsley, chopped
Sea salt and white pepper, to taste
½-pound sugar snap peas, trimmed
2 tomatillos, sliced
2 garlic cloves, minced

Place 1 cup of water and a metal rack in your Inner Pot.
Place all ingredients in a large sheet of foil.
Fold up the sides of the foil to make a bowl-like shape.
Lower the fish packet onto the rack.
Put on the pressure cooker's lid and turn the steam valve to "Sealing" position.
Press the "Steam" button one time to select "Less" option.
Use the Pressure Level button to adjust the pressure to "Low Pressure".
Once the cooking cycle is completed, quickly and carefully turn the steam release handle from Sealing position to the Venting position. When all the steam is released, remove the pressure lid from the top carefully.
Bon appétit!

Per Serving: Calories 584; Fat 15g; Sodium 441mg; Carbs 17g; Fiber 4.6g; Sugar 5g; Protein 29g

Seafood Quiche with Colby Cheese

Prep time: 15 minutes| **Cook time:** 10 minutes| **Serves:** 4

6 eggs
½ cup cream cheese
½ cup Greek-style yogurt
Himalayan salt and black pepper, to taste
1 teaspoon cayenne pepper
1 teaspoon dried basil
1 teaspoon dried oregano
1-pound crab meat, chopped
½-pound raw shrimp, chopped
1 cup Colby cheese, shredded

In a mixing bowl, whisk the eggs with the cream cheese and yogurt.
Season with salt, black pepper, cayenne pepper, basil, and oregano.
Stir in the seafood; stir to combine and spoon the mixture into a lightly greased baking pan.
Lastly, top with the shredded cheese.
Cover with a piece of aluminum foil.
Put on the pressure cooker's lid and turn the steam valve to "Sealing" position.
Press the "Steam" button one time to select "Normal" option.
Use the Pressure Level button to adjust the pressure to "Low Pressure".
Once the cooking cycle is completed, quickly and carefully turn the steam release handle from Sealing position to the Venting position. When all the steam is released, remove the pressure lid from the top carefully.
Bon appétit!

Per Serving: Calories 521; Fat 7.9g; Sodium 704mg; Carbs 6g; Fiber 3.6g; Sugar 6g; Protein 18g

Spanish Paella

Prep time: 15 minutes| **Cook time:** 6 minutes| **Serves:** 5

2 tablespoons olive oil
2 links (6-oz.) Spanish chorizo sausage, cut into slices
1 yellow onion, chopped
3 cloves garlic, minced
2 sweet peppers, sliced
1 Chiles de Árbol, minced
1 cup Arborio rice, rinsed
1 ½ lbs. shrimp, deveined
1 cup chicken broth
1 cup water
⅓ cup white wine
½ teaspoons curry paste
Sea salt and white pepper, to taste
1 cup green peas, fresh or thawed
¼ cup fresh parsley leaves, roughly chopped

Press the "Sauté" button two times to select "Normal" settings and then heat the oil until sizzling.
Cook the sausage for 2 minutes, stirring continuously to ensure even cooking.
Stir in the onions and garlic; cook for about a minute longer, stirring frequently.
Add the peppers, rice, shrimp, broth, water, wine, curry paste, salt, and white pepper.
Put on the pressure cooker's lid and turn the steam valve to "Sealing" position.
Press the "Pressure Cook" button two times to select "Less" option.
Use the "+/-" keys on the control panel to set the cooking time to 3 minutes.
Use the Pressure Level button to adjust the pressure to "High Pressure".
Once the cooking cycle is completed, quickly and carefully turn the steam release handle from Sealing position to the Venting position.
When all the steam is released, remove the pressure lid from the top carefully.
Add the green peas and seal the lid one more time; let it sit in the residual heat until warmed through.
Serve garnished with fresh parsley and enjoy!

Per Serving: Calories 397; Fat 7.9g; Sodium 704mg; Carbs 6g; Fiber 3.6g; Sugar 6g; Protein 18g

Crabs with Garlic Sauce

Prep time: 15 minutes| **Cook time:** 6 minutes| **Serves:** 5

1 ½ lbs. crabs
1 stick butter
2 cloves garlic, minced
1 teaspoon Old Bay seasoning
1 lemon, sliced

Place 1 cup water and a metal Steam Rack in the bottom of your Inner Pot.

Lower the crabs onto the Steam Rack.
Put on the pressure cooker's lid and turn the steam valve to "Sealing" position.
Press the "Steam" button two times to select "Less" option.
Use the Pressure Level button to adjust the pressure to "Low Pressure".
Once the cooking cycle is completed, quickly and carefully turn the steam release handle from Sealing position to the Venting position.
When all the steam is released, remove the pressure lid from the top carefully.
Empty the pot and keep the crab aside.
Press the "Sauté" button two times to select "Normal" settings and then melt butter.
Once hot, sauté the garlic and Old Bay seasoning for 2 to 3 minutes.
Add the cooked crabs and gently stir to combine.
Serve with lemon slices.
Bon appétit!

Per Serving: Calories 489; Fat 11g; Sodium 501mg; Carbs 8.9g; Fiber 4.6g; Sugar 8g; Protein 26g

Butter dipped Lobster Tails

Prep time: 15 minutes| **Cook time:** 3 minutes| **Serves:** 4

1 ½ lbs. lobster tails, halved
½ stick butter, at room temperature
Sea salt and black pepper, to taste
½ teaspoon red pepper flakes

Add a metal Steam Rack, steamer basket, and 1 cup of water in your Inner Pot.
Place the lobster tails, shell side down, in the prepared steamer basket.
Put on the pressure cooker's lid and turn the steam valve to "Sealing" position.
Press the "Steam" button one time to select "Less" option.
Use the Pressure Level button to adjust the pressure to "Low Pressure".
Once the cooking cycle is completed, quickly and carefully turn the steam release handle from Sealing position to the Venting position.
When all the steam is released, remove the pressure lid from the top carefully.
Empty the pot and keep the crab aside.
Drizzle with butter. Season with salt, black pepper, and red pepper and serve immediately.
Enjoy!

Per Serving: Calories 397; Fat 12.9g; Sodium 414mg; Carbs 11g; Fiber 5g; Sugar 9g; Protein 31g

Mussels in Scallion Sauce

Prep time: 15 minutes| **Cook time:** 5 minutes| **Serves:** 2

1 cup water
½ cup cooking wine
2 garlic cloves, sliced

1 ½ lbs. frozen mussels, cleaned and debearded
2 tablespoons butter
1 bunch scallion, chopped

Add the water, wine, and garlic to the Inner Pot. Add a metal rack to the Inner Pot.
Put the mussels into the steamer basket; lower the steamer basket onto the rack.
Put on the pressure cooker's lid and turn the steam valve to "Sealing" position.
Press the "Steam" button two times to select "Less" option.
Use the Pressure Level button to adjust the pressure to "Low Pressure".
Once the cooking cycle is completed, quickly and carefully turn the steam release handle from Sealing position to the Venting position.
When all the steam is released, remove the pressure lid from the top carefully.
Press the "Sauté" button two times to select "Normal" settings and add butter and scallions;
let it cook until the sauce is thoroughly heated and slightly thickened.
Press the "Cancel" button and add the mussels.
Serve warm. Bon appétit!

Per Serving: Calories 419; Fat 14g; Sodium 791mg; Carbs 8.9g; Fiber 4.6g; Sugar 8g; Protein 31g

Saucy Red Snapper

Prep time: 15 minutes| **Cook time:** 5 minutes| **Serves:** 4
1 tablespoon ghee, at room temperature
1 medium-sized leek, chopped
4 cloves garlic, minced
1 tablespoon capers
2 medium ripe tomatoes, chopped
1 cup chicken broth
1 red chili pepper, seeded and chopped
1 teaspoon basil
½ teaspoons oregano
½ teaspoons rosemary
3 (6-oz.) red snapper fillets
Coarse sea salt and black pepper, to taste
1 teaspoon Fish taco seasoning mix
1 lemon, cut into wedges

Press the "Sauté" button two times to select "Normal" settings and melt the ghee.
Once hot, sauté the leek and garlic until tender.
Add the remaining ingredients, except for the lemon wedges, to the Inner Pot.
Put on the pressure cooker's lid and turn the steam valve to "Sealing" position.
Press the "Pressure Cook" button two times to select "Less" option.
Use the "+/-" keys on the control panel to set the cooking time to 4 minutes.
Use the Pressure Level button to adjust the pressure to "High Pressure".
Once the cooking cycle is completed, quickly and carefully turn the steam release handle from Sealing position to the Venting position.

When all the steam is released, remove the pressure lid from the top carefully.
Serve in individual bowls, garnished with lemon wedges. Enjoy!

Per Serving: Calories 472; Fat 7.9g; Sodium 704mg; Carbs 6g; Fiber 3.6g; Sugar 6g; Protein 18g

Shrimp Salad

Prep time: 15 minutes| **Cook time:** 3 minutes| **Serves:** 4
1-pound shrimp, deveined
Kosher salt and white pepper, to taste
1 onion, thinly sliced
1 sweet pepper, thinly sliced
1 jalapeno pepper, deseeded and minced
2 heaping tablespoons fresh parsley, chopped
1 head romaine lettuce, torn into pieces
4 tablespoons olive oil
1 lime, juiced and zested
1 tablespoon Dijon mustard

Add a metal Steam Rack and 1 cup of water to your Inner Pot.
Put the shrimp into the steamer basket. Lower the steamer basket onto the Steam Rack.
Put on the pressure cooker's lid and turn the steam valve to "Sealing" position.
Press the "Steam" button one time to select "Less" option.
Use the Pressure Level button to adjust the pressure to "Low Pressure".
Once the cooking cycle is completed, quickly and carefully turn the steam release handle from Sealing position to the Venting position.
When all the steam is released, remove the pressure lid from the top carefully.
Transfer steamed shrimp to a salad bowl; toss your shrimp with the remaining ingredients.
Serve well chilled. Bon appétit!

Per Serving: Calories 461; Fat 7.9g; Sodium 704mg; Carbs 6g; Fiber 3.6g; Sugar 6g; Protein 18g

Crab Sliders

Prep time: 15 minutes| **Cook time:** 3 minutes| **Serves:** 4
10 oz. crabmeat
4 heaping tablespoons fresh chives, chopped
2 garlic cloves, minced
½ cup mayonnaise
½ teaspoons hot sauce
1 teaspoon Old Bay seasoning
½ cup celery stalk, chopped
1 tablespoon fresh lime juice
8 mini slider rolls
2 cups Iceberg lettuce, torn into pieces

Add 1 cup of water, metal Steam Rack, and a steamer basket to your Inner Pot.
Place the crabmeat in the prepared steamer basket.
Put on the pressure cooker's lid and turn the steam valve to "Sealing" position.

Press the "Steam" button one time to select "Less" option.
Use the Pressure Level button to adjust the pressure to "Low Pressure".
Once the cooking cycle is completed, quickly and carefully turn the steam release handle from Sealing position to the Venting position.
When all the steam is released, remove the pressure lid from the top carefully.
Add the chives, garlic, mayo, hot sauce, Old Bay seasoning, celery, and lime juice; stir to combine well.
Divide the mixture between slider rolls and garnish with lettuce.
Serve and enjoy!

Per Serving: Calories 407; Fat 19g; Sodium 354mg; Carbs 15g; Fiber 5.1g; Sugar 8.2g; Protein 32g

Vietnamese-Fish

Prep time: 15 minutes| **Cook time:** 10 minutes| **Serves:** 4
2 tablespoons coconut oil, melted
¼ cup brown sugar
2 tablespoons fish sauce
2 tablespoons soy sauce
1 (1-inch) ginger root, grated
Juice of ½ lime
Sea salt and white pepper, to taste
1 cup chicken broth
4 (7-oz.) sea bass fillets
2 tablespoons fresh chives, chopped

Press the "Sauté" button two times to select "Normal" settings and then heat the coconut oil.
Once hot, cook the brown sugar, fish sauce, soy sauce, ginger, lime, salt, white pepper, and broth.
Bring to a simmer and press the "Cancel" button. Add sea bass.
Put on the pressure cooker's lid and turn the steam valve to "Sealing" position.
Press the "Pressure Cook" button two times to select "Less" option.
Use the "+/-" keys on the control panel to set the cooking time to 4 minutes.
Use the Pressure Level button to adjust the pressure to "High Pressure".
Once the cooking cycle is completed, quickly and carefully turn the steam release handle from Sealing position to the Venting position.
When all the steam is released, remove the pressure lid from the top carefully.
Remove the sea bass fillets from the cooking liquid.
Press the "Sauté" button two times to select "Normal" settings.
Reduce the sauce until it is thick and syrupy.
Spoon the sauce over the reserved sea bass fillets.
Garnish with fresh chives.
Bon appétit!

Per Serving: Calories 403; Fat 10.9g; Sodium 354mg; Carbs 10.5g; Fiber 4.1g; Sugar 8.2g; Protein 26g

Fish and Couscous Pilaf

Prep time: 15 minutes| **Cook time:** 10 minutes| **Serves:** 4
2 tablespoons butter
1 yellow onion, chopped
2 cups couscous
2 cups water
1 cup vegetable broth
1 cup coconut milk
Sea salt and black pepper, to taste
1 teaspoon cayenne pepper
1 teaspoon dried basil
2 ripe tomatoes, pureed
1 ½ lbs. halibut, cut into chunks
1 teaspoon coriander
1 teaspoon curry paste
1 teaspoon ancho chili powder
2 bay leaves
4 cardamom pods
1 teaspoon garam masala
2 tablespoons almonds, slivered

Press the "Sauté" button two times to select "Normal" settings and melt the butter.
Once hot, cook the onions until tender and translucent.
Add the remaining ingredients, except for the slivered almonds, to the Inner Pot; stir to combine.
Put on the pressure cooker's lid and turn the steam valve to "Sealing" position.
Press the "Pressure Cook" button two times to select "Less" option.
Use the "+/-" keys on the control panel to set the cooking time to 4 minutes.
Use the Pressure Level button to adjust the pressure to "High Pressure".
Once the cooking cycle is completed, quickly and carefully turn the steam release handle from Sealing position to the Venting position.
When all the steam is released, remove the pressure lid from the top carefully.
Serve garnished with almonds.
Bon appétit!

Per Serving: Calories 382; Fat 7.9g; Sodium 704mg; Carbs 6g; Fiber 3.6g; Sugar 6g; Protein 18g

Salmon on Croissants

Prep time: 15 minutes| **Cook time:** 3 minutes| **Serves:** 2
1 ½ lbs. salmon fillets
1 red onion, thinly sliced
¼ cup prepared horseradish, drained
¼ cup mayonnaise
2 tablespoons sour cream
Salt and white pepper, to taste
½ teaspoons red pepper flakes, crushed
½ teaspoons dried rosemary, only leaves crushed
½ teaspoons dried oregano
1 cup cherry tomatoes, halved
2 cups Iceberg lettuce leaves, torn into pieces
6 croissants, split

Add 1 cup of water and metal Steam Rack to the Inner Pot.
Lower the salmon fillets onto the Steam Rack.
Put on the pressure cooker's lid and turn the steam valve to "Sealing" position.
Press the "Steam" button two times to select "Less" option.
Use the Pressure Level button to adjust the pressure to "Low Pressure".
Once the cooking cycle is completed, quickly and carefully turn the steam release handle from Sealing position to the Venting position.
When all the steam is released, remove the pressure lid from the top carefully.
Add the remaining ingredients and stir to combine well.
Place in your refrigerator until ready to serve.
Serve on croissants and enjoy!

Per Serving: Calories 412; Fat 20g; Sodium 491mg; Carbs 9g; Fiber 3g; Sugar 8g; Protein 31g

Tuna Steaks in Lime- Sauce

Prep time: 15 minutes| **Cook time:** 4 minutes| **Serves:** 3
3 tuna steaks
1 ½ tablespoons sesame oil, melted
½ teaspoons salt
¼ teaspoon black pepper, to taste
¼ teaspoon smoked paprika
1 cup water
1 tablespoon fresh cilantro, chopped
For the Sauce:
1 tablespoon butter, at room temperature
1 tablespoon fresh lime juice
1 teaspoon Worcestershire sauce

Brush the tuna steaks with sesame oil.
Season the tuna steaks with salt, black pepper, and smoked paprika.
Place the fish in the steaming basket; transfer it to the Inner Pot.
Pour 1 cup of water into the base of your Inner Pot.
Put on the pressure cooker's lid and turn the steam valve to "Sealing" position.
Press the "Pressure Cook" button two times to select "Less" option.
Use the "+/-" keys on the control panel to set the cooking time to 4 minutes.
Use the Pressure Level button to adjust the pressure to "Low Pressure".
Once the cooking cycle is completed, quickly and carefully turn the steam release handle from Sealing position to the Venting position.
When all the steam is released, remove the pressure lid from the top carefully.
Meanwhile, warm the butter over medium-low heat.
Add the lime juice and Worcestershire sauce; remove from the heat and stir.
Spoon the sauce over the tuna steaks, sprinkle with fresh cilantro leaves and serve.
Bon appétit!

Per Serving: Calories 471; Fat 10.9g; Sodium 454mg; Carbs 10g; Fiber 3.1g; Sugar 5.2g; Protein 20g

Beer-Steamed Mussels

Prep time: 15 minutes| **Cook time:** 5 minutes| **Serves:** 4
1 tablespoon olive oil
½ cup scallions, chopped
2 cloves garlic, minced
2 medium-sized ripe tomatoes, puréed
1 (12-oz.) bottles lager beer
1 cup water
1 tablespoon fresh cilantro, chopped
Sea salt and black pepper, to taste
2 Thai chili peppers, stemmed and split
1 ½ lbs. mussels, cleaned and debearded

Directions
Press the "Sauté" button two times to select "Normal" settings.
Heat the oil and cook the scallions until tender and fragrant.
Then, stir in the garlic and cook an additional 30 seconds or until fragrant.
Add the remaining ingredients.
Put on the pressure cooker's lid and turn the steam valve to "Sealing" position.
Press the "Pressure Cook" button two times to select "Less" option.
Use the "+/-" keys on the control panel to set the cooking time to 3 minutes.
Use the Pressure Level button to adjust the pressure to "Low Pressure".
Once the cooking cycle is completed, quickly and carefully turn the steam release handle from Sealing position to the Venting position.
When all the steam is released, remove the pressure lid from the top carefully.
Serve with garlic croutons.
Bon appétit!

Per Serving: Calories 384; Fat 7.9g; Sodium 704mg; Carbs 6g; Fiber 3.6g; Sugar 6g; Protein 18g

Fish Paprikash

Prep time: 15 minutes| **Cook time:** 7 minutes| **Serves:** 4
2 tablespoons butter, at room temperature
1 cup leeks, chopped
2 bell peppers, seeded and sliced
2 garlic cloves, minced
2 sprigs thyme
1 sprig rosemary
1 teaspoon sweet paprika
1 teaspoon hot paprika
Sea salt and black pepper, to taste
2 tomatoes, puréed
2 cups vegetable broth
2 cups water
1 ½ lbs. cod fish, cut into bite-sized chunks
2 tablespoons fresh cilantro, roughly chopped
1 cup sour cream, well-chilled

Press the "Sauté" button two times to select "Normal" settings.

Melt the butter and sauté the leeks until fragrant.

Then, stir in the peppers and garlic and continue to sauté an additional 40 seconds.

Add the thyme, rosemary, paprika, salt, black pepper, tomatoes, broth, water, and fish.

Put on the pressure cooker's lid and turn the steam valve to "Sealing" position.

Press the "Pressure Cook" button two times to select "Less" option.

Use the "+/-" keys on the control panel to set the cooking time to 6 minutes.

Use the Pressure Level button to adjust the pressure to "High Pressure".

Once the cooking cycle is completed, quickly and carefully turn the steam release handle from Sealing position to the Venting position. When all the steam is released, remove the pressure lid from the top carefully.

Ladle into individual bowls and serve garnished with fresh cilantro and well-chilled sour cream.

Bon appétit!

Per Serving: Calories 472; Fat 12.9g; Sodium 414mg; Carbs 11g; Fiber 5g; Sugar 9g; Protein 31g

Mahi-Mahi Fish with Guacamole

Prep time: 15 minutes| **Cook time:** 5 minutes| **Serves:** 4

1 cup water
4 mahi-mahi fillets
2 tablespoons olive oil
Sea salt and black pepper, to taste
½ teaspoons red pepper flakes, crushed
½ cup shallots, sliced
2 tablespoons fresh lemon juice
1 teaspoon epazote
¼ cup fresh coriander, chopped
1 teaspoon dried sage
For Cumin Guacamole:
2 medium tomatoes, chopped
1 large avocado, peeled, pitted and mashed
2 tablespoons salsa Verde
1 clove garlic, minced
Fresh juice of 1 lime
Sea salt to taste

Pour 1 cup of water to the base of your Inner Pot.

Brush the mahi-mahi fillets with olive oil; then, sprinkle with salt, black pepper, and red pepper flakes.

Place the mahi-mahi fillets in the steaming basket; transfer it to the Inner Pot.

Add the shallots on top; add the lemon juice, epazote, coriander, and sage.

Put on the pressure cooker's lid and turn the steam valve to "Sealing" position.

Press the "Pressure Cook" button two times to select "Less" option.

Use the "+/-" keys on the control panel to set the cooking time to 3 minutes.

Use the Pressure Level button to adjust the pressure to "Low Pressure".

Once the cooking cycle is completed, quickly and carefully turn the steam release handle from Sealing position to the Venting position. When all the steam is released, remove the pressure lid from the top carefully.

Next, mix all ingredients for the cumin guacamole; place in your refrigerator for at least 20 minutes.

Serve the mahi-mahi fillets with fresh cumin guacamole on the side.

Bon appétit!

Per Serving: Calories 478; Fat 7.9g; Sodium 704mg; Carbs 6g; Fiber 3.6g; Sugar 6g; Protein 18g

Halibut Steaks with Tomatoes

Prep time: 15 minutes| **Cook time:** 5 minutes| **Serves:** 4

2 tablespoons Worcestershire sauce
2 tablespoons oyster sauce
½ cup dry white wine
1 tablespoon Dijon mustard
1 (1-inch) piece fresh ginger, grated
4 halibut steaks
2 teaspoons olive oil
2 tomatoes, sliced
2 spring onions, sliced
2 garlic cloves, crushed
1 cup mixed salad greens, to serve

In a mixing bowl, whisk Worcestershire sauce, oyster sauce, white wine, mustard, and ginger.

Add the fish steaks and let them marinate for 30 minutes in your refrigerator.

Meanwhile, Press the "Sauté" button two times to select "Normal" settings on your Inner Pot.

Now, heat the olive oil and sauté the tomatoes with the spring onions and garlic until they are tender.

Add 2 cups of water to the base of your Inner Pot. Add the metal steamer insert to the Inner Pot.

Now, place the halibut steaks on top of the steamer insert.

Put on the pressure cooker's lid and turn the steam valve to "Sealing" position.

Press the "Pressure Cook" button two times to select "Less" option.

Use the "+/-" keys on the control panel to set the cooking time to 5 minutes.

Use the Pressure Level button to adjust the pressure to "Low Pressure".

Once the cooking cycle is completed, quickly and carefully turn the steam release handle from Sealing position to the Venting position. When all the steam is released, remove the pressure lid from the top carefully.

Serve the warm halibut steaks with the sautéed vegetables and mixed salad greens. Enjoy!

Per Serving: Calories 334; Fat 7.9g; Sodium 704mg; Carbs 6g; Fiber 3.6g; Sugar 6g; Protein 18g

Mayo Shrimp Salad

Prep time: 15 minutes| **Cook time:** 2 minutes| **Serves:** 4

1-pound shrimp, deveined and peeled
Fresh juice of 2 lemons
Salt and black pepper, to taste
1 red onion, chopped
1 stalk celery, chopped
1 tablespoon fresh dill, minced
½ cup mayonnaise
1 teaspoon Dijon mustard

Prepare your Inner Pot by adding 1 cup of water and steamer basket to the Inner Pot.
Now, add the shrimp to the steamer basket.
Top with lemon slices.
Put on the pressure cooker's lid and turn the steam valve to "Sealing" position.
Press the "Pressure Cook" button two times to select "Less" option.
Use the "+/-" keys on the control panel to set the cooking time to 2 minutes.
Use the Pressure Level button to adjust the pressure to "Low Pressure".
Once the cooking cycle is completed, quickly and carefully turn the steam release handle from Sealing position to the Venting position.
When all the steam is released, remove the pressure lid from the top carefully.
Add the remaining ingredients and toss to combine well.
Serve well chilled and enjoy!

Per Serving: Calories 489; Fat 11g; Sodium 501mg; Carbs 8.9g; Fiber 4.6g; Sugar 8g; Protein 26g

Risotto with Sea Bass

Prep time: 15 minutes| **Cook time:** 8 minutes| **Serves:** 4

2 tablespoons butter, melted
½ cup leeks, sliced
2 garlic cloves, minced
2 cups basmati rice
1 ½ lbs. sea bass fillets, diced
2 cups vegetable broth
1 cup water
Salt, to taste
½ teaspoon black pepper
1 teaspoon fresh ginger, grated

Press the "Sauté" button two times to select "Normal" settings.
Then, melt the butter and sweat the leeks for 2 to 3 minutes.
Stir in the garlic; continue to sauté an additional 40 seconds. Add the remaining ingredients.
Put on the pressure cooker's lid and turn the steam valve to "Sealing" position.
Press the "Pressure Cook" button two times to select "Less" option.
Use the "+/-" keys on the control panel to set the cooking time to 4 minutes.
Use the Pressure Level button to adjust the pressure to "Low Pressure".

Once the cooking cycle is completed, quickly and carefully turn the steam release handle from Sealing position to the Venting position.
When all the steam is released, remove the pressure lid from the top carefully.
Serve warm in individual bowls and enjoy!

Per Serving: Calories 449; Fat 2.9g; Sodium 511mg; Carbs 12g; Fiber 3g; Sugar 8g; Protein 27g

Fish Mélange

Prep time: 15 minutes| **Cook time:** 10 minutes| **Serves:** 4

1 tablespoon olive oil
2 shallots, diced
2 garlic cloves, smashed
2 carrots, diced
2 (6-oz.) cans crab, juice reserved
½-pound cod, cut into bite-sized chunks
Sea salt, to taste
½ teaspoons black pepper
2 bay leaves
1 tablespoon Creole seasoning
2 cups water
1 cup double cream
1 tablespoon lemon juice

Press the "Sauté" button two times to select "Normal" settings.
Then, heat the oil and sauté the shallots until tender.
Stir in the garlic and carrots; cook an additional minute or so.
Add the canned crab meat, cod, salt, black pepper, bay leaves, Creole seasoning, and water.
Put on the pressure cooker's lid and turn the steam valve to "Sealing" position.
Press the "Pressure Cook" button two times to select "Less" option.
Use the "+/-" keys on the control panel to set the cooking time to 6 minutes.
Use the Pressure Level button to adjust the pressure to "High Pressure".
Once the cooking cycle is completed, quickly and carefully turn the steam release handle from Sealing position to the Venting position.
When all the steam is released, remove the pressure lid from the top carefully.
Lastly, stir in the double cream and lemon juice.
Press the "Sauté" button two times to select "Normal" settings; let it simmer until heated through.
Enjoy!

Per Serving: Calories 521; Fat 19g; Sodium 354mg; Carbs 15g; Fiber 5.1g; Sugar 8.2g; Protein 32g

Fish Burritos

Prep time: 15 minutes| **Cook time:** 10 minutes| **Serves:** 4

2 tablespoons olive oil
4 catfish fillets

Sea salt to taste
⅓ teaspoon black pepper, to taste
½ teaspoons cayenne pepper
½ teaspoons ground bay leaf
1 teaspoon dried thyme
4 burrito-sized tortillas
1 cup fresh salsa
1 large-sized tomato, sliced

Directions
Prepare your Inner Pot by adding 1 ½ cups of water and a metal rack to its bottom.
Place the fish fillets in the center of a foil sheet.
Drizzle olive oil over the fish.
Season with salt, black pepper, cayenne pepper, ground bay leaf and dried thyme.
Wrap tightly and lower it onto the rack.
Put on the pressure cooker's lid and turn the steam valve to "Sealing" position.
Press the "Pressure Cook" button two times to select "Less" option.
Use the "+/-" keys on the control panel to set the cooking time to 10 minutes.
Use the Pressure Level button to adjust the pressure to "High Pressure".
Once the cooking cycle is completed, allow the steam to release naturally.
When all the steam is released, remove the pressure lid from the top carefully.
Divide the fish fillets among tortillas.
Top it with the salsa and tomatoes.
Roll each tortilla into a burrito and serve immediately.

Per Serving: Calories 380; Fat 7.9g; Sodium 704mg; Carbs 6g; Fiber 3.6g; Sugar 6g; Protein 18g

Saucy Clams

Prep time: 15 minutes| **Cook time:** 10 minutes| **Serves:** 4
½ cup bacon, smoked and cubed
2 onions, chopped
3 garlic cloves, minced
1 sprig thyme
3 (5-oz.) cans clams, chopped
⅓ cup tarty white wine
⅓ cup water
½ cup clam juice
A pinch of cayenne pepper
1 bay leaf
5 lime juice
2 tablespoons fresh chives, roughly chopped

Press the "Sauté" button two times to select "Normal" settings.
Add the cubed bacon. Once your bacon releases its fat, add the onions, garlic, and thyme.
Cook for 3 minutes more or until the onion is transparent.

Add the clams, white wine, water, clam juice, cayenne pepper, and bay leaf.
Put on the pressure cooker's lid and turn the steam valve to "Sealing" position.
Press the "Pressure Cook" button two times to select "Less" option.
Use the "+/-" keys on the control panel to set the cooking time to 4 minutes.
Use the Pressure Level button to adjust the pressure to "Low Pressure".
Once the cooking cycle is completed, allow the steam to release naturally.
When all the steam is released, remove the pressure lid from the top carefully.
Ladle into individual bowls and serve garnished with lime slices and fresh chives.
Bon appétit!

Per Serving: Calories 584; Fat 15g; Sodium 441mg; Carbs 17g; Fiber 4.6g; Sugar 5g; Protein 29g

Sole Fillets with Pickle

Prep time: 15 minutes| **Cook time:** 3 minutes| **Serves:** 4
1 ½ lbs. sole fillets
Sea salt and black pepper, to taste
1 teaspoon paprika
½ cup mayonnaise
1 tablespoon pickle juice
2 cloves garlic, smashed

Sprinkle the fillets with salt, black pepper, and paprika.
Add 1 ½ cups of water and a steamer basket to the Inner Pot. Place the fish in the steamer basket.
Put on the pressure cooker's lid and turn the steam valve to "Sealing" position.
Press the "Pressure Cook" button two times to select "Less" option.
Use the "+/-" keys on the control panel to set the cooking time to 3 minutes.
Use the Pressure Level button to adjust the pressure to "Low Pressure".
Once the cooking cycle is completed, quickly and carefully turn the steam release handle from Sealing position to the Venting position.
When all the steam is released, remove the pressure lid from the top carefully.
Then, make the sauce by mixing the mayonnaise with the pickle juice and garlic.
Serve the fish fillets with the well-chilled sauce on the side.
Bon appétit!

Per Serving: Calories 382; Fat 7.9g; Sodium 704mg; Carbs 6g; Fiber 3.6g; Sugar 6g; Protein 18g

Black Bean Soup with Avocado Salsa

Prep time: 15 minutes| **Cook time:** 35 minutes| **Serves:** 6-8

2 poblano peppers
2 tablespoons plus 1 teaspoon olive oil
1 large yellow onion, finely diced, ¼ cup reserved
1 bell pepper, finely diced
5 garlic cloves, minced
2 teaspoons ground cumin
2 teaspoons chili powder
1 teaspoon dried oregano
1 pound dried black beans, rinsed and picked over (discard any bad beans)
1 bay leaf
7 cups vegetable broth (try the recipe here)
Kosher salt
Black pepper
2 medium avocados, peeled, pitted, diced
1 tablespoon lime juice
1 large tomato or 2 small tomatoes, chopped
2 tablespoons chopped cilantro
1 lime, halved

Preheat the oven.
Rub the poblanos with 1 teaspoon of oil. Broil until blistered on all sides.
Once cool enough to handle, slide off any loose skin, remove the stem and seeds, and chop the poblanos.
Press the "Sauté" button two times to select "Normal" mode.
Once hot, add the remaining 2 tablespoons of oil followed by all but ¼ cup of the onion, the bell pepper, and the garlic.
Stir and cook for about 3 minutes, until the onion softens.
Add the roasted poblano, cumin, chili powder, and oregano. Stir and cook for 1 minute.
Add the beans, bay leaf, and broth, and season with salt and pepper.
Put on the pressure cooker's lid and turn the steam valve to "Sealing" position.
Press the "Pressure Cook" button two times to select "Normal" option.
Use the "+/-" keys on the control panel to set the cooking time to 30 minutes.
Use the Pressure Level button to adjust the pressure to "High Pressure".
Meanwhile, in a medium bowl, combine the avocados, tomato, the reserved ¼ cup of diced onion, the cilantro, and a squeeze of lime juice. Season with salt and pepper.
Once the cooking cycle is completed, allow the steam to release naturally.
When all the steam is released, remove the pressure lid from the top carefully.
Remove the bay leaf.
Add the remaining lime juice to the pot. The liquid will thicken upon standing.
If desired, purée up to half of the soup with an immersion blender or in a countertop blender.
Serve hot, topped with avocado salsa.

Per Serving: Calories 419; Fat 14g; Sodium 791mg; Carbs 8.9g; Fiber 4.6g; Sugar 8g; Protein 31g

Tomato Soup

Prep time: 15 minutes| **Cook time:** 25 minutes| **Serves:** 4

2 tablespoons olive oil
1 large red onion, chopped
1 large carrot, peeled and chopped
3 garlic cloves, smashed
3 lbs. ripe tomatoes, chopped
1 teaspoon sugar
1 tablespoon tomato paste
¾ cup vegetable or chicken broth
Kosher salt
Black pepper
⅓ cup heavy cream
Fresh basil, for garnish
Parmesan cheese, for garnish

Press the "Sauté" button two times to select "Normal" mode.
Once hot, add the oil followed by the onion and carrot.
Cook for 6 to 7 minutes, until the onion is translucent. Add the garlic and cook for 2 minutes more.
Add the tomatoes, sugar, tomato paste, and broth. Season with salt and pepper.
Put on the pressure cooker's lid and turn the steam valve to "Sealing" position.
Press the "Pressure Cook" button two times to select "Less" option.
Use the "+/-" keys on the control panel to set the cooking time to 15 minutes.
Use the Pressure Level button to adjust the pressure to "High Pressure".
Once the cooking cycle is completed, allow the steam to release naturally for 10 minutes, then turn the steam release handle to the Venting position.
When all the steam is released, remove the pressure lid from the top carefully.
Add the cream. Use an immersion blender to purée the soup or carefully purée in batches in a blender.
If there are chunks of peel and they bother you, strain the soup or run it through a food mill.
Add more broth if a thinner soup is desired.
Taste for seasoning. Serve topped with fresh basil and Parmesan.

Per Serving: Calories 479; Fat 10g; Sodium 891mg; Carbs 22.9g; Fiber 4g; Sugar 4g; Protein 23g

Cauliflower and Potato Soup

Prep time: 15 minutes| **Cook time:** 10 minutes| **Serves:** 4

1 tablespoon olive oil
1 medium yellow onion, diced

3 garlic cloves, smashed
1 medium cauliflower head, broken into large florets
1 pound Yukon Gold potatoes, peeled and cut into ½-inch cubes
4 cups vegetable or chicken broth
Kosher salt
Black pepper
1 cup whole milk or half-and-half
1 cup shredded sharp Cheddar cheese

Press the "Sauté" button two times to select "Normal" mode
Once hot, add the oil followed by the onion and garlic.
Stir and cook for about 3 minutes, until the onion begins to turn translucent.
Add the cauliflower, potatoes, and broth.
Season with salt and pepper.
Put on the pressure cooker's lid and turn the steam valve to "Sealing" position.
Press the "Pressure Cook" button two times to select "Less" option.
Use the "+/-" keys on the control panel to set the cooking time to 5 minutes.
Use the Pressure Level button to adjust the pressure to "High Pressure".
Once the cooking cycle is completed, allow the steam to release naturally for 10 minutes, then turn the steam release handle to the Venting position.
When all the steam is released, remove the pressure lid from the top carefully.
Add the milk or half-and-half and ½ cup of cheese.
Blend until smooth using an immersion blender.
Add more broth if you want a thinner soup.
Taste for seasoning. Serve topped with a sprinkle of the remaining Cheddar.

Per Serving: Calories 479; Fat 10g; Sodium 891mg; Carbs 22.9g; Fiber 4g; Sugar 4g; Protein 3g

Broccoli and Leek Soup

Prep time: 15 minutes| **Cook time:** 15 minutes| **Serves:** 4
4 tablespoons butter
2 large leeks, soaked, rinsed, and chopped
3 garlic cloves, smashed
1½ lbs. broccoli, cut into florets
3 cups vegetable or chicken broth
Kosher salt
Black pepper
2 pinches red pepper flakes
3 tablespoons all-purpose flour
1 cup milk
¼ cup grated Parmesan cheese, plus more for garnish

Press the "Sauté" button two times to select "Normal" mode
Once hot, add 1 tablespoon of butter.
Once melted, add the leeks and garlic and sauté for 5 minutes, or until the leeks are translucent.

Add the broccoli and broth, and season with salt and pepper. Add the red pepper flakes.
Put on the pressure cooker's lid and turn the steam valve to "Sealing" position.
Press the "Pressure Cook" button two times to select "Less" option.
Use the "+/-" keys on the control panel to set the cooking time to 6 minutes.
Use the Pressure Level button to adjust the pressure to "High Pressure".
Once the cooking cycle is completed, allow the steam to release naturally.
When all the steam is released, remove the pressure lid from the top carefully.
Meanwhile, in a small saucepan over medium-high heat, melt the remaining 3 tablespoons of butter on the stove.
Whisk in the flour, followed by the milk. Cook, stirring, until thick and bubbly.
Add the Parmesan. Purée the broccoli and broth using an immersion blender or countertop blender.
Return the broccoli mixture to the pot and add the milk mixture, stirring well.
Press the "Sauté" button two times to select "Normal" mode to reheat the soup.
Serve in bowls with a sprinkling of Parmesan on top.

Per Serving: Calories 380; Fat 10.9g; Sodium 454mg; Carbs 10g; Fiber 3.1g; Sugar 5.2g; Protein 20g

Matzo Ball Soup

Prep time: 15 minutes| **Cook time:** 25 minutes| **Serves:** 4
1 cup matzo meal
⅛ teaspoon baking powder
1½ teaspoons kosher salt, plus more for seasoning
¼ teaspoon black pepper, plus more for seasoning
Pinch ground nutmeg
4 eggs
5¼ cups water
¼ cup canola or vegetable oil
1 bone-in, skin-on chicken breast
1 bay leaf
6 cups homemade chicken broth (try the recipe here)
1 large carrot, finely diced
2 celery stalks, finely diced
1 tablespoon chopped fresh dill

In a small bowl, combine the matzo meal, baking powder, 1 teaspoon of salt, pepper, and nutmeg.
In a medium bowl, beat together the eggs, ¼ cup of water, and the oil.
Add the matzo mixture and mix well.
Add 1 tablespoon more matzo meal. Chill in the refrigerator for at least 30 minutes.
Meanwhile, add the chicken, 3 cups of water, the remaining ½ teaspoon salt, and the bay leaf to the Instant Pot.
Put on the pressure cooker's lid and turn the steam valve to "Sealing" position.

Press the "Pressure Cook" button two times to select "Less" option.
Use the "+/-" keys on the control panel to set the cooking time to 10 minutes.
Use the Pressure Level button to adjust the pressure to "High Pressure".
Once the cooking cycle is completed, quickly and carefully turn the steam release handle from Sealing position to the Venting position.
When all the steam is released, remove the pressure lid from the top carefully.
Remove the chicken and set aside. Remove the bay leaf and discard.
Add water until the liquid in the Instant Pot reaches 5 cups (about 2 cups more water).
Using a spoon and wet hands, form the matzo ball mixture into walnut-size balls (about 2 tablespoons).
As you form them, set them on a plate. Once all of the balls are formed, add them to the pot.
Make sure the balls are all separated without disturbing them too much.
Select Pressure Cook and cook at High Pressure for 10 minutes.
Meanwhile, in a large pot on the stove, heat the broth to a low simmer.
Add the carrot and celery and cook for 5 minutes. Season with salt and pepper and turn the heat to low.
Bone the chicken and discard the skin. Shred the meat.
Once the pressure cooking is complete, release the pressure naturally.
Ladle the broth and veggies into bowls and add the chicken.
Add 2 to 3 matzo balls per bowl and top with fresh dill.

Per Serving: Calories 419; Fat 14g; Sodium 791mg; Carbs 8.9g; Fiber 4.6g; Sugar 8g; Protein 3g

Chicken Noodle Soup

Prep time: 15 minutes| **Cook time:** 20 minutes| **Serves:** 4
2 tablespoons canola oil
2 medium yellow onions, halved
1 (2-inch) piece ginger, cut into ¼-inch slices
1 tablespoon coriander seeds
3 star anise pods
5 cloves
1 cinnamon stick
3 cardamom pods, lightly smashed
6 bone-in, skin-on chicken thighs
3 tablespoons fish sauce
1 tablespoon sugar
8 cups water
Kosher salt
Black pepper
4 servings rice noodles, cooked
Toppings
3 scallions, sliced
1 small handful fresh herbs, chopped
1 lime, cut into wedges
Handful of bean sprouts
1 jalapeño, thinly sliced

Press the "Sauté" button two times to select "More" mode
Once hot, add the oil to the pot. Add the onions, cut-side down, and the ginger.
Cook, without moving, until charred for 4 minutes.
Add the coriander, star anise, cloves, cinnamon stick, and cardamom.
Stir and cook for 1 minute more.
Add the chicken, fish sauce, and sugar and immediately pour over the water.
Put on the pressure cooker's lid and turn the steam valve to "Sealing" position.
Press the "Pressure Cook" button two times to select "Less" option.
Use the "+/-" keys on the control panel to set the cooking time to 15 minutes.
Use the Pressure Level button to adjust the pressure to "High Pressure".
Once the cooking cycle is completed, allow the steam to release naturally for 10 minutes, then turn the steam release handle to the Venting position.
When all the steam is released, remove the pressure lid from the top carefully.
Remove the chicken from the pot and carefully strain the broth. Season with salt and pepper as desired.
Place the cooked noodles in 4 bowls.
When the chicken is cool enough to handle, pick the meat off the bones and add to the bowls.
Pour over the broth and top with scallions, herbs, lime, and bean sprouts and jalapeño.

Per Serving: Calories 461; Fat 12.9g; Sodium 414mg; Carbs 11g; Fiber 5g; Sugar 9g; Protein 31g

French Onion Soup

Prep time: 20 minutes| **Cook time:** 15 minutes| **Serves:** 4
5 tablespoons butter
2 lbs. yellow onions, cut into ⅛-inch slices
Kosher salt
Black pepper
Pinch sugar
½ cup dry white wine
6 cups beef or chicken broth
2 fresh thyme sprigs
1 loaf French bread, cut into ¾-inch slices and toasted
1 cup grated Gruyère cheese

Press the "Sauté" button two times to select "Normal" mode.
Add and heat the butter.
Once the butter has melted, add the onions and stir.
Cover loosely with the lid and cook, stirring occasionally, until translucent, about 15 minutes.
Lower the heat to low. Season with salt and pepper and add the sugar.
Cook, stirring frequently, until the onions turn golden brown and become translucent, about 10 minutes.
Raise the heat back to medium. Add the wine.

Add the broth and thyme and season with salt and pepper.
Put on the pressure cooker's lid and turn the steam valve to "Sealing" position.
Press the "Pressure Cook" button two times to select "Less" option.
Use the "+/-" keys on the control panel to set the cooking time to 6 minutes.
Use the Pressure Level button to adjust the pressure to "High Pressure".
Once the cooking cycle is completed, quickly and carefully turn the steam release handle from Sealing position to the Venting position.
When all the steam is released, remove the pressure lid from the top carefully.
Preheat the oven.
Spoon the soup into ovenproof bowls and top with toasted bread.
Sprinkle the top with cheese and place under the broiler for 5 to 7 minutes until the cheese is bubbly.

Per Serving: Calories 479; Fat 10g; Sodium 891mg; Carbs 22.9g; Fiber 4g; Sugar 4g; Protein 3g

Butternut Squash Soup

Prep time: 20 minutes| **Cook time:** 21 minutes| **Serves:** 4
2 tablespoons olive oil
8 fresh sage leaves
10 oz. uncooked Italian-style pork or chicken sausage, without casing
½ large yellow onion, chopped
2 small celery stalks, chopped
2 large garlic cloves, smashed
1 medium butternut squash, peeled, seeded, and cut into 1-inch cubes (about 4 cups)
2 cups chicken or vegetable broth, plus more as needed
½ teaspoon baking soda
Kosher salt
Black pepper
½ cup heavy cream or half-and-half
Pinch ground nutmeg

Press the "Sauté" button two times to select "More" mode.
Once hot, add the oil followed by the sage leaves. Fry for 2 to 3 minutes until crispy. Remove and drain on a paper towel.
Add the sausage. Use a spoon or spatula to break up the sausage into small pieces as it cooks.
Continue until the sausage is cooked through. Use a slotted spoon to transfer the sausage to a plate.
Add the onion to the pot and cook for 1 minute.
Add the celery and garlic and cook, stirring occasionally, for about 3 minutes.
Add the squash, broth, and baking soda and stir. Season with salt and pepper.
Put on the pressure cooker's lid and turn the steam valve to "Sealing" position.
Press the "Pressure Cook" button two times to select "Less" option.

Use the "+/-" keys on the control panel to set the cooking time to 15 minutes.
Use the Pressure Level button to adjust the pressure to "High Pressure".
Once the cooking cycle is completed, quickly and carefully turn the steam release handle from Sealing position to the Venting position.
When all the steam is released, remove the pressure lid from the top carefully.
Add the cream and nutmeg, and purée with an immersion blender.
Add more broth or cream if you want a thinner soup. Add the sausage, and taste for seasoning.
Serve in bowls topped with crispy sage.

Per Serving: Calories 489; Fat 11g; Sodium 501mg; Carbs 8.9g; Fiber 4.6g; Sugar 8g; Protein 26g

Sweet Potato Kale Soup

Prep time: 20 minutes| **Cook time:** 25 minutes| **Serves:** 4
2 tablespoons olive oil
1 (10-oz.) fully cooked kielbasa, linguae, or Spanish chorizo, cut into ¼-inch slices
1 large onion, chopped
3 garlic cloves, minced
2 lbs. sweet potatoes, peeled and cut into 1-inch cubes
1 pound Yukon Gold or white potatoes (not russets), peeled and cut into 1-inch cubes
6 cups chicken broth
Kosher salt
Black pepper
1 small bunch kale, stemmed and roughly chopped

Press the "Sauté" button two times to select "Normal" mode.
Once hot, add the oil followed by the sausage. Cook, stirring, for about 7 minutes, until browned.
Remove and place on paper towels to drain.
Add the onion and garlic. Cook for 5 minutes, or until the onion is translucent.
Add the sweet potatoes, potatoes, and broth. Season with salt and pepper.
Put on the pressure cooker's lid and turn the steam valve to "Sealing" position.
Press the "Pressure Cook" button two times to select "Less" option.
Use the "+/-" keys on the control panel to set the cooking time to 8 minutes.
Use the Pressure Level button to adjust the pressure to "High Pressure".
Once the cooking cycle is completed, allow the steam to release naturally for 10 minutes, then turn the steam release handle to the Venting position.
When all the steam is released, remove the pressure lid from the top carefully.
Use a potato masher or immersion blender to mash about half of the potatoes, leaving some chunks.
Press the "Sauté" button two times to select "Normal" mode and then add the kale.

Cook for 5 minutes more until the kale is wilted. Add the sausage and serve.

Per Serving: Calories 334; Fat 7.9g; Sodium 704mg; Carbs 6g; Fiber 3.6g; Sugar 6g; Protein 18g

Ham Bone Soup

Prep time: 20 minutes| **Cook time:** 25 minutes| **Serves:** 4

2 tablespoons olive oil
½ cup onion, chopped
2 carrots, diced
1 rib celery, diced
1 parsnip, diced
1 ham bone
5 cups chicken stock
Sea salt and black pepper, to taste

Press the "Sauté" button two times to select "Normal" settings and heat the olive oil until sizzling.
Then, sauté the onion, carrot, celery, and parsnip until tender.
Add the ham bone, chicken stock, salt, and black pepper to the inner pot.
Put on the pressure cooker's lid and turn the steam valve to "Sealing" position.
Press the "Pressure Cook" button two times to select "Less" option.
Use the "+/-" keys on the control panel to set the cooking time to 15 minutes.
Use the Pressure Level button to adjust the pressure to "High Pressure".
Once the cooking cycle is completed, allow the steam to release naturally.
When all the steam is released, remove the pressure lid from the top carefully.
Remove the ham bone from the inner pot.
Chop the meat from the bone; add back into the soup.
Serve in individual bowls and enjoy!

Per Serving: Calories 412; Fat 20g; Sodium 491mg; Carbs 9g; Fiber 3g; Sugar 8g; Protein 31g

Chicken Tortilla Soup

Prep time: 20 minutes| **Cook time:** 8 minutes| **Serves:** 4

2 tablespoons olive oil
½ cup shallots, chopped
1 sweet pepper, chopped
1 Poblano chili pepper, chopped
½-pound chicken thighs, boneless and skinless
2 ripe tomatoes, chopped
1 can (10-oz.) red enchilada sauce
2 teaspoons ground cumin
1 teaspoon ground coriander
1 teaspoon chili powder
Seasoned salt and freshly cracked pepper, to taste
4 cups roasted vegetable broth
1 bay leaf
1 can (15-oz.) black beans, drained

4 (6-inch) corn tortillas, cut crosswise into ¼-inch strips
1 avocado, cut into ½-inch dice
1 cup cheddar cheese, shredded

Press the "Sauté" button two times to select "Normal" settings and heat the olive oil.
Once hot, sauté the shallots and peppers until tender and aromatic.
Add the chicken thighs, tomatoes, enchilada sauce, cumin, coriander, chili powder, salt, black pepper, vegetable broth, and bay leaf to the inner pot.
Put on the pressure cooker's lid and turn the steam valve to "Sealing" position.
Press the "Pressure Cook" button two times to select "Less" option.
Use the "+/-" keys on the control panel to set the cooking time to 8 minutes.
Use the Pressure Level button to adjust the pressure to "High Pressure".
Once the cooking cycle is completed, allow the steam to release naturally.
When all the steam is released, remove the pressure lid from the top carefully.
Stir in the canned beans and seal the lid; let it sit in the residual heat until everything is heated through.
Divide your soup between individual bowls and serve garnished with tortilla strips, avocado, and cheddar cheese.

Per Serving: Calories 584; Fat 15g; Sodium 441mg; Carbs 17g; Fiber 4.6g; Sugar 5g; Protein 29g

Lentil and Tomato Soup

Prep time: 20 minutes| **Cook time:** 10 minutes| **Serves:** 4

2 tablespoons butter
1 red onion, chopped
½ cup celery, chopped
1 teaspoon ground cumin
1 teaspoon ground coriander
1 teaspoon garlic powder
1 cup yellow lentils
1 teaspoon dried parsley flakes
2 cups roasted vegetable broth
2 cups tomato puree
2 green onions, sliced

Press the "Sauté" button two times to select "Normal" settings and melt the butter.
Once hot, cook the onion and celery until just tender.
Stir in the remaining ingredients, except for the green onions.
Put on the pressure cooker's lid and turn the steam valve to "Sealing" position.
Press the "Pressure Cook" button two times to select "Less" option.
Use the "+/-" keys on the control panel to set the cooking time to 8 minutes.
Use the Pressure Level button to adjust the pressure to "High Pressure".
Once the cooking cycle is completed, quickly and carefully turn the steam release handle from Sealing position to the Venting position.

When all the steam is released, remove the pressure lid from the top carefully.
Serve warm garnished with green onions.
Enjoy!

Per Serving: Calories 380; Fat 7.9g; Sodium 704mg; Carbs 6g; Fiber 3.6g; Sugar 6g; Protein 18g

Vegetable Wild Rice Soup

Prep time: 20 minutes| **Cook time:** 40 minutes| **Serves:** 4

3 carrots, chopped
3 stalks celery, chopped
1 turnip, chopped
1 shallot, chopped
1 ½ cups wild rice
10 oz. button mushrooms, sliced
5 cups vegetable broth
1 teaspoon granulated garlic
Sea salt and red pepper, to taste

Place the ingredients in the inner pot; stir to combine.
Put on the pressure cooker's lid and turn the steam valve to "Sealing" position.
Press the "Soup/Broth" button two times to select "Normal" option.
Use the "+/-" keys on the control panel to set the cooking time to 40 minutes.
Use the Pressure Level button to adjust the pressure to "High Pressure".
Once the cooking cycle is completed, quickly and carefully turn the steam release handle from Sealing position to the Venting position.
When all the steam is released, remove the pressure lid from the top carefully.
Serve warm garnished with a few drizzles of olive oil if desired.
Bon appétit!

Per Serving: Calories 380; Fat 7.9g; Sodium 704mg; Carbs 6g; Fiber 3.6g; Sugar 6g; Protein 18g

Noodle Soup

Prep time: 20 minutes| **Cook time:** 20 minutes| **Serves:** 6

2 tablespoons olive oil
2 carrots, diced
2 parsnips, diced
1 yellow onion, chopped
2 cloves garlic, minced
6 cups chicken bone broth
1 bay leaf
Salt and black pepper
2 lbs. chicken thighs drumettes
2 cups wide egg noodles
¼ cup fresh cilantro, roughly chopped

Press the "Sauté" button two times to select "Normal" settings and heat the oil.
Once hot, cook the carrots, parsnips, and onions until they are just tender.
Add the minced garlic and continue to cook for a minute more.

Add the chicken bone broth, bay leaf, salt, black pepper, and chicken to the inner pot.
Put on the pressure cooker's lid and turn the steam valve to "Sealing" position.
Press the "Pressure Cook" button two times to select "Less" option.
Use the "+/-" keys on the control panel to set the cooking time to 9 minutes.
Use the Pressure Level button to adjust the pressure to "High Pressure".
Once the cooking cycle is completed, quickly and carefully turn the steam release handle from Sealing position to the Venting position.
When all the steam is released, remove the pressure lid from the top carefully.
Shred the cooked chicken and set aside.
Stir in noodles and press the "Sauté" button two times to select "Normal" settings.
Cook approximately 5 minutes or until thoroughly heated.
Afterwards, add the chicken back into the soup. Serve garnished with fresh cilantro.
Bon appétit!

Per Serving: Calories 419; Fat 14g; Sodium 791mg; Carbs 8.9g; Fiber 4.6g; Sugar 8g; Protein 3g

Minestrone Soup

Prep time: 20 minutes| **Cook time:** 20 minutes| **Serves:** 4

2 tablespoons canola oil
1 onion, chopped
2 stalks celery, diced
2 carrots, diced
2 cloves garlic, pressed
2 lbs. tomatoes, pureed
2 cups chicken broth
1 cup pasta, uncooked
2 teaspoons Italian seasoning
Sea salt and black pepper, to taste
½ cup fresh corn kernels
2 cups cannellini beans, canned and rinsed
6 oz. Parmesan cheese, grated

Press the "Sauté" button two times to select "Normal" settings and heat oil until sizzling,
Then, sauté the onion, celery, and carrots for 3 to 4 minutes or until tender.
Add the garlic, tomatoes, broth, pasta, Italian seasoning, salt, and black pepper.
Put on the pressure cooker's lid and turn the steam valve to "Sealing" position.
Press the "Pressure Cook" button two times to select "Less" option.
Use the "+/-" keys on the control panel to set the cooking time to 5 minutes.
Use the Pressure Level button to adjust the pressure to "High Pressure".
Once the cooking cycle is completed, quickly and carefully turn the steam release handle from Sealing position to the Venting position.
When all the steam is released, remove the pressure lid from the top carefully.
Lastly, stir in the corn kernels and beans.
Seal the lid and let it sit in the residual heat for 5 to 8 minutes.

Ladle into individual bowls and serve topped with Parmesan cheese.
Bon appétit!

Per Serving: Calories 478; Fat 7.9g; Sodium 704mg; Carbs 6g; Fiber 3.6g; Sugar 6g; Protein 18g

Beef Soup with Vegetables

Prep time: 20 minutes| **Cook time:** 20 minutes| **Serves:** 4

2 tablespoons olive oil
1 ½ lbs. beef stew meat, cubed
Sea salt and black pepper, to taste
1 onion, chopped
2 celery stalks, chopped
2 carrots, chopped
2 cloves garlic, chopped
2 rosemary sprigs
2 thyme sprigs
¼ cup tamari sauce
2 bay leaves
5 cups beef bone broth
2 ripe tomatoes, pureed
6 oz. green beans, fresh or thawed

Press the "Sauté" button two times to select "Normal" settings and heat the oil until sizzling.
Now, brown the beef meat for 3 to 4 minutes, stirring frequently to ensure even cooking.
Add the remaining ingredients, except for the green beans.
Put on the pressure cooker's lid and turn the steam valve to "Sealing" position.
Press the "Pressure Cook" button two times to select "Less" option.
Use the "+/-" keys on the control panel to set the cooking time to 13 minutes.
Use the Pressure Level button to adjust the pressure to "High Pressure".
Once the cooking cycle is completed, allow the steam to release naturally.
When all the steam is released, remove the pressure lid from the top carefully.
Add the green beans.
Choose the "Pressure Cook" mode and cook for 2 minutes at High pressure.
Once cooking is complete, use a quick pressure release; carefully remove the lid.
Bon appétit!

Per Serving: Calories 380; Fat 19g; Sodium 354mg; Carbs 15g; Fiber 5.1g; Sugar 8.2g; Protein 32g

Acorn Squash Soup

Prep time: 20 minutes| **Cook time:** 15 minutes| **Serves:** 4

1 tablespoon butter, softened
2 cloves garlic, sliced
1 medium-sized leek, chopped
1 turnip, chopped
1 carrot, chopped
1 ½ lbs. acorn squash, chopped
2 cups vegetable broth

2 cups water
½ teaspoon ground allspice
1 sprig fresh thyme
Himalayan salt and black pepper, to taste

Press the "Sauté" button two times to select "Normal" settings and melt the butter.
Once hot, cook the garlic and leek until just tender and fragrant.
Add the remaining ingredients to the inner pot.
Put on the pressure cooker's lid and turn the steam valve to "Sealing" position.
Press the "Pressure Cook" button two times to select "Less" option.
Use the "+/-" keys on the control panel to set the cooking time to 10 minutes.
Use the Pressure Level button to adjust the pressure to "High Pressure".
Once the cooking cycle is completed, quickly and carefully turn the steam release handle from Sealing position to the Venting position.
When all the steam is released, remove the pressure lid from the top carefully.
Puree the soup in your blender until smooth and uniform.
Serve warm and enjoy!

Per Serving: Calories 334; Fat 7.9g; Sodium 704mg; Carbs 6g; Fiber 3.6g; Sugar 6g; Protein 18g

Pinot Grigio Soup

Prep time: 15 minutes| **Cook time:** 15 minutes| **Serves:** 4

2 slices bacon, chopped
1 medium leek, chopped
1 celery stalk, chopped
2 carrots, chopped
2 parsnips, chopped
⅓ cup Pinot Grigio
3 cups chicken broth
⅓ cup whole milk
½ pound frozen corn kernels, thawed
1 serrano pepper, minced
1 teaspoon granulated garlic
Seas salt and black pepper, to taste
1 pound shrimp, deveined

Press the "Sauté" button two times to select "Normal" settings and cook the bacon until it is crisp.
Chop the bacon and set aside.
Then, sauté the leeks, celery, carrots, and parsnips in the bacon drippings.
Cook for about 4 minutes or until they have softened. Add a splash of wine to deglaze the pot.
Press the "Cancel" button. Stir in the broth, milk, corn, pepper, granulated garlic, salt, and black pepper.
Put on the pressure cooker's lid and turn the steam valve to "Sealing" position.
Press the "Pressure Cook" button two times to select "Less" option.
Use the "+/-" keys on the control panel to set the cooking time to 2 minutes.

Use the Pressure Level button to adjust the pressure to "High Pressure".
Once the cooking cycle is completed, quickly and carefully turn the steam release handle from Sealing position to the Venting position. When all the steam is released, remove the pressure lid from the top carefully.
Stir in the shrimp and seal the lid again; allow it to stand in the residual heat for 5 to 10 minutes.
Garnish with the reserved crumbled bacon.
Bon appétit!

Per Serving: Calories 489; Fat 11g; Sodium 501mg; Carbs 8.9g; Fiber 4.6g; Sugar 8g; Protein 26g

Creamy Clam Chowder

Prep time: 15 minutes| **Cook time:** 15 minutes| **Serves:** 4

2 tablespoons butter
1 onion, chopped
1 garlic clove, minced
1 stalk celery, diced
1 carrot, diced
1 cup water
2 cups fish stock
Sea salt and white pepper, to taste
1-pound Russet potatoes, peeled and diced
1 teaspoon cayenne pepper
18 oz. canned clams, chopped with juice
1 cup heavy cream

Press the "Sauté" button two times to select "Normal" settings.
And melt the butter; once hot, cook the onion, garlic, celery, and carrot for 3 minutes.
Add the water, stock, salt, white pepper, potatoes, and cayenne pepper.
Put on the pressure cooker's lid and turn the steam valve to "Sealing" position.
Press the "Pressure Cook" button two times to select "Less" option.
Use the "+/-" keys on the control panel to set the cooking time to 2 minutes.
Use the Pressure Level button to adjust the pressure to "High Pressure".
Once the cooking cycle is completed, quickly and carefully turn the steam release handle from Sealing position to the Venting position. When all the steam is released, remove the pressure lid from the top carefully.
Press the "Sauté" button two times to select "Normal" settings and use the lowest setting.
Stir in the clams and heavy cream.
Let it simmer for about 5 minutes or until everything is thoroughly heated.
Bon appétit!

Per Serving: Calories 479; Fat 10g; Sodium 891mg; Carbs 22.9g; Fiber 4g; Sugar 4g; Protein 3g

Cod Tomato Soup

Prep time: 15 minutes| **Cook time:** 7 minutes| **Serves:** 4

½ stick butter, at room temperature
1 onion, chopped
2 garlic cloves, minced
2 ripe tomatoes, pureed
2 tablespoons tomato paste
1 cup shellfish stock
¼ cup cooking wine
1-pound cod fish, cut into bite-sized pieces
½ teaspoons basil
½ teaspoons dried dill weed
¼ teaspoon dried oregano
¼ teaspoon hot sauce
½ teaspoons paprika
Sea salt and black pepper, to taste

Press the "Sauté" button two times to select "Normal" settings.
And melt the butter; once hot, cook the onion and garlic for about 2 minutes.
Add the remaining ingredients.
Put on the pressure cooker's lid and turn the steam valve to "Sealing" position.
Press the "Pressure Cook" button two times to select "Less" option.
Use the "+/-" keys on the control panel to set the cooking time to 5 minutes.
Use the Pressure Level button to adjust the pressure to "High Pressure".
Once the cooking cycle is completed, quickly and carefully turn the steam release handle from Sealing position to the Venting position. When all the steam is released, remove the pressure lid from the top carefully.
Ladle into serving bowls and serve immediately.

Per Serving: Calories 382; Fat 10.9g; Sodium 354mg; Carbs 10.5g; Fiber 4.1g; Sugar 8.2g; Protein 26g

Beef Stroganoff Soup

Prep time: 15 minutes| **Cook time:** 50 minutes| **Serves:** 4

1-pound beef stew meat, cubed
5 cups beef bone broth
½ teaspoons dried basil
½ teaspoons dried oregano
½ teaspoons dried rosemary
1 teaspoon dried sage
1 teaspoon shallot powder
½ teaspoons porcini powder
1 teaspoon garlic powder
Sea salt and black pepper, to taste
7 oz. button mushrooms, sliced
½ cup sour cream
2 tablespoons potato starch, mixed with 4 tablespoons of cold water

In the inner pot, place the stew meat, broth, and spices.
Put on the pressure cooker's lid and turn the steam valve to "Sealing" position.
Press the "Soup/Broth" button three times to select "Normal" option.
Use the "+/-" keys on the control panel to set the cooking time to 50 minutes.
Use the Pressure Level button to adjust the pressure to "High Pressure".

Once the cooking cycle is completed, allow the steam to release naturally.
When all the steam is released, remove the pressure lid from the top carefully.
Add the mushrooms and sour cream to the inner pot.
Bring to a boil and add the potato starch slurry.
Continue to simmer until the soup thickens.
Ladle into serving bowls and serve immediately. Bon appétit!

Per Serving: Calories 449; Fat 2.9g; Sodium 511mg; Carbs 12g; Fiber 3g; Sugar 8g; Protein 7g

Cheesy Broccoli Soup

Prep time: 15 minutes| **Cook time:** 5 minutes| **Serves:** 4

4 tablespoons butter
2 cloves garlic, pressed
1 teaspoon shallot powder
4 cups cream of celery soup
1-pound small broccoli florets
Sea salt and black pepper, to taste
½ teaspoon chili powder
2 cups half and half
2 cups sharp cheddar cheese, freshly grated
2 scallions stalks, chopped

Add the butter, garlic, shallot powder, cream of celery soup, broccoli, salt, black pepper, and chili powder to the inner pot.
Put on the pressure cooker's lid and turn the steam valve to "Sealing" position.
Press the "Pressure Cook" button two times to select "Less" option.
Use the "+/-" keys on the control panel to set the cooking time to 2 minutes.
Use the Pressure Level button to adjust the pressure to "High Pressure".
Once the cooking cycle is completed, quickly and carefully turn the steam release handle from Sealing position to the Venting position.
When all the steam is released, remove the pressure lid from the top carefully.
Stir in the half and half and cheese. Let it simmer until everything is thoroughly heated.
Divide between serving bowls and serve garnished with chopped scallions.
Bon appétit!

Per Serving: Calories 352; Fat 12.9g; Sodium 414mg; Carbs 11g; Fiber 5g; Sugar 9g; Protein 31g

Sage Onion Soup

Prep time: 15 minutes| **Cook time:** 2 minutes| **Serves:** 4

4 tablespoons butter, melted
1 pound onions, thinly sliced
Kosher salt and ground white pepper, to taste
½ teaspoons dried sage
4 cups chicken bone broth
1 loaf French bread, sliced
1 cup mozzarella cheese, shredded

Press the "Sauté" button two times to select "Normal" settings and melt the butter.
Once hot, cook the onions until golden and caramelized.
Add the salt, pepper, sage, and chicken bone broth.
Put on the pressure cooker's lid and turn the steam valve to "Sealing" position.
Press the "Pressure Cook" button two times to select "Less" option.
Use the "+/-" keys on the control panel to set the cooking time to 2 minutes.
Use the Pressure Level button to adjust the pressure to "High Pressure".
Once the cooking cycle is completed, quickly and carefully turn the steam release handle from Sealing position to the Venting position.
When all the steam is released, remove the pressure lid from the top carefully.
Divide the soup between four oven safe bowls; top with the bread and shredded cheese.
Now, place the bowls under the broiler for about 4 minutes or until the cheese has melted.
Bon appétit!

Per Serving: Calories 472; Fat 10.9g; Sodium 454mg; Carbs 10g; Fiber 3.1g; Sugar 5.2g; Protein 20g

Meatball Noodle Soup

Prep time: 15 minutes| **Cook time:** 25 minutes| **Serves:** 4

Meatballs:
½-pound ground beef
½-pound ground turkey
½ cup panko crumbs
¼ cup Pecorino Romano cheese, grated
1 egg, beaten
2 cloves garlic, crushed
2 tablespoons cilantro, chopped
Sea salt and black pepper, to taste
Soup:
1 tablespoon olive oil
1 onion, chopped
1 celery stalk, chopped
2 cloves garlic, minced
2 tomatoes, crushed
4 cups chicken broth
2 bay leaves
6 oz. noodles

In a mixing bowl, thoroughly combine all ingredients for the meatballs.
Form the mixture into 20 meatballs.
Press the "Sauté" button two times to select "Normal" settings and heat the oil.
Now, brown the meatballs in batches; reserve.
Heat the olive oil; sauté the onion, celery, and garlic for 3 to 4 minutes or until they are fragrant.
Add the tomatoes, broth, and bay leaves to the inner pot.
Put on the pressure cooker's lid and turn the steam valve to "Sealing" position.

Press the "Pressure Cook" button two times to select "Less" option.
Use the "+/-" keys on the control panel to set the cooking time to 12 minutes.
Use the Pressure Level button to adjust the pressure to "High Pressure".
Once the cooking cycle is completed, quickly and carefully turn the steam release handle from Sealing position to the Venting position.
When all the steam is released, remove the pressure lid from the top carefully.
Next, sit in the noodles and secure the lid again.
Choose the "Pressure Cook" mode and cook for 5 minutes at High Pressure.
Once cooking is complete, use a quick pressure release; carefully remove the lid.
Bon appétit!

Per Serving: Calories 584; Fat 15g; Sodium 441mg; Carbs 17g; Fiber 4.6g; Sugar 5g; Protein 29g

Chipotle Chili Soup

Prep time: 15 minutes| **Cook time:** 33 minutes| **Serves:** 4

1 tablespoon canola oil
1-pound ground beef
2 cloves garlic, smashed
1 medium leek, chopped
2 chipotle chilis in adobo sauce, roughly chopped
1 (14 ½ -oz.) can tomatoes, diced
2 cups vegetable broth
16 oz. pinto beans, undrained
½ teaspoons cumin powder
1 teaspoon stone-ground mustard
1 teaspoon chili powder

Press the "Sauté" button two times to select "Normal" settings and heat the oil.
Brown the ground beef for 2 to 3 minutes, stirring frequently.
Add the remaining ingredients and stir to combine well.
Put on the pressure cooker's lid and turn the steam valve to "Sealing" position.
Press the "Bean/Chili" button two times to select "Normal" option.
Use the Pressure Level button to adjust the pressure to "High Pressure".
Once the cooking cycle is completed, allow the steam to release naturally.
When all the steam is released, remove the pressure lid from the top carefully.
Bon appétit!

Per Serving: Calories 419; Fat 14g; Sodium 791mg; Carbs 8.9g; Fiber 4.6g; Sugar 8g; Protein 3g

Corn and Chicken Soup

Prep time: 15 minutes| **Cook time:** 15 minutes| **Serves:** 4

1 tablespoon olive oil
1 yellow onion, chopped

1 celery stalk, diced
1 carrot, finely diced
1 turnip, diced
6 cups roasted vegetable broth
1-pound chicken breasts, skinless, boneless and diced
1 teaspoon garlic powder
1 teaspoon mustard powder
1 (15-oz.) can creamed corn
4 large eggs, whisked
Kosher salt and black pepper, to taste

Press the "Sauté" button two times to select "Normal" settings and heat the oil.
Now, sauté the onion until just tender and translucent.
Add the celery, carrot, turnip, vegetable broth, chicken, garlic powder, and mustard powder.
Put on the pressure cooker's lid and turn the steam valve to "Sealing" position.
Press the "Pressure Cook" button two times to select "Less" option.
Use the "+/-" keys on the control panel to set the cooking time to 9 minutes.
Use the Pressure Level button to adjust the pressure to "High Pressure".
Once the cooking cycle is completed, quickly and carefully turn the steam release handle from Sealing position to the Venting position.
When all the steam is released, remove the pressure lid from the top carefully.
Press the "Sauté" button two times to select "Less" settings.
Stir in the creamed corn and eggs; let it simmer, stirring continuously for about 5 minutes.
Season with salt and pepper to taste and serve warm.
Bon appétit!

Per Serving: Calories 351; Fat 7.9g; Sodium 704mg; Carbs 6g; Fiber 3.6g; Sugar 6g; Protein 18g

Kidney Bean Chicken Soup

Prep time: 15 minutes| **Cook time:** 17 minutes| **Serves:** 4

2 tablespoons butter, softened
1 onion, chopped
1 sweet pepper, deseeded and chopped
1 habanero pepper, deseeded and chopped
2 cloves garlic, minced
Sea salt and black pepper, to taste
1 teaspoon dried basil
1 teaspoon dried oregano
1 teaspoon cayenne pepper
4 cups vegetable broth
1-pound chicken thighs
2 cans (15-oz.) red kidney beans
¼ cup fresh cilantro, chopped
½ cup tortilla chips

Press the "Sauté" button two times to select "Normal" settings and melt the butter.
Once hot, cook the onion until tender and translucent.

122

Stir in the peppers and sauté for a few minutes more.
Add the minced garlic and continue to sauté for another minute.
Add the spices, vegetable broth, and chicken thighs to the inner pot.
Put on the pressure cooker's lid and turn the steam valve to "Sealing" position.
Press the "Pressure Cook" button two times to select "Less" option.
Use the "+/-" keys on the control panel to set the cooking time to 13 minutes.
Use the Pressure Level button to adjust the pressure to "High Pressure".
Once the cooking cycle is completed, quickly and carefully turn the steam release handle from Sealing position to the Venting position.
When all the steam is released, remove the pressure lid from the top carefully.
Remove the chicken to a cutting board. Add the kidney beans to the inner pot and seal the lid again.
Let it sit in the residual heat until thoroughly heated.
Shred the chicken and discard the bones; put it back into the soup.
Serve with fresh cilantro and tortilla chips. Enjoy!

Per Serving: Calories 479; Fat 10g; Sodium 891mg; Carbs 22.9g; Fiber 4g; Sugar 4g; Protein 3g

Sweet Potato Soup with Swiss Chard

Prep time: 15 minutes| **Cook time:** 10 minutes| **Serves:** 4

2 tablespoons butter, softened at room temperature
1 white onion, chopped
1 sweet pepper, deveined and chopped
2 cloves garlic, pressed
1 pound sweet potatoes, peeled and diced
2 ripe tomatoes, pureed
2 cups chicken bone broth
2 cups water
Kosher salt and black pepper, to taste
¼ cup peanut butter
2 cups Swiss chard, torn into pieces

Press the "Sauté" button two times to select "Normal" settings and melt the butter.
Once hot, cook the onion, pepper, and garlic until tender and fragrant.
Add the sweet potatoes and continue to sauté for about 3 minutes longer.
Now, stir in the tomatoes, broth, water, salt, and black pepper.
Put on the pressure cooker's lid and turn the steam valve to "Sealing" position.
Press the "Pressure Cook" button two times to select "Less" option.
Use the "+/-" keys on the control panel to set the cooking time to 4 minutes.
Use the Pressure Level button to adjust the pressure to "High Pressure".
Once the cooking cycle is completed, quickly and carefully turn the steam release handle from Sealing position to the Venting position.

When all the steam is released, remove the pressure lid from the top carefully.
Stir in the peanut butter and Swiss chard; seal the lid again and let it sit in the residual heat until your greens wilt.
Serve warm.

Per Serving: Calories 521; Fat 7.9g; Sodium 704mg; Carbs 6g; Fiber 3.6g; Sugar 6g; Protein 18g

Turkey and Basmati Rice Soup

Prep time: 15 minutes| **Cook time:** 15 minutes| **Serves:** 4

1 tablespoon sesame oil
1 onion, chopped
1 large thumb-sized pieces' fresh ginger, peeled and grated
1-pound turkey breast, boneless and cut into chunks
2 carrots, sliced
1 celery stalk, sliced
5 cups chicken broth
1 teaspoon garlic powder
1 teaspoon cumin seeds
1 teaspoon garam masala
1 teaspoon turmeric powder
1 cup basmati rice, rinsed
1 small handful of fresh coriander, roughly chopped

Press the "Sauté" button two times to select "Normal" settings.
And heat the sesame oil until sizzling. Now, sauté the onion and ginger until tender and aromatic.
Add the turkey, carrot, and celery to the inner pot; continue to cook for 3 to 4 minutes.
Add the chicken broth and spices to the inner pot.
Put on the pressure cooker's lid and turn the steam valve to "Sealing" position.
Press the "Pressure Cook" button two times to select "Less" option.
Use the "+/-" keys on the control panel to set the cooking time to 5 minutes.
Use the Pressure Level button to adjust the pressure to "High Pressure".
Once the cooking cycle is completed, quickly and carefully turn the steam release handle from Sealing position to the Venting position.
When all the steam is released, remove the pressure lid from the top carefully.
After that, stir in the basmati rice.
Choose the "Pressure Cook" mode and cook for 4 minutes at High Pressure.
Once cooking is complete, use a quick pressure release; carefully remove the lid.
Ladle into four serving bowls and serve with fresh coriander. Enjoy!

Per Serving: Calories 449; Fat 2.9g; Sodium 511mg; Carbs 12g; Fiber 3g; Sugar 8g; Protein 7g

Beef Barley Soup

Prep time: 15 minutes| **Cook time:** 25 minutes| **Serves:** 4

1 tablespoon canola oil
2 shallots, chopped
2 garlic cloves, minced
2 celery stalks, chopped
1 parsnip, chopped
1 cup tomato puree
4 cups beef broth
1 cup pearl barley
2 sprigs thyme
Sea salt and white pepper, to taste
1 teaspoon red pepper flakes, crushed

Press the "Sauté" button two times to select "Normal" settings and heat the canola oil.
Once hot, sauté the shallots, garlic, celery, and parsnip until tender and aromatic.
Add the remaining ingredients and stir to combine.
Put on the pressure cooker's lid and turn the steam valve to "Sealing" position.
Press the "Soup/Broth" button one time to select "Less" option.
Use the Pressure Level button to adjust the pressure to "High Pressure".
Once the cooking cycle is completed, quickly and carefully turn the steam release handle from Sealing position to the Venting position.
When all the steam is released, remove the pressure lid from the top carefully.
Serve in individual bowls.
Bon appétit!

Per Serving: Calories 382; Fat 7.9g; Sodium 704mg; Carbs 6g; Fiber 3.6g; Sugar 6g; Protein 18g

Peppery Ground Pork Soup

Prep time: 15 minutes| **Cook time:** 13 minutes| **Serves:** 4

1-pound ground pork
1 teaspoon Italian seasoning
1 teaspoon garlic powder
Sea salt and black pepper, to taste
2 sweet peppers, seeded and sliced
1 jalapeno pepper, seeded and minced
2 ripe tomatoes, pureed
4 cups chicken stock

Press the "Sauté" button two times to select "Normal" settings.
Then, brown the ground pork until no longer pink or about 3 minutes.
Add the remaining ingredients to the inner pot and stir.
Put on the pressure cooker's lid and turn the steam valve to "Sealing" position.
Press the "Pressure Cook" button two times to select "Less" option.
Use the "+/-" keys on the control panel to set the cooking time to 10 minutes.
Use the Pressure Level button to adjust the pressure to "Low Pressure".
Once the cooking cycle is completed, allow the steam to release naturally.

When all the steam is released, remove the pressure lid from the top carefully.
Serve warm. Bon appétit!

Per Serving: Calories 489; Fat 11g; Sodium 501mg; Carbs 8.9g; Fiber 4.6g; Sugar 8g; Protein 26g

Lima Bean Soup

Prep time: 15 minutes| **Cook time:** 15 minutes| **Serves:** 5

2 tablespoons sesame oil
1 pound cremini mushrooms, thinly sliced
1 large-sized eggplant, sliced into rounds
1 red onion, chopped
2 garlic cloves, chopped
2 carrots, sliced
2 sweet potatoes, peeled and diced
½ teaspoons red curry paste
½ teaspoons cayenne pepper
Sea salt and black pepper, to taste
2 sprigs thyme
2 sprigs rosemary
2 medium-sized tomatoes, pureed
5 cups roasted vegetable broth
16 oz. lima beans, soaked overnight
Juice of 1 fresh lemon

Press the "Sauté" button two times to select "Normal" settings and heat the oil until sizzling.
Now, cook the mushrooms, eggplant, onion, and garlic until just tender and fragrant.
Add the carrots, sweet potatoes, curry paste, spices, tomatoes, broth, and lima beans.
Put on the pressure cooker's lid and turn the steam valve to "Sealing" position.
Press the "Pressure Cook" button two times to select "Less" option.
Use the "+/-" keys on the control panel to set the cooking time to 13 minutes.
Use the Pressure Level button to adjust the pressure to "High Pressure".
Once the cooking cycle is completed, quickly and carefully turn the steam release handle from Sealing position to the Venting position.
When all the steam is released, remove the pressure lid from the top carefully.
Divide your soup between individual bowls; add a few drizzles of lemon juice to each serving and enjoy!

Per Serving: Calories 461; Fat 12.9g; Sodium 414mg; Carbs 11g; Fiber 5g; Sugar 9g; Protein 31g

Lobster Bisque

Prep time: 15 minutes| **Cook time:** 5 minutes| **Serves:** 4

1-pound lump lobster meat
2 tablespoons olive oil
1 yellow onion, chopped
1 celery stalk, diced
1 carrot, diced
2 cloves garlic, minced
1 teaspoon rosemary

1 teaspoon basil
1 teaspoon thyme
½ teaspoons turmeric powder
1 tomato, pureed
¼ cup cooking sherry
3 cups clam juice
1 tablespoon soy sauce
½ teaspoons smoked paprika
Sea salt and ground white pepper, to taste
1 teaspoon Tabasco sauce
1 cup heavy cream

In the Inner Pot of your Instant Pot, place the lobster meat, olive oil, onion, celery, carrot, garlic, rosemary, basil, thyme, turmeric, tomato puree, cooking sherry, and clam juice.
Put on the pressure cooker's lid and turn the steam valve to "Sealing" position.
Press the "Pressure Cook" button two times to select "Less" option.
Use the "+/-" keys on the control panel to set the cooking time to 4 minutes.
Use the Pressure Level button to adjust the pressure to "High Pressure".
Once the cooking cycle is completed, quickly and carefully turn the steam release handle from Sealing position to the Venting position.
When all the steam is released, remove the pressure lid from the top carefully.
Set the lobster meat aside and chop into small chunks.
Now, add in the soy sauce, smoked paprika, salt, white pepper, Tabasco sauce, and heavy cream.
Continue to stir and simmer until it's all blended together and heated through.
Put the lobster meat back into your bisque.
Serve in individual bowls and enjoy!

Per Serving: Calories 419; Fat 14g; Sodium 791mg; Carbs 8.9g; Fiber 4.6g; Sugar 8g; Protein 3g

Seafood Chowder with Bacon

Prep time: 15 minutes| **Cook time:** 10 minutes| **Serves:** 4
3 strips bacon, chopped
1 onion, chopped
2 carrots, diced
2 stalks celery, diced
2 cloves garlic, minced
1 tablespoon Creole seasoning
Sea salt and black pepper, to taste
3 cups seafood stock
2 ripe tomatoes, pureed
2 tablespoons tomato paste
2 bay leaves
1 pound clams, chopped
1 ½ tablespoons flaxseed meal

Press the "Sauté" button two times to select "Normal" settings.
Now, cook the bacon until it is crisp; crumble the bacon and set it aside.
Now, sauté the onion, carrot, celery, and garlic in bacon drippings.
Add the remaining ingredients, except for the chopped clams, to the inner pot.

Put on the pressure cooker's lid and turn the steam valve to "Sealing" position.
Press the "Pressure Cook" button two times to select "Less" option.
Use the "+/-" keys on the control panel to set the cooking time to 4 minutes.
Use the Pressure Level button to adjust the pressure to "High Pressure".
Once the cooking cycle is completed, quickly and carefully turn the steam release handle from Sealing position to the Venting position.
When all the steam is released, remove the pressure lid from the top carefully.
Stir in the chopped clams and flaxseed meal.
Press the "Sauté" button two times to select "Normal" settings.
And let it simmer for 2 to 3 minutes longer or until everything is heated through.
Serve in individual bowls topped with the reserved bacon.
Bon appétit!

Per Serving: Calories 350; Fat 19g; Sodium 354mg; Carbs 15g; Fiber 5.1g; Sugar 8.2g; Protein 32g

Potato Chowder

Prep time: 15 minutes| **Cook time:** 15 minutes| **Serves:** 4
2 tablespoons butter
1 sweet onion, chopped
2 garlic cloves, minced
1 sweet pepper, deveined and sliced
1 jalapeno pepper, deveined and sliced
4 tablespoons all-purpose flour
4 cups vegetable broth
1 pound potatoes, cut into bite-sized pieces
3 cups creamed corn kernels
1 cup double cream
Kosher salt and black pepper, to taste
½ teaspoons cayenne pepper

Press the "Sauté" button two times to select "Normal" settings and melt the butter.
Once hot, sauté the sweet onions, garlic, and peppers for about 3 minutes.
Sprinkle the flour over the vegetables; continue stirring for 4 minutes.
Add the broth and potatoes and gently stir to combine.
Put on the pressure cooker's lid and turn the steam valve to "Sealing" position.
Press the "Pressure Cook" button two times to select "Less" option.
Use the "+/-" keys on the control panel to set the cooking time to 5 minutes.
Use the Pressure Level button to adjust the pressure to "High Pressure".
Once the cooking cycle is completed, quickly and carefully turn the steam release handle from Sealing position to the Venting position.
When all the steam is released, remove the pressure lid from the top carefully.
Press the "Sauté" button two times to select "Normal" settings and use the lowest setting.
Stir in the creamed corn, double cream, salt, black pepper, and cayenne pepper.

Let it simmer, stirring continuously for about 5 minutes or until everything is thoroughly heated.
Taste and adjust the seasonings.
Bon appétit!

Per Serving: Calories 412; Fat 20g; Sodium 491mg; Carbs 9g; Fiber 3g; Sugar 8g; Protein 31g

Halibut Chowder

Prep time: 15 minutes| **Cook time:** 10 minutes| **Serves:** 5

2 tablespoons butter
1 medium-sized leek, sliced
1 carrot, shredded
1 celery stalk, shredded
2 cloves garlic, minced
5 cups chicken bone broth
2 ripe tomatoes, chopped
1 ½ lbs. halibut, cut into small cubes
Kosher salt and cracked black pepper, to taste
1 cup milk
½ cup double cream
1 cup Swiss cheese, shredded

Press the "Sauté" button two times to select "Normal" settings and melt the butter.
Once hot, sauté the leeks, carrot, celery, and garlic until they are just tender and fragrant.
Then, add the chicken bone broth, tomatoes, halibut, salt, and black pepper.
Put on the pressure cooker's lid and turn the steam valve to "Sealing" position.
Press the "Pressure Cook" button two times to select "Less" option.
Use the "+/-" keys on the control panel to set the cooking time to 5 minutes.
Use the Pressure Level button to adjust the pressure to "High Pressure".
Once the cooking cycle is completed, quickly and carefully turn the steam release handle from Sealing position to the Venting position.
When all the steam is released, remove the pressure lid from the top carefully.
Press the "Sauté" button two times to select "Less" setting.
Stir in the milk and double cream. Allow it to simmer for about 3 minutes or until heated through.
Ladle your chowder into five serving bowls; top with the shredded Swiss cheese and serve immediately.

Per Serving: Calories 479; Fat 10g; Sodium 891mg; Carbs 22.9g; Fiber 4g; Sugar 4g; Protein 3g

Red Lentil Spinach Soup

Prep time: 15 minutes| **Cook time:** 5 minutes| **Serves:** 5

2 cups red lentils, rinsed
1 onion, chopped
2 cloves garlic, minced
1 teaspoon cumin
1 teaspoon smoked paprika

Sea salt and black pepper, to taste
2 carrots, sliced
6 cups water
2 bay leaves
2 cups fresh spinach leaves, torn into small pieces

Place all ingredients, except for the fresh spinach, in the inner pot.
Put on the pressure cooker's lid and turn the steam valve to "Sealing" position.
Press the "Pressure Cook" button two times to select "Less" option.
Use the "+/-" keys on the control panel to set the cooking time to 3 minutes.
Use the Pressure Level button to adjust the pressure to "High Pressure".
Once the cooking cycle is completed, quickly and carefully turn the steam release handle from Sealing position to the Venting position.
When all the steam is released, remove the pressure lid from the top carefully.
Stir in the spinach and seal the lid again; let it sit until the spinach just starts to wilt.
Serve in individual bowls and enjoy!

Per Serving: Calories 349; Fat 10.9g; Sodium 454mg; Carbs 10g; Fiber 3.1g; Sugar 5.2g; Protein 20g

Chicken Vegetable Soup

Prep time: 15 minutes| **Cook time:** 20 minutes| **Serves:** 3

2 tablespoons butter, melted
½-pound chicken legs, boneless and skinless
1 onion, diced
1 teaspoon garlic, minced
1 teaspoon ginger, peeled and grated
3 cups chicken stock
½ teaspoons dried sage
½ teaspoons dried thyme leaves
Sea salt and black pepper, to taste
2 tablespoons tamari sauce
2 carrots, diced
2 parsnips, diced
2 cups cauliflower florets

Press the "Sauté" button two times to select "Normal" settings and melt the butter.
Once hot, sauté the chicken until golden brown; reserve.
Cook the onion, garlic, and ginger in pan drippings until just tender and aromatic.
Add the reserved chicken, stock, and spices.
Put on the pressure cooker's lid and turn the steam valve to "Sealing" position.
Press the "Pressure Cook" button two times to select "Less" option.
Use the "+/-" keys on the control panel to set the cooking time to 13 minutes.
Use the Pressure Level button to adjust the pressure to "High Pressure".
Once the cooking cycle is completed, quickly and carefully turn the steam release handle from Sealing position to the Venting position.
When all the steam is released, remove the pressure lid from the top carefully.

Now, add the tamari sauce and vegetables to the inner pot.
Choose the "Manual" mode and cook for 5 minutes at High Pressure.
Once cooking is complete, use a quick pressure release; carefully remove the lid. Serve immediately.

Per Serving: Calories 334; Fat 7.9g; Sodium 704mg; Carbs 6g; Fiber 3.6g; Sugar 6g; Protein 18g

Farmhouse Soup

Prep time: 15 minutes| **Cook time:** 10 minutes| **Serves:** 4

2 tablespoons canola oil
1 shallot, chopped
2 garlic cloves, minced
½ teaspoons dried oregano
½ teaspoons dried basil
½ teaspoons dried rosemary
4 oz. frozen carrots, chopped
4 oz. frozen green peas
8 oz. frozen broccoli, chopped
4 oz. frozen green beans
2 ripe tomatoes, pureed
4 cups vegetable broth
Sea salt and black pepper, to taste
½ teaspoons red pepper flakes

Press the "Sauté" button two times to select "Normal" settings and heat the oil.
Sauté the shallot until softened, approximately 4 minutes. Stir in the garlic and cook for 30 seconds more.
Add the dried herbs, frozen vegetables, tomatoes, vegetable broth, salt, and black pepper.
Put on the pressure cooker's lid and turn the steam valve to "Sealing" position.
Press the "Pressure Cook" button two times to select "Less" option.
Use the "+/-" keys on the control panel to set the cooking time to 4 minutes.
Use the Pressure Level button to adjust the pressure to "High Pressure".
Once the cooking cycle is completed, quickly and carefully turn the steam release handle from Sealing position to the Venting position.
When all the steam is released, remove the pressure lid from the top carefully.
Divide between serving bowls and garnish with red pepper flakes.
Bon appétit!

Per Serving: Calories 382; Fat 7.9g; Sodium 704mg; Carbs 6g; Fiber 3.6g; Sugar 6g; Protein 18g

Tomato Vegetable Soup

Prep time: 15 minutes| **Cook time:** 10 minutes| **Serves:** 4

1 tablespoon olive oil
1 cup green onions, chopped
2 stalks green garlic, chopped
1 celery stalk, diced
2 carrots, diced
2 cups vegetable broth
Sea salt and black pepper, to your liking
½ teaspoons cayenne pepper
1 teaspoon fresh basil, chopped
1 teaspoon fresh rosemary, chopped
1 (28-oz.) can tomatoes, crushed
½ cup double cream
½ cup feta cheese, cubed
1 tablespoon olive oil

Press the "Sauté" button two times to select "Normal" settings
And heat 1 tablespoon of olive oil. Sauté the green onions, garlic, celery, and carrots until softened.
Add the vegetable broth, salt, black pepper, cayenne pepper, basil, rosemary, and tomatoes to the inner pot.
Put on the pressure cooker's lid and turn the steam valve to "Sealing" position.
Press the "Pressure Cook" button two times to select "Less" option.
Use the "+/-" keys on the control panel to set the cooking time to 6 minutes.
Use the Pressure Level button to adjust the pressure to "High Pressure".
Once the cooking cycle is completed, allow the steam to release naturally.
When all the steam is released, remove the pressure lid from the top carefully.
Stir in the double cream and seal the lid again; let it sit for 10 minutes more.
Ladle into soup bowls; garnish with feta and 1 tablespoon of olive oil.
Bon appétit!

Per Serving: Calories 584; Fat 15g; Sodium 441mg; Carbs 17g; Fiber 4.6g; Sugar 5g; Protein 29g

Hang Wau Soup

Prep time: 15 minutes| **Cook time:** 55 minutes| **Serves:** 4

2 lbs. oxtails
4 cloves garlic, sliced
2 bay leaves
1 thyme sprig
2 rosemary sprigs
1 tablespoon soy sauce
1 teaspoon cumin powder
1 teaspoon paprika
2 potatoes, peeled and diced
2 carrots, diced
1 parsnip, diced
1 cup vegetable broth
2 bird's eye chilis, pounded in a mortar and pestle
2 star anis
Sea salt and black pepper, to taste

Place the oxtails in the inner pot. Cover the oxtails with water.
Stir in the garlic, bay leaves, thyme, rosemary, soy sauce, cumin, and paprika.
Put on the pressure cooker's lid and turn the steam valve to "Sealing" position.

Press the "Pressure Cook" button two times to select "More" option.
Use the "+/-" keys on the control panel to set the cooking time to 50 minutes.
Use the Pressure Level button to adjust the pressure to "High Pressure".
Once the cooking cycle is completed, allow the steam to release naturally.
When all the steam is released, remove the pressure lid from the top carefully.
After that, add the other ingredients to the inner pot.
Choose the "Manual" mode and cook for 4 minutes at High Pressure.
Once cooking is complete, use a quick pressure release; carefully remove the lid.
Serve with crusty bread and enjoy!

Per Serving: Calories 478; Fat 7.9g; Sodium 704mg; Carbs 6g; Fiber 3.6g; Sugar 6g; Protein 18g

Minty Asparagus Soup

Prep time: 15 minutes| **Cook time:** 10 minutes| **Serves:** 4

1 tablespoon butter
1 Asian shallot, chopped
2 garlic cloves, minced
2 lbs. asparagus stalks, trimmed and chopped
Kosher salt and black pepper, to taste
3 cups chicken broth
1 cup yogurt
2 tablespoons fresh mint leaves, chopped

Press the "Sauté" button two times to select "Normal" settings and melt the butter.
Once hot, cook the Asian shallots and garlic until just tender and fragrant.
Add the asparagus, salt, pepper, and broth.
Put on the pressure cooker's lid and turn the steam valve to "Sealing" position.
Press the "Pressure Cook" button two times to select "Less" option.
Use the "+/-" keys on the control panel to set the cooking time to 4 minutes.
Use the Pressure Level button to adjust the pressure to "High Pressure".
Once the cooking cycle is completed, quickly and carefully turn the steam release handle from Sealing position to the Venting position.
When all the steam is released, remove the pressure lid from the top carefully.
Add the yogurt and blend the soup until it is completely smooth. Taste and season with more salt if desired.
Ladle into individual bowls; then, top each bowl with fresh mint leaves and serve.

Per Serving: Calories 489; Fat 11g; Sodium 501mg; Carbs 8.9g; Fiber 4.6g; Sugar 8g; Protein 26g

Zucchini Quinoa Soup

Prep time: 15 minutes| **Cook time:** 10 minutes| **Serves:** 4

2 tablespoons olive oil

1 shallot, diced
1 teaspoon fresh garlic, minced
Sea salt and black pepper, to your liking
1-pound zucchini, cut into rounds
1 cup quinoa
4 cups vegetable broth
2 tablespoons fresh parsley leaves

Press the "Sauté" button two times to select "Normal" settings and heat the oil.
Once hot, sweat the shallot for 2 to 3 minutes.
Stir in the garlic and continue to cook for another 30 seconds or until aromatic.
Stir in the salt, black pepper, zucchini, quinoa, and vegetable broth.
Put on the pressure cooker's lid and turn the steam valve to "Sealing" position.
Press the "Pressure Cook" button two times to select "Less" option.
Use the "+/-" keys on the control panel to set the cooking time to 3 minutes.
Use the Pressure Level button to adjust the pressure to "High Pressure".
Once the cooking cycle is completed, quickly and carefully turn the steam release handle from Sealing position to the Venting position.
When all the steam is released, remove the pressure lid from the top carefully.
Ladle into soup bowls; serve garnished with fresh parsley leaves.
Enjoy!

Per Serving: Calories 449; Fat 2.9g; Sodium 511mg; Carbs 12g; Fiber 3g; Sugar 8g; Protein 28g

Shrimp Vegetable Bisque

Prep time: 15 minutes| **Cook time:** 10 minutes| **Serves:** 4

2 tablespoons butter
½ cup white onion, chopped
1 celery rib, chopped
1 parsnip, chopped
1 carrot, chopped
2 tablespoons all-purpose flour
¼ cup sherry wine
Sea salt and black pepper
1 cup tomato puree
3 cups chicken bone broth
16 oz. shrimp, deveined
1 cup heavy whipping cream

Press the "Sauté" button two times to select "Normal" settings and melt the butter.
Once hot, cook the onion, celery, parsnip, and carrot until softened.
Add the flour and cook for 3 minutes more or until everything is well coated.
Pour in sherry wine to deglaze the pot.
Now, add the salt, pepper, tomato puree, and broth.
Put on the pressure cooker's lid and turn the steam valve to "Sealing" position.
Press the "Pressure Cook" button two times to select "Less" option.
Use the "+/-" keys on the control panel to set the cooking time to 5 minutes.

Use the Pressure Level button to adjust the pressure to "High Pressure".
Once the cooking cycle is completed, quickly and carefully turn the steam release handle from Sealing position to the Venting position.
When all the steam is released, remove the pressure lid from the top carefully.
Now, add the shrimp and heavy cream.
Cook on the "Sauté" function for a further 2 to 3 minutes or until everything is heated through
Bon appétit!

Per Serving: Calories 479; Fat 10g; Sodium 891mg; Carbs 22.9g; Fiber 4g; Sugar 4g; Protein 3g

Borscht Soup

Prep time: 15 minutes| **Cook time:** 15 minutes| **Serves:** 4
2 tablespoons safflower oil
1 red onion, chopped
2 cloves garlic, minced
1 pound Yukon potatoes, peeled and diced
2 carrots, chopped
1 small red bell pepper, finely chopped
½-pound red bee roots, grated
1 tablespoon cider vinegar
2 tablespoons tomato paste
Sea salt and black pepper, to taste
2 bay leaves
½ teaspoons ground cumin
4 cups chicken stock

Press the "Sauté" button two times to select "Normal" settings and heat the oil.
Once hot, cook the onion for about 2 minutes or until softened.
Add the garlic, potatoes, carrots, bell pepper, and beets to the inner pot.
Add the remaining ingredients to the inner pot and stir until everything is well combined.
Put on the pressure cooker's lid and turn the steam valve to "Sealing" position.
Press the "Pressure Cook" button two times to select "Less" option.
Use the "+/-" keys on the control panel to set the cooking time to 10 minutes.
Use the Pressure Level button to adjust the pressure to "High Pressure".
Once the cooking cycle is completed, allow the steam to release naturally.
When all the steam is released, remove the pressure lid from the top carefully.
To serve, add more salt and vinegar if desired.
Bon appétit!

Per Serving: Calories 419; Fat 14g; Sodium 791mg; Carbs 8.9g; Fiber 4.6g; Sugar 8g; Protein 3g

Alfredo Ditalini Soup

Prep time: 15 minutes| **Cook time:** 25 minutes| **Serves:** 4
2 tablespoons coconut oil, melted

1-pound chicken breast, skinless and boneless
1 white onion, chopped
2 cloves garlic, pressed
12 serrano pepper, minced
¼ cup all-purpose flour
4 cups vegetable broth
2 cups cauliflower florets, frozen
2 cups Ditalini pasta
1 cup heavy cream
Sea salt and black pepper, to taste

Press the "Sauté" button two times to select "Normal" settings and heat the oil.
Once hot, brown the chicken for 3 to 4 minutes per side; set aside.
Then, sauté the onion, garlic, and serrano pepper in pan drippings.
Add the flour and continue to stir until your veggies are well coated.
Add the vegetable broth, cauliflower, and pasta to the inner pot; put the chicken back into the inner pot.
Put on the pressure cooker's lid and turn the steam valve to "Sealing" position.
Press the "Pressure Cook" button two times to select "Less" option.
Use the "+/-" keys on the control panel to set the cooking time to 6 minutes.
Use the Pressure Level button to adjust the pressure to "High Pressure".
Once the cooking cycle is completed, quickly and carefully turn the steam release handle from Sealing position to the Venting position.
When all the steam is released, remove the pressure lid from the top carefully.
Stir in the cauliflower and Ditalini pasta.
Choose the "Manual" mode and cook for 5 minutes at High Pressure.
Once cooking is complete, use a quick pressure release; carefully remove the lid.
Shred the cooked chicken and add it back into the soup.
Afterwards, add the heavy cream, salt, and black pepper.
Seal the lid and let it sit in the residual heat for 5 minutes.
Bon appétit!

Per Serving: Calories 584; Fat 15g; Sodium 441mg; Carbs 17g; Fiber 4.6g; Sugar 5g; Protein 29g

Hamburger Soup

Prep time: 20 minutes| **Cook time:** 15 minutes| **Serves:** 5
1 tablespoon olive oil
1-pound ground beef
1 leek, diced
2 cloves garlic, sliced
2 tablespoons cooking sherry
4 cups beef broth
1 can condensed tomato soup
1 teaspoon fish sauce
1 teaspoon basil
½ teaspoons oregano
2 bay leaves
¼ teaspoon paprika
Sea salt and black pepper, to taste

Press the "Sauté" button two times to select "Normal" settings and heat the oil.

Once hot, brown the ground beef for 2 to 3 minutes, stirring and crumbling with a wooden spoon.

Stir in the leeks and garlic; continue to sauté an additional 2 minutes, stirring continuously.

Add a splash of cooking sherry to deglaze the pot. Add the other ingredients to the inner pot.

Put on the pressure cooker's lid and turn the steam valve to "Sealing" position.

Press the "Pressure Cook" button two times to select "Less" option.

Use the "+/-" keys on the control panel to set the cooking time to 10 minutes.

Use the Pressure Level button to adjust the pressure to "High Pressure".

Once the cooking cycle is completed, allow the steam to release naturally.

When all the steam is released, remove the pressure lid from the top carefully.

Serve warm with crusty bread, if desired. Bon appétit!

Per Serving: Calories 449; Fat 2.9g; Sodium 511mg; Carbs 12g; Fiber 3g; Sugar 8g; Protein 28g

Sausage and Cabbage Soup

Prep time: 20 minutes| **Cook time:** 15 minutes| **Serves:** 5

2 tablespoons olive oil
1-pound beef sausage, thinly sliced
1 onion, chopped
3 cloves garlic. minced
1 stalk celery, chopped
1 carrot, peeled and chopped
¼ cup Italian cooking wine
1 (1-pound) head cabbage, shredded into small pieces
5 cups beef bone broth
1 tablespoon Italia seasoning blend
1 teaspoon cayenne pepper
1 bay leaf
Salt and cracked black pepper, to taste

Press the "Sauté" button two times to select "Normal" settings and heat the oil.

Once hot, cook the beef sausage until no longer pink.

Now, stir in the onion and garlic; continue to sauté until they are fragrant.

Add a splash of cooking wine, scraping up any browned bits from the bottom of the inner pot.

Add the remaining ingredients.

Put on the pressure cooker's lid and turn the steam valve to "Sealing" position.

Press the "Pressure Cook" button two times to select "Less" option.

Use the "+/-" keys on the control panel to set the cooking time to 6 minutes.

Use the Pressure Level button to adjust the pressure to "High Pressure".

Once the cooking cycle is completed, quickly and carefully turn the steam release handle from Sealing position to the Venting position.

When all the steam is released, remove the pressure lid from the top carefully.

Choose the "Manual" mode and cook for 6 minutes at High Pressure.

Once cooking is complete, use a quick pressure release; carefully remove the lid.

Divide between soup bowls and serve immediately

Per Serving: Calories 479; Fat 10g; Sodium 891mg; Carbs 22.9g; Fiber 4g; Sugar 4g; Protein 3g

Duck Millet Soup

Prep time: 20 minutes| **Cook time:** 20 minutes| **Serves:** 4

2 tablespoons olive oil
1-pound duck portions with bones
2 garlic cloves, minced
4 cups water
1 tablespoon chicken bouillon granules
½ cup millet, rinsed
Salt and freshly cracked black pepper, to taste
¼ cup fresh scallions, chopped

Press the "Sauté" button two times to select "Normal" settings and heat the oil.

Once hot, brown your duck for 4 to 5 minutes; stir in the garlic and cook an additional 30 seconds.

Add the remaining ingredients.

Put on the pressure cooker's lid and turn the steam valve to "Sealing" position.

Press the "Pressure Cook" button two times to select "Less" option.

Use the "+/-" keys on the control panel to set the cooking time to 12 minutes.

Use the Pressure Level button to adjust the pressure to "High Pressure".

Once the cooking cycle is completed, quickly and carefully turn the steam release handle from Sealing position to the Venting position.

When all the steam is released, remove the pressure lid from the top carefully.

Remove the cooked duck to a cutting board. Shred the meat and discard the bones.

Put your duck back into the inner pot. Stir and serve immediately.

Bon appétit!

Per Serving: Calories 489; Fat 11g; Sodium 501mg; Carbs 8.9g; Fiber 4.6g; Sugar 8g; Protein 26g

Beef Potato Stew

Prep time: 20 minutes| **Cook time:** 33 minutes| **Serves:** 8

3 tablespoons olive oil
2½ lbs. beef chuck roast, cut into 1½-inch pieces
1 large onion, diced
1½ cups chopped celery
2 tablespoons minced garlic
¼ cup balsamic vinegar
3 cups beef broth
3 tablespoons tomato paste
4 cups halved baby potatoes
1½ cups peeled and chopped carrots
2 teaspoons salt
2 teaspoons black pepper
1 teaspoon dried thyme
1 teaspoon dried rosemary
1 teaspoon dried oregano

Turn on the Sauté function on Normal mode, and when the inner pot is hot, pour in the oil.
Add the meat, working in batches if necessary, and brown it 2 to 3 minutes on each side.
Add the onion and celery and cook until the onion is translucent, 3 to 4 minutes.
Add the garlic and cook until fragrant, about 1 minute.
Pour in the balsamic vinegar and deglaze the pot, stirring to scrape up the browned bits from the bottom.
Add the remaining ingredients. Put on the pressure cooker's lid and turn the steam valve to "Sealing" position.
Set the Instant Pot to Pressure Cook.
Use the Pressure Level button to adjust the pressure to "High".
Use the "+/-" keys on the control panel to set the cooking time to 30 minutes.
Once the cooking cycle is completed, allow the steam to release naturally for 10 minutes and then quick-release the remaining pressure.
When all the steam is released, remove the pressure lid from the top carefully.
Serve.

Per Serving: Calories 479; Fat 10g; Sodium 891mg; Carbs 22.9g; Fiber 4g; Sugar 4g; Protein 33g

White Chicken Chili

Prep time: 20 minutes| **Cook time:** 20 minutes| **Serves:** 8

2 large boneless, skinless chicken breasts
1 (15-oz.) can black beans, drained
1 (15-oz.) can white beans, drained
1 medium onion, chopped
2 cups frozen corn
1 (10-oz.) can diced tomatoes and green chiles
1 cup chicken broth
1 teaspoon chili powder
1 teaspoon ground cumin
1 (0.4-oz.) packet ranch dressing mix
8 oz. cream cheese, cut into 6 pieces

Combine the chicken, black beans, white beans, onion, corn, tomatoes, and chicken broth in the inner pot.
Sprinkle with the chili powder, cumin, and ranch dressing mix and stir well.
Put on the pressure cooker's lid and turn the steam valve to "Sealing" position.
Set the Instant Pot to Pressure Cook.
Use the "+/-" keys on the control panel to set the cooking time to 20 minutes.
Use the Pressure Level button to adjust the pressure to "High".
Once the cooking cycle is completed, allow the steam to release naturally for 10 minutes and then quick-release the remaining pressure.
When all the steam is released, remove the pressure lid from the top carefully.
Transfer the chicken to a plate and shred it with a fork.
Add the cream cheese to the bean mixture and stir until the cheese is melted and combined.
Return the chicken to the pot and stir well.

Per Serving: Calories 472; Fat 10.9g; Sodium 454mg; Carbs 10g; Fiber 3.1g; Sugar 5.2g; Protein 20g

Beef Peas Stew

Prep time: 20 minutes| **Cook time:** 27 minutes| **Serves:** 4-6

2 tablespoons olive oil
1 ½ lbs. beef stew meat, cut bite-sized pieces
1 red onion, chopped
4 cloves garlic, minced
1 carrot, cut into rounds
1 parsnip, cut into rounds
2 stalks celery, diced
Sea salt and black pepper, to taste
1 teaspoon cayenne pepper
4 cups beef bone broth
½ cup tomato paste
1 tablespoon fish sauce
2 bay leaves
1 cup frozen green peas

Press the "Sauté" button twice to select "Normal" settings and heat the oil.
Once hot, brown the beef stew meat for 4 to 5 minutes; set aside.
Then, cook the onion in pan drippings until tender and translucent; stir in the garlic and cook for 30 seconds.
Add the carrots, parsnip, celery, salt, black pepper, cayenne pepper, beef broth, tomato paste, fish sauce, and bay leaves.
Stir in the reserved beef stew meat.
Put on the pressure cooker's lid and turn the steam valve to "Sealing" position.
Set the Instant Pot to "Meat/Stew".

Use the "+/-" keys on the control panel to set the cooking time to 20 minutes.
Use the Pressure Level button to adjust the pressure to "High".
Once the cooking cycle is completed, quick-release the steam.
When all the steam is released, remove the pressure lid from the top carefully.
Stir in the green peas, cover, and let it sit in for 5 to 7 minutes.
Serve and enjoy!

Per Serving: Calories 334; Fat 19g; Sodium 354mg; Carbs 15g; Fiber 5.1g; Sugar 8.2g; Protein 32g

Italian Beef Stew

Prep time: 20 minutes| **Cook time:** 20 minutes| **Serves:** 4-6
2 lbs. beef top round, cut into bite-sized chunks
¼ cup all-purpose flour
1 tablespoon Italian seasoning
Sea salt and black pepper, to taste
1 tablespoon lard, at room temperature
1 onion, chopped
4 cloves garlic, pressed
¼ cup cooking wine
¼ cup tomato paste
1 pound sweet potatoes, diced
½ pound carrots, sliced into rounds
2 bell peppers, deveined and sliced
1 teaspoon fish sauce
2 bay leaves
4 cups beef broth
2 tablespoons fresh Italian parsley, roughly chopped

Toss the beef chunks with the flour, Italian seasoning, salt, and pepper until well coated.
Press the "Sauté" button twice to select "Normal" settings and melt the lard.
Then, sauté the onion and garlic for a minute or so; add the wine and stir. Scrape up all the browned bits off the inner pot.
Brown the beef chunks on all sides, stirring frequently; reserve.
Add the beef back into the inner pot. Stir in the tomato paste, sweet potatoes, carrots, bell peppers, fish sauce, bay leaves, and beef broth.
Put on the pressure cooker's lid and turn the steam valve to "Sealing" position.
Set the Instant Pot to "Meat/Stew".
Use the "+/-" keys on the control panel to set the cooking time to 20 minutes.
Use the Pressure Level button to adjust the pressure to "High".
Once the cooking cycle is completed, allow the steam to release naturally for 10 minutes.
When all the steam is released, remove the pressure lid from the top carefully.
Serve garnished with Italian parsley.

Per Serving: Calories 344; Fat 7.9g; Sodium 704mg; Carbs 6g; Fiber 3.6g; Sugar 6g; Protein 18g

Bosnian Pot Stew

Prep time: 20 minutes| **Cook time:** 35 minutes| **Serves:** 4-6
2 tablespoons safflower oil
2 lbs. pork loin roast, cut into cubes
2 garlic cloves, chopped
1 onion, chopped
2 carrots, cut into chunks
2 celery ribs, cut into chunks
1 pound potatoes, cut into chunks
sea salt and black pepper, to taste
1 teaspoon paprika
2 tomatoes, pureed
2 cups chicken bone broth
½ pound green beans, cut into 1-inch pieces
2 tablespoons fresh parsley leaves, roughly chopped

Press the "Sauté" button twice to select "Normal" settings and heat the oil until sizzling.
Once hot, cook the pork until it is no longer pink on all sides.
Add the garlic and onion and cook for a minute or so, stirring frequently.
Stir in the carrots, celery, potatoes, salt, black pepper, paprika, tomatoes, and chicken bone broth.
Put on the pressure cooker's lid and turn the steam valve to "Sealing" position.
Set the Instant Pot to "Meat/Stew".
Use the "+/-" keys on the control panel to set the cooking time to 35 minutes.
Use the Pressure Level button to adjust the pressure to "High".
Once the cooking cycle is completed, quick-release the steam.
When all the steam is released, remove the pressure lid from the top carefully.
Add the green beans to the inner pot.
Press the "Sauté" button twice to select "Normal" settings again and let it simmer for a few minutes.
Serve in individual bowls garnished with fresh parsley.

Per Serving: Calories 421; Fat 10.9g; Sodium 354mg; Carbs 10.5g; Fiber 4.1g; Sugar 8.2g; Protein 26g

Chickpea Stew

Prep time: 20 minutes| **Cook time:** 35 minutes| **Serves:** 4-6
2 tablespoons olive oil
1 large-sized leek, chopped
3 cloves garlic, pressed
3 potatoes, diced
2 carrots, diced
1 sweet pepper, seeded and chopped
1 jalapeno pepper, seeded and chopped
1 cup tomato puree
½ teaspoons cumin powder
½ teaspoons turmeric powder
1 teaspoon mustard seeds
2 cups roasted vegetable broth
1 ½ cups chickpeas, soaked overnight

Press the "Sauté" button twice to select "Normal" settings and heat the oil until sizzling.

Once hot, cook the leeks and garlic for 2 to 3 minutes or until they are just tender.

Add the remaining ingredients and stir to combine well.

Put on the pressure cooker's lid and turn the steam valve to "Sealing" position.

Set the Instant Pot to Pressure Cook.

Use the "+/-" keys on the control panel to set the cooking time to 35 minutes.

Use the Pressure Level button to adjust the pressure to "High".

Once the cooking cycle is completed, quick-release the steam.

When all the steam is released, remove the pressure lid from the top carefully.

Serve in individual bowls.

Bon appétit!

Per Serving: Calories 382; Fat 7.9g; Sodium 704mg; Carbs 6g; Fiber 3.6g; Sugar 6g; Protein 18g

Sausage and Bean Stew

Prep time: 20 minutes| **Cook time:** 25 minutes| **Serves:** 4-6

1 tablespoon olive oil
10 oz. smoked beef sausage, sliced
2 carrots, chopped
1 onion, chopped
2 garlic cloves, minced
Sea salt and black pepper, to taste
½ teaspoons fresh rosemary, chopped
1 teaspoon fresh basil, chopped
1 cup canned tomatoes, crushed
1 cup chicken broth
20 oz. pinto beans, soaked overnight
6 oz. kale, torn into pieces

Press the "Sauté" button twice to select "Normal" settings and heat the oil.

Once hot, brown the sausage for 3 to 4 minutes.

Add the remaining ingredients, except for the kale, to the inner pot.

Put on the pressure cooker's lid and turn the steam valve to "Sealing" position.

Set the Instant Pot to Pressure Cook.

Use the "+/-" keys on the control panel to set the cooking time to 25 minutes.

Use the Pressure Level button to adjust the pressure to "High".

Once the cooking cycle is completed, quick-release the steam.

When all the steam is released, remove the pressure lid from the top carefully.

Next, stir in the kale and seal the lid. Let it sit for 5 minutes before serving.

Bon appétit!

Per Serving: Calories 421; Fat 7.9g; Sodium 704mg; Carbs 6g; Fiber 3.6g; Sugar 6g; Protein 18g

Chicken Stew with Apples

Prep time: 20 minutes| **Cook time:** 10 minutes| **Serves:** 4-6

2 tablespoons olive oil
2 lbs. chicken thighs
1 onion, chopped
2 garlic cloves, minced
1 (1-inch) piece fresh ginger, peeled and minced
Kosher salt and black pepper, to taste
1 teaspoon paprika
1 tablespoon fresh sage, chopped
1 pound winter squash, peeled and cubed
2 carrots, trimmed and diced
1 cup apple cider
1 cup chicken stock
2 cups chopped peeled Granny Smith apple

Press the "Sauté" button twice to select "Normal" settings and heat the oil.

Once hot, sear the chicken thighs for about 2 minutes per side; reserve.

Add the onion, garlic, and ginger and sauté them for 2 to 3 minutes or until just tender.

Add the salt, pepper, paprika, sage, winter squash, carrots, apple cider, and chicken stock.

Add the reserved chicken thighs.

Put on the pressure cooker's lid and turn the steam valve to "Sealing" position.

Set the Instant Pot to Pressure Cook.

Use the "+/-" keys on the control panel to set the cooking time to 10 minutes.

Use the Pressure Level button to adjust the pressure to "High".

Once the cooking cycle is completed, allow the steam to release naturally for 10 minutes.

When all the steam is released, remove the pressure lid from the top carefully.

Remove the chicken thighs and shred with two forks; discard the bones.

Add the shredded chicken back into the inner pot.

Afterwards, stir in the apples; Press the "Sauté" button twice to select "Normal" settings and let it simmer for 10 to 12 minutes longer or until the apples are tender. Serve.

Per Serving: Calories 584; Fat 15g; Sodium 441mg; Carbs 17g; Fiber 4.6g; Sugar 5g; Protein 29g

Chicken and Shrimp Gumbo

Prep time: 20 minutes| **Cook time:** 7 minutes| **Serves:** 4-6

2 tablespoons olive oil
1 onion, diced
1 teaspoon garlic, minced
½ pound chicken breasts, boneless, skinless and cubed
½ pound smoked chicken sausage, cut into slices
2 sweet peppers, diced
1 jalapeno pepper, minced
1 celery stalk, diced
2 cups chicken bone broth

2 tomatoes, chopped
1 tablespoon Creole seasoning
Sea salt and black pepper, to taste
1 teaspoon cayenne pepper
1 tablespoon oyster sauce
1 bay leaf
1 pound shrimp, deveined
½ pound okra, frozen
2 stalks green onions, sliced thinly
1 tablespoon fresh lemon juice

Press the "Sauté" button two times to select "Normal" settings and heat the oil.
Sweat the onion and garlic until tender and aromatic or about 3 minutes; reserve.
Then, heat the remaining tablespoon of olive oil and cook the chicken and sausage until no longer pink, about 4 minutes.
Make sure to stir periodically to ensure even cooking.
Stir in the peppers, celery, broth, tomatoes, Creole seasoning, salt, black pepper, cayenne pepper, oyster sauce, and bay leaf. Add the reserved onion mixture.
Put on the pressure cooker's lid and turn the steam valve to "Sealing" position.
Set the Instant Pot to Pressure Cook.
Use the Pressure Level button to adjust the pressure to "High".
Use the "+/-" keys on the control panel to set the cooking time to 7 minutes.
Once the cooking cycle is completed, allow the steam to release naturally.
When all the steam is released, remove the pressure lid from the top carefully.
Afterwards, stir in the shrimp and okra.
Set the Instant Pot on Pressure Cook. Cook for 3 minutes at High pressure.
Once cooking is complete, use a natural pressure release; carefully remove the lid.
Divide between individual bowls and garnish with green onions.
Drizzle lemon juice over each serving. Bon appétit!

Per Serving: Calories 419; Fat 14g; Sodium 791mg; Carbs 8.9g; Fiber 4.6g; Sugar 8g; Protein 3g

Steak Kidney Bean Chili

Prep time: 20 minutes| **Cook time:** 18 minutes| **Serves:** 4-6
2 lbs. beef steak, cut into bite-sized cubes
4 tablespoons all-purpose flour
2 tablespoons vegetable oil
1 onion, chopped
2 cloves garlic, minced
1 jalapeño pepper, seeded and minced
2 cups beef broth
Sea salt and black pepper, to taste
1 teaspoon paprika
1 teaspoon celery seeds
1 teaspoon mustard seeds
2 tablespoons ground cumin
1 tablespoon brown sugar
2 cups red kidney beans, soaked overnight and rinsed
1 cup tomato sauce

2 tablespoons cornstarch, mixed with 4 tablespoons of water

Toss the beef steak with the flour.
Press the "Sauté" button twice to select "Normal" settings and heat the oil until sizzling.
Now, cook the beef steak in batches until browned on all side. Reserve.
Then, cook the onion, garlic, and jalapeño until they soften.
Scrape the bottom of the pot with a splash of beef broth.
Add the beef broth, spices, sugar, beans, and tomato sauce to the inner pot; stir to combine well.
Put on the pressure cooker's lid and turn the steam valve to "Sealing" position.
Set the Instant Pot to Pressure Cook.
Use the "+/-" keys on the control panel to set the cooking time to 18 minutes.
Use the Pressure Level button to adjust the pressure to "High".
Once the cooking cycle is completed, allow the steam to release naturally.
When all the steam is released, remove the pressure lid from the top carefully.
Press the "Sauté" button twice to select "Normal" settings.
Stir in the cornstarch slurry; stir for a few minutes to thicken the cooking liquid.
Bon appétit!

Per Serving: Calories 479; Fat 10g; Sodium 891mg; Carbs 22.9g; Fiber 4g; Sugar 4g; Protein 33g

Marsala Fish Stew

Prep time: 20 minutes| **Cook time:** 5 minutes| **Serves:** 4-6
2 tablespoons canola oil
1 onion, sliced
3 garlic cloves, sliced
½ cup Marsala wine
1 ½ cups shellfish stock
1 cup water
1 pound Yukon Gold potatoes, diced
2 ripe tomatoes, pureed
Sea salt and black pepper, to taste
2 bay leaves
1 teaspoon smoked paprika
½ teaspoons hot sauce
2 lbs. halibut, cut into bite-sized pieces
2 tablespoons fresh cilantro, chopped

Press the "Sauté" button twice to select "Normal" settings and heat the oil.
Once hot, cook the onions until softened; stir in the garlic and continue to sauté an additional 30 seconds.
Add the wine to deglaze the bottom of the inner pot, scraping up any browned bits.
Add the shellfish stock, water, potatoes, tomatoes, salt, black pepper, bay leaves, paprika, hot sauce, and halibut to the inner pot.
Put on the pressure cooker's lid and turn the steam valve to "Sealing" position.

Set the Instant Pot to Pressure Cook.
Use the "+/-" keys on the control panel to set the cooking time to 5 minutes.
Use the Pressure Level button to adjust the pressure to "High".
Once the cooking cycle is completed, quick-release the steam.
When all the steam is released, remove the pressure lid from the top carefully.
Serve with fresh cilantro and enjoy!

Per Serving: Calories 492; Fat 12.9g; Sodium 414mg; Carbs 11g; Fiber 5g; Sugar 9g; Protein 31g

Bœuf À La Bourguignonne

Prep time: 20 minutes| **Cook time:** 26 minutes| **Serves:** 4-6
4 thick slices bacon, diced
2 lbs. beef round roast, cut into 1-inch cubes
Sea salt and black pepper, to taste
1 cup red Burgundy wine
2 onions, thinly sliced
2 carrots, diced
2 celery stalks, diced
4 cloves garlic, minced
2 tablespoons tomato paste
2 thyme sprigs
2 bay leaves
2 cups beef broth
2 tablespoons bouquet garni, chopped

Press the "Sauté" button twice to select "Normal" settings.
Cook the bacon until it is golden-brown; reserve.
Add the beef to the inner pot; sear the beef until browned or about 3 minutes per side.
Stir in the other ingredients; stir to combine well.
Put on the pressure cooker's lid and turn the steam valve to "Sealing" position.
Set the Instant Pot to Pressure Cook.
Use the "+/-" keys on the control panel to set the cooking time to 20 minutes.
Use the Pressure Level button to adjust the pressure to "High".
Once the cooking cycle is completed, quick-release the steam.
When all the steam is released, remove the pressure lid from the top carefully.
Serve in individual bowls topped with the reserved bacon. Bon appétit!

Per Serving: Calories 489; Fat 11g; Sodium 501mg; Carbs 8.9g; Fiber 4.6g; Sugar 8g; Protein 26g

Hungarian Beef Goulash

Prep time: 20 minutes| **Cook time:** 20 minutes| **Serves:** 4-6
2 tablespoons olive oil
2 lbs. beef chuck, cut into bite-sized pieces
¼ cup Hungarian red wine
2 onions, sliced
2 garlic cloves, crushed
1 red chili pepper, minced
Sea salt and black pepper, to taste
1 tablespoon Hungarian paprika
1 beef stock cube
2 cups water
2 ripe tomatoes, puréed
2 bay leaves

Press the "Sauté" button twice to select "Normal" settings and heat the oil.
Once hot, cook the beef until no longer pink.
Add the red wine and stir with a wooden spoon.
Stir in the remaining ingredients.
Put on the pressure cooker's lid and turn the steam valve to "Sealing" position.
Set the Instant Pot to Pressure Cook.
Use the "+/-" keys on the control panel to set the cooking time to 20 minutes.
Use the Pressure Level button to adjust the pressure to "High".
Once the cooking cycle is completed, quick-release the steam.
When all the steam is released, remove the pressure lid from the top carefully.
Serve in individual bowls and enjoy!

Per Serving: Calories 521; Fat 10.9g; Sodium 354mg; Carbs 10.5g; Fiber 4.1g; Sugar 8.2g; Protein 26g

Pork Chile Verde

Prep time: 20 minutes| **Cook time:** 20 minutes| **Serves:** 4-6
1 pound tomatillos, halved
4 garlic cloves, sliced
2 chili peppers, minced
2 heaping tablespoons cilantro, chopped
2 tablespoons olive oil
3 lbs. pork stew meat, cut into 2-inch cubes
1 onion, chopped
1 bell pepper, deveined and sliced
Salt and black pepper, to taste
2 cups vegetable broth

Place the tomatillos under a preheated broiler for about 6 minutes. Let cool enough to handle.
Purée the tomatillos with the garlic, chili peppers, and cilantro in your blender; process until chopped.
Press the "Sauté" button twice to select "Normal" settings and heat the oil.
Once hot, cook the pork until no longer pink.
Add the onion and cook for a few minutes more or until it is tender and translucent.
Add the remaining ingredients, including tomatillo sauce, to the inner pot.
Put on the pressure cooker's lid and turn the steam valve to "Sealing" position.
Set the Instant Pot to "Meat/Stew".
Use the "+/-" keys on the control panel to set the cooking time to 20 minutes.
Use the Pressure Level button to adjust the pressure to "High".
Once the cooking cycle is completed, quick-release the steam.

When all the steam is released, remove the pressure lid from the top carefully.
Ladle into serving bowls and garnish with tortillas if desired.
Bon appétit!

Per Serving: Calories 412; Fat 20g; Sodium 491mg; Carbs 9g; Fiber 3g; Sugar 8g; Protein 31g

Italian Beef Ragù

Prep time: 20 minutes| **Cook time:** 10 minutes| **Serves:** 4-6

2 tablespoons butter, melted
1 medium leek, diced
2 carrots, diced
1 stalk celery, diced
5 oz. bacon, diced
1 pound ground chuck
½ cup Italian red wine
¼ cup tomato puree
2 cups chicken stock
1 tablespoon Italian seasoning blend
½ teaspoons kosher salt
½ teaspoons black pepper

Press the "Sauté" button twice to select "Normal" settings and melt the butter.
Sauté the leek, carrot, celery and garlic for 2 to 3 minutes.
Add the bacon and ground beef to the inner pot; continue to cook an additional 3 minutes, stirring frequently.
Add the remaining ingredients to the inner pot.
Put on the pressure cooker's lid and turn the steam valve to "Sealing" position.
Set the Instant Pot to Pressure Cook.
Use the "+/-" keys on the control panel to set the cooking time to 5 minutes.
Use the Pressure Level button to adjust the pressure to "High".
Once the cooking cycle is completed, quick-release the steam.
When all the steam is released, remove the pressure lid from the top carefully.
Serve with hot pasta if desired.
Bon appétit!

Per Serving: Calories 449; Fat 2.9g; Sodium 511mg; Carbs 12g; Fiber 3g; Sugar 8g; Protein 28g

Brunswick Stew

Prep time: 20 minutes| **Cook time:** 12 minutes| **Serves:** 4-6

2 tablespoons lard, melted
1 onion, diced
2 cloves garlic, minced
1 pound chicken breast, cut into 1-inch cubes
2 cups lima beans, soaked
1 (14 ½-oz.) can tomatoes, diced
2 cups chicken broth
1 tablespoon Worcestershire sauce
1 teaspoon Creole seasoning
Sea salt and black pepper, to taste

1 teaspoon hot sauce
1 cup corn kernels

Press the "Sauté" button twice to select "Normal" settings and melt the lard.
Once hot, cook the onion and garlic until just tender and aromatic.
Now, add the chicken and cook an additional 3 minutes, stirring frequently.
Add the lima beans, tomatoes, broth, Worcestershire sauce, Creole seasoning, salt, black pepper, and hot sauce to the inner pot.
Put on the pressure cooker's lid and turn the steam valve to "Sealing" position.
Set the Instant Pot to Pressure Cook.
Use the "+/-" keys on the control panel to set the cooking time to 12 minutes.
Use the Pressure Level button to adjust the pressure to "High".
Once the cooking cycle is completed, allow the steam to release naturally.
When all the steam is released, remove the pressure lid from the top carefully.
Stir in the corn kernels and seal the lid. Let it sit in the residual heat until heated through. Enjoy!

Per Serving: Calories 419; Fat 14g; Sodium 791mg; Carbs 8.9g; Fiber 4.6g; Sugar 8g; Protein 3g

Traditional Polish Stew

Prep time: 20 minutes| **Cook time:** 15 minutes| **Serves:** 4-6

2 slices smoked bacon, diced
1 pound Kielbasa, sliced
½ pound pork stew meat, cubed
1 onion, chopped
4 garlic cloves, sliced
2 carrots, trimmed and diced
1 pound sauerkraut, drained
1 pound fresh cabbage, shredded
1 teaspoon dried thyme
1 teaspoon dried basil
2 bay leaves
1 tablespoon cayenne pepper
1 teaspoon mustard seeds
1 teaspoon caraway seeds, crushed
Sea salt, to taste
½ teaspoons black peppercorns
½ cup dry red wine
2 ½ cups beef stock
½ cup tomato puree

Press the "Sauté" button twice to select "Normal" settings.
Now, cook the bacon, Kielbasa, and pork stew meat until the bacon is crisp; reserve.
Add the onion and garlic, and sauté them until they're softened and starting to brown.
Add the remaining ingredients to the inner pot, including the reserved meat mixture.
Put on the pressure cooker's lid and turn the steam valve to "Sealing" position.
Set the Instant Pot to Pressure Cook.
Use the "+/-" keys on the control panel to set the cooking time to 15 minutes.

Use the Pressure Level button to adjust the pressure to "High".
Once the cooking cycle is completed, quick-release the steam. .
When all the steam is released, remove the pressure lid from the top carefully.
Ladle into individual bowls and serve warm.

Per Serving: Calories 584; Fat 15g; Sodium 441mg; Carbs 17g; Fiber 4.6g; Sugar 5g; Protein 29g

Vegan Pottage Stew

Prep time: 20 minutes| **Cook time:** 15 minutes| **Serves:** 4-6

2 tablespoons olive oil
1 onion, chopped
2 garlic cloves, minced
2 carrots, diced
2 parsnips, diced
1 turnip, diced
4 cups vegetable broth
2 bay leaves
2 thyme sprigs
2 rosemary sprigs
Kosher salt and black pepper, to taste
¼ cup red wine
1 cup porridge oats

Press the "Sauté" button twice to select "Normal" settings and heat the olive oil until sizzling.
Now, sauté the onion and garlic until just tender and fragrant.
Add the remaining ingredients to the inner pot; stir to combine.
Put on the pressure cooker's lid and turn the steam valve to "Sealing" position.
Set the Instant Pot to Pressure Cook.
Use the "+/-" keys on the control panel to set the cooking time to 10 minutes.
Use the Pressure Level button to adjust the pressure to "High".
Once the cooking cycle is completed, quick-release the steam.
When all the steam is released, remove the pressure lid from the top carefully.
Ladle into individual bowls and serve immediately.
Bon appétit!

Per Serving: Calories 382; Fat 7.9g; Sodium 704mg; Carbs 6g; Fiber 3.6g; Sugar 6g; Protein 18g

Mulligan Stew

Prep time: 20 minutes| **Cook time:** 20 minutes| **Serves:** 8

1 tablespoon lard, melted
2 lbs. pork butt roast, cut into 2-inch pieces
2 lbs. beef stew meat, cut into 2-inch pieces
2 chicken thighs, boneless
2 bell peppers, chopped
1 red chili pepper, chopped
1 onion, chopped
2 carrots, chopped

4 garlic cloves, chopped
4 cups beef bone broth
1 cup beer
1 (28-oz.) can tomatoes, crushed
Sea salt and black pepper, to taste
1 pound frozen corn kernels
3 tablespoons Worcestershire sauce

Press the "Sauté" button twice to select "Normal" settings and melt the lard. Once hot, brown the meat in batches. Remove the browned meats to a bowl.
Then, sauté the peppers, onion, carrots for about 3 minutes or until tender and fragrant. Add the garlic and continue to cook for 30 seconds more.
Add the meat back to the Instant Pot. Stir in the remaining ingredients, except for the corn kernels.
Put on the pressure cooker's lid and turn the steam valve to "Sealing" position.
Set the Instant Pot to "Meat/Stew".
Use the "+/-" keys on the control panel to set the cooking time to 20 minutes.
Use the Pressure Level button to adjust the pressure to "High".
Once the cooking cycle is completed, allow the steam to release naturally.
When all the steam is released, quick-release the steam.
Lastly, stir in the corn and continue to cook for a few minutes more on the "Sauté" function.
Serve immediately.

Per Serving: Calories 334; Fat 10.9g; Sodium 454mg; Carbs 10g; Fiber 3.1g; Sugar 5.2g; Protein 20g

Irish Bean Cabbage Stew

Prep time: 20 minutes| **Cook time:** 25 minutes| **Serves:** 4-6

2 cups white beans, soaked and rinsed
½ cup pearled barley
4 cups roasted vegetable broth
1 shallot, chopped
2 carrots, chopped
2 ribs celery, chopped
1 sweet pepper, chopped
1 serrano pepper, chopped
4 cloves garlic, minced
1 pound cabbage, chopped
½ pound potatoes, diced
2 bay leaves
½ teaspoons mustard seeds
½ teaspoons caraway seeds
1 teaspoon cayenne pepper
Sea salt and black pepper, to taste
1 (14 ½-oz.) can tomatoes, diced

Place the white beans, barley, and vegetable broth in the inner pot.
Put on the pressure cooker's lid and turn the steam valve to "Sealing" position.
Set the Instant Pot to "Bean/Chili".
Use the "+/-" keys on the control panel to set the cooking time to 25 minutes.

Use the Pressure Level button to adjust the pressure to "High".

Once the cooking cycle is completed, quick-release the steam.

When all the steam is released, remove the pressure lid from the top carefully.

Add the remaining ingredients and stir to combine.

Set the Instant Pot to Pressure Cook and cook for 5 minutes at High pressure.

Once cooking is complete, use a quick pressure release; carefully remove the lid.

Serve in individual bowls and enjoy!

Per Serving: Calories 449; Fat 2.9g; Sodium 511mg; Carbs 12g; Fiber 3g; Sugar 8g; Protein 28g

Rich Chicken Purloo

Prep time: 20 minutes| **Cook time:** 10 minutes| **Serves:** 8

1 tablespoon olive oil
1 onion, chopped
3 lbs. chicken legs, boneless and skinless
2 garlic cloves, minced
5 cups water
2 carrots, diced
2 celery ribs, diced
2 bay leaves
1 teaspoon mustard seeds
¼ teaspoon marjoram
Seasoned salt and black pepper, to taste
1 teaspoon cayenne pepper
2 cups white long-grain rice

Press the "Sauté" button twice to select "Normal" settings and heat the olive oil.

Now, add the onion and chicken legs; cook until the onion is translucent or about 4 minutes.

Stir in the minced garlic and continue to cook for a minute more. Add the water.

Put on the pressure cooker's lid and turn the steam valve to "Sealing" position.

Set the Instant Pot to Pressure Cook.

Use the "+/-" keys on the control panel to set the cooking time to 10 minutes.

Use the Pressure Level button to adjust the pressure to "High".

Once the cooking cycle is completed, quick-release the steam.

When all the steam is released, remove the pressure lid from the top carefully.

Add the remaining ingredients.

Set the Instant Pot to Pressure Cook and cook for 5 minutes at High pressure.

Once cooking is complete, use a quick pressure release; carefully remove the lid.

Serve warm.

Per Serving: Calories 479; Fat 10g; Sodium 891mg; Carbs 22.9g; Fiber 4g; Sugar 4g; Protein 33g

Almond Lentil Vegetable Stew

Prep time: 20 minutes| **Cook time:** 10 minutes| **Serves:** 4-6

1 tablespoon olive oil
1 onion, chopped
1 teaspoon fresh garlic, minced
1 dried chili pepper, crushed
1 pound potatoes, cut into 1-inch pieces
1 pound cauliflower, broken into florets
1 cup green lentils
3 cups tomato juice
3 cups vegetable broth
Seasoned salt and black pepper, to taste
1 teaspoon cayenne pepper
½ cup almond butter
2 heaping tablespoons cilantro, roughly chopped
1 heaping tablespoon parsley, roughly chopped

Press the "Sauté" button twice to select "Normal" settings and heat the olive oil.

Now, sauté the onion until it is transparent.

Add garlic and continue to sauté an additional minute.

Stir in the chili pepper, potatoes, cauliflower, lentils, tomato juice, vegetable broth, salt, black pepper, and cayenne pepper.

Put on the pressure cooker's lid and turn the steam valve to "Sealing" position.

Set the Instant Pot to Pressure Cook.

Use the "+/-" keys on the control panel to set the cooking time to 10 minutes.

Use the Pressure Level button to adjust the pressure to "High".

Once the cooking cycle is completed, quick-release the steam.

When all the steam is released, remove the pressure lid from the top carefully.

Stir in the almond butter. Press the "Sauté" button on "Less" settings.

And simmer for about 3 minutes.

Garnish with cilantro and parsley.

Bon appétit!

Per Serving: Calories 461; Fat 7.9g; Sodium 704mg; Carbs 6g; Fiber 3.6g; Sugar 6g; Protein 18g

Catalan Shellfish Stew

Prep time: 20 minutes| **Cook time:** 10 minutes| **Serves:** 4-6

4 tablespoons olive oil
1 onion, chopped
3 cloves garlic, minced
4 oz. prosciutto, diced
1 ½ lbs. shrimp
1 ½ lbs. clams
1 Chile de Arbol, minced
½ cup dry white wine
4 cups clam juice
1 laurel (bay leaf)
Sea salt and black pepper, to taste
1 teaspoon guindilla (cayenne pepper)
1 teaspoon rosemary, chopped
1 teaspoon basil, chopped
2 tomatoes, pureed

1 fresh lemon, sliced

Press the "Sauté" button two times to select "Normal" settings and heat the olive oil.
Now, sauté the onion until it is transparent.
Add the garlic and continue to sauté an additional 1 minute.
Add the prosciutto and cook an additional 3 minutes. Add the remaining ingredients, except for the lemon.
Put on the pressure cooker's lid and turn the steam valve to "Sealing" position.
Set the Instant Pot to Pressure Cook.
Use the "+/-" keys on the control panel to set the cooking time to 10 minutes.
Use the Pressure Level button to adjust the pressure to "High".
Once the cooking cycle is completed, allow the steam to release naturally for 10 minutes.
When all the steam is released, remove the pressure lid from the top carefully.
Serve in individual bowls garnished with lemon slices.
Enjoy!

Per Serving: Calories 478; Fat 7.9g; Sodium 704mg; Carbs 6g; Fiber 3.6g; Sugar 6g; Protein 18g

Beef and Potato Stew

Prep time: 20 minutes| **Cook time:** 20 minutes| **Serves:** 4-6
1 tablespoon lard, melted
2 lbs. chuck roast, cut into 2-inch cubes
2 onions, chopped
2 cloves garlic, minced
2 tablespoons Hungarian paprika
4 bell peppers, deveined and chopped
1 chili pepper, chopped
1 cup tomato puree
4 potatoes, diced
4 cups beef broth
2 bay leaves
Seasoned salt and black pepper, to taste

Press the "Sauté" button twice to select "Normal" settings and melt the lard.
Once hot, cook the beef until no longer pink.
Add a splash of broth and stir with a wooden spoon, scraping up the browned bits on the bottom of the inner pot.
Add the onion to the inner pot; continue sautéing an additional 3 minutes.
Now, stir in the garlic and cook for 30 seconds more.
Stir in the remaining ingredients.
Put on the pressure cooker's lid and turn the steam valve to "Sealing" position.
Set the Instant Pot on "Meat/Stew".
Use the Pressure Level button to adjust the pressure to "High".
Use the "+/-" keys on the control panel to set the cooking time to 20 minutes.
Once the cooking cycle is completed, quick-release the steam.
When all the steam is released, remove the pressure lid from the top carefully.

Discard the bay leaves and serve in individual bowls.
Bon appétit!

Per Serving: Calories 492; Fat 12.9g; Sodium 414mg; Carbs 11g; Fiber 5g; Sugar 9g; Protein 31g

Hungarian Chicken Stew

Prep time: 20 minutes| **Cook time:** 15 minutes| **Serves:** 4-6
2 tablespoons lard, at room temperature
2 lbs. chicken, cut into pieces
2 onions, chopped
2 cloves garlic, minced
1 cup tomato puree
1 Hungarian pepper, diced
2 tablespoons Hungarian paprika
2 cups chicken stock
Kosher salt and cracked black pepper
3 tablespoons all-purpose flour
1 cup full-fat sour cream

Press the "Sauté" button twice to select "Normal" settings and melt the lard.
Once hot, cook the chicken for about 3 minutes or until no longer pink.
Add the onion to the inner pot; continue sautéing an additional 3 minutes.
Now, stir in the garlic and cook for 30 seconds more.
Add the tomato puree, Hungarian pepper, paprika, chicken stock, salt, and black pepper to the inner pot.
Put on the pressure cooker's lid and turn the steam valve to "Sealing" position.
Set the Instant Pot to Pressure Cook.
Use the "+/-" keys on the control panel to set the cooking time to 15 minutes.
Use the Pressure Level button to adjust the pressure to "High".
Once the cooking cycle is completed, quick-release the steam.
When all the steam is released, remove the pressure lid from the top carefully.
Remove the chicken from the inner pot; shred the chicken and discard the bones.
In a mixing bowl, stir the flour into the sour cream.
Add the flour/cream mixture to the cooking liquid, stirring constantly with a wire whisk.
Let it simmer until the sauce is thickened.
Return the chicken to your paprika, stir and press the "Cancel" button.
Enjoy!

Per Serving: Calories 584; Fat 15g; Sodium 441mg; Carbs 17g; Fiber 4.6g; Sugar 5g; Protein 29g

Indian Bean Stew

Prep time: 20 minutes| **Cook time:** 26 minutes| **Serves:** 4-6
2 tablespoons sesame oil
1 onion, sliced
4 cloves garlic, finely chopped

1 (1-inch) piece fresh ginger root, peeled and grated
2 cups red kidney beans, soaked overnight
2 Bhut jolokia peppers, minced
1 teaspoon red curry paste
5 cups vegetable broth
1 teaspoon coriander seeds
1/2 teaspoons cumin seeds
¼ teaspoon ground cinnamon
Seasoned salt and black pepper, to taste
2 tomatoes, pureed
2 tablespoons fresh coriander, chopped

Press the "Sauté" button twice to select "Normal" settings and heat the oil.
Now, sauté the onion until it is transparent.
Add the garlic and ginger and continue to sauté an additional 1 minute.
Add the beans, peppers, curry paste, vegetable broth spices, and tomatoes.
Put on the pressure cooker's lid and turn the steam valve to "Sealing" position.
Set the Instant Pot to Pressure Cook.
Use the "+/-" keys on the control panel to set the cooking time to 25 minutes.
Use the Pressure Level button to adjust the pressure to "High".
Once the cooking cycle is completed, quick-release the pressure.
When all the steam is released, remove the pressure lid from the top carefully.
Serve in individual bowls garnished with fresh coriander.
Enjoy!

Per Serving: Calories 472; Fat 10.9g; Sodium 354mg; Carbs 10.5g; Fiber 4.1g; Sugar 8.2g; Protein 26g

Mediterranean Chicken Stew

Prep time: 20 minutes| **Cook time:** 15 minutes| **Serves:** 4
2 tablespoons olive oil
1 onion, chopped
1 stalk celery, chopped
2 carrots, chopped
1 teaspoon garlic, minced
4 chicken legs, boneless skinless
¼ cup dry red wine
2 ripe tomatoes, pureed
2 cups chicken bone broth
2 bay leaves
Sea salt and black pepper, to taste
½ teaspoon dried basil
1 teaspoon dried oregano
½ cup Kalamata olives, pitted and sliced

Press the "Sauté" button twice to select "Normal" settings and heat the oil.
Now, sauté the onion, celery, and carrot for 4 to 5 minutes or until they are tender.
Add the other ingredients, except for the Kalamata olives, and stir to combine.
Put on the pressure cooker's lid and turn the steam valve to "Sealing" position.
Set the Instant Pot to Pressure Cook.
Use the "+/-" keys on the control panel to set the cooking time to 15 minutes.

Use the Pressure Level button to adjust the pressure to "High".
Once the cooking cycle is completed, allow the steam to release naturally.
When all the steam is released, remove the pressure lid from the top carefully.
Serve warm garnished with Kalamata olives.
Bon appétit!

Per Serving: Calories 479; Fat 10g; Sodium 891mg; Carbs 22.9g; Fiber 4g; Sugar 4g; Protein 33g

Seafood Vegetable Ragout

Prep time: 20 minutes| **Cook time:** 10 minutes| **Serves:** 4-6
2 tablespoons olive oil
1 shallot, diced
2 carrots, diced
1 parsnip, diced
1 teaspoon fresh garlic, minced
½ cup dry white wine
2 cups fish stock
1 tomato, pureed
1 bay leaf
1 pound shrimp, deveined
½ pound scallops
Seasoned salt and pepper, to taste
1 tablespoon paprika
2 tablespoons fresh parsley, chopped
1 lime, sliced

Press the "Sauté" button twice to select "Normal" settings and heat the oil.
Now, sauté the shallot, carrot, and parsnip for 4 to 5 minutes or until they are tender.
Stir in the garlic and continue to sauté an additional 30 second or until aromatic.
Stir in the white wine, stock, tomato, bay leaf, shrimp, scallops, salt, black pepper, and paprika.
Put on the pressure cooker's lid and turn the steam valve to "Sealing" position.
Set the Instant Pot to Pressure Cook.
Use the "+/-" keys on the control panel to set the cooking time to 5 minutes.
Use the Pressure Level button to adjust the pressure to "High".
Once the cooking cycle is completed, allow the steam to release naturally for 5 minutes.
When all the steam is released, remove the pressure lid from the top carefully.
Enjoy!

Per Serving: Calories 449; Fat 2.9g; Sodium 511mg; Carbs 12g; Fiber 3g; Sugar 8g; Protein 28g

Spanish Olla Podrida

Prep time: 20 minutes| **Cook time:** 20 minutes| **Serves:** 4-6
2 ½ lbs. meaty pork ribs in adobo
½ pound Spanish chorizo sausage, sliced
1 tablespoon olive oil
2 onions, chopped
2 carrots, sliced

2 garlic cloves, sliced
Salt and black pepper, to taste
1 pound alubias de Ibeas beans, soaked
overnight

Place the pork and sausage in the inner pot;
cover with water.
Add the other ingredients and stir to combine.
Put on the pressure cooker's lid and turn the
steam valve to "Sealing" position.
Set the Instant Pot to Pressure Cook.
Use the "+/-" keys on the control panel to set
the cooking time to 20 minutes.
Use the Pressure Level button to adjust the
pressure to "High".
Once the cooking cycle is completed, quick-
release the pressure.
When all the steam is released, remove the
pressure lid from the top carefully.
Serve hot with corn tortilla if desired.
Enjoy!

Per Serving: Calories 492; Fat 7.9g; Sodium
704mg; Carbs 6g; Fiber 3.6g; Sugar 6g;
Protein 18g

Basque Squid Stew

Prep time: 20 minutes| **Cook time:** 10
minutes| **Serves:** 4-6
2 tablespoons olive oil
1 onion, finely diced
2 cloves garlic, minced
1 thyme sprig, chopped
1 rosemary sprig, chopped
1 serrano pepper, deseeded and chopped
2 tomatoes, pureed
½ cup clam juice
1 cup chicken stock
½ cup cooking sherry
1 pound fresh squid, cleaned and sliced into
rings
Sea salt and black pepper, to taste
1 teaspoon cayenne pepper
1 bay leaf
¼ teaspoon saffron
1 lemon, cut into wedges

Press the "Sauté" button twice to select
"Normal" settings and heat the oil.
Now, sauté the onion until tender and
translucent.
Now, add the garlic and continue to sauté an
additional minute.
Add the remaining ingredients, except for the
lemon.
Put on the pressure cooker's lid and turn the
steam valve to "Sealing" position.
Set the Instant Pot to Pressure Cook.
Use the "+/-" keys on the control panel to set
the cooking time to 10 minutes.
Use the Pressure Level button to adjust the
pressure to "High".
Once the cooking cycle is completed, quick-
release the pressure.
When all the steam is released, remove the
pressure lid from the top carefully.
Serve garnished with lemon wedges.
Bon appétit!

Per Serving: Calories 493; Fat 12.9g;
Sodium 414mg; Carbs 11g; Fiber 5g; Sugar
9g; Protein 31g

Slumgullion Stew

Prep time: 20 minutes| **Cook time:** 10
minutes| **Serves:** 4-6
1 tablespoon canola oil
1 leek, chopped
2 garlic cloves, minced
2 carrots, chopped
½ (16-oz.) package macaroni
½ pound ground beef
½ pound pork sausage, crumbled
1 ½ cups tomato puree
1 ½ cups chicken broth
Seasoned salt and black pepper, to taste
1 (15-oz.) can stewed tomatoes
2 cups green beans, cut into thirds

Press the "Sauté" button twice to select
"Normal" settings and heat the oil.
Now, sauté the leek, garlic and carrot until
they have softened.
Then, add the macaroni, ground beef,
sausage, tomato puree, chicken broth, salt,
and black pepper to the inner pot.
Put on the pressure cooker's lid and turn the
steam valve to "Sealing" position.
Set the Instant Pot to Pressure Cook.
Use the "+/-" keys on the control panel to set
the cooking time to 10 minutes.
Use the Pressure Level button to adjust the
pressure to "High".
Once the cooking cycle is completed, quick-
release the pressure.
When all the steam is released, remove the
pressure lid from the top carefully.
After that, add the canned tomatoes and
green beans; let it simmer on the "Sauté"
function for 2 to 3 minutes.
Bon appétit!

Per Serving: Calories 405; Fat 19g; Sodium
354mg; Carbs 15g; Fiber 5.1g; Sugar 8.2g;
Protein 32g

Lentil Vegetable Hotpot

Prep time: 20 minutes| **Cook time:** 15
minutes| **Serves:** 4-6
1 tablespoon olive oil
1 onion, chopped
3 cloves garlic, minced
1 carrot, chopped
1 stalk celery, chopped
1 parsnip, chopped
2 cups brown lentils
2 tomatoes, pureed
1 sprig thyme, chopped
1 sprig rosemary, chopped
1 teaspoon basil
Kosher salt and black pepper, to taste
2 cups vegetable broth
3 cups Swiss chard, torn into pieces

Press the "Sauté" button twice to select "Normal" settings and heat the oil.
Sauté the onion until tender and translucent or about 4 minutes.
Then, stir in the garlic and cook an additional 30 seconds or until fragrant.
Now, stir in the carrot, celery, parsnip, lentils, tomatoes, spices, and broth.
Afterwards, add the Swiss chard to the inner pot.
Put on the pressure cooker's lid and turn the steam valve to "Sealing" position.
Set the Instant Pot to Pressure Cook.
Use the "+/-" keys on the control panel to set the cooking time to 10 minutes.
Use the Pressure Level button to adjust the pressure to "High".
Once the cooking cycle is completed, quick-release the pressure.
When all the steam is released, remove the pressure lid from the top carefully.
Bon appétit!

Per Serving: Calories 419; Fat 14g; Sodium 791mg; Carbs 8.9g; Fiber 4.6g; Sugar 8g; Protein 3g

Vegetarian Ratatouille

Prep time: 20 minutes| **Cook time:** 15 minutes| **Serves:** 4-6
1 pound eggplant, cut into rounds
1 tablespoon sea salt
3 tablespoons olive oil
1 red onion, sliced
4 cloves garlic, minced
4 sweet peppers, seeded and chopped
1 red chili pepper, seeded and minced
Sea salt and black pepper, to taste
1 teaspoon capers
½ teaspoons celery seeds
2 tomatoes, pureed
1 cup roasted vegetable broth
2 tablespoons coriander, chopped

Toss the eggplant with 1 tablespoon of sea salt; allow it to drain in a colander.
Press the "Sauté" button twice to select "Normal" settings and heat the olive oil.
Sauté the onion until tender and translucent, about 4 minutes.
Add the garlic and continue to sauté for 30 seconds more or until fragrant.
Add the remaining ingredients to the inner pot, including the drained eggplant.
Press the "Sauté" button two times to select "Normal" setting and cook for 7 minutes.
Bon appétit!

Per Serving: Calories 584; Fat 15g; Sodium 441mg; Carbs 17g; Fiber 4.6g; Sugar 5g; Protein 29g

French Pot-Au-Feu

Prep time: 20 minutes| **Cook time:** 20 minutes| **Serves:** 4-6
2 tablespoons olive oil

2 lbs. beef pot roast, cut into 2-inch pieces
1 onion, chopped
2 carrots, chopped
3 garlic cloves, pressed
2 tomatoes, pureed
1 cup dry red wine
3 cups beef broth
½ teaspoons marjoram
½ teaspoons sage
Sea salt and black pepper, to taste
1 shallot, sliced
1 pound cremini mushrooms, sliced
1 cup chèvres cheese, crumbled

Press the "Sauté" button twice to select "Normal" settings and heat the olive oil.
Cook the beef in batches and transfer to a bowl.
Then, cook the onion in pan drippings.
Stir in the carrots and garlic and continue to cook an additional 3 minutes.
Add the tomatoes, wine, broth, marjoram, sage, salt, and black pepper. Add the browned beef.
Put on the pressure cooker's lid and turn the steam valve to "Sealing" position.
Set the Instant Pot on "Meat/Stew".
Use the "+/-" keys on the control panel to set the cooking time to 45 minutes.
Use the Pressure Level button to adjust the pressure to "High".
Once the cooking cycle is completed, quick-release the pressure.
When all the steam is released, remove the pressure lid from the top carefully.
Now, add the shallot and mushrooms; continue to cook on the "Sauté" function for 10 minutes.
Transfer your stew to a lightly greased casserole dish.
Top with the cheese and place under a preheated broiler for 10 minutes or until the cheese melts.
Serve warm.

Per Serving: Calories 489; Fat 11g; Sodium 501mg; Carbs 8.9g; Fiber 4.6g; Sugar 8g; Protein 26g

Chicken Fricassee with Wine

Prep time: 20 minutes| **Cook time:** 15 minutes| **Serves:** 4-6
2 tablespoons canola oil
6 chicken wings
1 onion, chopped
2 garlic cloves, minced
Kosher salt and black pepper, to taste
1 teaspoon cayenne pepper
1 teaspoon celery seeds
½ teaspoon mustard powder
2 carrots, chopped
2 celery stalks, chopped
3 cups vegetable broth
½ cup cooking sherry
2 tablespoons all-purpose flour
1 cup double cream

Press the "Sauté" button twice to select "Normal" settings and heat 1 tablespoon of olive oil.
Now, cook the chicken wings for 2 to 3 minutes per side; set aside.
Add a splash of cooking sherry to deglaze the pot.
Then, heat the remaining tablespoon of olive oil; sauté the onion until just tender or about 3 minutes.
Stir in the garlic and continue to cook an additional minute, stirring frequently.
Add the reserved chicken, salt, black pepper, cayenne pepper, celery seeds, mustard powder, carrots, celery, broth, and sherry to the inner pot.
Put on the pressure cooker's lid and turn the steam valve to "Sealing" position.
Set the Instant Pot on "Poultry".
Use the "+/-" keys on the control panel to set the cooking time to 15 minutes.
Use the Pressure Level button to adjust the pressure to "High".
Once the cooking cycle is completed, quick-release the pressure.
When all the steam is released, remove the pressure lid from the top carefully.
Mix the flour with the double cream.
Add the flour mixture to the hot cooking liquid.
Seal the lid and let it sit in the residual heat until thoroughly warmed.
Ladle into individual bowls and serve.
Bon appétit!

Per Serving: Calories 334; Fat 7.9g; Sodium 704mg; Carbs 6g; Fiber 3.6g; Sugar 6g; Protein 18g

Barley Pottage

Prep time: 20 minutes| **Cook time:** 20 minutes| **Serves:** 4-6
1 tablespoon olive oil
1 onion, chopped
2 cloves garlic, minced
1 red chili pepper, minced
2 sweet peppers, seeded and chopped
1 ½ cups pearled barley
2 cups water
4 cups vegetable broth
2 stalks celery, chopped
2 carrots, chopped
2 tomatoes, pureed
1 teaspoon red pepper flakes
Sea salt and black pepper, to taste

Press the "Sauté" button twice to select "Normal" settings and heat the olive oil.
Now, sauté the onion until tender and translucent.
Then, stir in the garlic and peppers and cook an additional 3 minutes. Stir in the pearled barley.
Pour in water and broth.
Add the remaining ingredients to the inner pot.
Put on the pressure cooker's lid and turn the steam valve to "Sealing" position.

Set the Instant Pot to Pressure Cook.
Use the "+/-" keys on the control panel to set the cooking time to 15 minutes.
Use the Pressure Level button to adjust the pressure to "High".
Once the cooking cycle is completed, quick-release the steam.
When all the steam is released, remove the pressure lid from the top carefully.
Bon appétit!

Per Serving: Calories 405; Fat 10.9g; Sodium 454mg; Carbs 10g; Fiber 3.1g; Sugar 5.2g; Protein 20g

Hyderabadi- Lentil Stew

Prep time: 20 minutes| **Cook time:** 10 minutes| **Serves:** 4-6
2 tablespoons canola oil
1 teaspoon cumin seeds
1 onion, chopped
1 teaspoon garlic paste
2 cups yellow lentils, soaked for 30 minutes and rinsed
½ teaspoons tamarind paste
½ teaspoons red chili powder
10 curry leaves
1 cup tomato sauce
Kosher salt and white pepper, to taste

Press the "Sauté" button twice to select "Normal" settings and heat the oil.
Then, sauté the cumin seeds for 1 to 2 minutes, stirring frequently.
Then, add the onion and cook an additional 2 minutes. Stir in the remaining ingredients.
Put on the pressure cooker's lid and turn the steam valve to "Sealing" position.
Set the Instant Pot to Pressure Cook.
Use the "+/-" keys on the control panel to set the cooking time to 5 minutes.
Use the Pressure Level button to adjust the pressure to "High".
Once the cooking cycle is completed, allow the steam to release naturally for 10 minutes.
When all the steam is released, remove the pressure lid from the top carefully.
Ladle into individual bowls and serve immediately.
Bon appétit!

Per Serving: Calories 405; Fat 12.9g; Sodium 414mg; Carbs 11g; Fiber 5g; Sugar 9g; Protein 31g

Kentucky Burgoo

Prep time: 20 minutes| **Cook time:** 55 minutes| **Serves:** 8
2 tablespoons lard, melted
2 onions, chopped
1 pound pork shank, cubed
2 lbs. beef shank, cubed
1 pound chicken legs
½ cup Kentucky bourbon
4 cups chicken broth
2 cups dry lima beans, soaked

2 cups tomato puree
1 pound potatoes, diced
2 carrots, sliced thickly
2 parsnips, sliced thickly
1 celery rib, sliced thickly
2 sweet peppers, seeded and sliced
1 jalapeno pepper, seeded and minced
1 teaspoon dried sage, crushed
1 teaspoon dried basil, crushed
Salt and black pepper, to taste

Press the "Sauté" button two times to select "Normal" settings and melt 1 tablespoon of lard.
Once hot, sauté the onion until tender and translucent; reserve.
Add the remaining tablespoon of lard; brown the meat in batches until no longer pink or about 4 minutes.
Add a splash of Kentucky bourbon to deglaze the pot. Pour chicken broth into the inner pot.
Put on the pressure cooker's lid and turn the steam valve to "Sealing" position.
Set the Instant Pot on "Meat/Stew".
Use the "+/-" keys on the control panel to set the cooking time to 45 minutes.
Use the Pressure Level button to adjust the pressure to "High".
Once the cooking cycle is completed, quick-release the pressure.
When all the steam is released, remove the pressure lid from the top carefully.
Shred chicken meat and discard the bones; add the chicken back to the inner pot.
Next, stir in lima beans and tomato puree.
Set the Instant Pot on Pressure Cook. Cook for 5 minutes at High pressure.
Once cooking is complete, use a quick pressure release; carefully remove the lid.
Then, stir in the remaining ingredients, including the sautéed onion.
Set the Instant Pot on Pressure Cook again. Cook for 5 minutes at High pressure.
Once cooking is complete, use a quick pressure release; carefully remove the lid.
Serve with cornbread if desired.

Per Serving: Calories 382; Fat 7.9g; Sodium 704mg; Carbs 6g; Fiber 3.6g; Sugar 6g; Protein 18g

Thai Curry Stew

Prep time: 20 minutes| **Cook time:** 44 minutes| **Serves:** 4-6
2 tablespoons sesame oil
2 lbs. beef chuck, cubed
2 onions, thinly sliced
2 cloves garlic, pressed
1 (2-inch) galangal piece, peeled and sliced
1 Bird's eye chili pepper, seeded and minced
½ cup tomato paste
4 cups chicken bone broth
¼ cup Thai red curry paste
1 tablespoon soy sauce
½ teaspoons ground cloves
½ teaspoons cardamom
½ teaspoons cumin
1 cinnamon quill

Sea salt and ground white pepper, to taste
½ (15-oz.) can full-fat coconut milk
2 cups cauliflower florets
2 tablespoons fresh cilantro, roughly chopped

Press the "Sauté" button twice to select "Normal" settings and heat the sesame oil.
When the oil starts to sizzle, cook the meat until browned on all sides.
Add a splash of broth and use a spoon to scrape the brown bits from the bottom of the pot.
Next, stir in the onion, garlic, galangal, chili pepper, tomato paste, broth, curry paste, soy sauce, and spices.
Put on the pressure cooker's lid and turn the steam valve to "Sealing" position.
Set the Instant Pot on "Soup/Broth".
Use the "+/-" keys on the control panel to set the cooking time to 40 minutes.
Use the Pressure Level button to adjust the pressure to "High".
Once the cooking cycle is completed, quick-release the steam.
When all the steam is released, remove the pressure lid from the top carefully.
After that, add the coconut milk and cauliflower to the inner pot.
Set the Instant Pot on Pressure Cook again and cook for 4 minutes at High pressure.
Once cooking is complete, use a quick pressure release; carefully remove the lid.
Serve garnished with fresh cilantro.
Enjoy!

Per Serving: Calories 479; Fat 10g; Sodium 891mg; Carbs 22.9g; Fiber 4g; Sugar 4g; Protein 33g

Oyster Stew with Chorizo

Prep time: 20 minutes| **Cook time:** 10 minutes| **Serves:** 4-6
2 tablespoons olive oil
8 oz. Spanish chorizo sausage, sliced
1 onion, chopped
1 teaspoon ginger-garlic paste
½ teaspoons dried rosemary
½ teaspoons smoked paprika
½ pound fresh oysters, cleaned
Sea salt and black pepper, to taste
3 cups chicken broth
2 cups kale leaves, washed
1 cup heavy cream

Press the "Sauté" button twice to select "Normal" settings and heat the sesame oil.
When the oil starts to sizzle, cook the sausage until no longer pink.
Add the onion to the inner pot and continue to sauté for a further 3 minutes or until tender and translucent.
Now, stir in the ginger-garlic paste, rosemary, paprika, oysters, salt, pepper, and chicken broth.
Put on the pressure cooker's lid and turn the steam valve to "Sealing" position.
Set the Instant Pot to Pressure Cook.

Use the "+/-" keys on the control panel to set the cooking time to 6 minutes.
Use the Pressure Level button to adjust the pressure to "High".
Once the cooking cycle is completed, quick-release the steam.
When all the steam is released, remove the pressure lid from the top carefully.
Add the kale leaves and heavy cream, seal the lid again, and let it sit in the residual heat.
Serve warm and enjoy!

Per Serving: Calories 412; Fat 20g; Sodium 491mg; Carbs 9g; Fiber 3g; Sugar 8g; Protein 31g

Lentil Curry Stew

Prep time: 20 minutes| **Cook time:** 15 minutes| **Serves:** 4-6

Dahl:
2 tablespoons butter
1 brown onion, chopped
4 garlic cloves, minced
1 (1-inch) piece ginger, peeled and grated
1 red chili pepper, deseeded and minced
6 fresh curry leaves
2 tomatoes, chopped
½ teaspoons ground cumin
¼ teaspoon ground cardamom
1 ½ cups dried chana dal, soaked
4 cups vegetable broth
½ teaspoons turmeric powder
Kosher salt and black pepper, to taste
Tadka (Tempering):
1 tablespoon butter
A pinch of asafetida
½ teaspoons cumin seeds
1 teaspoon mustard seeds
½ onion, sliced
1 bay leaf
2 dried chili peppers, seeded and cut in half

Press the "Sauté" button twice to select "Normal" settings and melt 2 tablespoons of butter.
Once hot, cook the onion until tender and translucent or about 3 minutes.
Then, stir in the garlic and ginger; continue to cook an additional minute or until they are fragrant.
Add the remaining ingredients for the Dahl.
Put on the pressure cooker's lid and turn the steam valve to "Sealing" position.
Set the Instant Pot to Pressure Cook.
Use the "+/-" keys on the control panel to set the cooking time to 10 minutes.
Use the Pressure Level button to adjust the pressure to "High".
Once the cooking cycle is completed, quick-release the pressure.
When all the steam is released, remove the pressure lid from the top carefully.
Clean the inner pot and Press the "Sauté" button two times to select "Normal" settings again.
Melt 1 tablespoon of butter.
Now, add a pinch of asafetida, cumin seeds, mustard seeds, onion and bay leaf; sauté for a minute.
Stir in the dried chili peppers and cook for 30 seconds longer.
Pour the hot tadka over the hot dal and serve.

Per Serving: Calories 305; Fat 7.9g; Sodium 704mg; Carbs 6g; Fiber 3.6g; Sugar 6g; Protein 18g

Chicken Stock

Prep time: 20 minutes| **Cook time:** 60 minutes| **Serves:** 8

2 lbs. chicken bones and parts
1 yellow onion, quartered
1 large garlic clove, smashed
1 carrot, cut into large chunks
1 bay leaf
½ teaspoon kosher salt
1 teaspoon whole black peppercorns
8 cups water

Add the chicken, onion, garlic, carrot, bay leaf, salt, and peppercorns to the pot. Pour the water over.
Put on the pressure cooker's lid and turn the steam valve to "Sealing" position.
Set the Instant Pot to Pressure Cook.
Use the Pressure Level button to adjust the pressure to "High".
Use the "+/-" keys on the control panel to set the cooking time to 60 minutes.
Once the cooking cycle is completed, allow the steam to release naturally.
When all the steam is released, remove the pressure lid from the top carefully.
Carefully strain the broth through a fine-mesh strainer or cheesecloth.
Store the stock in the refrigerator for a few days or freeze for up to 3 months.

Per Serving: Calories 19; Fat 14g; Sodium 91mg; Carbs 8.9g; Fiber 4.6g; Sugar 8g; Protein 3g

Vegetable Stock

Prep time: 20 minutes| **Cook time:** 60minutes| **Serves:** 8

2 onions, quartered
2 celery stalks, quartered
2 carrots, cut into large chunks
10 button mushrooms
4 garlic cloves, smashed
1 small bunch fresh parsley
1 bay leaf
8 cups water
Kosher salt

Add the onions, celery, carrots, mushrooms, garlic, parsley, bay leaf, and water to the Instant Pot.
Put on the pressure cooker's lid and turn the steam valve to "Sealing" position.
Set the Instant Pot to Pressure Cook.
Use the Pressure Level button to adjust the pressure to "High".
Use the "+/-" keys on the control panel to set the cooking time to 60 minutes.
Once the cooking cycle is completed, allow the steam to release naturally.
When all the steam is released, remove the pressure lid from the top carefully.

Carefully strain the stock using a fine-mesh strainer or cheesecloth. Season with salt.
Store the stock in the refrigerator for a few days or freeze for up to 3 months.

Per Serving: Calories 54; Fat 7.9g; Sodium 704mg; Carbs 6g; Fiber 3.6g; Sugar 6g; Protein 18g

Beef Bone Broth

Prep time: 20 minutes| **Cook time:** 1 hr. 30 minutes| **Serves:** 8

2½ lbs. beef bones, including short ribs, knuckles, oxtails, and more
1 teaspoon olive oil
1 yellow onion, quartered
2 celery stalks, quartered
1 carrot, cut into large chunks
1 bay leaf
2 teaspoons apple cider vinegar
1 tablespoon fish sauce
8 cups water

Preheat the oven to 400°F.
Toss the bones with the oil on a baking sheet and roast for 30 minutes.
Once cool enough to handle, add the bones, onion, celery, carrot, bay leaf, vinegar, fish sauce, and water to the Instant Pot.
Put on the pressure cooker's lid and turn the steam valve to "Sealing" position.
Set the Instant Pot to Pressure Cook.
Use the "+/-" keys on the control panel to set the cooking time to 1 hour 30 minutes.
Use the Pressure Level button to adjust the pressure to "High".
Once the cooking cycle is completed, allow the steam to release naturally.
When all the steam is released, remove the pressure lid from the top carefully.
Skim any fat off the top of the stock, if desired.
Carefully strain the broth using a fine-mesh strainer or cheesecloth.
Store the broth in the refrigerator for a few days or freeze for up to 3 months.

Per Serving: Calories 79; Fat 10g; Sodium 891mg; Carbs 22.9g; Fiber 4g; Sugar 4g; Protein 33g

Spicy Chicken Bone Broth

Prep time: 20 minutes| **Cook time:** 1 hr. 30 minutes| **Serves:** 8

2½ lbs. mixed chicken bones and feet
1 yellow onion, quartered
1 celery stalk, quartered
1 carrot, cut into large chunks
1 (1½-inch) piece ginger, peeled and cut into ¼-inch slices
1 teaspoon whole black peppercorns
1 tablespoon fish sauce
1 teaspoon apple cider vinegar

8 cups water

Add the bones, onion, celery, carrot, ginger, peppercorns, fish sauce, vinegar, and water to the Instant Pot.
Put on the pressure cooker's lid and turn the steam valve to "Sealing" position.
Set the Instant Pot to Pressure Cook.
Use the Pressure Level button to adjust the pressure to "High".
Use the "+/-" keys on the control panel to set the cooking time to 1 hour 30 minutes.
Once the cooking cycle is completed, allow the steam to release naturally.
When all the steam is released, remove the pressure lid from the top carefully.
Skim any fat off the top of the stock, if desired. Carefully strain the broth using a fine-mesh strainer or cheesecloth.
Store the broth in the refrigerator for a few days or freeze for up to 3 months.

Per Serving: Calories 78; Fat 19g; Sodium 354mg; Carbs 15g; Fiber 5.1g; Sugar 8.2g; Protein 32g

Homemade Ketchup

Prep time: 20 minutes| **Cook time:** 15 minutes| **Serves:** 8
2 tablespoons olive oil
1 medium onion, finely chopped
4 garlic cloves, smashed
1 (28-oz.) can whole tomatoes with juice
½ cup red wine vinegar
1 tablespoon tomato paste
1 teaspoon Worcestershire sauce
⅓ cup packed brown sugar
½ teaspoon paprika
¼ teaspoon white pepper
⅛ teaspoon ground allspice
Pinch kosher salt

Press the "Sauté" button twice to select "Normal" mode.
Once hot, add the oil followed by the onion.
Cook for 3 minutes until the onion is starting to turn translucent. Add the garlic and sauté 1 minute more.
Add the tomatoes with juice, crushing the tomatoes with your hand as you add them.
Add the vinegar, tomato paste, Worcestershire sauce, brown sugar, paprika, white pepper, and allspice and bring to a simmer. Add a pinch of salt.
Put on the pressure cooker's lid and turn the steam valve to "Sealing" position.
Set the Instant Pot to Pressure Cook.
Use the "+/-" keys on the control panel to set the cooking time to 15 minutes.
Use the Pressure Level button to adjust the pressure to "High".
Once the cooking cycle is completed, allow the steam to release naturally.
When all the steam is released, remove the pressure lid from the top carefully.
Remove the lid and stir. Taste for seasoning.

Press the "Sauté" button twice to select "Normal" mode and cook, for 15 to 20 minutes.
Use an immersion blender to blend until smooth, or blend in a food processor.
Let it cool and store it in the refrigerator for up to 1 month or the freezer for several months.

Per Serving: Calories 84; Fat 15g; Sodium 441mg; Carbs 17g; Fiber 4.6g; Sugar 5g; Protein 29g

Sweet and Tangy Barbecue Sauce

Prep time: 20 minutes| **Cook time:** 15 minutes| **Serves:** 8
4 tablespoons butter
1 small onion, finely chopped
3 garlic cloves, minced
1 cup tomato sauce
½ cup ketchup
½ cup apple cider vinegar
½ cup brown sugar
3 tablespoons molasses
1 tablespoon Dijon mustard
1 teaspoon liquid smoke
¼ teaspoon cayenne
¼ teaspoon black pepper

Press the "Sauté" button two times to select "Normal" mode
Once hot, add the butter and let it melt. Add the onion and cook for 3 minutes until it is starting to turn translucent. Add the garlic and sauté 1 minute more.
Add the tomato sauce, ketchup, vinegar, brown sugar, molasses, mustard, liquid smoke, cayenne, and pepper.
Put on the pressure cooker's lid and turn the steam valve to "Sealing" position.
Set the Instant Pot to Pressure Cook.
Use the "+/-" keys on the control panel to set the cooking time to 15 minutes.
Use the Pressure Level button to adjust the pressure to "High".
Once the cooking cycle is completed, allow the steam to release naturally.
When all the steam is released, remove the pressure lid from the top carefully.
Stir and taste for seasoning. If a thicker sauce is desired.
Press the "Sauté" button two times to select "Normal" mode and cook, stirring occasionally, for 10 to 15 minutes.
Let it cool and store it in the refrigerator for up to 2 weeks or the freezer for several months.

Per Serving: Calories 32; Fat 10.9g; Sodium 354mg; Carbs 10.5g; Fiber 4.1g; Sugar 8.2g; Protein 26g

Marinara Sauce

Prep time: 20 minutes| **Cook time:** 30 minutes| **Serves:** 8
2 tablespoons olive oil

1 medium onion, grated
1 large carrot, peeled and grated
5 garlic cloves, grated
1 (28-oz.) can crushed tomatoes with juice
½ teaspoon dried oregano
Pinch sugar
Kosher salt
Black pepper

Press the "Sauté" button twice to select "Normal" mode.
Once hot, add the oil followed by the onion and carrot.
Sauté for 2 minutes until the onion is translucent. Add the garlic and cook for 30 seconds.
Add the tomatoes with juice and stir. Add the oregano.
Put on the pressure cooker's lid and turn the steam valve to "Sealing" position.
Set the Instant Pot to Pressure Cook.
Use the "+/-" keys on the control panel to set the cooking time to 30 minutes.
Use the Pressure Level button to adjust the pressure to "High".
Once the cooking cycle is completed, allow the steam to release naturally.
When all the steam is released, remove the pressure lid from the top carefully.
Stir and taste for seasoning. Add the sugar, and season with salt and pepper as desired.
Store for up to a week in the refrigerator or freezer for several months.

Per Serving: Calories 42; Fat 19g; Sodium 354mg; Carbs 15g; Fiber 5.1g; Sugar 8.2g; Protein 2g

Puttanesca Sauce

Prep time: 20 minutes| **Cook time:** 20 minutes| **Serves:** 8
2 tablespoons olive oil
1 small onion, finely chopped
4 garlic cloves, minced
1 (28-oz.) can whole tomatoes with juice
½ cup chopped pitted Kalamata olives
4 anchovy fillets, drained and minced
1 tablespoon tomato paste
1 tablespoon drained capers
¼ teaspoon red pepper flakes
Kosher salt
Black pepper

Press the "Sauté" button two times to select "Normal" mode
Once hot, add the oil followed by the onion.
Sauté for 3 minutes, then add the garlic.
Sauté 1 minute more.
Add the tomatoes with juice, squishing each one with your hand as it goes into the pot.
Add the olives, anchovies, tomato paste, capers, and red pepper flakes. Season with salt and pepper.
Put on the pressure cooker's lid and turn the steam valve to "Sealing" position.
Set the Instant Pot to Pressure Cook.
Use the Pressure Level button to adjust the pressure to "High".

Use the "+/-" keys on the control panel to set the cooking time to 20 minutes.
Once the cooking cycle is completed, allow the steam to release naturally.
When all the steam is released, remove the pressure lid from the top carefully.
If a thicker sauce is desired, press the "Sauté" button twice to select "Normal" mode and simmer for 5 minutes. Serve over pasta.

Per Serving: Calories 41; Fat 10.9g; Sodium 454mg; Carbs 10g; Fiber 3.1g; Sugar 5.2g; Protein 05g

Broccoli Pesto

Prep time: 20 minutes| **Cook time:** 3 minutes| **Serves:** 8
1 bunch broccoli (about 1 pound), cut into florets (reserve stems for vegetable stock)
3 cups water
⅓ cup toasted walnuts
3 garlic cloves, minced
1 packed cup fresh basil leaves
¼ cup olive oil
2 tablespoons lemon juice
¼ cup grated Parmesan cheese
Kosher salt
Black pepper

Add the broccoli and water to the Instant Pot.
Put on the pressure cooker's lid and turn the steam valve to "Sealing" position.
Set the Instant Pot to Pressure Cook.
Use the Pressure Level button to adjust the pressure to "High".
Use the "+/-" keys on the control panel to set the cooking time to 3 minutes.
Once the cooking cycle is completed, quick-release pressure.
When all the steam is released, remove the pressure lid from the top carefully.
Meanwhile, combine the walnuts and garlic in a food processor.
Pulse several times until crumbly, but before the walnuts turn to butter.
Remove the broccoli and rinse with cold water.
Drain well and add to the food processor, along with the basil, oil, and lemon juice.
Pulse until well mixed. Add ¼ cup of cooking liquid and the Parmesan, and season with salt and pepper.
Process until smooth. Add more cooking liquid as needed.
Per Serving: Calories 49; Fat 11g; Sodium 501mg; Carbs 8.9g; Fiber 4.6g; Sugar 8g; Protein 26g

Onion Gravy

Prep time: 20 minutes| **Cook time:** 10 minutes| **Serves:** 8
3 tablespoons butter
1 large sweet onion, finely chopped
2 cups chicken broth (try the recipe here)
2 fresh thyme sprigs
1 bay leaf

2 tablespoons all-purpose flour
Kosher salt
Black pepper

Press the "Sauté" button twice to select "Normal" mode.
Once hot, add 1 tablespoon of butter followed by the onion.
Sauté for 6 minutes, until translucent and starting to brown.
Add the broth, thyme, and bay leaf.
Put on the pressure cooker's lid and turn the steam valve to "Sealing" position.
Set the Instant Pot to Pressure Cook.
Use the Pressure Level button to adjust the pressure to "High".
Use the "+/-" keys on the control panel to set the cooking time to 10 minutes.
Once the cooking cycle is completed, allow the steam to release naturally.
When all the steam is released, remove the pressure lid from the top carefully.
Press the "Sauté" button twice to select "Normal" mode.
In a small bowl, knead together the remaining 2 tablespoons of butter with the flour until a pasty ball forms.
Add to the simmering broth and stir until the paste is dissolved and the gravy is thick, about 5 minutes.
Season with salt and pepper as desired.

Per Serving: Calories 33; Fat 7.9g; Sodium 704mg; Carbs 6g; Fiber 3.6g; Sugar 6g; Protein 18g

Mango-Apple Chutney

Prep time: 20 minutes| **Cook time:** 11 minutes| **Serves:** 8
1 tablespoon canola oil
1 large red onion, finely chopped
1 heaping tablespoon grated fresh ginger
1 red Thai chile, cut into a few pieces
2 large mangos, peeled and diced
2 apples, cored, partially peeled, and diced
1 red bell pepper, diced
½ cup golden raisins
1¼ cups sugar
½ cup apple cider vinegar
1 teaspoon kosher salt
1½ teaspoons curry powder
½ teaspoon ground cinnamon
1 tablespoon lemon juice

Press the "Sauté" button twice to select "Normal" mode. Add the oil.
Once hot, add the onion and sauté for 3 minutes. Add the ginger and chile, and cook for 1 minute.
Add the mangos, apples, bell pepper, raisins, sugar, vinegar, salt, curry powder, and cinnamon.
Put on the pressure cooker's lid and turn the steam valve to "Sealing" position.
Set the Instant Pot to Pressure Cook.
Use the Pressure Level button to adjust the pressure to "High".

Use the "+/-" keys on the control panel to set the cooking time to 7 minutes.
Once the cooking cycle is completed, allow the steam to release naturally.
When all the steam is released, remove the pressure lid from the top carefully.
Press the "Sauté" button two times to select "Normal" mode and simmer for 10 minutes.
Add the lemon juice and stir.
Store in airtight containers in the refrigerator for up to a month or in the freezer for up to a year.

Per Serving: Calories 49; Fat 2.9g; Sodium 511mg; Carbs 12g; Fiber 3g; Sugar 8g; Protein 28g

Cranberry Sauce

Prep time: 20 minutes| **Cook time:** 15 minutes| **Serves:** 8
4 cups washed cranberries, fresh or frozen
1 (1-inch) piece ginger, peeled and cut into ⅛-inch slices
½ cup orange juice
Zest from ½ orange
Juice and zest from ½ lemon
1 cup sugar

Add the cranberries, ginger, orange juice, orange zest, lemon juice, lemon zest, and sugar to the Instant Pot.
Put on the pressure cooker's lid and turn the steam valve to "Sealing" position.
Set the Instant Pot to Pressure Cook.
Use the Pressure Level button to adjust the pressure to "Low".
Use the "+/-" keys on the control panel to set the cooking time to 15 minutes.
Once the cooking cycle is completed, allow the steam to release naturally.
When all the steam is released, remove the pressure lid from the top carefully.
Let cool and remove the ginger if desired.
Store the sauce in the refrigerator for up to 3 weeks.

Per Serving: Calories 51; Fat 12.9g; Sodium 414mg; Carbs 11g; Fiber 5g; Sugar 9g; Protein 31g

Cinnamon Applesauce

Prep time: 20 minutes| **Cook time:** 4 minutes| **Serves:** 8
10 to 12 medium apples, peeled, cored, and diced
½ cup apple cider, apple juice, or water
1 cinnamon stick, broken in half
Up to ¼ cup honey
1 tablespoon lemon juice

Add the apples, cider or juice or water, and both halves of the cinnamon stick to the Instant Pot.
Put on the pressure cooker's lid and turn the steam valve to "Sealing" position.

Set the Instant Pot to Pressure Cook.
Use the Pressure Level button to adjust the pressure to "Low".
Use the "+/-" keys on the control panel to set the cooking time to 4 minutes.
Once the cooking cycle is completed, allow the steam to release naturally.
When all the steam is released, remove the pressure lid from the top carefully.
Stir and remove the cinnamon stick halves. If the applesauce isn't sweet enough, add honey.
Serve.

Per Serving: Calories 84; Fat 5g; Sodium 41mg; Carbs 7g; Fiber 7.6g; Sugar 5g; Protein 2g

Orange and Lemon Marmalade

Prep time: 20 minutes| **Cook time:** 14 minutes| **Serves:** 8

1½ lbs. sweet oranges
8 oz. lemons, such as Meyer lemons
1 cup water
3 lbs. sugar

Cut the oranges and lemons into ⅛-inch slices.
Discard the end pieces that are all peel or pith, and remove the seeds and set aside for use later. Cut the slices into 4 or 5 pieces.
Add the fruit and water to the Instant Pot.
Put on the pressure cooker's lid and turn the steam valve to "Sealing" position.
Set the Instant Pot to Pressure Cook.
Use the "+/-" keys on the control panel to set the cooking time to 14 minutes.
Use the Pressure Level button to adjust the pressure to "Low".
Once the cooking cycle is completed, allow the steam to release naturally.
When all the steam is released, remove the pressure lid from the top carefully.
Add the sugar and stir until dissolved.
Place the seeds in a tea bag or gauze packet, cinch, and place in the mixture. Taste for sweetness.
Press the "Sauté" button two times to select "More" mode and boil for about 5 minutes.
Pour into clean jars and let them sit at room temperature until totally cooled.
Store in jars in the refrigerator for up to 3 weeks or the freezer for several months.

Per Serving: Calories 19; Fat 14g; Sodium 791mg; Carbs 8.9g; Fiber 4.6g; Sugar 8g; Protein 3g

Triple-Berry Jam

Prep time: 20 minutes| **Cook time:** 11 minutes| **Serves:** 8

8 oz. fresh strawberries, hulled and halved
8 oz. fresh blueberries
8 oz. fresh raspberries
1 cup sugar
2 teaspoons lemon juice

1 teaspoon grated lemon zest
Up to ¼ cup honey

Add the strawberries, blueberries, raspberries, and sugar to the Instant Pot and stir.
Let it sit for at least 15 minutes or up to 1 hour.
Press the "Sauté" button twice to select "Normal" mode and bring the mixture to a boil for 3 minutes.
Put on the pressure cooker's lid and turn the steam valve to "Sealing" position.
Set the Instant Pot to Pressure Cook.
Use the "+/-" keys on the control panel to set the cooking time to 8 minutes.
Use the Pressure Level button to adjust the pressure to "High".
Once the cooking cycle is completed, allow the steam to release naturally.
When all the steam is released, remove the pressure lid from the top carefully.
Remove the lid and Press the "Sauté" button two times to select "Normal" mode.
Add the lemon juice and zest. Carefully taste the jam and add honey if needed.
Boil for 3 to 4 minutes, stirring frequently, or until the gel point is reached.
Select Cancel. Mash the jam if a smoother texture is desired.
Carefully transfer to lidded containers, close, and let them cool.
The jam could be kept in the refrigerator for up to 3 weeks or the freezer for at least 6 months.

Per Serving: Calories 42; Fat 11g; Sodium 91mg; Carbs 4g; Fiber 3g; Sugar 8g; Protein 3g

Apple Butter

Prep time: 20 minutes| **Cook time:** 30 minutes| **Serves:** 8

4 lbs. apples, peeled, cored, and roughly chopped
½ cup apple cider
1 tablespoon lemon juice
1 cup brown sugar
1 teaspoon ground cinnamon
Pinch ground cloves or nutmeg
Pinch kosher salt

Add the apples and cider to the Instant Pot.
Put on the pressure cooker's lid and turn the steam valve to "Sealing" position.
Set the Instant Pot to Pressure Cook.
Use the "+/-" keys on the control panel to set the cooking time to 30 minutes.
Use the Pressure Level button to adjust the pressure to "High".
Once the cooking cycle is completed, allow the steam to release naturally.
When all the steam is released, remove the pressure lid from the top carefully.
Add the lemon juice, brown sugar, cinnamon, cloves or nutmeg, and salt and stir.
Press the "Sauté" button two times to select "Normal" mode and cook for about 30 minutes.

Store in an airtight container in the refrigerator for up to a week or in the freezer for up to 3 months.

Per Serving: Calories 79; Fat 10g; Sodium 891mg; Carbs 22.9g; Fiber 4g; Sugar 4g; Protein 33g

Vegetable Broth

Prep time: 20 minutes| **Cook time:** 40 minutes| **Serves:** 8

2 medium onions, halved
2 celery stalks with leaves, roughly chopped
2 large carrots, scrubbed and roughly chopped
8 oz. white button or cremini mushrooms, whole
12 cups water
1 head garlic, halved crosswise
1 bunch parsley stems
2 bay leaves
5 to 7 whole black peppercorns

Press the "Sauté" button two time on the Instant pot to select "Normal" settings.
Sauté the onions, celery, carrots, and mushrooms for 3 to 5 minutes.
Add the water, garlic, parsley, bay leaves, and peppercorns.
Put on the pressure cooker's lid and turn the steam valve to "Sealing" position.
Set the Instant Pot to Pressure Cook.
Use the "+/-" keys on the control panel to set the cooking time to 40 minutes.
Use the Pressure Level button to adjust the pressure to "High".
Once the cooking cycle is completed, quick-release pressure.
When all the steam is released, remove the pressure lid from the top carefully.
When the cook time is complete, quick-release the pressure and carefully remove the lid.
Strain the broth through a fine-mesh sieve into a large bowl and discard the solids.
Store the broth in a covered container in the fridge for up to 4 days or in the freezer for up to 6 months.

Per Serving: Calories 61; Fat 7.9g; Sodium 704mg; Carbs 6g; Fiber 3.6g; Sugar 6g; Protein 18g

Oil-Free Marinara Sauce

Prep time: 20 minutes| **Cook time:** 12 minutes| **Serves:** 8

1 medium onion, diced
4 tablespoons water, as needed
4 garlic cloves, minced
1 tablespoon dried basil
1 tablespoon dried oregano
¼ to 1 teaspoon red pepper flakes
2 (28-oz.) cans no-salt-added crushed tomatoes
½ cup Easy Vegetable Broth or no-salt-added vegetable broth
Black pepper

Salt

Press the "Sauté" button twice on the Instant pot to select "Normal" settings.
Sauté the onion for 1 to 2 minutes, until slightly browned, adding water as needed to prevent sticking.
Add the garlic, basil, oregano, and red pepper flakes to taste and stir for 30 seconds, until fragrant.
Stir in the tomatoes and broth, scraping up any browned bits from the bottom of the pot.
Season to taste with black pepper and salt.
Put on the pressure cooker's lid and turn the steam valve to "Sealing" position.
Set the Instant Pot to Pressure Cook.
Use the "+/-" keys on the control panel to set the cooking time to 12 minutes.
Use the Pressure Level button to adjust the pressure to "High".
Once the cooking cycle is completed, allow the steam to release naturally.
When all the steam is released, remove the pressure lid from the top carefully.
Store in a covered container in the fridge for up to 4 weeks or in the freezer for up to 3 months.

Per Serving: Calories 54; Fat 10.9g; Sodium 354mg; Carbs 10.5g; Fiber 4.1g; Sugar 8.2g; Protein 26g

Maple Barbecue Sauce

Prep time: 20 minutes| **Cook time:** 6 minutes| **Serves:** 8

2 tablespoons minced onion
2 garlic cloves, minced
1 teaspoon smoked paprika
1 teaspoon ground allspice
1 cup water
1 (15-oz.) can no-salt-added tomato sauce
¼ cup maple syrup
2 tablespoons stone-ground mustard
2 tablespoons apple cider vinegar
½ teaspoon salt

Press the "Sauté" button twice on the Instant pot to select "Normal" settings. Sauté the onion for 2 minutes.
Add the garlic, paprika, and allspice and stir for 30 seconds, until fragrant.
Stir in the water, scraping up any browned bits from the bottom of the pot.
Add the tomato sauce, maple syrup, mustard, vinegar, and salt. Whisk to combine.
Put on the pressure cooker's lid and turn the steam valve to "Sealing" position.
Set the Instant Pot to Pressure Cook.
Use the Pressure Level button to adjust the pressure to "High".
Use the "+/-" keys on the control panel to set the cooking time to 4 minutes.
Once the cooking cycle is completed, quick-release pressure.
When all the steam is released, remove the pressure lid from the top carefully.
Store in the refrigerator for up to 4 weeks in a covered container.

Per Serving: Calories 34; Fat 9g; Sodium 354mg; Carbs 5g; Fiber 5.1g; Sugar 8.2g; Protein 2g

Fresh Tomato Ketchup

Prep time: 20 minutes| **Cook time:** 15 minutes| **Serves:** 8

2 lbs. plum tomatoes, roughly chopped
5 pitted dates
6 tablespoons distilled white vinegar
1 tablespoon gluten-free vegan Worcestershire sauce
1 tablespoon paprika
1 teaspoon onion powder
1 teaspoon salt
½ teaspoon mustard powder
¼ teaspoon celery seed
¼ teaspoon garlic powder
Pinch of ground cloves
2 tablespoons water
1 tablespoon arrowroot powder or cornstarch

In your Instant Pot, combine the tomatoes, dates, vinegar, Worcestershire sauce, paprika, onion powder, salt, mustard powder, celery seed, garlic powder, and cloves.
Using a potato masher, mash the tomatoes until they have released much of their liquid.
Put on the pressure cooker's lid and turn the steam valve to "Sealing" position.
Set the Instant Pot to Pressure Cook.
Use the "+/-" keys on the control panel to set the cooking time to 5 minutes.
Use the Pressure Level button to adjust the pressure to "High".
Once the cooking cycle is completed, quick-release pressure.
When all the steam is released, remove the pressure lid from the top carefully.
Select the Sauté function and simmer about 10 minutes, until reduced, stirring often.
In a small bowl, whisk together the water and arrowroot and add to the simmering ketchup for 2 to 4 minutes.
Strain the ketchup through a fine-mesh sieve.
Store in the fridge for up to 6 months in a covered container.

Per Serving: Calories 84; Fat 5g; Sodium 41mg; Carbs 7g; Fiber 7.6g; Sugar 5g; Protein 2g

Hot Pepper Sauce

Prep time: 20 minutes| **Cook time:** 2 minutes| **Serves:** 8

12 to 16 oz. fresh hot red peppers, stems removed, halved
1 cup distilled white vinegar
¼ cup apple cider vinegar
3 garlic cloves, smashed

In your Instant Pot, stir together the peppers, white vinegar, cider vinegar, and garlic.
Put on the pressure cooker's lid and turn the steam valve to "Sealing" position.

Set the Instant Pot to Pressure Cook.
Use the "+/-" keys on the control panel to set the cooking time to 2 minutes.
Use the Pressure Level button to adjust the pressure to "High".
Once the cooking cycle is completed, allow the steam to release naturally.
When all the steam is released, remove the pressure lid from the top carefully.
Using an immersion blender, food processor, or blender, blend the sauce until smooth.
Strain through a fine-mesh sieve and store in glass bottles or jars at room temperature for up to 6 months.

Per Serving: Calories 78; Fat 10.9g; Sodium 454mg; Carbs 10g; Fiber 3.1g; Sugar 5.2g; Protein 05g

Nut-Free Cheese Sauce

Prep time: 20 minutes| **Cook time:** 7 minutes| **Serves:** 8

3 medium yellow potatoes, cut into 1-inch chunks
1 large carrot, cut into 1-inch chunks
2 cups water
¼ cup nutritional yeast
2 tablespoons lemon juice
2 teaspoons chickpea miso paste
½ teaspoon onion powder
½ teaspoon garlic powder
½ teaspoon mustard powder
¼ teaspoon ground turmeric

In your Instant Pot, combine the potatoes, carrot, and water.
Put on the pressure cooker's lid and turn the steam valve to "Sealing" position.
Set the Instant Pot to Pressure Cook.
Use the Pressure Level button to adjust the pressure to "High".
Use the "+/-" keys on the control panel to set the cooking time to 7 minutes.
Once the cooking cycle is completed, allow the steam to release naturally for 10 minutes and then quick-release the remaining pressure.
When all the steam is released, remove the pressure lid from the top carefully.
Using a slotted spoon, remove the potatoes and carrots to a blender, then add ½ cup of the cooking water along with the nutritional yeast, lemon juice, miso, onion powder, garlic powder, mustard powder, and turmeric.
Blend until smooth and creamy, adding more cooking water as necessary to thin.
Store in the fridge for up to 4 days in a covered container.

Per Serving: Calories 32; Fat 9g; Sodium 34mg; Carbs 2g; Fiber 5.1g; Sugar 2g; Protein 2g

Applesauce

Prep time: 20 minutes| **Cook time:** 4 minutes| **Serves:** 8

3 lbs. apples, cored, cut into large chunks

⅓ cup water
1 tablespoon lemon juice

In your Instant Pot, combine the apples, water, and lemon juice.
Put on the pressure cooker's lid and turn the steam valve to "Sealing" position.
Set the Instant Pot to Pressure Cook.
Use the Pressure Level button to adjust the pressure to "High".
Use the "+/-" keys on the control panel to set the cooking time to 4 minutes.
Once the cooking cycle is completed, allow the steam to release naturally for 10 minutes and then quick-release the remaining pressure.
When all the steam is released, remove the pressure lid from the top carefully.
Using a potato masher, mash the apples to your desired chunkiness.
Using a pair of tongs or a fork, transfer the apple peels to a deep, narrow container and blend using an immersion blender. Return to the pot and stir to combine. Store in the fridge for up to 4 weeks in a covered container.

Per Serving: Calories 34; Fat 19g; Sodium 354mg; Carbs 25g; Fiber 5.1g; Sugar 8.2g; Protein 2g

Strawberry Compote

Prep time: 20 minutes| **Cook time:** 4 minutes| **Serves:** 8

4 cups frozen strawberries
¼ cup sugar
1 tablespoon lemon juice

In your Instant Pot, combine the strawberries, sugar, and lemon juice. Stir to coat the berries.
Put on the pressure cooker's lid and turn the steam valve to "Sealing" position.
Set the Instant Pot to Pressure Cook.
Use the Pressure Level button to adjust the pressure to "High".
Use the "+/-" keys on the control panel to set the cooking time to 4 minutes.
Once the cooking cycle is completed, allow the steam to release naturally for 10 minutes and then quick-release the remaining pressure.
When all the steam is released, remove the pressure lid from the top carefully.
Using a potato masher, mash the berries until they are broken down completely.
Pour into a container and chill. The compote will thicken as it cools.
Store in the fridge for up to 4 weeks in a covered container.

Per Serving: Calories 42; Fat 11g; Sodium 91mg; Carbs 4g; Fiber 3g; Sugar 8g; Protein 3g

Bone Broth

Prep time: 20 minutes| **Cook time:** 120 minutes| **Serves:** 8

2-3 lbs. bones (2-3 lbs. beef, lamb, pork, or 1 carcass of chicken)
½ onion
3 carrots, cut into large chunks
2 stalks celery, cut into large chunks
Fresh herbs
1 teaspoon sea salt
1-2 tablespoon apple cider vinegar
Water as needed

Add the bones to the Instant Pot. Add all of the veggies, herbs, salt and vinegar.
Pour in the water to fill the pot 2/3 full.
Put on the pressure cooker's lid and turn the steam valve to "Sealing" position.
Press the "Soup" button one time to select "Less" option.
Use the "+/-" keys on the control panel to set the cooking time to 120 minutes.
Once the cooking cycle is completed, allow the steam to release naturally.
When all the steam is released, remove the pressure lid from the top carefully.
Strain the broth and pour into jars. Store in the refrigerator or freeze.

Per Serving: Calories 79; Fat 10g; Sodium 891mg; Carbs 2.9g; Fiber 4g; Sugar 4g; Protein 3g

Pork Broth

Prep time: 20 minutes| **Cook time:** 60 minutes| **Serves:** 8

3 lbs. pork bones
8 cups water
3 large carrots, cut into large chunks
3 large stalks celery, cut into large chunks
1 bay leaf
2 cloves garlic, sliced
1 tablespoon apple cider vinegar
1 teaspoon whole peppercorns
Salt to taste

Dump all of the ingredients into the Instant Pot and give it a little stir to mix everything evenly.
Put on the pressure cooker's lid and turn the steam valve to "Sealing" position.
Set the Instant Pot to Pressure Cook.
Use the "+/-" keys on the control panel to set the cooking time to 60 minutes.
Use the Pressure Level button to adjust the pressure to "High".
Once the cooking cycle is completed, allow the steam to release naturally.
When all the steam is released, remove the pressure lid from the top carefully.
Strain the broth and pour into jars. Store in the refrigerator or freeze.

Per Serving: Calories 61; Fat 7.9g; Sodium 704mg; Carbs 6g; Fiber 3.6g; Sugar 6g; Protein 18g

Mushroom Broth

Prep time: 20 minutes| **Cook time:** 15 minutes| **Serves:** 8

4 oz. dried mushrooms, soaked and rinsed
8 cups water
½ cup carrots, chopped
½ cup celery, chopped
1 onion, quartered
4 cloves garlic, crushed
4 bay leaves
Salt and black pepper to taste.

Put all of the ingredients into the Instant Pot.
Put on the pressure cooker's lid and turn the steam valve to "Sealing" position.
Set the Instant Pot to Pressure Cook.
Use the Pressure Level button to adjust the pressure to "High".
Use the "+/-" keys on the control panel to set the cooking time to 15 minutes.
Once the cooking cycle is completed, quick-release pressure.
When all the steam is released, remove the pressure lid from the top carefully.
Season with salt and pepper to taste.
Strain the broth and pour into jars. Store in the refrigerator or freeze.

Per Serving: Calories 34; Fat 12.9g; Sodium 44mg; Carbs 11g; Fiber 5g; Sugar 9g; Protein 31g

Chicken Stock

Prep time: 20 minutes| **Cook time:** 60 minutes| **Serves:** 8

1 chicken carcass
10 cups water
1 onion, quartered
2 large carrots, cut into chunks
12 whole pieces peppercorns
2 bay leaves
2 tablespoons apple cider vinegar
1 sprig thyme
Salt to taste

Put all of the ingredients into the Instant Pot.
Put on the pressure cooker's lid and turn the steam valve to "Sealing" position.
Set the Instant Pot to Pressure Cook.
Use the Pressure Level button to adjust the pressure to "High".
Use the "+/-" keys on the control panel to set the cooking time to 60 minutes.
Once the cooking cycle is completed, allow the steam to release naturally.
When all the steam is released, remove the pressure lid from the top carefully.
Season with salt to taste. Strain the stock and pour into jars.
Store in the refrigerator or freeze.

Per Serving: Calories 84; Fat 5g; Sodium 41mg; Carbs 7g; Fiber 7.6g; Sugar 5g; Protein 2g

Chicken Feet Stock

Prep time: 20 minutes| **Cook time:** 60 minutes| **Serves:** 8

1½ lbs. chicken feet, cleaned and rinsed
8 cups water
2 carrots, cut into chunks
1 onion, quartered
2 stalks celery, cut in half
1 teaspoon black peppercorns
1 bay leaf

Put all of the ingredients into the Instant Pot.
Put on the pressure cooker's lid and turn the steam valve to "Sealing" position.
Set the Instant Pot to Pressure Cook.
Use the Pressure Level button to adjust the pressure to "High".
Use the "+/-" keys on the control panel to set the cooking time to 60 minutes.
Once the cooking cycle is completed, allow the steam to release naturally for 10 minutes and then release the remaining steam manually.
When all the steam is released, remove the pressure lid from the top carefully.
Strain the stock and pour into jars. Store in the refrigerator or freeze.

Per Serving: Calories 44; Fat 2.2g; Sodium 811mg; Carbs 12g; Fiber 3g; Sugar 8g; Protein 8g

Turkey Stock

Prep time: 20 minutes| **Cook time:** 45 minutes| **Serves:** 6

1 bag turkey giblet
6 cups water
1 stalk celery, cut in half
1 carrot, cut into chunks
1 onion, quartered
1 bay leaf
1 teaspoon whole black peppercorns

Put all of the ingredients into the Instant Pot.
Put on the pressure cooker's lid and turn the steam valve to "Sealing" position.
Set the Instant Pot to Pressure Cook.
Use the "+/-" keys on the control panel to set the cooking time to 45 minutes.
Use the Pressure Level button to adjust the pressure to "High".
Once the cooking cycle is completed, allow the steam to release naturally for 10 minutes and then release the remaining pressure manually.
When all the steam is released, remove the pressure lid from the top carefully.
Strain the stock and pour into jars. Store in the refrigerator or freeze.

Per Serving: Calories 42; Fat 11g; Sodium 91mg; Carbs 4g; Fiber 3g; Sugar 8g; Protein 3g

Fish Stock

Prep time: 20 minutes| **Cook time:** 45 minutes| **Serves:** 10

2 salmon heads, large-sized, cut into quarters
1 tablespoon olive oil
2 lemongrass stalks, roughly chopped
1 cup carrots, roughly chopped
1 cup celery, roughly chopped
2 cloves garlic, sliced
Handful fresh thyme, including stems
Water as needed

Wash the fish heads and pat them dry.
Press the "Sauté" button two times to select "Normal" mode. Add and heat the oil.
Add the salmon heads and lightly sear the fish on both sides.
Put all of the ingredients into the Instant Pot and pour the water to cover mix.
Put on the pressure cooker's lid and turn the steam valve to "Sealing" position.
Set your Instant Pot to Soup/Broth.
Use the "+/-" keys on the control panel to set the cooking time to 45 minutes.
Use the Pressure Level button to adjust the pressure to "High".
Once the cooking cycle is completed, allow the steam to release naturally for 15 minutes and then release the remaining pressure manually.
When all the steam is released, remove the pressure lid from the top carefully.
Strain the stock and pour into jars. Store in the refrigerator or freeze.

Per Serving: Calories 72; Fat 9g; Sodium 354mg; Carbs 2g; Fiber 5.1g; Sugar 8.2g; Protein 2g

Seafood Soup Stock

Prep time: 20 minutes| **Cook time:** 30 minutes| **Serves:** 8

Shells and heads from ½ lb. prawns
8 cups water
4 onions, quartered
4 carrots, cut into chunks
3 cloves garlic, sliced
2 bay leaves
1 teaspoon whole black peppercorns

Put all of the ingredients into the Instant Pot.
Put on the pressure cooker's lid and turn the steam valve to "Sealing" position.
Set the Instant Pot to Pressure Cook.
Use the Pressure Level button to adjust the pressure to "High".
Use the "+/-" keys on the control panel to set the cooking time to 30 minutes.
Once the cooking cycle is completed, allow the steam to release naturally for 15 minutes and then release the remaining pressure manually.
When all the steam is released, remove the pressure lid from the top carefully.
Strain the stock and pour into jars. Store in the refrigerator or freeze.

Per Serving: Calories 89; Fat 11g; Sodium 51mg; Carbs 8.9g; Fiber 4.6g; Sugar 8g; Protein 26g

Herb Stock

Prep time: 20 minutes| **Cook time:** 15 minutes| **Serves:** 8

4 cups water
3 bay leaves
2 cloves garlic, crushed
1 teaspoon whole black peppercorns
A handful of rosemary
2 sprigs parsley
½ teaspoon salt

Put all of the ingredients, except salt, into the Instant Pot.
Put on the pressure cooker's lid and turn the steam valve to "Sealing" position.
Set the Instant Pot to Pressure Cook.
Use the Pressure Level button to adjust the pressure to "High".
Use the "+/-" keys on the control panel to set the cooking time to 15 minutes.
Once the cooking cycle is completed, allow the steam to release naturally for 10 minutes and then release the remaining steam manually.
When all the steam is released, remove the pressure lid from the top carefully.
Season with salt to taste.
Strain the stock and pour into jars. Store in the refrigerator or freeze.

Per Serving: Calories 84; Fat 5g; Sodium 41mg; Carbs 7g; Fiber 7.6g; Sugar 5g; Protein 2g

Homemade Salsa

Prep time: 20 minutes| **Cook time:** 30 minutes| **Serves:** 8

6 cups fresh tomatoes, diced, peeled and seeded
1½ green bell peppers, diced
2 yellow onions, diced
1 cup jalapeno peppers, seeded and chopped
1½ cans (6-oz.) tomato paste
¼ cup vinegar
1½ tablespoon sugar
½ tablespoon kosher salt
1 tablespoon garlic powder
1 tablespoon cayenne pepper

Put all of the ingredients into the Instant Pot.
Stir well to combine.
Put on the pressure cooker's lid and turn the steam valve to "Sealing" position.
Set the Instant Pot to Pressure Cook.
Use the Pressure Level button to adjust the pressure to "High".
Use the "+/-" keys on the control panel to set the cooking time to 30 minutes.
Once the cooking cycle is completed, allow the steam to release naturally for 10 minutes and then release the remaining pressure manually.
When all the steam is released, remove the pressure lid from the top carefully.

Serve warm or cool.

Per Serving: Calories 34; Fat 10.9g; Sodium 354mg; Carbs 10.5g; Fiber 4.1g; Sugar 8.2g; Protein 26g

Bolognese Sauce

Prep time: 20 minutes| **Cook time:** 15 minutes| **Serves:** 4

½ tablespoon unsalted butter
2 teaspoons garlic, minced
1 carrot, chopped
1 stalk celery, chopped
1 lb. ground beef
1 can pasta sauce
1 tablespoon sugar
½ teaspoon kosher salt
¼ teaspoon black pepper
¼ teaspoon basil, dried
¼ cup half and half cream
⅛ cup parsley, chopped

Press the "Sauté" button two times to select "Normal" mode. Once hot, add the butter and melt it.
Add the garlic and sauté for 30 seconds.
Add the carrots and celery and sauté for 6-8 minutes, or until soft.
Add the ground beef and cook for another 4-5 minutes until browned, stirring occasionally.
Add the pasta sauce, sugar, salt, pepper, and basil. Stir well.
Put on the pressure cooker's lid and turn the steam valve to "Sealing" position.
Set the Instant Pot to Pressure Cook.
Use the Pressure Level button to adjust the pressure to "High".
Use the "+/-" keys on the control panel to set the cooking time to 15 minutes.
Once the cooking cycle is completed, allow the steam to release naturally for 10 minutes, and then release the remaining pressure manually.
When all the steam is released, remove the pressure lid from the top carefully.
Add the half and half to the pot. Stir to combine.
Top with parsley and serve.

Per Serving: Calories 42; Fat 11g; Sodium 91mg; Carbs 4g; Fiber 3g; Sugar 8g; Protein 3g

Cranberry Apple Sauce

Prep time: 20 minutes| **Cook time:** 5 minutes| **Serves:** 2

1-2 apples, peeled, cored, and then cut into chunks
10 oz. cranberries, frozen or fresh, preferably organic
1 teaspoon cinnamon
½ cup maple syrup or honey
¼ cup lemon juice
¼ teaspoon sea salt

Combine all of the ingredients in the Instant Pot.

Put on the pressure cooker's lid and turn the steam valve to "Sealing" position.
Set the Instant Pot to Pressure Cook.
Use the "+/-" keys on the control panel to set the cooking time to 1 minute.
Use the Pressure Level button to adjust the pressure to "High".
Once the cooking cycle is completed, allow the steam to release naturally for 15 minutes and then release the remaining pressure manually.
When all the steam is released, remove the pressure lid from the top carefully.
Using a wooden spoon, mash the fruit a bit.
Press the "Sauté" button twice to select "Normal" mode and simmer for 1-2 minutes to evaporate some water, stirring occasionally.
Once the sauce begins to thicken, press the CANCEL key to stop the SAUTE function.
Pour into clean jars and refrigerate.

Per Serving: Calories 82; Fat 10.9g; Sodium 454mg; Carbs 10g; Fiber 3.1g; Sugar 5.2g; Protein 05g

Tabasco Sauce

Prep time: 20 minutes| **Cook time:** 1 minutes| **Serves:** 8

18 oz. fresh hot peppers or any kind, stems removed, chopped
3 teaspoon smoked or plain salt
1¾ cups apple cider

Combine all of the ingredients in the Instant Pot.
Put on the pressure cooker's lid and turn the steam valve to "Sealing" position.
Set the Instant Pot to Pressure Cook.
Use the Pressure Level button to adjust the pressure to "High".
Use the "+/-" keys on the control panel to set the cooking time to 1 minute.
Once the cooking cycle is completed, allow the steam to release naturally for 15 minutes and then release the remaining pressure manually.
When all the steam is released, remove the pressure lid from the top carefully.
Using an immersion blender, puree the mixture.
Pour into clean and sterilized bottles and refrigerate.

Per Serving: Calories 51; Fat 10.9g; Sodium 354mg; Carbs 10.5g; Fiber 4.1g; Sugar 8.2g; Protein 6g

Vegan Alfredo Sauce

Prep time: 20 minutes| **Cook time:** 3 minutes| **Serves:** 8

1½ tablespoon olive oil
10 cloves garlic, minced
¾ cup raw cashews
6 cups cauliflower florets
2 cups asparagus
6 cups vegetable broth
½ teaspoon salt

Press the "Sauté" button twice to select "Normal" mode. and heat the oil.
Add the garlic and sauté for 1-2 minutes, until fragrant.
Add the cashews, cauliflower, asparagus, and broth. Press Cancel to stop heating.
Put on the pressure cooker's lid and turn the steam valve to "Sealing" position.
Set the Instant Pot to Pressure Cook.
Use the Pressure Level button to adjust the pressure to "High".
Use the "+/-" keys on the control panel to set the cooking time to 3 minutes.
Once the cooking cycle is completed, quick-release steam.
When all the steam is released, remove the pressure lid from the top carefully.
Transfer to a blender. Season with salt and blend until smooth.
Serve with pasta or brow rice.

Per Serving: Calories 84; Fat 5g; Sodium 41mg; Carbs 7g; Fiber 7.6g; Sugar 5g; Protein 2g

Tomato Basil Sauce

Prep time: 20 minutes| **Cook time:** 15 minutes| **Serves:** 4

1 tablespoon olive oil
3 cloves garlic, minced
2½ lbs. Roma tomatoes, diced
½ cup chopped basil
¼ cup vegetable broth
Salt to taste

Press the "Sauté" button twice to select "Normal" mode on the Instant Pot and heat the oil.
Add the garlic and sauté for 1 minute.
Add the tomatoes, basil, and broth. Mix well.
Put on the pressure cooker's lid and turn the steam valve to "Sealing" position.
Set the Instant Pot to Pressure Cook.
Use the "+/-" keys on the control panel to set the cooking time to 10 minutes.
Use the Pressure Level button to adjust the pressure to "High".
Once the cooking cycle is completed, quick-release steam.
When all the steam is released, remove the pressure lid from the top carefully.
Press the "Sauté" button twice to select "Normal" mode again and cook for 5 minutes more. Turn off heat.
Using an immersion blender, blend until smooth.
Taste and season with salt if necessary.
Serve.

Per Serving: Calories 79; Fat 10g; Sodium 891mg; Carbs 22.9g; Fiber 4g; Sugar 4g; Protein 3g

Caramel Sauce

Prep time: 20 minutes| **Cook time:** 15 minutes| **Serves:** 4

1 cup sugar
⅓ cup water
3 tablespoon coconut oil
⅓ cup condensed coconut milk
1 teaspoon vanilla extract

Press the "Sauté" button twice to select "Normal" mode.
In the Instant Pot, combine the sugar and water. Cook for 12 minutes.
Add the coconut oil, milk, and vanilla. Stir well.
Cook, stirring occasionally, until the mixture is smooth.
Press the CANCEL key to stop the SAUTÉ function.
Transfer to a heatproof container.
Let it cool and serve.

Per Serving: Calories 7; Fat 10g; Sodium 891mg; Carbs 22.9g; Fiber 4g; Sugar 4g; Protein 3g

Mushroom Gravy Sauce

Prep time: 20 minutes| **Cook time:** 3 minutes| **Serves:** 8

2 tablespoon butter
¼ cup shallots, chopped
1 package button mushrooms, sliced
2 cups beef broth
2 tablespoon flour
¼ cup half and half
Salt to taste
½ teaspoon black pepper

Press the "Sauté" button twice to select "Normal" mode
Once hot, add the butter and melt it.
Add the shallots and mushrooms. Cook until fragrant.
Whisk in the broth and flour. Whisk until smooth.
Simmer the mixture for 5 minutes.
Pour in half and half, stir well. Season with salt and pepper.
Put on the pressure cooker's lid and turn the steam valve to "Sealing" position.
Set the Instant Pot to Pressure Cook.
Use the "+/-" keys on the control panel to set the cooking time to 3 minutes.
Use the Pressure Level button to adjust the pressure to "High".
Once the cooking cycle is completed, allow the steam to release naturally for 10 minutes and then release the remaining pressure manually.
When all the steam is released, remove the pressure lid from the top carefully.
Serve.

Per Serving: Calories 72; Fat 10g; Sodium 891mg; Carbs 22.9g; Fiber 4g; Sugar 4g; Protein 3g

Chili Sauce

Prep time: 15 minutes| **Cook time:** 8 minutes| **Serves:** 4

4 medium-sized Ancho chili peppers
½ teaspoon cumin, ground
½ teaspoon dried oregano, ground
2 teaspoons kosher salt
1½ teaspoon sugar
1½ cups water
2 tablespoon apple cider vinegar
2 cloves garlic, crushed
2 tablespoons heavy cream

Cut the peppers in half and remove the stems and seeds. Chop into small pieces.
Add the peppers, cumin, oregano, salt, and sugar to the Instant Pot.
Pour in the water and stir well.
Put on the pressure cooker's lid and turn the steam valve to "Sealing" position.
Set the Instant Pot to Pressure Cook.
Use the "+/-" keys on the control panel to set the cooking time to 8 minutes.
Use the Pressure Level button to adjust the pressure to "High".
Once the cooking cycle is completed, allow the steam to release naturally for 10 minutes and then release the remaining pressure manually.
When all the steam is released, remove the pressure lid from the top carefully.
Transfer the mixture to a food processor.
Add the vinegar, garlic, and heavy cream.
Pulse until smooth and creamy.
Serve.

Per Serving: Calories 78; Fat 7.9g; Sodium 704mg; Carbs 6g; Fiber 3.6g; Sugar 6g; Protein 18g

White Sauce

Prep time: 15 minutes| **Cook time:** 3 minutes| **Serves:** 8

12 oz. cauliflower florets
2 tablespoons almond milk
¼ teaspoon garlic salt
½ cup water
¼ teaspoon pepper

In the Instant Pot, combine the cauliflower florets, garlic salt, pepper, and water.

Put on the pressure cooker's lid and turn the steam valve to "Sealing" position.
Set the Instant Pot to Pressure Cook.
Use the "+/-" keys on the control panel to set the cooking time to 3 minutes.
Use the Pressure Level button to adjust the pressure to "High".
Once the cooking cycle is completed, quick-release the steam.
When all the steam is released, remove the pressure lid from the top carefully.
Using an immersion blender, blend until smooth.
Pour in the almond milk and mix well.
Serve.

Per Serving: Calories 84; Fat 5g; Sodium 41mg; Carbs 7g; Fiber 7.6g; Sugar 5g; Protein 2g

Strawberry Applesauce

Prep time: 15 minutes| **Cook time:** 5 minutes| **Serves:** 6

8 peeled apples, cored and sliced
3 cups strawberries, hulled and chopped
2 tablespoons lemon juice
¼ teaspoon cinnamon powder
2 tablespoons sugar

Combine all of the ingredients in the Instant Pot and stir to mix.
Put on the pressure cooker's lid and turn the steam valve to "Sealing" position.
Set the Instant Pot to Pressure Cook.
Use the Pressure Level button to adjust the pressure to "High".
Use the "+/-" keys on the control panel to set the cooking time to 5 minutes.
Once the cooking cycle is completed, allow the steam to release naturally for 15 minutes and then release the remaining pressure manually.
When all the steam is released, remove the pressure lid from the top carefully.
Use a potato masher to mash the mixture and get the consistency you like.

Per Serving: Calories 32; Fat 2.9g; Sodium 41mg; Carbs 11g; Fiber 5g; Sugar 9g; Protein 31g

Dandelion Greens

Prep time: 15 minutes| **Cook time:** 1 minutes| **Serves:** 8

4 lbs. dandelion greens, stalks cut and, and greens washed
½ cup water
¼ cup olive oil
¼ cup lemon juice
½ teaspoon salt
½ teaspoon black pepper

Add dandelion greens and water to the Instant Pot.
Put on the pressure cooker's lid and turn the steam valve to "Sealing" position.
Set the Instant Pot to Pressure Cook.
Use the Pressure Level button to adjust the pressure to "Low".
Use the "+/-" keys on the control panel to set the cooking time to 1 minute.
Once the cooking cycle is completed, allow the steam to release quickly.
When all the steam is released, remove the pressure lid from the top carefully.
Combine olive oil, lemon juice, salt, and pepper in a small bowl.
Pour over greens and toss to coat.

Per Serving: Calories 305; Fat 12.9g; Sodium 754mg; Carbs 21g; Fiber 6.1g; Sugar 4.2g; Protein 11g

Greek-Style Peas

Prep time: 15 minutes| **Cook time:** 9 minutes| **Serves:** 4

3 tablespoons olive oil
1 large russet potato, peeled and cut into ½" pieces
1 medium white onion, peeled and diced
1 medium carrot, peeled and diced
3 medium tomatoes, seeded and diced
1 clove garlic, peeled and minced
1 pound fresh or frozen green peas
¼ cup chopped fresh dill
¼ teaspoon salt
¼ teaspoon black pepper
⅓ cup crumbled feta cheese

Press the "Sauté" button two time to select "Normal" temperature setting on the Instant Pot and heat oil.
Add potato, onion, and carrot, and cook until onion and carrot are tender, about 8 minutes.
Add tomatoes and garlic, and cook until garlic is fragrant, about 1 minute. Add peas.
Put on the pressure cooker's lid and turn the steam valve to "Sealing" position.
Set the Instant Pot to Pressure Cook.
Use the "+/-" keys on the control panel to set the cooking time to 1 minute.
Use the Pressure Level button to adjust the pressure to "Low".

Once the cooking cycle is completed, allow the steam to release quickly.
When all the steam is released, remove the pressure lid from the top carefully.
Stir in dill, salt, and pepper. Top with feta and serve hot.

Per Serving: Calories 242; Fat 11g; Sodium 91mg; Carbs 4g; Fiber 3g; Sugar 8g; Protein 3g

Braised Eggplant

Prep time: 15 minutes| **Cook time:** 25 minutes| **Serves:** 4

2 large eggplants, cut into 1" pieces
1¾ teaspoons salt
3 tablespoons olive oil
1 medium yellow onion, peeled and diced
3 cloves garlic, peeled and minced
2 cups diced fresh tomatoes
1 cup water
1 tablespoon dried oregano
½ teaspoon black pepper
2 tablespoons minced fresh basil

Place eggplant in a colander and sprinkle with 1½ teaspoons salt.
Place colander over a plate. Let stand 30 minutes to drain.
Press the "Sauté" button twice to select "Normal" temperature setting on the Instant Pot and heat 2 tablespoons oil.
Add onion and cook until soft, about 5 minutes. Add garlic and cook until fragrant, about 30 seconds.
Add tomatoes and water. Press the Cancel button. Rinse eggplant well and drain. Add to pot.
Put on the pressure cooker's lid and turn the steam valve to "Sealing" position.
Set the Instant Pot to Pressure Cook.
Use the "+/-" keys on the control panel to set the cooking time to 8 minutes.
Use the Pressure Level button to adjust the pressure to "Low".
Once the cooking cycle is completed, allow the steam to release quickly.
When all the steam is released, remove the pressure lid from the top carefully.
Add oregano, pepper, and remaining ¼ teaspoon salt.
Add remaining 1 tablespoon oil to pot and stir well.
Press the "Sauté" button twice to select "Normal" temperature setting and simmer for 15 minutes to thicken.
Add basil and serve hot.

Per Serving: Calories 334; Fat 7.9g; Sodium 704mg; Carbs 6g; Fiber 3.6g; Sugar 6g; Protein 18g

Roasted Spaghetti Squash

Prep time: 15 minutes| **Cook time:** 10 minutes| **Serves:** 4

1 bulb garlic, top sliced off
3 tablespoons olive oil
1 (3-pound) spaghetti squash
1 cup water
½ teaspoon salt
½ teaspoon black pepper
¼ cup chopped fresh flat-leaf parsley
¼ cup grated Parmesan cheese

At 400 degrees F, preheat your oven.
Place garlic bulb on a sheet of aluminum foil.
Drizzle with 1 tablespoon oil.
Wrap bulb tightly and roast directly on the oven rack for 30–40 minutes, or until bulb is tender.
Unwrap and let bulb rest while you prepare squash.
Slice spaghetti squash in half lengthwise.
Scoop out seeds with a spoon and discard.
Place the rack in the Instant Pot, add water, and place spaghetti squash on rack.
Put on the pressure cooker's lid and turn the steam valve to "Sealing" position.
Set the Instant Pot to Pressure Cook.
Use the Pressure Level button to adjust the pressure to "Low".
Use the "+/-" keys on the control panel to set the cooking time to 7 minutes.
Once the cooking cycle is completed, allow the steam to release naturally.
When all the steam is released, remove the pressure lid from the top carefully.
Clean and dry pot. Press the "Sauté" button twice to select "Normal" temperature setting and heat remaining 2 tablespoons of oil.
Squeeze garlic into pot and cook for 30 seconds, then add squash, salt, and pepper and cook until squash is thoroughly coated in the garlic.
Transfer to a serving bowl and top with parsley and cheese.
Serve immediately.

Per Serving: Calories 442; Fat 11g; Sodium 91mg; Carbs 14g; Fiber 3g; Sugar 8g; Protein 13g

Tomato Basil Soup

Prep time: 15 minutes| **Cook time:** 12 minutes| **Serves:** 4

1 tablespoon olive oil
1 small onion, peeled and diced
1 stalk celery, sliced
8 medium heirloom tomatoes, seeded and quartered
¼ cup julienned fresh basil
½ teaspoon salt
3 cups low-sodium chicken broth
1 cup heavy cream
1 teaspoon black pepper

Press the "Sauté" button twice to select "Normal" temperature setting on the Instant Pot and heat oil.

Add onion and celery and cook until translucent, about 5 minutes.
Add tomatoes and cook for 3 minutes, or until tomatoes are tender and start to break down.
Add basil, salt, and broth. Press the Cancel button.
Put on the pressure cooker's lid and turn the steam valve to "Sealing" position.
Set the Instant Pot to Pressure Cook.
Use the "+/-" keys on the control panel to set the cooking time to 7 minutes.
Use the Pressure Level button to adjust the pressure to "Low".
Once the cooking cycle is completed, allow the steam to release naturally.
When all the steam is released, remove the pressure lid from the top carefully.
Add cream and pepper. Purée soup with an immersion blender, or purée in batches in a blender.
Ladle into bowls and serve warm.

Per Serving: Calories 472; Fat 7.9g; Sodium 704mg; Carbs 6g; Fiber 3.6g; Sugar 6g; Protein 18g

Artichokes Provençal

Prep time: 15 minutes| **Cook time:** 7 minutes| **Serves:** 4

4 large artichokes
1 medium lemon, cut in half
2 tablespoons olive oil
½ medium white onion, peeled and sliced
4 cloves garlic, peeled and chopped
2 tablespoons chopped fresh oregano
2 tablespoons chopped fresh basil
2 sprigs fresh thyme
2 medium tomatoes, seeded and chopped
¼ cup chopped Kalamata olives
¼ cup red wine
¼ cup water
¼ teaspoon salt
¼ teaspoon black pepper

Run artichokes under running water, making sure water runs between leaves to flush out any debris.
Slice off top ⅓ of artichoke, trim stem, and pull away any tough outer leaves.
Rub all cut surfaces with lemon.
Press the "Sauté" button twice to select "Normal" temperature setting on the Instant Pot and heat oil.
Add onion and cook until just tender, about 2 minutes. Add garlic, oregano, basil, and thyme, and cook until fragrant, about 30 seconds.
Add tomatoes and olives and gently mix, then add wine and water and cook for 30 seconds.
Press the Cancel button, then add artichokes cut side down to the Instant Pot.
Put on the pressure cooker's lid and turn the steam valve to "Sealing" position.
Set the Instant Pot to Pressure Cook.
Use the "+/-" keys on the control panel to set the cooking time to 5 minutes.
Use the Pressure Level button to adjust the pressure to "Low".

Once the cooking cycle is completed, allow the steam to release quickly.
When all the steam is released, remove the pressure lid from the top carefully.
Pour sauce over top, then season with salt and pepper. Serve warm.

Per Serving: Calories 272; Fat 10g; Sodium 891mg; Carbs 22.9g; Fiber 4g; Sugar 4g; Protein 3g

Hearty Minestrone Soup

Prep time: 15 minutes| **Cook time:** 20 minutes| **Serves:** 4

2 cups dried Great Northern beans, soaked overnight and drained
1 cup orzo
2 large carrots, peeled and diced
1 bunch Swiss chard, ribs removed and roughly chopped
1 medium zucchini, trimmed and diced
2 stalks celery, diced
1 medium onion, peeled and diced
1 teaspoon minced garlic
1 tablespoon Italian seasoning
1 teaspoon salt
½ teaspoon black pepper
2 bay leaves
1 (15-oz.) can diced tomatoes, including juice
4 cups vegetable broth
1 cup tomato juice

Place all ingredients in the Instant Pot and stir to combine.
Put on the pressure cooker's lid and turn the steam valve to "Sealing" position.
Set the Instant Pot to Pressure Cook.
Use the "+/-" keys on the control panel to set the cooking time to 20 minutes.
Use the Pressure Level button to adjust the pressure to "Low".
Once the cooking cycle is completed, allow the steam to release naturally for 10 minutes and then quick-release the remaining pressure.
When all the steam is released, remove the pressure lid from the top carefully. Remove and discard bay leaves.
Ladle into bowls and serve warm.

Per Serving: Calories 384; Fat 5g; Sodium 41mg; Carbs 7g; Fiber 7.6g; Sugar 5g; Protein 2g

Spaghetti Squash with Mushrooms

Prep time: 15 minutes| **Cook time:** 15 minutes| **Serves:** 4

1 (3-pound) spaghetti squash
1 cup water
2 tablespoons olive oil
4 cups sliced button mushrooms
2 cloves garlic, peeled and minced
1 tablespoon chopped fresh oregano
1 tablespoon chopped fresh basil
¼ teaspoon crushed red pepper flakes
1 cup marinara sauce
½ cup shredded Parmesan cheese

Slice spaghetti squash in half lengthwise.
Scoop out seeds with a spoon and discard.
Place the rack in the Instant Pot, add water, and place spaghetti squash on rack.
Put on the pressure cooker's lid and turn the steam valve to "Sealing" position.
Set the Instant Pot to Pressure Cook.
Use the "+/-" keys on the control panel to set the cooking time to 7 minutes.
Use the Pressure Level button to adjust the pressure to "Low".
Once the cooking cycle is completed, allow the steam to release quickly.
When all the steam is released, remove the pressure lid from the top carefully.
Wash and dry pot. Press the "Sauté" button two time to select "Normal" temperature setting and heat oil.
Add mushrooms and cook until tender and any juices have evaporated, about 8 minutes.
Add garlic and cook until fragrant, about 30 seconds.
Add spaghetti squash to pot and toss to mix.
Add oregano, basil, red pepper flakes, and marinara sauce and toss to coat.
Press the Cancel button. Top with cheese and close the lid. Let stand 5 minutes until cheese melts. Serve hot.

Per Serving: Calories 305; Fat 10.9g; Sodium 454mg; Carbs 10g; Fiber 3.1g; Sugar 5.2g; Protein 05g

Artichoke Soup

Prep time: 15 minutes| **Cook time:** 30 minutes| **Serves:** 8

18 large fresh artichokes, trimmed, halved, and chokes removed
1 medium lemon, halved
6 tablespoons lemon juice
2 tablespoons olive oil
6 medium leeks, trimmed, cut lengthwise, and sliced
¾ teaspoon salt
½ teaspoon pepper
3 large potatoes, peeled and quartered
10 cups vegetable stock
½ cup low-fat plain Greek yogurt
½ cup chopped fresh chives

Rinse artichokes under running water, making sure water runs between leaves to flush out any debris.
Rub all cut surfaces with lemon. In a large bowl, combine artichokes, enough water to cover them, and 3 tablespoons lemon juice. Set aside.
Press the "Sauté" button two time to select "Normal" temperature setting on the Instant Pot and heat oil.
Add leeks, ½ teaspoon salt, and ¼ teaspoon pepper. Cook for 10 minutes or until leeks are softened.
Drain artichokes and add to leeks along with potatoes and stock. Add remaining ¼ teaspoon each salt and pepper.

Put on the pressure cooker's lid and turn the steam valve to "Sealing" position.
Set the Instant Pot to Pressure Cook.
Use the "+/-" keys on the control panel to set the cooking time to 20 minutes.
Use the Pressure Level button to adjust the pressure to "Low".
Once the cooking cycle is completed, allow the steam to release naturally.
When all the steam is released, remove the pressure lid from the top carefully.
Using an immersion blender, or in batches in a regular blender, purée the soup until smooth. Stir in remaining 3 tablespoons lemon juice.
Serve soup with a dollop of yogurt and a sprinkle of chives.

Per Serving: Calories 361; Fat 19g; Sodium 354mg; Carbs 25g; Fiber 5.1g; Sugar 8.2g; Protein 2g

Green Beans with Tomatoes and Potatoes

Prep time: 15 minutes| **Cook time:** 4 minutes| **Serves:** 8
1 pound small new potatoes
1 cup water
1 teaspoon salt
2 lbs. fresh green beans, trimmed
2 medium tomatoes, seeded and diced
2 tablespoons olive oil
1 tablespoon red wine vinegar
1 clove garlic, peeled and minced
½ teaspoon dry mustard powder
¼ teaspoon smoked paprika
¼ teaspoon black pepper

Place potatoes in a steamer basket.
Place the rack in the Instant Pot, add water, and then top with the steamer basket.
Put on the pressure cooker's lid and turn the steam valve to "Sealing" position.
Set the Instant Pot to Pressure Cook.
Use the "+/-" keys on the control panel to set the cooking time to 4 minutes.
Use the Pressure Level button to adjust the pressure to "Low".
Once the cooking cycle is completed, allow the steam to release quickly.
When all the steam is released, remove the pressure lid from the top carefully.
Add salt, green beans, and tomatoes to the Instant Pot.
Transfer mixture to a serving platter or large bowl.
In a small bowl, whisk oil, vinegar, garlic, mustard, paprika, and pepper. Pour dressing over vegetables and gently toss to coat.
Serve hot.

Per Serving: Calories 489; Fat 11g; Sodium 501mg; Carbs 8.9g; Fiber 4.6g; Sugar 8g; Protein 26g

Cabbage Soup

Prep time: 15 minutes| **Cook time:** 20 minutes| **Serves:** 8
2 tablespoons olive oil
3 medium onions, peeled and chopped
1 large carrot, peeled, quartered, and sliced
1 stalk celery, chopped
3 bay leaves
1 teaspoon smoked paprika
3 cups sliced white cabbage
1 teaspoon fresh thyme leaves
3 cloves garlic, peeled and minced
½ cup chopped roasted red pepper
1 (15-oz.) can white navy beans, drained
1½ cups low-sodium vegetable cocktail beverage
7 cups low-sodium vegetable stock
1 dried chili pepper
2 medium zucchini, trimmed, halved lengthwise, and thinly sliced
1 teaspoon salt
½ teaspoon black pepper

Press the "Sauté" button two time to select "Normal" temperature setting on the Instant Pot and heat oil.
Add onions, carrot, celery, and bay leaves.
Cook for 7–10 minutes or until vegetables are soft.
Add paprika, cabbage, thyme, garlic, roasted red pepper, and beans.
Stir to combine and cook for 2 minutes. Add vegetable cocktail beverage, stock, and chili pepper.
Put on the pressure cooker's lid and turn the steam valve to "Sealing" position.
Set the Instant Pot to Pressure Cook.
Use the "+/-" keys on the control panel to set the cooking time to 20 minutes.
Use the Pressure Level button to adjust the pressure to "Low".
Once the cooking cycle is completed, allow the steam to release quickly.
When all the steam is released, remove the pressure lid from the top carefully.
Remove and discard bay leaves.
Add zucchini, close lid, and let stand on the Keep Warm setting for 15 minutes.
Season with salt and pepper.
Serve hot.

Per Serving: Calories 374; Fat 5g; Sodium 41mg; Carbs 7g; Fiber 7.6g; Sugar 5g; Protein 2g

Eggplant Caponata

Prep time: 15 minutes| **Cook time:** 5 minutes| **Serves:** 8
¼ cup olive oil
¼ cup white wine
2 tablespoons red wine vinegar
1 teaspoon ground cinnamon
1 large eggplant, peeled and diced
1 medium onion, peeled and diced
1 medium green bell pepper, seeded and diced
1 medium red bell pepper, seeded and diced

2 cloves garlic, peeled and minced
1 (15-oz.) can diced tomatoes
3 stalks celery, diced
½ cup chopped oil-cured olives
½ cup golden raisins
2 tablespoons capers, rinsed and drained
½ teaspoon salt
½ teaspoon black pepper

Place all ingredients in the Instant Pot. Stir well to mix.
Put on the pressure cooker's lid and turn the steam valve to "Sealing" position.
Set the Instant Pot to Pressure Cook.
Use the "+/-" keys on the control panel to set the cooking time to 5 minutes.
Use the Pressure Level button to adjust the pressure to "Low".
Once the cooking cycle is completed, allow the steam to release quickly.
When all the steam is released, remove the pressure lid from the top carefully.
Serve warm.

Per Serving: Calories 478; Fat 7.9g; Sodium 704mg; Carbs 6g; Fiber 3.6g; Sugar 6g; Protein 18g

Pureed Cauliflower Soup

Prep time: 15 minutes| **Cook time:** 21 minutes| **Serves:** 6
2 tablespoons olive oil
1 medium onion, peeled and chopped
1 stalk celery, chopped
1 medium carrot, peeled and chopped
3 sprigs fresh thyme
4 cups cauliflower florets
2 cups vegetable stock
½ cup half-and-half
¼ cup low-fat plain Greek yogurt
2 tablespoons chopped fresh chives

Press the "Sauté" button twice to select "Normal" temperature setting on the Instant Pot and heat oil.
Add onion, celery, and carrot. Cook until just tender, about 6 minutes.
Add thyme, cauliflower, and stock. Stir well, then press the Cancel button.
Put on the pressure cooker's lid and turn the steam valve to "Sealing" position.
Set the Instant Pot to Pressure Cook.
Use the "+/-" keys on the control panel to set the cooking time to 5 minutes.
Use the Pressure Level button to adjust the pressure to "Low".
Once the cooking cycle is completed, allow the steam to release naturally.
When all the steam is released, remove the pressure lid from the top carefully.
Open lid, remove and discard thyme stems, and with an immersion blender, purée soup until smooth.
Stir in half-and-half and yogurt. Garnish with chives and serve immediately.

Per Serving: Calories 484; Fat 5g; Sodium 41mg; Carbs 7g; Fiber 7.6g; Sugar 5g; Protein 2g

Spicy Corn On the Cob

Prep time: 15 minutes| **Cook time:** 2 minutes| **Serves:** 4
2 tablespoons olive oil
¼ teaspoon smoked paprika
¼ teaspoon ground cumin
¼ teaspoon black pepper
⅛ teaspoon cayenne pepper
1 cup water
4 large ears corn, husk and silks removed
½ teaspoon flaky sea salt

In a small bowl, whisk together olive oil, paprika, cumin, black pepper, and cayenne pepper. Set aside.
Place the rack in the Instant Pot, pour in water, and place corn on the rack.
Put on the pressure cooker's lid and turn the steam valve to "Sealing" position.
Set the Instant Pot to Pressure Cook.
Use the "+/-" keys on the control panel to set the cooking time to 2 minutes.
Use the Pressure Level button to adjust the pressure to "Low".
Once the cooking cycle is completed, allow the steam to release naturally.
When all the steam is released, remove the pressure lid from the top carefully.
Carefully transfer corn to a platter and brush with spiced olive oil.
Serve immediately with sea salt.

Per Serving: Calories 242; Fat 11g; Sodium 91mg; Carbs 14g; Fiber 3g; Sugar 8g; Protein 13g

Gingered Sweet Potatoes

Prep time: 15 minutes| **Cook time:** 10 minutes| **Serves:** 6
2½ lbs. sweet potatoes, peeled and chopped
2 cups water
1 tablespoon minced fresh ginger
½ teaspoon salt
1 tablespoon maple syrup
1 tablespoon unsalted butter
¼ cup whole milk

Place sweet potatoes and water in the Instant Pot.
Put on the pressure cooker's lid and turn the steam valve to "Sealing" position.
Set the Instant Pot to Pressure Cook.
Use the "+/-" keys on the control panel to set the cooking time to 10 minutes.
Use the Pressure Level button to adjust the pressure to "Low".
Once the cooking cycle is completed, allow the steam to release naturally.
When all the steam is released, remove the pressure lid from the top carefully.

Drain water from the Instant Pot. Add ginger, salt, maple syrup, butter, and milk to sweet potatoes.
Using an immersion blender, cream the potatoes until desired consistency is reached. Serve warm.

Per Serving: Calories 419; Fat 14g; Sodium 791mg; Carbs 8.9g; Fiber 4.6g; Sugar 8g; Protein 3g

Zucchini Pomodoro

Prep time: 15 minutes| **Cook time:** 6 minutes| **Serves:** 4-6
1 tablespoon vegetable oil
1 large onion, peeled and diced
3 cloves garlic, peeled and minced
1 (28-oz.) can diced tomatoes, including juice
½ cup water
1 tablespoon Italian seasoning
½ teaspoon salt
½ teaspoon black pepper
2 medium zucchini, trimmed and spiralized

Press the "Sauté" button twice to select "Normal" temperature setting on the Instant Pot and heat oil.
Add onion and cook until translucent, about 5 minutes. Add garlic and cook for an additional 30 seconds.
Add tomatoes, water, Italian seasoning, salt, and pepper. Add zucchini and toss to combine.
Put on the pressure cooker's lid and turn the steam valve to "Sealing" position.
Set the Instant Pot to Pressure Cook.
Use the "+/-" keys on the control panel to set the cooking time to 1 minute.
Use the Pressure Level button to adjust the pressure to "Low".
Once the cooking cycle is completed, allow the steam to release naturally for 5 minutes and then quick-release the remaining pressure.
When all the steam is released, remove the pressure lid from the top carefully.
Transfer zucchini to four bowls.
Press the Sauté button, then adjust the temperature setting to Less, and simmer sauce in the Instant Pot uncovered for 5 minutes.
Ladle over zucchini and serve immediately.

Per Serving: Calories 272; Fat 10g; Sodium 891mg; Carbs 22.9g; Fiber 4g; Sugar 4g; Protein 3g

Burgundy Mushrooms

Prep time: 15 minutes| **Cook time:** 20 minutes| **Serves:** 8
¼ cup olive oil
3 cloves garlic, peeled and halved
16 oz. whole white mushrooms
16 oz. whole baby bella mushrooms
1½ cups dry red wine
1 teaspoon Worcestershire sauce
1 teaspoon dried thyme

1 tablespoon Dijon mustard
1 teaspoon ground celery seed
½ teaspoon black pepper
3 cups beef broth
2 slices bacon

Press the "Sauté" button twice to select "Normal" temperature setting on the Instant Pot and heat oil.
Add garlic and mushrooms, and cook until mushrooms start to get tender, about 3 minutes.
Add wine and simmer for 3 minutes.
Add Worcestershire sauce, thyme, mustard, celery seed, pepper, broth, and bacon to pot.
Put on the pressure cooker's lid and turn the steam valve to "Sealing" position.
Set the Instant Pot to Pressure Cook.
Use the Pressure Level button to adjust the pressure to "Low".
Use the "+/-" keys on the control panel to set the cooking time to 20 minutes.
Once the cooking cycle is completed, allow the steam to release naturally.
When all the steam is released, remove the pressure lid from the top carefully.
Remove and discard bacon and garlic halves.
Transfer mushrooms to a serving bowl.
Serve warm.

Per Serving: Calories 484; Fat 5g; Sodium 41mg; Carbs 7g; Fiber 7.6g; Sugar 5g; Protein 2g

Wild Mushroom Soup

Prep time: 15 minutes| **Cook time:** 10 minutes| **Serves:** 8
3 tablespoons olive oil
1 stalk celery, diced
1 medium carrot, peeled and diced
½ medium yellow onion, peeled and diced
1 clove garlic, peeled and minced
1 (8-oz.) container hen of the woods mushrooms, sliced
1 (8-oz.) container porcini or chanterelle mushrooms, sliced
2 cups sliced shiitake mushrooms
2 tablespoons dry sherry
4 cups vegetable broth
2 cups water
1 tablespoon chopped fresh tarragon
½ teaspoon salt
½ teaspoon black pepper

Press the "Sauté" button twice to select "Normal" temperature setting on the Instant Pot and heat oil.
Add celery, carrot, and onion. Cook, stirring often, until softened, about 5 minutes.
Add garlic and cook 30 seconds until fragrant, then add mushrooms and cook for 5 minutes.
Add sherry, broth, water, tarragon, salt, and pepper to pot, and stir well. Press the Cancel button.
Put on the pressure cooker's lid and turn the steam valve to "Sealing" position.
Set the Instant Pot to Pressure Cook.

Use the "+/-" keys on the control panel to set the cooking time to 5 minutes.
Use the Pressure Level button to adjust the pressure to "Low".
Once the cooking cycle is completed, allow the steam to release naturally.
When all the steam is released, remove the pressure lid from the top carefully.
Serve hot.

Per Serving: Calories 199; Fat 5g; Sodium 41mg; Carbs 7g; Fiber 7.6g; Sugar 5g; Protein 2g

Stuffed Acorn Squash

Prep time: 15 minutes| **Cook time:** 25 minutes| **Serves:** 2

1 cup water
1 (1-pound) acorn squash, halved and seeded
2 tablespoons olive oil
½ medium white onion, peeled and sliced
1 stalk celery, sliced
2 cloves garlic, peeled and chopped
1 tablespoon chopped fresh sage
1 tablespoon chopped fresh flat-leaf parsley
1 teaspoon chopped fresh rosemary
1 teaspoon fresh thyme leaves
¼ teaspoon salt
¼ teaspoon black pepper
½ cup wild rice
¾ cup vegetable stock
¼ cup chopped toasted walnuts
¼ cup golden raisins
¼ cup dried cranberries
¼ cup crumbled goat cheese

Place the rack in the Instant Pot and add water.
Place squash halves on the rack.
Put on the pressure cooker's lid and turn the steam valve to "Sealing" position.
Set the Instant Pot to Pressure Cook.
Use the "+/-" keys on the control panel to set the cooking time to 10 minutes.
Use the Pressure Level button to adjust the pressure to "Low".
Once the cooking cycle is completed, allow the steam to release naturally for 10 minutes and then quick-release the remaining pressure.
Insert a paring knife into the squash to check for doneness. Once it pierces easily, it is cooked. Then transfer the squash to a platter and cover with foil to keep warm.
Wash and dry the inner pot. Set your Instant Pot to Sauté on "Normal" temperature setting. Heat oil.
Add garlic, sage, parsley, rosemary, and thyme. Then cook until fragrant, about 30 seconds.
Add salt and pepper and stir well to season.
Then add wild rice and stock. Press the Cancel button.
Close the lid and turn the handle to "Sealing" position.
Set your Instant Pot to Pressure Cook.
Use the "+/-" keys on the control panel to set the cooking time to 25 minutes.

Use the Pressure Level button to adjust the pressure to "Low".
Once the cooking cycle is completed, quick-release the pressure.
When all the steam is released, remove the pressure lid from the top carefully.
Add walnuts, raisins, and cranberries, and stir well.
Close lid and let stand on the Keep Warm setting for 10 minutes.
Spoon mixture into acorn squash halves and top with goat cheese.
Serve warm.

Per Serving: Calories 305; Fat 12.9g; Sodium 754mg; Carbs 21g; Fiber 6.1g; Sugar 4.2g; Protein 11g

Herbed Potato Salad

Prep time: 15 minutes| **Cook time:** 25 minutes| **Serves:** 10

¼ cup olive oil
3 tablespoons red wine vinegar
¼ cup chopped fresh flat-leaf parsley
2 tablespoons chopped fresh dill
2 tablespoons chopped fresh chives
1 clove garlic, peeled and minced
½ teaspoon dry mustard powder
¼ teaspoon black pepper
2 lbs. baby Yukon Gold potatoes
1 cup water
1 teaspoon salt

Whisk together oil, vinegar, parsley, dill, chives, garlic, mustard, and pepper in a small bowl. Set aside.
Place potatoes in a steamer basket.
Place the rack in the Instant Pot, add water and salt, then top with the steamer basket.
Put on the pressure cooker's lid and turn the steam valve to "Sealing" position.
Set the Instant Pot to Pressure Cook.
Use the Pressure Level button to adjust the pressure to "Low".
Use the "+/-" keys on the control panel to set the cooking time to 4 minutes.
Once the cooking cycle is completed, allow the steam to quick-release pressure.
When all the steam is released, remove the pressure lid from the top carefully.
Transfer hot potatoes to a serving bowl. Pour dressing over potatoes and gently toss to coat.
Serve warm or at room temperature.

Per Serving: Calories 382; Fat 7.9g; Sodium 704mg; Carbs 6g; Fiber 3.6g; Sugar 6g; Protein 18g

Steamed Cauliflower with Herbs

Prep time: 15 minutes| **Cook time:** 10 minutes| **Serves:** 6

1 head cauliflower, cut into florets (about 6 cups)
1 cup water
4 tablespoons olive oil

1 clove garlic, peeled and minced
2 tablespoons chopped fresh oregano
1 teaspoon chopped fresh thyme leaves
1 teaspoon chopped fresh sage
¼ teaspoon salt
¼ teaspoon black pepper

Place cauliflower florets in a steamer basket.
Place the rack in the Instant Pot, add water,
then top with the steamer basket.
Put on the pressure cooker's lid and turn the
steam valve to "Sealing" position.
Set the Instant Pot to Pressure Cook.
Use the Pressure Level button to adjust the
pressure to "Low".
Use the "+/-" keys on the control panel to set
the cooking time to 10 minute.
Once the cooking cycle is completed, quick-
release the steam.
When all the steam is released, remove the
pressure lid from the top carefully.
While cauliflower cooks, prepare the dressing.
Whisk together olive oil, garlic, oregano,
thyme, sage, salt, and pepper.
Carefully transfer cauliflower to a serving bowl
and immediately pour dressing over
cauliflower.
Carefully toss to coat. Let stand for 5 minutes.
Serve hot.

Per Serving: Calories 272; Fat 10g; Sodium
891mg; Carbs 22.9g; Fiber 4g; Sugar 4g;
Protein 3g

Maple Dill Carrots

Prep time: 15 minutes| **Cook time:** 5
minutes| **Serves:** 6
1 pound carrots, peeled and cut into quarters,
or whole baby carrots
1 tablespoon minced fresh dill
1 tablespoon maple syrup
1 tablespoon ghee
½ teaspoon salt
½ cup water

Place all ingredients in the Instant Pot.
Put on the pressure cooker's lid and turn the
steam valve to "Sealing" position.
Set the Instant Pot to Pressure Cook.
Use the "+/-" keys on the control panel to set
the cooking time to 5 minutes.
Use the Pressure Level button to adjust the
pressure to "Low".
Once the cooking cycle is completed, let the
steam release naturally for 5 minutes and
then quick-release the remaining pressure.
When all the steam is released, remove the
pressure lid from the top carefully.
Transfer to a serving dish and serve warm.

Per Serving: Calories 472; Fat 10.9g;
Sodium 354mg; Carbs 10.5g; Fiber 4.1g;
Sugar 8.2g; Protein 6g

Ratatouille

Prep time: 15 minutes| **Cook time:** 25
minutes| **Serves:** 8
1 medium eggplant, cut into 1" pieces
2 teaspoons salt
4 tablespoons olive oil
1 medium white onion, peeled and chopped
1 medium green bell pepper, seeded and
chopped
1 medium red bell pepper, seeded and
chopped
1 medium zucchini, trimmed and chopped
1 medium yellow squash, chopped
4 cloves garlic, peeled and minced
4 large tomatoes, cut into 1" pieces
2 teaspoons Italian seasoning
¼ teaspoon crushed red pepper flakes
6 fresh basil leaves, thinly sliced

Place eggplant in a colander and sprinkle
evenly with salt.
Let stand 30 minutes, then rinse and dry
eggplant. Set aside.
Press the "Sauté" button twice to select
"Normal" temperature setting on the Instant
Pot and heat 1 tablespoon oil.
Add onion and bell peppers. Cook, stirring
often, until vegetables are just tender, about
5 minutes.
Transfer to a large bowl and set aside.
Add 1 tablespoon oil to pot and heat for 30
seconds, then add zucchini and squash.
Cook, stirring constantly, until vegetables are
tender, about 5 minutes.
Add garlic and cook until fragrant, about 30
seconds. Transfer to bowl with onion and
peppers.
Add 1 tablespoon oil to pot and heat for 30
seconds.
Add eggplant and cook, stirring constantly,
until eggplant is golden brown, about 8
minutes.
Add tomatoes and cook until they are tender
and releasing juice, about 4 minutes.
Return reserved vegetables to pot and stir in
Italian seasoning and red pepper flakes.
Put on the pressure cooker's lid and turn the
steam valve to "Sealing" position.
Set the Instant Pot to Pressure Cook.
Use the "+/-" keys on the control panel to set
the cooking time to 5 minutes.
Use the Pressure Level button to adjust the
pressure to "Low".
Once the cooking cycle is completed, quick-
release the steam.
When all the steam is released, remove the
pressure lid from the top carefully.
Serve topped with basil and remaining 1
tablespoon oil.

Per Serving: Calories 334; Fat 10.9g;
Sodium 354mg; Carbs 10.5g; Fiber 4.1g;
Sugar 8.2g; Protein 6g

Steamed Broccoli

Prep time: 5 minutes| **Cook time:** 1 minutes| **Serves:** 6

6 cups broccoli florets

Pour 1½ cups water into the inner pot of the Instant Pot. Place a steam rack inside.
Place the broccoli florets inside a steamer basket and place the basket on the steam rack.
Put on the pressure cooker's lid and turn the steam valve to "Sealing" position.
Set the Instant Pot on "Steam".
Use the "+/-" keys on the control panel to set the cooking time to 1 minute.
Use the Pressure Level button to adjust the pressure to "Low".
Once the cooking cycle is completed, quick-release the pressure.
When all the steam is released, remove the pressure lid from the top carefully.
Remove the steamer basket and serve.

Per Serving: Calories 305; Fat 10.9g; Sodium 454mg; Carbs 10g; Fiber 3.1g; Sugar 5.2g; Protein 05g

Boiled Cabbage

Prep time: 15 minutes| **Cook time:** 5 minutes| **Serves:** 6

1 large head green cabbage, cored and chopped
3 cups vegetable broth
1 teaspoon salt
½ teaspoon black pepper

Place the cabbage, broth, salt, and pepper in the inner pot.
Put on the pressure cooker's lid and turn the steam valve to "Sealing" position.
Set the Instant Pot to Pressure Cook.
Use the Pressure Level button to adjust the pressure to "Low".
Use the "+/-" keys on the control panel to set the cooking time to 5 minutes.
Once the cooking cycle is completed, allow the steam to release naturally.
When all the steam is released, remove the pressure lid from the top carefully.
Serve the cabbage with a little of the cooking liquid.

Per Serving: Calories 199; Fat 5g; Sodium 41mg; Carbs 7g; Fiber 7.6g; Sugar 5g; Protein 2g

Vegetable Cheese Sauce

Prep time: 15 minutes| **Cook time:** 6 minutes| **Serves:** 6

1 small yellow onion, peeled and chopped
1 medium zucchini, peeled and sliced
6 cloves garlic, chopped
2¼ cups vegetable broth
¼ teaspoon paprika
1 medium sweet potato, peeled and chopped
½ cup nutritional yeast

Place the onion, zucchini, garlic, and ¼ cup broth into the inner pot.
Press the "Sauté" button two time to select "Normal" mode and let the vegetables sauté until soft, 5 minutes.
Add the remaining 2 cups broth, paprika, and sweet potato.
Put on the pressure cooker's lid and turn the steam valve to "Sealing" position.
Set the Instant Pot to Pressure Cook.
Use the Pressure Level button to adjust the pressure to "Low".
Use the "+/-" keys on the control panel to set the cooking time to 6 minutes.
Once the cooking cycle is completed, quick-release the pressure.
When all the steam is released, remove the pressure lid from the top carefully.
Allow to cool for a few minutes and then transfer the mixture to a large blender.
Add the nutritional yeast to the blender with the other ingredients and blend on high until smooth.
Serve warm as a topping for the vegetables of your choice.

Per Serving: Calories 521; Fat 7.9g; Sodium 704mg; Carbs 6g; Fiber 3.6g; Sugar 6g; Protein 18g

Purple Cabbage Salad

Prep time: 15 minutes| **Cook time:** 2 minutes| **Serves:** 8

½ cup dry quinoa
1 (10-oz.) bag frozen shelled edamame
1 cup vegetable broth
¼ cup reduced sodium tamari
¼ cup natural almond butter
3 tablespoons toasted sesame seed oil
½ teaspoon pure stevia powder
1 head purple cabbage, cored and chopped

Place the quinoa, edamame, and broth in the inner pot of your Instant Pot.
Put on the pressure cooker's lid and turn the steam valve to "Sealing" position.
Set the Instant Pot to Pressure Cook.
Use the "+/-" keys on the control panel to set the cooking time to 2 minutes.
Use the Pressure Level button to adjust the pressure to "Low".
Once the cooking cycle is completed, quick-release the pressure.
When all the steam is released, remove the pressure lid from the top carefully.
Meanwhile, in a small bowl, whisk together the tamari, almond butter, sesame seed oil, and stevia. Set aside.
Use a fork to fluff the quinoa, and then transfer the mixture to a large bowl.
Allow the quinoa and edamame to cool, and then add the purple cabbage to the bowl and toss to combine.
Add the dressing and toss again until everything is evenly coated.
Serve.

Per Serving: Calories 242; Fat 11g; Sodium 91mg; Carbs 14g; Fiber 3g; Sugar 8g; Protein 13g

Steamed Cauliflower

Prep time: 15 minutes| **Cook time:** 2 minutes| **Serves:** 6

1 large head cauliflower, cored and cut into large florets

Pour 2 cups water into the inner pot of the Instant Pot. Place a steam rack inside.
Place the cauliflower florets inside a steamer basket and place the basket on the steam rack.
Put on the pressure cooker's lid and turn the steam valve to "Sealing" position.
Set the Instant Pot on "Steam".
Use the "+/-" keys on the control panel to set the cooking time to 2 minutes.
Use the Pressure Level button to adjust the pressure to "Low".
Once the cooking cycle is completed, allow the steam to release naturally.
When all the steam is released, remove the pressure lid from the top carefully.
Carefully remove the steamer basket and serve.

Per Serving: Calories 378; Fat 19g; Sodium 354mg; Carbs 25g; Fiber 5.1g; Sugar 8.2g; Protein 2g

Saucy Brussels Sprouts and Carrots

Prep time: 15 minutes| **Cook time:** 13 minutes| **Serves:** 4

1 tablespoon coconut oil
12 oz. Brussels sprouts, tough ends removed and cut in half
12 oz. carrots (about 4 medium), peeled, ends removed, and cut into 1" chunks
¼ cup fresh lime juice
¼ cup apple cider vinegar
½ cup coconut aminos
¼ cup almond butter

Press the "Sauté" button twice to select "Normal" mode and melt the oil in the inner pot.
Add the Brussels sprouts and carrots and sauté until browned, about 5–7 minutes.
While the vegetables are browning, make the sauce.
In a small bowl, whisk together the lime juice, vinegar, coconut aminos, and almond butter.
Pour the sauce over the vegetables and press the Cancel button.
Put on the pressure cooker's lid and turn the steam valve to "Sealing" position.
Set the Instant Pot to Pressure Cook.
Use the Pressure Level button to adjust the pressure to "Low".
Use the "+/-" keys on the control panel to set the cooking time to 6 minutes.

Once the cooking cycle is completed, allow the steam to release quickly.
When all the steam is released, remove the pressure lid from the top carefully.
Serve.

Per Serving: Calories 272; Fat 10g; Sodium 891mg; Carbs 22.9g; Fiber 4g; Sugar 4g; Protein 3g

Simple Spaghetti Squash

Prep time: 15 minutes| **Cook time:** 25 minutes| **Serves:** 4

1 medium spaghetti squash
2 tablespoons olive oil
⅛ teaspoon salt
⅛ teaspoon black pepper

Place 1½ cups water in the inner pot of your Instant Pot. Place the steam rack inside.
Wash squash with soap and water and dry it.
Place the whole uncut squash on top of the steam rack inside the inner pot.
Put on the pressure cooker's lid and turn the steam valve to "Sealing" position.
Set the Instant Pot to Pressure Cook.
Use the "+/-" keys on the control panel to set the cooking time to 25 minutes.
Use the Pressure Level button to adjust the pressure to "Low".
Once the cooking cycle is completed, quick-release the pressure.
When all the steam is released, remove the pressure lid from the top carefully.
Allow the squash to cool, and then carefully remove it from the pot.
Use a sharp knife to cut the squash in half lengthwise.
Spoon out the seeds and discard. Use a fork to scrape out the squash strands into a medium bowl.
Drizzle with the oil, add the salt and pepper, and serve.

Per Serving: Calories 382; Fat 19g; Sodium 354mg; Carbs 25g; Fiber 5.1g; Sugar 8.2g; Protein 2g

Baked Sweet Potatoes

Prep time: 15 minutes| **Cook time:** 18 minutes| **Serves:** 4

4 medium sweet potatoes
2 tablespoons coconut oil
½ teaspoon ground cinnamon

Pour 1½ cups water into the Instant Pot and place the steam rack inside.
Place the sweet potatoes on the rack. It's okay if they overlap.
Put on the pressure cooker's lid and turn the steam valve to "Sealing" position.
Set the Instant Pot to Pressure Cook.
Use the "+/-" keys on the control panel to set the cooking time to 18 minutes.
Use the Pressure Level button to adjust the pressure to "Low".

Once the cooking cycle is completed, quick-release pressure.
When all the steam is released, remove the pressure lid from the top carefully.
Carefully remove the sweet potatoes from the pot.
Use a knife to cut each sweet potato lengthwise and open the potato slightly.
Add ½ tablespoon coconut oil and ⅛ teaspoon cinnamon to each potato and serve.

Per Serving: Calories 199; Fat 5g; Sodium 41mg; Carbs 7g; Fiber 7.6g; Sugar 5g; Protein 2g

Lemony Cauliflower Rice

Prep time: 15 minutes| **Cook time:** 7 minutes| **Serves:** 4

1 tablespoon avocado oil
1 small yellow onion, peeled and diced
1 teaspoon minced garlic
4 cups riced cauliflower
Juice from 1 small lemon
½ teaspoon salt
¼ teaspoon black pepper

Press the Sauté button, add the oil to the pot, and heat 1 minute.
Add the onion and sauté 5 minutes.
Add the garlic and sauté 1 more minute. Press the Cancel button.
Add the cauliflower rice, lemon juice, salt, and pepper and stir to combine.
Put on the pressure cooker's lid and turn the steam valve to "Sealing" position.
Set the Instant Pot to Pressure Cook.
Use the Pressure Level button to adjust the pressure to "Low".
Use the "+/-" keys on the control panel to set the cooking time to 1 minute.
Once the cooking cycle is completed, quick-release pressure.
When all the steam is released, remove the pressure lid from the top carefully.
Serve.

Per Serving: Calories 334; Fat 7.9g; Sodium 704mg; Carbs 6g; Fiber 3.6g; Sugar 6g; Protein 18g

Lemony Steamed Asparagus

Prep time: 15 minutes| **Cook time:** 1minutes| **Serves:** 4-6
1 pound asparagus, woody ends removed
Juice from ½ large lemon
¼ teaspoon kosher salt

Add ½ cup water to the inner pot and add the steam rack.
Add the asparagus to the steamer basket and place the basket on top of the rack.
Put on the pressure cooker's lid and turn the steam valve to "Sealing" position.
Set the Instant Pot on "Steam".
Use the "+/-" keys on the control panel to set the cooking time to 1 minute.

Use the Pressure Level button to adjust the pressure to "Low".

Once the cooking cycle is completed, quick-release pressure.
When all the steam is released, remove the pressure lid from the top carefully.
Transfer the asparagus to a plate and top with lemon juice and salt.

Per Serving: Calories 44; Fat 2.2g; Sodium 811mg; Carbs 12g; Fiber 3g; Sugar 8g; Protein 8g

Lemon Garlic Red Chard

Prep time: 15 minutes| **Cook time:** 7 minutes| **Serves:** 4
1 tablespoon avocado oil
1 small yellow onion, peeled and diced
1 bunch red chard, leaves and stems chopped
3 cloves garlic, minced
¾ teaspoon salt
Juice from ½ medium lemon

1 teaspoon lemon zest

Add the oil to the inner pot of the Instant Pot and allow it to heat 1 minute.
Add the onion and chard stems and sauté 5 minutes.
Add the garlic and sauté another 30 seconds.
Add the chard leaves, salt, and lemon juice and stir to combine. Press the Cancel button.
Put on the pressure cooker's lid and turn the steam valve to "Sealing" position.
Set the Instant Pot to Pressure Cook.
Use the Pressure Level button to adjust the pressure to "Low".
Use the "+/-" keys on the control panel to set the cooking time to 1 minute.
Once the cooking cycle is completed, quick-release pressure.
When all the steam is released, remove the pressure lid from the top carefully.
Spoon the chard mixture into a serving bowl and top with lemon zest.

Per Serving: Calories 203; Fat 12.9g; Sodium 754mg; Carbs 21g; Fiber 6.1g; Sugar 4.2g; Protein 11g

Ginger Broccoli and Carrots

Prep time: 15 minutes| **Cook time:** 5 minutes| **Serves:** 6
1 tablespoon avocado oil
1" fresh ginger, peeled and thinly sliced
1 clove garlic, minced
2 broccoli crowns, stems removed and cut into large florets
2 large carrots, peeled and thinly sliced
½ teaspoon kosher salt
Juice from ½ large lemon
¼ cup water

Add the oil to the inner pot.

Press the "Sauté" button twice to select "Normal" mode and heat oil 2 minutes.
Add the ginger and garlic and sauté 1 minute.
Add the broccoli, carrots, and salt and stir to combine. Press the Cancel button.
Add the lemon juice and water and use a wooden spoon to scrape up any brown bits.
Put on the pressure cooker's lid and turn the steam valve to "Sealing" position.
Set the Instant Pot to Pressure Cook.
Use the Pressure Level button to adjust the pressure to "Low".
Use the "+/-" keys on the control panel to set the cooking time to 2 minutes.
Once the cooking cycle is completed, quick-release pressure.
When all the steam is released, remove the pressure lid from the top carefully.
Serve immediately.

Per Serving: Calories 419; Fat 14g; Sodium 791mg; Carbs 28.9g; Fiber 4.6g; Sugar 8g; Protein 3g

Spinach Salad with Quinoa

Prep time: 15 minutes| **Cook time:** 6 minutes| **Serves:** 6
¼ cup olive oil
2 tablespoons fresh lemon juice
¼ teaspoon pure stevia powder
1 teaspoon Dijon mustard
¼ teaspoon salt
⅛ teaspoon black pepper
1 tablespoon avocado oil
1 small yellow onion, peeled and diced
1 large carrot, peeled and diced
1 medium stalk celery, ends removed and sliced
½ cup dry quinoa
1 cup vegetable broth
10 oz. baby spinach leaves

In a small bowl, whisk together the olive oil, lemon juice, stevia, mustard, salt, and pepper. Set aside.
Add the avocado oil to the inner pot of the Instant Pot and press the Sauté button.
Allow the oil to heat 1 minute and then add the onion, carrot, and celery.
Cook the vegetables until they are softened, about 5 minutes.
Rinse the quinoa in a fine-mesh strainer under water until the water runs clear.
Add the quinoa to the inner pot and stir to combine with the vegetables. Press the Cancel button.
Add the vegetable broth to the inner pot.
Put on the pressure cooker's lid and turn the steam valve to "Sealing" position.
Set the Instant Pot to Pressure Cook.
Use the "+/-" keys on the control panel to set the cooking time to 1 minute.
Use the Pressure Level button to adjust the pressure to "Low".
Once the cooking cycle is completed, quick-release pressure.
When all the steam is released, remove the pressure lid from the top carefully.

Place the spinach leaves in a large bowl and top with the quinoa mixture.
Drizzle with the dressing and toss to combine.
Serve warm.

Per Serving: Calories 371; Fat 10.9g; Sodium 454mg; Carbs 10g; Fiber 3.1g; Sugar 5.2g; Protein 05g

Curried Mustard Greens

Prep time: 15 minutes| **Cook time:** 10 minutes| **Serves:** 6
1 tablespoon avocado oil
1 medium white onion, peeled and chopped
1 tablespoon peeled and chopped ginger
3 cloves garlic, minced
2 tablespoons curry powder
½ teaspoon salt
¼ teaspoon black pepper
2 cups vegetable broth
½ cup coconut cream
1 large bunch mustard greens (about 1 pound), tough stems removed and roughly chopped

Add the oil to the inner pot.
Press the "Sauté" button two time to select "Normal" mode and heat the oil 2 minutes.
Add the onion and sauté until softened, about 5 minutes.
Add the ginger, garlic, curry, salt, and pepper and sauté 1 more minute.
Stir in the vegetable broth and coconut cream until combined and then allow it to come to a boil, about 2–3 minutes more.
Stir in the mustard greens until everything is well combined.
Put on the pressure cooker's lid and turn the steam valve to "Sealing" position.
Set the Instant Pot to Pressure Cook.
Use the Pressure Level button to adjust the pressure to "Low".
Use the "+/-" keys on the control panel to set the cooking time to 1 minute.
Once the cooking cycle is completed, quick-release pressure.
When all the steam is released, remove the pressure lid from the top carefully.
Transfer to a bowl and serve.

Per Serving: Calories 272; Fat 10g; Sodium 891mg; Carbs 22.9g; Fiber 4g; Sugar 4g; Protein 3g

Cheesy Brussels Sprouts and Carrots

Prep time: 15 minutes| **Cook time:** 10 minutes| **Serves:** 4
1 pound Brussels sprouts, tough ends removed and cut in half
1 pound baby carrots
1 cup chicken stock
2 tablespoons lemon juice
½ cup nutritional yeast
¼ teaspoon salt

Add the Brussels sprouts, carrots, stock, lemon juice, nutritional yeast, and salt to the inner pot of your Instant Pot. Stir well to combine.

Put on the pressure cooker's lid and turn the steam valve to "Sealing" position.

Set the Instant Pot to Pressure Cook.

Use the "+/-" keys on the control panel to set the cooking time to 10 minutes.

Use the Pressure Level button to adjust the pressure to "Low".

Once the cooking cycle is completed, quick-release pressure.

When all the steam is released, remove the pressure lid from the top carefully.

Transfer the vegetables and sauce to a bowl and serve.

Per Serving: Calories 382; Fat 19g; Sodium 354mg; Carbs 25g; Fiber 5.1g; Sugar 8.2g; Protein 2g

Garlic Green Beans

Prep time: 15 minutes| **Cook time:** 5 minutes| **Serves:** 4

12 oz. green beans, ends trimmed
4 cloves garlic, minced
1 tablespoon avocado oil
½ teaspoon salt
1 cup water

Place the green beans in a medium bowl and toss with the garlic, oil, and salt.

Transfer this mixture to the steamer basket.

Pour 1 cup water into the inner pot and place the steam rack inside.

Place the steamer basket with the green beans on top of the steam rack.

Put on the pressure cooker's lid and turn the steam valve to "Sealing" position.

Set the Instant Pot to Pressure Cook.

Use the "+/-" keys on the control panel to set the cooking time to 5 minutes.

Use the Pressure Level button to adjust the pressure to "Low".

Once the cooking cycle is completed, allow the steam to release naturally.

When all the steam is released, remove the pressure lid from the top carefully.

Transfer to a bowl for serving.

Per Serving: Calories 199; Fat 5g; Sodium 41mg; Carbs 7g; Fiber 7.6g; Sugar 5g; Protein 2g

Simple Beet Salad

Prep time: 15 minutes| **Cook time:** 5 minutes| **Serves:** 8

6 medium beets, peeled and cut into small cubes
1 cup water
¼ cup olive oil
¼ cup apple cider vinegar
1 teaspoon Dijon mustard
¼ teaspoon pure stevia powder
½ teaspoon salt

¼ teaspoon black pepper
1 large shallot, peeled and diced
1 large stalk celery, ends removed and thinly sliced

Place the beets into the steamer basket.

Pour 1 cup water into the inner pot and place the steam rack inside.

Place the steamer basket with the beets on top of the steam rack.

Meanwhile, in a small container or jar with a tight lid add the oil, vinegar, mustard, stevia, salt, and pepper and shake well to combine. Set aside.

Put on the pressure cooker's lid and turn the steam valve to "Sealing" position.

Set the Instant Pot to Pressure Cook.

Use the "+/-" keys on the control panel to set the cooking time to 5 minutes.

Use the Pressure Level button to adjust the pressure to "Low".

Once the cooking cycle is completed, allow the steam to release naturally.

When all the steam is released, remove the pressure lid from the top carefully.

Carefully remove the basket from the Instant Pot and let the beets cool completely.

Place the shallot and celery in a large bowl and then add the cooked, cooled beets.

Drizzle with the dressing and toss to coat.

Per Serving: Calories 203; Fat 2.2g; Sodium 811mg; Carbs 12g; Fiber 3g; Sugar 8g; Protein 8g

Spinach Salad with Beets

Prep time: 15 minutes| **Cook time:** 5 minutes| **Serves:** 4

3 medium beets, peeled and cut into small cubes
1 cup water
½ small shallot, peeled and finely chopped
⅓ cup olive oil
2 tablespoons apple cider vinegar
2½ tablespoons fresh orange juice
¼ teaspoon orange zest
5 oz. baby spinach leaves
¼ cup sliced almonds
⅛ teaspoon coarse salt
⅛ teaspoon black pepper

Place the beets into the steamer basket.

Pour 1 cup water into the inner pot and place the steam rack inside.

Place the steamer basket with the beets on top of the steam rack.

Meanwhile, in a container or jar with a tight lid add the shallot, oil, vinegar, orange juice, and orange zest and shake well to combine. Set aside.

Put on the pressure cooker's lid and turn the steam valve to "Sealing" position.

Set the Instant Pot to Pressure Cook.

Use the "+/-" keys on the control panel to set the cooking time to 5 minutes.

Use the Pressure Level button to adjust the pressure to "Low".

Once the cooking cycle is completed, quick-release pressure.
When all the steam is released, remove the pressure lid from the top carefully.
Place the spinach and almonds in a large bowl and add the cooked beets.
Drizzle with the dressing and toss to coat. Top the salad with salt and pepper and serve.

Per Serving: Calories 216; Fat 7.9g; Sodium 704mg; Carbs 6g; Fiber 3.6g; Sugar 6g; Protein 18g

Mashed Sweet Potatoes

Prep time: 15 minutes| **Cook time:** 8 minutes| **Serves:** 6

1 cup water
3 large sweet potatoes, peeled and cut into cubes
2 tablespoons olive oil
1 teaspoon dried thyme
1 teaspoon dried rosemary, crushed
¼ teaspoon garlic salt

Pour 1 cup water into the inner pot of the Instant Pot and place a steam rack inside.
Place the sweet potato into a steamer basket and place it on top of the steam rack.
Put on the pressure cooker's lid and turn the steam valve to "Sealing" position.
Set the Instant Pot to Pressure Cook.
Use the "+/-" keys on the control panel to set the cooking time to 8 minutes.
Use the Pressure Level button to adjust the pressure to "Low".
Once the cooking cycle is completed, quick-release pressure.
When all the steam is released, remove the pressure lid from the top carefully.
Carefully remove the steamer basket from the inner pot and transfer the sweet potatoes to a large bowl.
Add the olive oil, thyme, rosemary, and garlic salt and use a potato masher to mash the potatoes.

Serve.

Per Serving: Calories 242; Fat 11g; Sodium 91mg; Carbs 14g; Fiber 3g; Sugar 8g; Protein 13g

Mashed Cauliflower

Prep time: 15 minutes| **Cook time:** 3 minutes| **Serves:** 4

1 large cauliflower crown, core removed and roughly chopped
2 cups chicken stock
2 tablespoons olive oil plus ½ teaspoon for serving
½ teaspoon salt
½ teaspoon garlic powder
¾ cup nutritional yeast
¼ teaspoon black pepper

Add the cauliflower and stock to the inner pot.
Put on the pressure cooker's lid and turn the steam valve to "Sealing" position.
Set the Instant Pot to Pressure Cook.
Use the Pressure Level button to adjust the pressure to "Low".
Use the "+/-" keys on the control panel to set the cooking time to 3 minutes.
Once the cooking cycle is completed, quick-release pressure.
When all the steam is released, remove the pressure lid from the top carefully.
Use a slotted spoon to transfer the cauliflower to a food processor.
Add the 2 tablespoons oil, salt, garlic powder, and nutritional yeast to the food processor and process until silky smooth.
Transfer to a medium bowl, drizzle with ½ teaspoon olive oil, sprinkle with the pepper, and serve.

Per Serving: Calories 216; Fat 10.9g; Sodium 354mg; Carbs 10.5g; Fiber 4.1g; Sugar 8.2g; Protein 6g

Pumpkin Pie Bites

Prep time: 5 minutes| **Cook time:** 20 minutes| **Serves:** 1

¼ cup pumpkin puree
3 tablespoons sugar
¼ cup heavy cream
1 large egg
¼ teaspoon pumpkin pie spice
1/16 teaspoon salt
1 cup water
2 tablespoons sweetened whipped cream

Grease three cups of a silicone egg bites mold. Set aside.
In a small bowl, whisk together pumpkin, sugar, heavy cream, egg, pumpkin pie spice, and salt until combined.
Equally divide the mixture among prepared egg bite mold cups. Cover tightly with foil.
Pour water into Instant Pot and add the trivet. Place mold on trivet. Alternatively, place the mold on a silicone sling and lower into the Instant Pot.
Put on the pressure cooker's lid and turn the steam valve to "Sealing" position.
Set the Instant Pot to Pressure Cook.
Use the "+/-" keys on the control panel to set the timer to 20 minutes.
Use the Pressure Level button to adjust the pressure to "Low".
Once the cooking cycle is completed, allow the steam to release naturally.
When all the steam is released, remove the pressure lid from the top carefully.
Allow pie bites to cool to room temperature, then refrigerate 4–8 hours until set.
Remove foil, invert pie bites onto a plate, and enjoy with whipped cream.

Per Serving: Calories 334; Fat 10.9g; Sodium 454mg; Carbs 10g; Fiber 3.1g; Sugar 5.2g; Protein 05g

Gooey Chocolate Chip Cookie Sundae

Prep time: 5 minutes| **Cook time:** 20 minutes| **Serves:** 1

1 ½ tablespoons butter, melted
1 tablespoon brown sugar
1 tablespoon granulated sugar
1 large egg yolk
½ teaspoon vanilla extract
⅓ cup all-purpose flour
⅛ teaspoon baking soda
1/16 teaspoon salt
1 tablespoon mini semisweet chocolate chips
1 cup water
¼ cup vanilla bean ice cream
1 tablespoon chopped pecans
1 tablespoon chocolate syrup

Grease an 8-oz. ramekin. Set aside.
In a small bowl, combine butter with brown sugar and granulated sugar until dissolved.
Add egg yolk and vanilla and mix until smooth.
Add flour, baking soda, and salt; combine to make a dough. Mix in chocolate chips.
Scrape dough into prepared ramekin and press into the bottom of the ramekin. Cover with foil.
Pour water into Instant Pot and add the trivet. Place ramekin on trivet.
Put on the pressure cooker's lid and turn the steam valve to "Sealing" position.
Set your Instant Pot on Pressure Cook. Use the "+/-" keys on the control panel to set the cooking time to 20 minutes.
Use the Pressure Level button to adjust the pressure to "Low".
Once the cooking cycle is completed, allow the steam to release naturally.
When all the steam is released, remove the pressure lid from the top carefully.
Carefully remove ramekin from the pot.
Remove foil and cool 3–5 minutes.
Top warm cookie with ice cream, pecans, and chocolate syrup. Serve immediately.

Per Serving: Calories 489; Fat 11g; Sodium 501mg; Carbs 8.9g; Fiber 4.6g; Sugar 8g; Protein 26g

Berry Almond Crisp

Prep time: 15 minutes| **Cook time:** 25 minutes| **Serves:** 4-6

¾ cup frozen berry mix
½ teaspoon almond extract
2 tablespoons granulated sugar
½ tablespoon cornstarch
1 tablespoon cold butter, cut up
1 tablespoon brown sugar
1/16 teaspoon ground cinnamon
1/16 teaspoon nutmeg
1 ½ tablespoons all-purpose flour
1 ½ tablespoons rolled oats
1 cup water
¼ cup vanilla ice cream

In a small bowl, toss together berries, almond extract, granulated sugar, and cornstarch.
Pour into an 8-oz. ramekin.
In a separate small bowl, using a fork, combine butter, brown sugar, cinnamon, nutmeg, flour, and oats until mixture resembles large crumbs.
Crumble over berry mixture and cover with foil.
Pour water into Instant Pot and add the trivet. Place ramekin on trivet.
Put on the pressure cooker's lid and turn the steam valve to "Sealing" position.
Set the Instant Pot to Pressure Cook. Use the "+/-" keys on the control panel to set the cooking time to 25 minutes.
Use the Pressure Level button to adjust the pressure to "Low".
Once the cooking cycle is completed, allow the steam to release naturally.

When all the steam is released, remove the pressure lid from the top carefully.
Carefully remove ramekin from the Instant Pot, then remove foil and let cool 5 minutes. Top with ice cream and serve immediately.

Per Serving: Calories 199; Fat 5g; Sodium 41mg; Carbs 7g; Fiber 7.6g; Sugar 5g; Protein 2g

Mango Sticky Rice

Prep time: 15 minutes| **Cook time:** 5 minutes| **Serves:** 4-6

Sticky Rice
½ cup uncooked jasmine rice
¾ cup canned unsweetened full-fat coconut milk
⅛ teaspoon salt
Coconut Sauce
½ cup canned unsweetened full-fat coconut milk
4 teaspoons sugar
1/16 teaspoon salt
½ tablespoon cornstarch
½ tablespoon cold water
For Serving
½ cup ripe mango slices, chilled
½ teaspoon toasted sesame seeds

To the Instant Pot, add all Sticky Rice ingredients.
Put on the pressure cooker's lid and turn the steam valve to "Sealing" position.
Set the Instant Pot to Pressure Cook. Use the "+/-" keys on the control panel to set the cooking time to 3 minutes.
Use the Pressure Level button to adjust the pressure to "Low".
Once the cooking cycle is completed, allow the steam to release naturally.
When all the steam is released, remove the pressure lid from the top carefully.
While the rice is cooking, make the Coconut Sauce.
In a small saucepan over medium heat, combine coconut milk, sugar, and salt.
In a small bowl, mix together cornstarch and cold water to make a slurry.
When coconut milk mixture comes to a boil, whisk in the slurry about 1–2 minutes until thickened.
Remove from heat and allow to cool to room temperature.
Add ¼ cup Coconut Sauce to the rice in the Instant Pot and stir to combine.
Replace the lid and let cool 10 minutes.
To serve, spoon rice into a bowl and arrange mango slices over rice.
Pour remaining coconut sauce over the top and sprinkle with sesame seeds. Serve.

Per Serving: Calories 489; Fat 11g; Sodium 501mg; Carbs 28.9g; Fiber 4.6g; Sugar 8g; Protein 6g

Stuffed Baked Apple À La Mode

Prep time: 15 minutes| **Cook time:** 7 minutes| **Serves:** 1
1 medium Honeycrisp apple
1 tablespoon brown sugar
1 tablespoon butter
½ teaspoon ground cinnamon
1 tablespoon chopped pecans
1 tablespoon sweetened dried cranberries
1 cup water
¼ cup vanilla ice cream

Core apple and scrape out center to create a cavity in the middle about 1" in diameter.
In a small bowl, mix together brown sugar, butter, cinnamon, pecans, and cranberries into a paste.
Scoop paste into apple and cover the top with a small piece of foil.
Pour water into Instant Pot and add the trivet. Place apple on trivet.
Put on the pressure cooker's lid and turn the steam valve to "Sealing" position.
Set the Instant Pot to Pressure Cook.
Use the Pressure Level button to adjust the pressure to "Low".
Use the "+/-" keys on the control panel to set the cooking time to 7 minutes.
Once the cooking cycle is completed, allow the steam to release naturally.
When all the steam is released, remove the pressure lid from the top carefully.
Using tongs, carefully remove apple from the Instant Pot and transfer to a bowl. Let cool 5 minutes.
Top with ice cream and serve immediately.

Per Serving: Calories 334; Fat 10.9g; Sodium 354mg; Carbs 25g; Fiber 4.1g; Sugar 8.2g; Protein 6g

Cinnamon-Vanilla Rice Pudding

Prep time: 20 minutes| **Cook time:** 8 minutes| **Serves:** 1
½ cup uncooked long-grain white rice
1 cup water
1/16 teaspoon salt
2 ½ tablespoons sugar
1 cup whole milk
1 large egg
½ tablespoon butter
½ tablespoon vanilla extract
2 tablespoons heavy cream
⅛ teaspoon ground cinnamon

To the Instant Pot, add rice, water, and salt.
Put on the pressure cooker's lid and turn the steam valve to "Sealing" position.
Set the Instant Pot to Pressure Cook. Use the "+/-" keys on the control panel to set the cooking time to 3 minutes.
Use the Pressure Level button to adjust the pressure to "Low".
Once the cooking cycle is completed, allow the steam to release naturally.
When all the steam is released, remove the pressure lid from the top carefully.

Fluff rice, then add sugar and stir to dissolve. Press Sauté button and adjust to Less. Whisk in ½ cup milk and bring to a low simmer.
In a liquid measuring cup, measure remaining ½ cup milk and whisk together with egg until completely combined.
While whisking, pour egg mixture into the pot until completely incorporated.
Whisk about 5 minutes until thickened. Press Cancel button to turn off the heat.
Stir in butter, vanilla, and cream. Scoop into a bowl and serve with a sprinkle of cinnamon.

Per Serving: Calories 199; Fat 5g; Sodium 41mg; Carbs 7g; Fiber 7.6g; Sugar 5g; Protein 2g

Carrot Cake with Cream Cheese Frosting

Prep time: 20 minutes| **Cook time:** 65 minutes| **Serves:** 1
Carrot Cake
¼ cup granulated sugar
¼ cup brown sugar
2 tablespoons canola oil
1 large egg, lightly beaten
1 teaspoon vanilla extract
½ cup all-purpose flour
¾ teaspoon ground cinnamon
⅛ teaspoon ground nutmeg
⅛ teaspoon ground cloves
½ teaspoon baking soda
1 cup shredded carrots
½ cup pecans
⅓ cup chopped pineapple
¼ cup sweetened shredded coconut
1 cup water
Cream Cheese Frosting
4 oz. cream cheese, softened
3 tablespoons butter
1 ½ teaspoons vanilla extract
1/16 teaspoon salt
2 cups confectioners' sugar

Grease a 6" cake pan. Set aside.
In a medium bowl, combine granulated sugar, brown sugar, and oil.
Add egg and vanilla and stir until combined.
Sift in flour, cinnamon, nutmeg, cloves, and baking soda. Stir to combine.
Add carrots, pecans, pineapple, and coconut. Stir well, then let rest 5 minutes to allow the moisture from the carrots and pineapple to soften the batter.
Pour batter into prepared cake pan and cover tightly with foil.
Pour water into Instant Pot and add the trivet. Place pan on trivet.
Put on the pressure cooker's lid and turn the steam valve to "Sealing" position.
Set the Instant Pot to Pressure Cook. Use the "+/-" keys on the control panel to set the cooking time to 60 minutes.
Use the Pressure Level button to adjust the pressure to "Low".
Once the cooking cycle is completed, allow the steam to release naturally.
When all the steam is released, remove the pressure lid from the top carefully.

Carefully remove pan and let cool 15 minutes before placing in the refrigerator at least 5 hours, preferably overnight.
To make the Cream Cheese Frosting, in a medium bowl, combine all ingredients except confectioners' sugar. Whisk together or blend using an electric mixer until smooth.
Add confectioners' sugar 1 cup at a time. Incorporate each cup before adding the next.
Remove cake from pan and frost with Cream Cheese Frosting. Serve.

Per Serving: Calories 322; Fat 11g; Sodium 491mg; Carbs 24g; Fiber 3g; Sugar 8g; Protein 3g

Vanilla Crème Brulee

Prep time: 20 minutes| **Cook time:** 8 minutes| **Serves:** 1
½ cup heavy cream
½ teaspoon vanilla bean paste
2 large egg yolks
2 tablespoons sugar
1 cup water
3 whole raspberries

In a small saucepan over medium-high heat, combine cream and vanilla bean paste until steaming. Do not boil and then remove from heat.
In a small bowl, whisk egg yolks and 1 tablespoon sugar until light and smooth.
While whisking, slowly pour hot cream into egg yolks and whisk to combine.
Pour cream mixture through a fine-mesh strainer into an 8-oz. ramekin. Cover with foil.
Pour water into Instant Pot and add the trivet. Place ramekin on trivet.
Put on the pressure cooker's lid and turn the steam valve to "Sealing" position.
Set the Instant Pot to Pressure Cook. Use the "+/-" keys on the control panel to set the cooking time to 8 minutes.
Use the Pressure Level button to adjust the pressure to "Low".
Once the cooking cycle is completed, allow the steam to release naturally.
When all the steam is released, remove the pressure lid from the top carefully.
Remove ramekin to cooling rack. Let cool and then refrigerate 6–8 hours.
To serve, remove foil. Sprinkle remaining 1 tablespoon sugar over the top of the crème Brûlée.
Using a kitchen torch, quickly torch the sugar in small circles until sugar is completely caramelized.
Cool 1 minute, then top with raspberries and serve.

Per Serving: Calories 334; Fat 10.9g; Sodium 354mg; Carbs 25g; Fiber 4.1g; Sugar 8.2g; Protein 11g

Crème Caramel (Purin)

Prep time: 20 minutes| **Cook time:** 9 minutes| **Serves:** 1

4 tablespoons sugar
1 cup plus 2 tablespoons and 1 teaspoon water
½ cup whole milk
1 large egg yolk
½ teaspoon vanilla extract
1 tablespoon sweetened whipped cream
1 maraschino cherry

To a small saucepan over medium heat, add 3 tablespoons sugar and 2 tablespoons water.
Tilt the pot and swirl to combine the mixture—do not stir—and cook about 6 minutes until dark amber in color and caramelized.
Remove from heat and carefully add 1 teaspoon water to the caramel to thin.
Quickly and carefully pour the hot caramel into an 8-oz. ramekin and set aside.
In a separate small saucepan over medium heat, heat milk until steaming, then remove from heat.
In a small bowl, whisk egg yolk and remaining 1 tablespoon sugar until creamy.
Slowly pour hot milk mixture into egg yolk mixture while constantly whisking.
Whisk in vanilla, then pour mixture over caramel in the ramekin and cover with foil.
Pour remaining 1 cup water into Instant Pot and add the trivet. Place ramekin on trivet.
Put on the pressure cooker's lid and turn the steam valve to "Sealing" position.
Set the Instant Pot to Pressure Cook. Use the "+/-" keys on the control panel to set the cooking time to 9 minutes.
Use the Pressure Level button to adjust the pressure to "Low".
Once the cooking cycle is completed, allow the steam to release naturally.
When all the steam is released, remove the pressure lid from the top carefully.
Carefully remove ramekin from the Instant Pot and let cool to room temperature.
Then refrigerate 6–8 hours or overnight.
When ready to serve, slide a wet knife around the edges of custard, then invert onto a plate.
Serve with whipped cream and cherry.

Per Serving: Calories 272; Fat 10g; Sodium 891mg; Carbs 22.9g; Fiber 4g; Sugar 4g; Protein 3g

Bread Pudding with Rum Sauce

Prep time: 20 minutes| **Cook time:** 35 minutes| **Serves:** 1

Bread Pudding
1 large egg
¾ cup heavy cream
¼ cup granulated sugar
2 teaspoons vanilla extract
4 slices Texas Toast bread, dried overnight and diced into 1" cubes
⅛ teaspoon ground cinnamon
1 cup water
Buttered Rum Sauce

2 tablespoons granulated sugar
1 tablespoon apple juice
1 ½ tablespoons brown sugar
2 tablespoons heavy cream
¼ teaspoon rum extract
⅛ teaspoon vanilla extract
2 tablespoons butter

Grease a 6" cake pan. Set aside.
In a small saucepan over medium heat, whisk together egg, ¾ cup cream, and ¼ cup granulated sugar until mixture starts to bubble slightly on the sides and steam.
Add 2 teaspoons vanilla and remove from heat.
Arrange bread pieces in prepared cake pan, then pour cream mixture over the top and let soak 5 minutes.
Sprinkle cinnamon on top. Cover pan tightly with foil.
Pour water into Instant Pot and add the trivet. Place pan on trivet.
Put on the pressure cooker's lid and turn the steam valve to "Sealing" position.
Set the Instant Pot to Pressure Cook. Use the "+/-" keys on the control panel to set the cooking time to 35 minutes.
Use the Pressure Level button to adjust the pressure to "Low".
Once the cooking cycle is completed, allow the steam to release naturally.
When all the steam is released, remove the pressure lid from the top carefully.
Prepare the Buttered Rum Sauce: In a separate small saucepan over medium heat, combine 2 tablespoons granulated sugar, apple juice, brown sugar, and 2 tablespoons cream.
Boil 5 minutes. Remove from heat, then add rum extract, ⅛ teaspoon vanilla, and butter, whisking constantly.
Remove pan, remove foil, and serve immediately with Buttered Rum Sauce.

Per Serving: Calories 382; Fat 7.9g; Sodium 704mg; Carbs 6g; Fiber 3.6g; Sugar 6g; Protein 18g

Brown Butter–Cinnamon Rice Treat

Prep time: 20 minutes| **Cook time:** 4 minutes| **Serves:** 1

½ tablespoon butter
½ cup mini marshmallows
⅛ teaspoon vanilla extract
1/16 teaspoon ground cinnamon
1 cup crispy rice cereal
1/16 teaspoon coarse sea salt

Lightly grease a medium bowl or line a small baking sheet with waxed paper.
On the Instant Pot, press Sauté button and adjust to Normal.
Add butter and cook about 4 minutes until slightly golden and browned.
Adjust the Instant Pot Sauté setting to Low and add marshmallows.
When melted, press Cancel button to turn off the heat and add vanilla and cinnamon.

Stir to combine, then add cereal and mix until completely combined.
Scrape mixture into prepared bowl or onto lined baking sheet. Lightly pat down to shape. Immediately sprinkle with salt, then cool at least 10 minutes and serve.

Per Serving: Calories 489; Fat 11g; Sodium 501mg; Carbs 28.9g; Fiber 4.6g; Sugar 8g; Protein 6g

Molten Chocolate Lava Cake

Prep time: 20 minutes| **Cook time:** 7 minutes| **Serves:** 1

½ cup semisweet chocolate chips
2 tablespoons butter
½ cup confectioners' sugar
1 large egg
¼ teaspoon vanilla extract
1 tablespoon all-purpose flour
½ tablespoon cocoa powder
1 cup water

In a medium microwave-safe bowl, combine chocolate chips and butter.
Microwave in 10-second intervals until completely melted.
Add sugar and combine until smooth.
Add egg and beat until completely combined.
Add vanilla, flour, and cocoa powder.
Stir to combine. Pour into a greased 8-oz. ramekin.
Pour water into Instant Pot and add the trivet. Place ramekin on trivet.
Put on the pressure cooker's lid and turn the steam valve to "Sealing" position.
Set the Instant Pot to Pressure Cook. Use the "+/-" keys on the control panel to set the cooking time to 7 minutes.
Use the Pressure Level button to adjust the pressure to "Low".
Once the cooking cycle is completed, allow the steam to release quickly.
When all the steam is released, remove the pressure lid from the top carefully.
Invert cake onto a plate and serve immediately.

Per Serving: Calories 272; Fat 10g; Sodium 891mg; Carbs 12.9g; Fiber 4g; Sugar 4g; Protein 3g

Cherry Cheesecake Bites

Prep time: 20 minutes| **Cook time:** 5 minutes| **Serves:** 1

Crust
4 ½ tablespoons graham cracker crumbs
2 tablespoons butter, melted
½ tablespoon all-purpose flour
⅛ teaspoon ground cinnamon
½ tablespoon sugar
Cheesecake Filling
8 oz. cream cheese, softened
5 tablespoons sugar
½ teaspoon vanilla extract
1 large egg, lightly beaten

1 tablespoon sour cream
1 cup water
Topping
2 tablespoons sour cream
6 tablespoons cherry pie filling

To make the Crust, in a medium bowl, combine all Crust ingredients.
Add ½ tablespoon mixture into each cup of a silicone egg bites mold.
To make the Filling, in a separate medium bowl, mix together cream cheese and sugar until sugar is completely dissolved.
Add vanilla, egg, and sour cream, and whisk until just combined. Do not overmix.
Pour filling evenly on top of crust. Place a paper towel on top of the mold, then cover tightly with foil.
Pour water into Instant Pot and add the trivet. Place mold on trivet.
Put on the pressure cooker's lid and turn the steam valve to "Sealing" position.
Set the Instant Pot to Pressure Cook. Use the "+/-" keys on the control panel to set the cooking time to 5 minutes.
Use the Pressure Level button to adjust the pressure to "Low".
Once the cooking cycle is completed, allow the steam to release naturally.
When all the steam is released, remove the pressure lid from the top carefully.
Remove foil and paper towel, and cool to room temperature 1–2 hours, then refrigerate overnight.
To serve, invert cheesecakes onto a plate or scoop them out with a large spoon and place on a plate.
Spread a thin layer of sour cream over each bite, and top with cherry pie filling.
Serve.

Per Serving: Calories 378; Fat 19g; Sodium 354mg; Carbs 21g; Fiber 5.1g; Sugar 8.2g; Protein 2g

Key Lime Pie

Prep time: 20 minutes| **Cook time:** 10 minutes| **Serves:** 1

Crust
¼ cup graham cracker crumbs
½ tablespoon sugar
1 tablespoon butter, melted
1/16 teaspoon ground cinnamon
Filling
1 large egg yolk
½ cup sweetened condensed milk
2 tablespoons lime juice
½ teaspoon lime zest
1 cup water
For Serving
2 tablespoons sweetened whipped cream
¼ teaspoon lime zest

In a medium bowl, mix together all Crust ingredients and press into an 8-oz. ramekin. Set aside.

In a separate medium bowl, mix together all Filling ingredients (except water) and pour over crust.
Cover with foil. Pour water into Instant Pot and add the trivet. Place ramekin on trivet.
Put on the pressure cooker's lid and turn the steam valve to "Sealing" position.
Set the Instant Pot to Pressure Cook. Use the "+/-" keys on the control panel to set the cooking time to 10 minutes.
Use the Pressure Level button to adjust the pressure to "Low".
Once the cooking cycle is completed, allow the steam to release naturally.
When all the steam is released, remove the pressure lid from the top carefully.
Let pie cool to room temperature, then refrigerate at least 6–8 hours or overnight.
Serve garnished with whipped cream and ¼ teaspoon lime zest.

Per Serving: Calories 199; Fat 5g; Sodium 41mg; Carbs 7g; Fiber 7.6g; Sugar 5g; Protein 2g

White Chocolate Crème Brûlée

Prep time: 20 minutes| **Cook time:** 16 minutes| **Serves:** 1
3 tablespoons white chocolate chips
½ cup heavy cream
2 large egg yolks
1 tablespoon sugar
1 cup water
1 tablespoon crushed candy cane, crushed into a fine powder

To a small bowl, add chocolate chips. In a small saucepan over medium-high heat, warm cream until steaming.
Do not boil. Remove from heat and pour over chocolate chips and stir until melted.
In a separate small bowl, whisk egg yolks and sugar until light and smooth.
While whisking, slowly pour hot cream into egg yolks to temper the eggs. Whisk until completely combined.
Pour cream mixture through a fine-mesh strainer into an 8-oz. ramekin. Cover with foil.
Pour water into Instant Pot and add the trivet. Place ramekin on trivet.
Put on the pressure cooker's lid and turn the steam valve to "Sealing" position.
Set the Instant Pot to Pressure Cook. Use the "+/-" keys on the control panel to set the cooking time to 16 minutes.
Use the Pressure Level button to adjust the pressure to "Low".
Once the cooking cycle is completed, allow the steam to release naturally.
When all the steam is released, remove the pressure lid from the top carefully.
Sprinkle peppermint candy evenly over the top of crème Brûlée and shake to distribute it evenly.
Using a kitchen torch, quickly torch candy in small circles until completely caramelized.
Keep the torch moving to evenly melt candy.
Cool 1 minute, then serve immediately.

Per Serving: Calories 361; Fat 12.9g; Sodium 754mg; Carbs 21g; Fiber 6.1g; Sugar 4.2g; Protein 11g

Dairy-Free Rice Pudding

Prep time: 20 minutes| **Cook time:** 3 minutes| **Serves:** 1
½ cup uncooked long-grain white rice
1 cup water
1/16 teaspoon salt
2 tablespoons brown sugar
¼ cup cream of coconut
1 cup canned unsweetened full-fat coconut milk
1 large egg
½ teaspoon vanilla extract
⅛ teaspoon ground cinnamon
½ tablespoon toasted shredded coconut

To the Instant Pot, add rice, water, and salt.
Put on the pressure cooker's lid and turn the steam valve to "Sealing" position.
Set the Instant Pot to Pressure Cook. Use the "+/-" keys on the control panel to set the cooking time to 3 minutes.
Use the Pressure Level button to adjust the pressure to "Low".
Once the cooking cycle is completed, allow the steam to release naturally.
When all the steam is released, remove the pressure lid from the top carefully.
Fluff rice, then add brown sugar and cream of coconut. Stir to dissolve.
Press Sauté button and adjust to Less.
Add ½ cup coconut milk and bring to a low simmer, whisking constantly.
In a liquid measuring cup, measure remaining ½ cup coconut milk and whisk together with egg.
While whisking, pour egg mixture into the pot until completely incorporated.
Whisk about 5 minutes until thickened. Press Cancel button to turn off heat.
Stir in vanilla. Scoop into a bowl and serve with a sprinkle of cinnamon and toasted coconut.

Per Serving: Calories 334; Fat 7.9g; Sodium 704mg; Carbs 6g; Fiber 3.6g; Sugar 6g; Protein 18g

White Chocolate–Lemon Pie

Prep time: 20 minutes| **Cook time:** 10 minutes| **Serves:** 1
Crust
¼ cup graham cracker crumbs
½ tablespoon sugar
1 tablespoon butter, melted
Filling
2 tablespoons white chocolate chips
¼ cup sweetened condensed milk
1 large egg yolk
2 tablespoons lemon juice
½ teaspoon lemon zest
1 cup water

178

To make Crust, in a small bowl, mix together all Crust ingredients and press into an 8-oz. ramekin.

To make Filling, in a separate small microwave-safe bowl, microwave chocolate chips in 15-second intervals until melted. Whisk in condensed milk, egg yolk, lemon juice, and lemon zest. Pour over the crust. Cover with foil.

Pour water into Instant Pot and add the trivet. Place ramekin on trivet.

Put on the pressure cooker's lid and turn the steam valve to "Sealing" position.

Set the Instant Pot to Pressure Cook. Use the "+/-" keys on the control panel to set the cooking time to 10 minutes.

Use the Pressure Level button to adjust the pressure to "Low".

Once the cooking cycle is completed, allow the steam to release naturally.

When all the steam is released, remove the pressure lid from the top carefully.

Let pie cool to room temperature, then refrigerate at least 6–8 hours or overnight, and then serve.

Per Serving: Calories 372; Fat 20g; Sodium 891mg; Carbs 29g; Fiber 3g; Sugar 8g; Protein 10g

Chocolate Peanut Butter Popcorn

Prep time: 5 minutes| **Cook time:** 6 minutes| **Serves:** 4-6

1 tablespoon coconut oil
¼ cup popcorn kernels
1 tablespoon creamy peanut butter
2 tablespoons dairy-free dark chocolate chips

Press the "Sauté" button two times to select "Normal" temperature on the Instant Pot and pour in the coconut oil.

When the oil is hot, add the popcorn kernels. Cook until the kernels stop popping on a regular basis about 5 to 6 minutes.

Remove the lid and stir in the peanut butter, using the heat of the pot to help it melt and coat the popcorn.

Stir in the chocolate chips. Serve warm or let the chocolate set at room temperature before eating.

Per Serving: Calories 472; Fat 7.9g; Sodium 704mg; Carbs 6g; Fiber 3.6g; Sugar 6g; Protein 18g

Stuffed Apples

Prep time: 20 minutes| **Cook time:** 6 minutes| **Serves:** 4-6

¼ cup chopped walnuts
¼ cup gluten-free rolled oats
3 teaspoons coconut oil
1 teaspoon maple syrup
1 teaspoon ground cinnamon
⅛ teaspoon salt
4 apples, cored

In a small bowl, combine the walnuts, oats, coconut oil, maple syrup, cinnamon, and salt. Spoon the mixture into the cored apples.

Pour 1 cup of water into the Instant Pot and insert the trivet. Place the apples on the trivet.

Put on the pressure cooker's lid and turn the steam valve to "Sealing" position.

Set the Instant Pot to Pressure Cook. Use the "+/-" keys on the control panel to set the cooking time to 6 minutes.

Use the Pressure Level button to adjust the pressure to "High".

Once the cooking cycle is completed, allow the steam to release quickly.

When all the steam is released, remove the pressure lid from the top carefully.

Serve the apples warm.

Per Serving: Calories 199; Fat 5g; Sodium 41mg; Carbs 7g; Fiber 7.6g; Sugar 5g; Protein 2g

Vanilla Bean Custard

Prep time: 20 minutes| **Cook time:** 7 minutes| **Serves:** 4-6

4 large egg yolks
1 cup whole milk
2 tablespoons honey
1 vanilla bean, scraped, or ¼ teaspoon vanilla extract

In a medium bowl, whisk together the egg yolks, milk, honey, and vanilla until smooth. Divide among four 4-oz. ramekins. Cover the tops with aluminum foil.

Pour 1 cup of water into the Instant Pot and insert the trivet. Place the ramekins on the trivet.

Put on the pressure cooker's lid and turn the steam valve to "Sealing" position.

Set the Instant Pot to Pressure Cook. Use the "+/-" keys on the control panel to set the cooking time to 7 minutes.

Use the Pressure Level button to adjust the pressure to "High".

Once the cooking cycle is completed, allow the steam to release naturally.

When all the steam is released, remove the pressure lid from the top carefully.

Serve warm or chilled.

Per Serving: Calories 489; Fat 11g; Sodium 501mg; Carbs 28.9g; Fiber 4.6g; Sugar 8g; Protein 6g

Peach Cobbler

Prep time: 20 minutes| **Cook time:** 10 minutes| **Serves:** 4-6

1 cup spelt flour
1 tablespoon baking powder
2 teaspoons coconut sugar
⅛ teaspoon kosher salt
1 cup buttermilk
2 lbs. frozen sliced peaches

¼ cup water
½ teaspoon ground cinnamon
¼ teaspoon ground coriander

In a medium bowl, combine the flour, baking powder, coconut sugar, and salt.
Stir in the buttermilk to form a thick dough.
In the Instant Pot, combine the peaches, water, cinnamon, and coriander.
Drop the dough, a tablespoon at a time, on top of the peaches, being careful to not let the dough touch the bottom or sides of the pot.
Put on the pressure cooker's lid and turn the steam valve to "Sealing" position.
Set the Instant Pot to Pressure Cook. Use the "+/-" keys on the control panel to set the cooking time to 10 minutes.
Use the Pressure Level button to adjust the pressure to "High".
Once the cooking cycle is completed, allow the steam to release quickly.
When all the steam is released, remove the pressure lid from the top carefully.
Let the cobbler cool for 5 to 10 minutes before serving.

Per Serving: Calories 334; Fat 7.9g; Sodium 704mg; Carbs 6g; Fiber 3.6g; Sugar 6g; Protein 18g

Lemon Bars

Prep time: 20 minutes| **Cook time:** 12 minutes| **Serves:** 4-6
¾ cup gluten-free rolled oats
¾ cup almond flour
¼ cup melted coconut oil
2 tablespoons honey, plus ⅓ cup
1 teaspoon vanilla extract
¼ teaspoon kosher salt
2 large eggs, beaten
Zest and juice of 2 lemons
1 teaspoon arrowroot powder or cornstarch

Line a 6-inch square cake pan with aluminum foil.
In a medium bowl, combine the oats, almond flour, coconut oil, 2 tablespoons of honey, the vanilla, and ⅛ teaspoon of salt to form a stiff dough.
Press the dough into the bottom of the prepared pan.
In a separate bowl, whisk together the eggs, lemon zest and juice, arrowroot powder, ⅓ cup of honey, and the remaining ⅛ teaspoon of salt.
Pour the mixture over the crust. Cover the pan with foil.
Pour 1 cup of water into the Instant Pot and insert the trivet.
Place the pan on top of the trivet.
Put on the pressure cooker's lid and turn the steam valve to "Sealing" position.
Set the Instant Pot to Pressure Cook. Use the "+/-" keys on the control panel to set the cooking time to 12 minutes.
Use the Pressure Level button to adjust the pressure to "High".

Once the cooking cycle is completed, allow the steam to release naturally for 15 minutes and then quick release the remaining pressure.
When all the steam is released, remove the pressure lid from the top carefully.
Lift out the pan. Chill the lemon bars in the refrigerator for at least 2 hours before slicing them into six portions and serving.

Per Serving: Calories 389; Fat 11g; Sodium 501mg; Carbs 28.9g; Fiber 4.6g; Sugar 8g; Protein 6g

Carrot Date Cake

Prep time: 20 minutes| **Cook time:** 45 minutes| **Serves:** 4-6
Nonstick cooking spray
1 cup almond flour
2 teaspoons ground cinnamon
1 teaspoon baking soda
¼ teaspoon ground nutmeg
¼ teaspoon kosher salt
2 eggs, beaten
¼ cup pure maple syrup
½ teaspoon vanilla extract
1 cup (about 2 medium) shredded carrots
¼ cup (about 5) pitted and chopped dates

Grease a 6-inch cake pan with nonstick cooking spray. Set aside.
In a medium bowl, combine the almond flour, cinnamon, baking soda, nutmeg, and salt.
In a separate bowl, whisk together the eggs, maple syrup, and vanilla.
Pour the egg mixture into the flour mixture and combine to form a batter. Fold in the carrots and dates.
Pour the batter into the prepared cake pan.
Cover the pan with a paper towel and then cover the top of the pan with foil.
Pour 1 cup of water into the Instant Pot and insert the trivet. Place the cake pan on top of the trivet.
Put on the pressure cooker's lid and turn the steam valve to "Sealing" position.
Set the Instant Pot to Pressure Cook. Use the "+/-" keys on the control panel to set the cooking time to 45 minutes.
Use the Pressure Level button to adjust the pressure to "High".
Once the cooking cycle is completed, allow the steam to release naturally for 10 minutes and then quickly release the remaining pressure.
When all the steam is released, remove the pressure lid from the top carefully.
Lift out the cake pan. Remove the foil and paper towel and let the cake cool on the trivet for 1 hour.
Cut the cake into six slices and serve.

Per Serving: Calories 334; Fat 10.9g; Sodium 454mg; Carbs 20g; Fiber 3.1g; Sugar 5.2g; Protein 05g

Berry Almond Bundt Cake

Prep time: 1 hour 10 minutes| **Cook time:** 45 minutes| **Serves:** 4-6

Nonstick cooking spray
1½ cups almond flour, plus 1 tablespoon
1 teaspoon baking soda
¼ teaspoon kosher salt
2 eggs, beaten
½ cup buttermilk
¼ cup pure maple syrup
½ teaspoon pure almond extract
1 cup fresh berries

Grease a 7-inch Bundt pan with nonstick cooking spray.
In a medium bowl, combine 1½ cups of almond flour, the baking soda, and salt.
In a separate bowl, whisk together the eggs, buttermilk, maple syrup, and almond extract.
Pour the egg mixture into the flour mixture and combine to form a batter.
In a small bowl, mix the berries with 1 tablespoon of almond flour until thoroughly coated.
Fold the berry mixture into the batter.
Pour the batter into the prepared Bundt pan and cover the top with aluminum foil.
Pour 1 cup of water into the Instant Pot and insert the trivet. Place the Bundt pan on top of the trivet.
Put on the pressure cooker's lid and turn the steam valve to "Sealing" position.
Set the Instant Pot to Pressure Cook. Use the "+/-" keys on the control panel to set the cooking time to 45 minutes.
Use the Pressure Level button to adjust the pressure to "High".
Once the cooking cycle is completed, allow the steam to release naturally for 10 minutes and quickly release the remaining pressure.
When all the steam is released, remove the pressure lid from the top carefully.
Lift out the Bundt pan. Remove the foil and let the cake cool on the trivet for 1 hour.
Cut the cake into six slices and serve.

Per Serving: Calories 366; Fat 10.9g; Sodium 354mg; Carbs 25g; Fiber 4.1g; Sugar 8.2g; Protein 11g

Brownies

Prep time: 1 hour 10 minutes| **Cook time:** 45 minutes| **Serves:** 4-6

Nonstick cooking spray
1 large egg plus 1 egg yolk
⅓ cup maple syrup
½ teaspoon vanilla extract
⅓ cup coconut oil, at room temperature
⅔ cup almond flour
3 tablespoons unsweetened cocoa powder
¼ teaspoon baking powder
¼ teaspoon kosher salt

Line a 6-inch cake pan with aluminum foil and grease it with nonstick cooking spray.
In a medium bowl, whisk together the egg, egg yolk, maple syrup, and vanilla.

Mix in the coconut oil until smooth. Stir in the almond flour, cocoa powder, baking powder, and salt.
Pour the batter into the prepared cake pan and cover it loosely with foil.
Pour 1 cup of water into the Instant Pot and insert the trivet. Place the cake pan on top of the trivet.
Put on the pressure cooker's lid and turn the steam valve to "Sealing" position.
Set the Instant Pot to Pressure Cook. Use the "+/-" keys on the control panel to set the cooking time to 45 minutes.
Use the Pressure Level button to adjust the pressure to "High".
Once the cooking cycle is completed, allow the steam to release naturally for 15 minutes and then quick release the remaining pressure.
When all the steam is released, remove the pressure lid from the top carefully.
Lift out the pan. Remove the foil and let the brownies cool on the trivet for 1 hour.
Cut the brownies into six portions and serve.

Per Serving: Calories 371; Fat 7.9g; Sodium 704mg; Carbs 6g; Fiber 3.6g; Sugar 6g; Protein 18g

Banana Pudding Cake

Prep time: 20 minutes| **Cook time:** 20 minutes| **Serves:** 6

3 tablespoons ground golden flaxseed meal
10 tablespoons water
1¾ cups mashed banana (about 3 bananas)
¼ cup avocado oil
1 teaspoon pure vanilla extract
2 cups almond flour
½ cup erythritol
1 teaspoon baking powder
¼ teaspoon salt
½ cup chopped pecans
½ teaspoon ground cinnamon

In a small bowl, combine the flaxseed and 9 tablespoons water and give it time to gel.
In a large bowl, whisk together the flaxseed and water mixture, banana, oil, and vanilla.
Add the flour, erythritol, baking powder, and salt and stir to combine well.
Spray a 7" cake pan with nonstick cooking spray. Pour the batter into the pan.
In a small bowl, combine the chopped pecans, cinnamon, and 1 tablespoon water.
Sprinkle on top of the cake batter.
Pour 1 cup water into the inner pot and place a steam rack inside. Place the pan on top of the steam rack.
Put on the pressure cooker's lid and turn the steam valve to "Sealing" position.
Set the Instant Pot to Pressure Cook. Use the "+/-" keys on the control panel to set the cooking time to 20 minutes.
Use the Pressure Level button to adjust the pressure to "Low".
Once the cooking cycle is completed, allow the steam to release naturally.
When all the steam is released, remove the pressure lid from the top carefully.

Spoon into six bowls and serve.

Per Serving: Calories 372; Fat 20g; Sodium 891mg; Carbs 29g; Fiber 3g; Sugar 8g; Protein 10g

Coconut Cake

Prep time: 20 minutes| **Cook time:** 40 minutes| **Serves:** 4-6

1 cup almond flour
½ cup unsweetened shredded coconut
⅓ cup erythritol
1 teaspoon baking powder
1 teaspoon ground cinnamon
½ teaspoon ground ginger
2 large eggs lightly whisked
¼ cup coconut oil, melted
½ cup unsweetened full-fat canned coconut milk

In a large bowl, whisk together the flour, coconut, erythritol, baking powder, cinnamon, and ginger.
Add the eggs, coconut oil, and coconut milk and stir until well combined.
Spray a 6" springform pan with nonstick cooking spray. Pour the cake batter into the pan.
Add 2 cups water to the inner pot and place a steam rack inside. Place the pan on top of the steam rack.
Put on the pressure cooker's lid and turn the steam valve to "Sealing" position.
Set the Instant Pot to Pressure Cook. Use the "+/-" keys on the control panel to set the cooking time to 40 minutes.
Use the Pressure Level button to adjust the pressure to "Low".
Once the cooking cycle is completed, allow the steam to release naturally for 10 minutes and then quick release the remaining pressure.
When all the steam is released, remove the pressure lid from the top carefully.
Allow the cake to cool 5–10 minutes before slicing to serve.

Per Serving: Calories 199; Fat 5g; Sodium 41mg; Carbs 7g; Fiber 7.6g; Sugar 5g; Protein 2g

Apple Crisp

Prep time: 20 minutes| **Cook time:** 17 minutes| **Serves:** 4
For the Filling
4 large apples, peeled, cored, and cut into wedges
2 tablespoons lemon juice
¼ cup erythritol
¼ teaspoon ground cinnamon
1 teaspoon pure vanilla extract
2 tablespoons almond flour
For the Topping
1 cup almond flour
⅓ cup erythritol
1 cup old fashioned rolled oats
½ cup chopped pecans

¾ teaspoon ground cinnamon
1½ teaspoons vanilla extract
¼ cup coconut oil
2 tablespoons water

In a medium bowl, combine the filling ingredients: apples, lemon juice, erythritol, cinnamon, vanilla, and almond flour.
Transfer to a 6" cake pan and set aside.
In a large bowl, combine the topping ingredients: almond flour, erythritol, oats, pecans, cinnamon, vanilla extract, oil, and water.
Use your hands to incorporate the coconut oil into the rest of the ingredients evenly.
Pour the topping over the apple filling.
Pour 2 cups water into the inner pot and place the steam rack inside.
Put on the pressure cooker's lid and turn the steam valve to "Sealing" position.
Set the Instant Pot to Pressure Cook. Use the "+/-" keys on the control panel to set the cooking time to 17 minutes.
Use the Pressure Level button to adjust the pressure to "Low".
Once the cooking cycle is completed, allow the steam to release naturally.
When all the steam is released, remove the pressure lid from the top carefully.
Spoon into four bowls and serve.

Per Serving: Calories 389; Fat 11g; Sodium 501mg; Carbs 28.9g; Fiber 4.6g; Sugar 8g; Protein 6g

Blueberry Crisp

Prep time: 20 minutes| **Cook time:** 17 minutes| **Serves:** 4
For the Filling
1 (10-oz.) bag frozen blueberries
2 tablespoons fresh orange juice
¼ cup erythritol
1 teaspoon pure vanilla extract
2 tablespoons almond flour
1 teaspoon orange zest
For the Topping
1 cup almond flour
⅓ cup erythritol
1 cup old fashioned rolled oats
½ cup sliced almonds
1½ teaspoons pure vanilla extract
¼ cup coconut oil
2 tablespoons fresh orange juice

In a medium bowl, combine the filling ingredients: the blueberries, orange juice, erythritol, vanilla, flour, and orange zest.
Transfer to a 6" cake pan and set aside.
In another bowl, combine the topping ingredients: the flour, erythritol, oats, almonds, vanilla, oil, and orange juice.
Use your hands to incorporate the oil into the rest of the ingredients evenly.
Pour the topping over the blueberry filling.
Pour 2 cups water into the inner pot and place the steam rack inside.
Place the cake pan on top of the steam rack.

Put on the pressure cooker's lid and turn the steam valve to "Sealing" position.
Set the Instant Pot to Pressure Cook.
Use the "+/-" keys on the control panel to set the cooking time to 17 minutes.
Use the Pressure Level button to adjust the pressure to "Low".
Once the cooking cycle is completed, allow the steam to release naturally.
When all the steam is released, remove the pressure lid from the top carefully.
Spoon into four bowls and serve.

Per Serving: Calories 334; Fat 19g; Sodium 354mg; Carbs 21g; Fiber 5.1g; Sugar 8.2g; Protein 2g

Cinnamon Apples

Prep time: 20 minutes| **Cook time:** 10 minutes| **Serves:** 4-6
1 tablespoon coconut oil
5 medium apples, peeled, cored, and cut into large chunks
1½ teaspoons ground cinnamon
1 tablespoon water
1 tablespoon lemon juice

Press the "Sauté" button two time to select "Normal" mode and put the oil in the inner pot to melt.
Once the oil is melted, add the apples, cinnamon, water, and lemon juice and stir to combine.
Put on the pressure cooker's lid and turn the steam valve to "Sealing" position.
Set the Instant Pot to Pressure Cook.
Use the Pressure Level button to adjust the pressure to "Low".
Use the "+/-" keys on the control panel to set the cooking time to 10 minute.
Once the cooking cycle is completed, allow the steam to release naturally.
When all the steam is released, remove the pressure lid from the top carefully.
Serve warm.

Per Serving: Calories 389; Fat 5g; Sodium 41mg; Carbs 27g; Fiber 7.6g; Sugar 5g; Protein 2g

Cinnamon Pineapple

Prep time: 20 minutes| **Cook time:** 2 minutes| **Serves:** 6
2 tablespoons coconut oil
1 large pineapple, cored and cut into 2" pieces
1½ teaspoons ground cinnamon

Press the "Sauté" button two time to select "Normal" mode and add the oil to the inner pot.
When the oil is melted, add the pineapple and cinnamon and stir to combine.
Put on the pressure cooker's lid and turn the steam valve to "Sealing" position.
Set the Instant Pot to Pressure Cook.

Use the "+/-" keys on the control panel to set the cooking time to 2 minutes.
Use the Pressure Level button to adjust the pressure to "Low".
Once the cooking cycle is completed, allow the steam to release naturally.
When all the steam is released, remove the pressure lid from the top carefully.
Serve.

Per Serving: Calories 322; Fat 11g; Sodium 491mg; Carbs 24g; Fiber 3g; Sugar 8g; Protein 3g

Banana Chocolate Chip Bundt Cake

Prep time: 20 minutes| **Cook time:** 55 minutes| **Serves:** 8
½ cup room temperature coconut oil
1 cup monk fruit sweetener
2 large eggs, room temperature
3 medium bananas, mashed
2 cups oat flour
1½ teaspoons baking soda
½ teaspoon salt
½ cup stevia-sweetened chocolate chips

In a large bowl of a stand mixer with a paddle attachment, add the oil, sweetener, and eggs and beat together on medium speed until well combined.
Add the mashed banana and beat until combined.
Add the flour, baking soda, and salt and beat again until combined.
Remove the paddle attachment and stir in the chocolate chips.
Spray a 6" Bundt cake pan with cooking oil.
Transfer the batter into the pan.
Place a paper towel over the top of the pan and then cover with aluminum foil.
Add 1½ cups water to the Instant Pot inner pot and then place a steam rack inside.
Place the Bundt pan on the steam rack.
Put on the pressure cooker's lid and turn the steam valve to "Sealing" position.
Set the Instant Pot to Pressure Cook.
Use the "+/-" keys on the control panel to set the cooking time to 55 minutes.
Use the Pressure Level button to adjust the pressure to "Low".
Once the cooking cycle is completed, allow the steam to release naturally for 10 minutes and then quick release the remaining pressure.
When all the steam is released, remove the pressure lid from the top carefully.
Allow to cool completely before removing from pan and slicing to serve.

Per Serving: Calories 382; Fat 7.9g; Sodium 704mg; Carbs 6g; Fiber 3.6g; Sugar 6g; Protein 18g

Warm Caramel Apple Dip

Prep time: 20 minutes| **Cook time:** 1 minutes| **Serves:** 10
2 cups pitted dates

½ cup tahini
¼ cup maple syrup
¼ cup water

Place the dates, tahini, maple syrup and ¼ cup water in the inner pot of the Instant Pot and stir to combine.
Put on the pressure cooker's lid and turn the steam valve to "Sealing" position.
Set the Instant Pot to Pressure Cook. Use the "+/-" keys on the control panel to set the cooking time to 1 minute.
Use the Pressure Level button to adjust the pressure to "Low".
Once the cooking cycle is completed, allow the steam to release quickly.
When all the steam is released, remove the pressure lid from the top carefully.
Allow the mixture to cool slightly, and then transfer to a blender.
Blend the mixture on high until super smooth, adding additional water as needed, 1 tablespoon at a time.
Serve.

Per Serving: Calories 334; Fat 7.9g; Sodium 704mg; Carbs 6g; Fiber 3.6g; Sugar 6g; Protein 18g

Pumpkin Pudding

Prep time: 20 minutes| **Cook time:** 5 minutes| **Serves:** 6
1 (13.66-oz.) can unsweetened full-fat coconut milk
1 large egg
½ cup canned pumpkin purée
½ cup pure maple syrup
1 tablespoon pure vanilla extract
2 teaspoons pumpkin pie spice
2 teaspoons arrowroot powder

In a medium bowl, whisk together the coconut milk, egg, pumpkin purée, maple syrup, and vanilla until you have a very smooth mixture.
Stir in the pumpkin pie spice and arrowroot powder.
Transfer the mixture to a 6" cake pan.
Pour 2 cups water into the inner pot and place the steam rack inside.
Place the cake pan on top of the steam rack.
Put on the pressure cooker's lid and turn the steam valve to "Sealing" position.
Set the Instant Pot to Pressure Cook.
Use the "+/-" keys on the control panel to set the cooking time to 5 minutes.
Use the Pressure Level button to adjust the pressure to "Low".
Once the cooking cycle is completed, allow the steam to release naturally.
When all the steam is released, remove the pressure lid from the top carefully.
Stir the pudding and then transfer it to a glass container with a lid.
Chill in the refrigerator 1 hour or more before serving.

Per Serving: Calories 361; Fat 12.9g; Sodium 754mg; Carbs 21g; Fiber 6.1g; Sugar 4.2g; Protein 11g

Orange Walnut Coffee Cake

Prep time: 20 minutes| **Cook time:** 40 minutes| **Serves:** 4
3 large eggs
4½ tablespoons pure maple syrup
Zest from 1 medium orange
1 tablespoon fresh orange juice
1 teaspoon pure vanilla extract
1⅓ cups almond flour
1 teaspoon baking powder
¾ teaspoon ground cinnamon
½ teaspoon salt
½ cup walnut pieces

In a medium bowl, whisk the eggs, 4 tablespoons maple syrup, orange zest, orange juice, and vanilla.
Add in the flour, baking powder, ½ teaspoon cinnamon, and salt.
Transfer the mixture to a 6" cake pan.
In a small bowl, mix together the walnuts, ¼ teaspoon cinnamon, and ½ tablespoon maple syrup.
Sprinkle on the top of the cake and cover it with aluminum foil.
Pour 1 cup water into the inner pot and place a steam rack inside.
Place the cake pan on top of the steam rack.
Put on the pressure cooker's lid and turn the steam valve to "Sealing" position.
Set the Instant Pot to Pressure Cook.
Use the "+/-" keys on the control panel to set the cooking time to 40 minutes.
Use the Pressure Level button to adjust the pressure to "Low".
Once the cooking cycle is completed, allow the steam to release quickly.
When all the steam is released, remove the pressure lid from the top carefully.
Allow the cake to cool completely before slicing.

Per Serving: Calories 378; Fat 10.9g; Sodium 354mg; Carbs 25g; Fiber 4.1g; Sugar 8.2g; Protein 11g

Caramelized Plantains

Prep time: 20 minutes| **Cook time:** 10 minutes| **Serves:** 4-6
1 tablespoon coconut oil
3 medium ripe plantains, peeled and sliced thickly on the diagonal
¼ teaspoon salt
1 teaspoon ground cinnamon
2 tablespoons pure maple syrup
¼ cup water

Put the oil in the inner pot and press the Sauté button. Set the temperature to Normal setting.
Once the oil is melted, add the plantains, salt, and cinnamon.

Stir until the plantains are coated in the oil and cinnamon. Press the Cancel button.
Stir in the maple syrup and water.
Put on the pressure cooker's lid and turn the steam valve to "Sealing" position.
Set the Instant Pot to Pressure Cook.
Use the Pressure Level button to adjust the pressure to "Low".
Use the "+/-" keys on the control panel to set the cooking time to 10 minute.
Once the cooking cycle is completed, allow the steam to release naturally.
When all the steam is released, remove the pressure lid from the top carefully.
Transfer to bowls for serving.

Per Serving: Calories 334; Fat 10.9g; Sodium 454mg; Carbs 20g; Fiber 3.1g; Sugar 5.2g; Protein 05g

Blueberry Pudding Cake

Prep time: 20 minutes| **Cook time:** 20 minutes| **Serves:** 6

3 tablespoons ground golden flaxseed meal
9 tablespoons water
1¼ cups unsweetened cinnamon applesauce
¼ cup avocado oil
1 teaspoon pure vanilla extract
2¼ cups almond flour
¾ cup erythritol
1 teaspoon baking powder
¼ teaspoon salt
½ cup sliced almonds
½ teaspoon ground cinnamon
1½ cups blueberries

In a small bowl, combine the flaxseed and water and give it time to gel.
In a large bowl, whisk together the flaxseed and water mixture, applesauce, oil, and vanilla.
Add 2 cups flour, ½ cup erythritol, baking powder, and salt and stir to combine well.
Spray a 7" cake pan with nonstick cooking spray. Pour the batter into the pan.
In a small bowl, combine the almonds, cinnamon, blueberries, remaining ¼ cup flour, and ¼ cup erythritol. Sprinkle mixture on top of the cake batter.
Pour 1 cup water into the inner pot and place a steam rack inside. Place the pan on top of the steam rack.
Put on the pressure cooker's lid and turn the steam valve to "Sealing" position.
Set the Instant Pot to Pressure Cook.
Use the "+/-" keys on the control panel to set the cooking time to 20 minutes.
Use the Pressure Level button to adjust the pressure to "Low".
Once the cooking cycle is completed, allow the steam to release quickly.
When all the steam is released, remove the pressure lid from the top carefully.
Spoon into six bowls and serve.

Per Serving: Calories 366; Fat 7.9g; Sodium 704mg; Carbs 6g; Fiber 3.6g; Sugar 6g; Protein 18g

Maple Pecan Pears

Prep time: 15 minutes| **Cook time:** 10 minutes| **Serves:** 4-6

2 large ripe but firm d'Anjou pears
1½ tablespoons coconut oil, melted
1 tablespoon pure maple syrup
½ teaspoon ground cinnamon
¼ cup chopped pecans

Peel the pears and cut them in half lengthwise. Carefully scoop out the core and seeds from each half.
Press the "Sauté" button two time to select "Normal" temperature setting and add the oil to the inner pot.
Once the oil melts, place the pears in the inner pot, cut side down, and cook them until they are starting to get browned, about 2–3 minutes.
Carefully transfer the pears to a steamer basket.
Add ½ cup water to the inner pot and use a spoon to scrape any brown bits.
Place the steam rack inside, and place the steamer basket with the pears on top.
Put on the pressure cooker's lid and turn the steam valve to "Sealing" position.
Set the Instant Pot to Pressure Cook.
Use the "+/-" keys on the control panel to set the cooking time to 10 minutes.
Use the Pressure Level button to adjust the pressure to "Low".
Once the cooking cycle is completed, allow the steam to release quickly.
When all the steam is released, remove the pressure lid from the top carefully.
Remove the water and dry the inner pot.
Press Sauté button and add the maple syrup and cinnamon.
Stir to combine and heat to warm, about 1 minute.
Drizzle the heated maple syrup and cinnamon onto the pears.
Then sprinkle with chopped pecans and serve.

Per Serving: Calories 372; Fat 20g; Sodium 891mg; Carbs 29g; Fiber 3g; Sugar 8g; Protein 10g

Strawberry Chocolate Chip Cakes

Prep time: 15 minutes| **Cook time:** 15 minutes| **Serves:** 4

4 large eggs
2 teaspoons pure vanilla extract
1⅓ cups almond flour
¼ cup erythritol
1 teaspoon baking powder
¼ teaspoon salt
1 cup strawberry chunks
½ cup stevia-sweetened chocolate chips

In a medium bowl, whisk the eggs and vanilla.
Add the flour, erythritol, baking powder, and salt, and stir to combine.
Fold in the strawberries and chocolate chips.
Spray four (6-oz.) glass Mason jars with cooking oil.

Divide the batter into the jars and cover them with aluminum foil.
Pour 1 cup water into the inner pot. Place the steam rack inside and place the Mason jars on the rack.
Put on the pressure cooker's lid and turn the steam valve to "Sealing" position.
Set the Instant Pot to Pressure Cook.
Use the "+/-" keys on the control panel to set the cooking time to 15 minutes.
Use the Pressure Level button to adjust the pressure to "Low".
Once the cooking cycle is completed, allow the steam to release quickly.
When all the steam is released, remove the pressure lid from the top carefully.
Carefully remove the Mason jars from the inner pot and allow to cool before serving.

Per Serving: Calories 389; Fat 11g; Sodium 501mg; Carbs 28.9g; Fiber 4.6g; Sugar 8g; Protein 6g

Red Velvet Cake

Prep time: 15 minutes| **Cook time:** 12 minutes| **Serves:** 4-6

Nonstick cooking spray
1 cup water
1½ cups all-purpose flour
⅓ cup unsweetened cocoa powder
1 teaspoon baking powder
1 teaspoon baking soda
¼ teaspoon salt
¾ cup granulated sugar
½ cup buttermilk
4 tablespoons (½ stick) plus 2 tablespoons unsalted butter, divided, at room temperature
1 large egg
2 tablespoons plain unsweetened Greek yogurt
1 teaspoon red food coloring
1 cup confectioners' sugar
4 oz. cream cheese, at room temperature
1 tablespoon heavy cream
¼ teaspoon vanilla extract

Spray the cups of two silicone egg molds with nonstick cooking spray.
Pour the water into the pressure cooker pot and place a steamer rack trivet in the bottom.
In a medium bowl, whisk together the flour, cocoa powder, baking powder, baking soda, and salt.
In a large bowl, beat together the granulated sugar, buttermilk, 4 tablespoons of butter, egg, and yogurt with a hand mixer until smooth.
Add the dry ingredients to the wet ingredients and mix with the hand mixer until well combined.
Add the red food coloring and beat until the color is fully incorporated into the batter
Fill the cups of the egg molds halfway with batter.
Lay a paper towel over the top of each mold.
Then cover the paper towel and egg bite molds loosely with aluminum foil.
Stack the two molds on top of each other and place on the trivet inside the pot.

Put on the pressure cooker's lid and turn the steam valve to "Sealing" position.
Set the Instant Pot to Pressure Cook.
Use the "+/-" keys on the control panel to set the cooking time to 12 minutes.
Use the Pressure Level button to adjust the pressure to "High".
Once the cooking cycle is completed, allow the steam to release naturally.
When all the steam is released, remove the pressure lid from the top carefully.
Remove the molds from the pressure cooker and cool on a wire rack before using a spoon to remove the cake bites from the molds.
In a small bowl, whip the confectioners' sugar, cream cheese, remaining 2 tablespoons of butter, heavy cream, and vanilla together with the hand mixer until fluffy, about 1 minute.
Dip each cake bite halfway into the cream cheese frosting.
Serve.

Per Serving: Calories 334; Fat 10.9g; Sodium 454mg; Carbs 20g; Fiber 3.1g; Sugar 5.2g; Protein 05g

Apple Bundt Cake

Prep time: 15 minutes| **Cook time:** 55 minutes| **Serves:** 4-6

½ cup room temperature coconut oil
1 cup monk fruit sweetener
2 large eggs, room temperature
1 cup unsweetened apple sauce
2 cups oat flour
1½ teaspoons baking soda
1 teaspoon ground cinnamon
½ teaspoon salt
1 large apple, peeled, cored, and diced

In a large bowl of a stand mixer with a paddle attachment, beat together the oil, sweetener, and eggs on medium speed until well combined.
Add the applesauce and beat until combined.
Add the flour, baking soda, cinnamon, and salt and beat again until combined.
Remove the paddle attachment and stir in the diced apple.
Spray a 6" Bundt cake pan with cooking oil.
Transfer the batter into the pan.
Place a paper towel over the top of the pan and then cover with aluminum foil.
Add 1½ cups water to the Instant Pot inner pot and then place a steam rack inside.
Place the Bundt pan on the steam rack.
Put on the pressure cooker's lid and turn the steam valve to "Sealing" position.
Set the Instant Pot to Pressure Cook.
Use the "+/-" keys on the control panel to set the cooking time to 55 minutes.
Use the Pressure Level button to adjust the pressure to "Low".
Once the cooking cycle is completed, allow the steam to release naturally for 10 minutes and then quick-release the remaining pressure.
When all the steam is released, remove the pressure lid from the top carefully.
Allow to cool completely before removing from pan and slicing to serve.

Per Serving: Calories 389; Fat 5g; Sodium 41mg; Carbs 27g; Fiber 7.6g; Sugar 5g; Protein 2g

Banana Sundae with Strawberry Sauce

Prep time: 15 minutes| **Cook time:** 1 minutes| **Serves:** 6

1 pound strawberries, hulled and chopped
2 tablespoons fresh lemon juice
½ cup erythritol
1 teaspoon arrowroot powder
½ teaspoon water
6 large ripe bananas, sliced and frozen

Add the strawberries, lemon juice, and erythritol to the inner pot.
Put on the pressure cooker's lid and turn the steam valve to "Sealing" position.
Set the Instant Pot to Pressure Cook.
Use the "+/-" keys on the control panel to set the cooking time to 1 minute.
Use the Pressure Level button to adjust the pressure to "Low".
Once the cooking cycle is completed, allow the steam to release naturally for 5 minutes and then quick-release the remaining pressure.
When all the steam is released, remove the pressure lid from the top carefully.
In a small bowl, mix the arrowroot powder with water to create a slurry.
Allow the strawberries to sit 5 minutes, and then stir in the arrowroot slurry.
Meanwhile, remove the bananas from the freezer and place them in your food processor.
Process the bananas until you have a thick, creamy mixture.
Spoon the mixture into six bowls, and spoon some strawberry sauce on the top of each bowl.

Per Serving: Calories 366; Fat 10.9g; Sodium 354mg; Carbs 25g; Fiber 4.1g; Sugar 8.2g; Protein 11g

Peanut Butter Pudding

Prep time: 15 minutes| **Cook time:** 8 minutes| **Serves:** 4

1 cup milk
1 cup half-and-half
⅓ cup sugar
2 tablespoons cornstarch
¼ teaspoon salt
½ cup creamy peanut butter
1 teaspoon vanilla extract
1 cup water

Press the "Sauté" button two time on the Instant pot to select "Normal" temperature settings.
Whisk the milk, half-and-half, sugar, cornstarch, and salt together in the pressure cooker pot. Simmer, for 7 minutes.
Whisk in the peanut butter and vanilla until the peanut butter is melted and mixed in completely.

Press cancel or turn off the burner. Transfer the pudding to a heat-safe bowl and cover with aluminum foil.
When the pot is cool enough to handle, wash and dry it.
Pour the water into the pressure cooker pot and place a steamer rack trivet in the bottom. Place the bowl of pudding on the trivet.
Put on the pressure cooker's lid and turn the steam valve to "Sealing" position.
Set the Instant Pot to Pressure Cook.
Use the "+/-" keys on the control panel to set the cooking time to 8 minutes.
Use the Pressure Level button to adjust the pressure to "High".
Once the cooking cycle is completed, allow the steam to release quickly.
When all the steam is released, remove the pressure lid from the top carefully.
Carefully remove the bowl from the pressure cooker and stir the pudding.
Let it cool on the counter, then serve.

Per Serving: Calories 472; Fat 12.9g; Sodium 754mg; Carbs 21g; Fiber 6.1g; Sugar 4.2g; Protein 11g

Zucchini Cake

Prep time: 15 minutes| **Cook time:** 40 minutes| **Serves:** 4

½ cup almond flour
¼ cup coconut flour
⅓ cup erythritol
¼ teaspoon salt
1 teaspoon ground cinnamon
¾ teaspoon baking powder
3 large eggs
¼ cup avocado oil
1 teaspoon pure vanilla extract
½ cup shredded zucchini

In a medium bowl, whisk together the almond flour, coconut flour, erythritol, salt, cinnamon, and baking powder.
In a separate large bowl, whisk together the eggs, oil, and vanilla.
Add the dry ingredients to the wet ingredients and stir to combine. Fold in the zucchini.
Transfer the batter to a 6" cake pan and cover with aluminum foil.
Pour 1 cup water into the inner pot and add the steam rack inside. Place the cake pan on the rack.
Put on the pressure cooker's lid and turn the steam valve to "Sealing" position.
Set the Instant Pot to Pressure Cook.
Use the "+/-" keys on the control panel to set the cooking time to 40 minutes.
Use the Pressure Level button to adjust the pressure to "Low".
Once the cooking cycle is completed, allow the steam to release naturally.
When all the steam is released, remove the pressure lid from the top carefully.
Allow the cake to cool completely before slicing and serving.

Per Serving: Calories 334; Fat 7.9g; Sodium 704mg; Carbs 6g; Fiber 3.6g; Sugar 6g; Protein 18g

Blueberry Almond Cakes

Prep time: 15 minutes| **Cook time:** 15 minutes| **Serves:** 4

4 large eggs
2 teaspoons pure vanilla extract
1⅓ cups almond flour
¼ cup erythritol
1 teaspoon baking powder
¼ teaspoon salt
1 cup blueberries
¼ cup sliced almonds

In a medium bowl, whisk the eggs and vanilla. Add the flour, erythritol, baking powder, and salt, and stir to combine. Fold in the blueberries.
Spray four (6-oz.) glass Mason jars with cooking oil.
Divide the batter into the jars, top each jar with some of the almonds, and cover them with aluminum foil.
Pour 1 cup water into the inner pot. Place the steam rack inside and place the Mason jars on the rack.
Put on the pressure cooker's lid and turn the steam valve to "Sealing" position.
Set the Instant Pot to Pressure Cook.
Use the "+/-" keys on the control panel to set the cooking time to 15 minutes.
Use the Pressure Level button to adjust the pressure to "Low".
Once the cooking cycle is completed, allow the steam to release quickly.
When all the steam is released, remove the pressure lid from the top carefully.
Carefully remove the Mason jars from the inner pot and allow to cool before serving.

Per Serving: Calories 419; Fat 14g; Sodium 791mg; Carbs 28.9g; Fiber 4.6g; Sugar 8g; Protein 3g

Chocolate Rice Pudding

Prep time: 15 minutes| **Cook time:** 8 minutes| **Serves:** 4-6

1 cup Arborio rice
1½ cups water
¼ teaspoon salt
2 cups unsweetened full-fat canned coconut milk
½ cup erythritol
2 large eggs
½ teaspoon pure vanilla extract
¾ cup stevia-sweetened chocolate chips

Add the rice, water, and salt to the inner pot.
Put on the pressure cooker's lid and turn the steam valve to "Sealing" position.
Set the Instant Pot to Pressure Cook.
Use the "+/-" keys on the control panel to set the cooking time to 3 minutes.
Use the Pressure Level button to adjust the pressure to "Low".

Once the cooking cycle is completed, allow the steam to release naturally.
When all the steam is released, remove the pressure lid from the top carefully.
Add 1½ cups coconut milk and erythritol to rice in the inner pot; stir to combine.
In a small bowl, whisk eggs with remaining ½ cup coconut milk, and vanilla.
Pour through a fine-mesh strainer into the inner pot.
Press the "Sauté" button two time to select "Normal" temperature setting and cook, for 5 minutes. Turn off the heat.
Stir in the chocolate chips and spoon into bowls.

Per Serving: Calories 371; Fat 19g; Sodium 354mg; Carbs 21g; Fiber 5.1g; Sugar 8.2g; Protein 2g

Walnut Brownies

Prep time: 15 minutes| **Cook time:** 50 minutes| **Serves:** 6

Nonstick cooking spray
1½ cups water
1 cup sugar
½ cup all-purpose flour
⅓ cup unsweetened cocoa powder
¼ teaspoon baking powder
8 tablespoons (1 stick) unsalted butter, melted
2 large eggs
½ teaspoon vanilla extract
½ cup chopped walnuts

Spray a heat-safe bowl with nonstick cooking spray.
Pour the water into the pressure cooker pot and place a steamer rack trivet in the bottom.
In a medium bowl, whisk together the sugar, flour, cocoa powder, and baking powder.
In a large bowl, whisk together the melted butter, eggs, and vanilla.
Add the dry ingredients to the wet ingredients and mix until well combined. Fold in the chopped walnuts.
Pour the batter into the prepared heat-safe bowl and smooth the top with a spatula.
Lay a paper towel over the top of the bowl, then cover the paper towel and bowl loosely with aluminum foil.
Place the bowl on the trivet inside the pot.
Put on the pressure cooker's lid and turn the steam valve to "Sealing" position.
Set the Instant Pot to Pressure Cook.
Use the "+/-" keys on the control panel to set the cooking time to 50 minutes.
Use the Pressure Level button to adjust the pressure to "High".
Once the cooking cycle is completed, allow the steam to release naturally for 10 minutes and then quick-release the remaining presssure.
When all the steam is released, remove the pressure lid from the top carefully.
Carefully remove the bowl from the pot and cool on a wire rack before slicing.

Per Serving: Calories 389; Fat 5g; Sodium 41mg; Carbs 27g; Fiber 7.6g; Sugar 5g; Protein 2g

4 Weeks Meal Plan

Week 1

Day 1:
Breakfast: Feta Frittata
Lunch: Vegetarian Loaf
Snack: Cider Collard Greens
Dinner: Butter dipped Lobster Tails
Dessert: White Chocolate–Lemon Pie

Day 2:
Breakfast: Breakfast Grits
Lunch: Simple Spaghetti Squash
Snack: Hot Cauliflower Bites
Dinner: Sesame Chicken
Dessert: Carrot Date Cake

Day 3:
Breakfast: Sausage Pancake Bites
Lunch: Lemony Steamed Asparagus
Snack: Tamari Edamame
Dinner: Tuna Steaks in Lime- Sauce
Dessert: Coconut Cake

Day 4:
Breakfast: Chocolate Oatmeal
Lunch: Pasta Primavera
Snack: Quinoa Energy Balls
Dinner: Mayo Shrimp Salad
Dessert: Banana Chocolate Chip Bundt Cake

Day 5:
Breakfast: Banana Walnut Oats
Lunch: Burgundy Mushrooms
Snack: Avocado Deviled Eggs
Dinner: Chicken Cacciatore
Dessert: Crème Caramel (Purin)

Day 6:
Breakfast: Banana Date Porridge
Lunch: Chili-Spiced Beans
Snack: Lemon Eggplant in Vegetable Broth
Dinner: Shrimp Salad
Dessert: Stuffed Baked Apple À La Mode

Day 7:
Breakfast: Almond Granola
Lunch: Black Bean Sliders
Snack: Lentil Balls
Dinner: Teriyaki Fish Steaks
Dessert: Vanilla Crème Brulee

Week 2

Day 1:
Breakfast: Cinnamon Oatmeal Muffins
Lunch: Lemony Steamed Asparagus
Snack: Classic Black Beans
Dinner: Lemon Mustard Chicken with Potatoes
Dessert: Berry Almond Crisp

Day 2:
Breakfast: Apple Steel Cut Oats
Lunch: Herbed Lima Beans
Snack: Hard-Boiled Eggs
Dinner: Sausage and Prawn Boil
Dessert: Pumpkin Pie Bites

Day 3:
Breakfast: Almond Granola
Lunch: Boiled Cabbage
Snack: Jalapeño Peppers with Cashews
Dinner: Stuffed Chicken Parmesan
Dessert: Dairy-Free Rice Pudding

Day 4:
Breakfast: 5-Ingredient Oatmeal
Lunch: Vegetarian Loaf
Snack: Honey Sweet Potatoes
Dinner: Beef and Potato Stew
Dessert: Zucchini Cake

Day 5:
Breakfast: Root Vegetable Casserole
Lunch: Simple Spaghetti Squash
Snack: Sweet Potatoes with Maple Syrup
Dinner: Brunswick Stew
Dessert: Chocolate Rice Pudding

Day 6:
Breakfast: Bacon-Cheddar Egg Bites
Lunch: Israeli Pasta Salad
Snack: Corn with Tofu Crema
Dinner: Game Hens with Garlic
Dessert: Peanut Butter Pudding

Day 7:
Breakfast: Vanilla Bean Yogurt
Lunch: Lemony Steamed Asparagus
Snack: Refried Beans
Dinner: Seafood Quiche with Colby Cheese
Dessert: Cinnamon Pineapple

189

Week 3	Week 4

Day 1:
Breakfast: Maple Steel-Cut Oats
Lunch: Three-Bean Chili
Snack: Spicy Chicken Wings
Dinner: Rich Chicken Purloo
Dessert: Lemon Bars

Day 2:
Breakfast: Vegetable Egg White
Lunch: Steamed Cauliflower
Snack: Hot Cauliflower Bites
Dinner: Chicken Puttanesca
Dessert: Dairy-Free Rice Pudding

Day 3:
Breakfast: Sausage Pancake Bites
Lunch: Dill Black-Eyed Peas
Snack: Dijon Brussels Sprouts
Dinner: Basque Squid Stew
Dessert: White Chocolate Crème Brûlée

Day 4:
Breakfast: Vegetable Breakfast Bowls
Lunch: Braised Eggplant
Snack: Honey Sweet Potatoes
Dinner: Trout Salad
Dessert: Berry Almond Crisp

Day 5:
Breakfast: Eggs with Asparagus
Lunch: Chickpea Salad
Snack: Avocado Deviled Eggs
Dinner: Brunswick Stew
Dessert: Gooey Chocolate Chip Cookie Sundae

Day 6:
Breakfast: Blueberry Coffee Cake
Lunch: Tomato Basil Soup
Snack: Garlic Baby Potatoes
Dinner: Greek-Shrimp with Feta Cheese
Dessert: Cinnamon-Vanilla Rice Pudding

Day 7:
Breakfast: Vanilla Yogurt with Granola
Lunch: Hearty Minestrone Soup
Snack: Cinnamon Acorn Squash
Dinner: Chicken Stew with Apples
Dessert: Banana Pudding Cake

Day 1:
Breakfast: Pumpkin Quinoa
Lunch: Herbed Lima Beans
Snack: Tamari Edamame
Dinner: Sole Fillets with Vegetables
Dessert: Vanilla Bean Custard

Day 2:
Breakfast: Poppy Seed Oatmeal Cups
Lunch: Bean and Lentil Chili
Snack: Cauliflower Queso with Bell Pepper
Dinner: Ocean Trout Fillets
Dessert: Dairy-Free Rice Pudding

Day 3:
Breakfast: Cheddar Egg Puff
Lunch: Boiled Cabbage
Snack: Broccoli Bites
Dinner: Marsala Fish Stew
Dessert: Maple Pecan Pears

Day 4:
Breakfast: Banana Date Porridge
Lunch: Zucchini Pomodoro
Snack: Cinnamon Almonds
Dinner: Chickpea Stew
Dessert: Chocolate Rice Pudding

Day 5:
Breakfast: Poppy Seed Oatmeal Cups
Lunch: Black Bean Sliders
Snack: Corn with Tofu Crema
Dinner: Beef Peas Stew
Dessert: Caramelized Plantains

Day 6:
Breakfast: Cinnamon Breakfast Loaf
Lunch: Hearty Minestrone Soup
Snack: Coconut Brown Rice
Dinner: Pina Colada Chicken
Dessert: Warm Caramel Apple Dip

Day 7:
Breakfast: Sausage Pancake Bites
Lunch: Salty Edamame
Snack: Polenta with Mushroom Ragù
Dinner: Italian Beef Ragù
Dessert: Blueberry Crisp

The Instant Pot appliance has two programs: Pressure cooking and Non-pressure cooking. Pressure cook, steam, rice, porridge, bean/chili, meat/stew, and soup/stock are included in pressure cooking. In non-pressure cooking, sauté, slow cook, and yogurt are included. It comes with a cooker base, inner pot, stealing ring, and steam-release valve, float valve, condensation collector, and pressure lid. This cookbook is filled with delicious pressure cooking and non-pressure cooking recipes. It is a wonderful appliance because you can cook food in very little time. You didn't need to purchase separate appliances. You can select your favorite recipe, adjust the pressure level, cooking time, and temperatures, put ingredients, close the lid, and press the start/stop button to start cooking. It has user-friendly operating buttons. The cleaning process is pretty simple. The install and removal process of accessories are super easy. Thank you for reading this book.

Stay safe and happy cooking!!!

Appendix 1 Measurement Conversion Chart

WEIGHT EQUIVALENTS

US STANDARD	METRIC (APPROXIMATE)
1 ounce	28 g
2 ounces	57 g
5 ounces	142 g
10 ounces	284 g
15 ounces	425 g
16 ounces (1 pound)	455 g
1.5pounds	680 g
2pounds	907 g

VOLUME EQUIVALENTS (LIQUID)

US STANDARD	US STANDARD (OUNCES)	METRIC
2 tablespoons	1 fl.oz	30 mL
¼ cup	2 fl.oz	60 mL
½ cup	4 fl.oz	120 mL
1 cup	8 fl.oz	240 mL
1½ cup	12 fl.oz	355 mL
2 cups or 1 pint	16 fl.oz	475 mL
4 cups or 1 quart	32 fl.oz	1 L
1 gallon	128 fl.oz	4 L

VOLUME EQUIVALENTS (DRY)

US STANDARD	METRIC (APPROXIMATE)
⅛ teaspoon	0.5 mL
¼ teaspoon	1 mL
½ teaspoon	2 mL
¾ teaspoon	4 mL
1 teaspoon	5 mL
1 teaspoon	15 mL
¼ cup	59 mL
½ cup	118 mL
¾ cup	177 mL
1 cup	235 mL
2 cups	475 mL
3 cups	700 mL
4 cups	1 L

TEMPERATURES EQUIVALENTS

FAHRENHEIT(F)	CELSIUS© (APPROXIMATE)
225 °F	107 °C
250 °F	120 °C
275 °F	135 °C
300 °F	150 °C
325 °F	160 °C
350 °F	180 °C
375 °F	190 °C
400 °F	205 °C
425 °F	220 °C
450 °F	235 °C
475 °F	245 °C
500 °F	260 °C

Appendix 2 Recipes Index

5-Ingredient Oatmeal 30
8-Ingredient Chicken 78

A

Acorn Squash Soup 119
Alfredo Ditalini Soup 129
Almond Butter Chocolate Chip Granola Bars 39
Almond Granola 27
Almond Lentil Vegetable Stew 138
Angel Hair Pasta with Spinach and White Wine 62
Apple Bundt Cake 186
Apple Butter 150
Apple Crisp 182
Apple Steel Cut Oats 28
Applesauce 152
Apricot Chicken 84
Artichoke Egg Casserole 27
Artichoke Soup 161
Artichokes Provençal 160
Avgolemono 64
Avocado Deviled Eggs 44
Avocado Hummus 43
Avocado Toast with Boiled Egg 19

B

Bacon-Cheddar Egg Bites 20
Baked Fish with Parmesan 93
Baked Sweet Potatoes 168
Banana Bites 28
Banana Chocolate Chip Bundt Cake 183
Banana Date Porridge 26
Banana Oatmeal 23
Banana Pudding Cake 181
Banana Sundae with Strawberry Sauce 187
Banana Walnut Oats 26
Barley Pottage 143
Basque Squid Stew 141
BBQ Chicken with Potatoes 85
Bean and Lentil Chili 54
Beans with Tomato and Parsley 52
Beef and Potato Stew 139
Beef Barley Soup 124
Beef Bone Broth 146
Beef Peas Stew 131
Beef Potato Stew 131
Beef Soup with Vegetables 119
Beef Stroganoff Soup 120
Beefsteak Tomatoes with Cheese 57
Beer-Steamed Mussels 109
Beet Hummus 47
Berry Almond Bundt Cake 181
Berry Almond Crisp 173
Berry Steel Cut Oats 28
Biscuit Dumplings and Gravy 33
Black Bean Dip 41
Black Bean Sliders 51
Black Bean Soup with Avocado Salsa 113
Black Beans with Corn and Tomato Relish 52
Blue Crabs with Wine and Herbs 98
Blueberry Almond Cakes 188
Blueberry Coffee Cake 32
Blueberry Crisp 182
Blueberry French Toast Bake 23
Blueberry- Oatmeal 21
Blueberry Pudding Cake 185

Blueberry Quinoa Porridge 25
Bœuf A La Bourguignonne 135
Boiled Cabbage 167
Bolognese Sauce 156
Bone Broth 153
Borscht Soup 129
Bosnian Pot Stew 132
Bowtie Pesto Pasta Salad 60
Braised Eggplant 159
Bread Pudding with Rum Sauce 176
Breakfast Biscuits and Gravy 21
Breakfast Grits 22
Broccoli and Leek Soup 114
Broccoli Bites 43
Broccoli Pesto 148
Brown Butter–Cinnamon Rice Treat 176
Brown Sugar Quinoa 20
Brownies 181
Brunswick Stew 136
Buckwheat Granola 25
Buffalo Chicken 83
Buffalo Chicken Dip 40
Burgundy Mushrooms 164
Butter dipped Lobster Tails 106
Butter Grouper 94
Butternut Squash Soup 116

C

Cabbage Soup 162
Cajun Chicken with Rice 86
Calamari with Pimentos 90
Cannellini Bean Salads 50
Caramel Sauce 157
Caramelized Plantains 184
Carp Pilaf 90
Carrot Cake with Cream Cheese Frosting 175
Carrot Date Cake 180
Catalan Shellfish Stew 138
Cauliflower and Potato Soup 113
Cauliflower Hummus 40
Cauliflower Queso with Bell Pepper 44
Cheddar Egg Puff 19
Cheesy Broccoli Soup 121
Cheesy Brussels Sprouts and Carrots 170
Cherry Cheesecake Bites 177
Chicken Adobo 80
Chicken and Shrimp Gumbo 133
Chicken Burrito Bowls 73
Chicken Cacciatore 79
Chicken Coconut Curry 79
Chicken Congee 81
Chicken Curry 79
Chicken Drumsticks 82
Chicken Dumplings 66
Chicken Enchiladas 65
Chicken Feet Stock 154
Chicken Fricassee with Wine 142
Chicken Nachos 80
Chicken Noodle Soup 115
Chicken Penne Puttanesca 72
Chicken Piccata 80
Chicken Pot Pie 65
Chicken Puttanesca 81
Chicken Stew with Apples 133
Chicken Stock 146
Chicken Stock 154
Chicken Tikka Masala 67
Chicken Tomato Drumsticks 82

Chicken Tortilla Soup   117
Chicken Vegetable Soup   126
Chicken Wings   66
Chicken with Black Bean Garlic Sauce   74
Chicken with Potatoes   81
Chicken with Potatoes and Peas   65
Chicken–Stuffed Sweet Potatoes   71
Chickpea Mushrooms   49
Chickpea Salad   49
Chickpea Soup   56
Chickpea Stew   132
Chili Lime Chicken   88
Chili Sauce   158
Chili-Spiced Beans   55
Chipotle Chili Soup   122
Chocolate Chip Banana Bread   32
Chocolate Oatmeal   26
Chocolate Peanut Butter Popcorn   179
Chocolate Rice Pudding   188
Chunky Tilapia Stew   92
Cider Collard Greens   37
Cilantro-Lime Brown Rice   36
Cinnamon Acorn Squash   38
Cinnamon Almonds   42
Cinnamon Apples   183
Cinnamon Applesauce   149
Cinnamon Breakfast Loaf   29
Cinnamon Oatmeal Muffins   26
Cinnamon Pineapple   183
Cinnamon Raisin Granola Bars   38
Cinnamon-Vanilla Rice Pudding   174
Classic Black Beans   35
Classic Hummus   35
Coca Cola Chicken   87
Coconut Brown Rice   36
Coconut Cake   182
Coconut Oatmeal   21
Cod Fish with Goat Cheese   97
Cod Tomato Soup   120
Codfish with Scallions   102
Corn and Chicken Soup   122
Corn with Tofu Crema   47
Couscous with Crab   58
Couscous with Olives   59
Couscous with Tomatoes   58
Crab Dip   97
Crab Sliders   107
Crabs with Garlic Sauce   106
Crack Chicken   83
Cranberry Apple Sauce   156
Cranberry Sauce   149
Cream Cheese Chicken   87
Creamed Spinach with Cashews   48
Creamy Chicken with Bacon   85
Creamy Clam Chowder   120
Creamy Oatmeal   21
Creamy Pumpkin Yogurt   23
Creamy White Bean Soup   53
Crème Caramel (Purin)   176
Creole Gumbo   98
Curried Halibut Steaks   90
Curried Mustard Greens   170

D

Dairy-Free Rice Pudding   178
Dandelion Greens   159
Denver Omelet   24
Dijon Brussels Sprouts   45
Dill Black-Eyed Peas   51
Dill Pasta Salad   62

Duck Millet Soup   130
Duck with Vegetables   70

E

Egg Bites   34
Egg Kale Casserole   24
Eggplant Caponata   162
Eggs with Asparagus   30

F

Farmhouse Soup   127
Faux-Tesserae Chicken Dinner   73
Feta Chickpea Salad   36
Feta Frittata   20
Fish and Couscous Pilaf   108
Fish and Vegetables   100
Fish Burritos   111
Fish Mélange   111
Fish Paprikash   109
Fish Stock   155
Fish Tacos   103
Foil-Packet Fish with Aioli   93
French Fish En Papillote   105
French Onion Soup   115
French Pot-Au-Feu   142
Fresh Tomato Ketchup   152

G

Game Hens with Garlic   75
Garlic Baby Potatoes   47
Garlic Collard Greens in Vegetable Broth   45
Garlic Green Beans   171
Garlicky Black-Eyed Pea Soup   50
Garlicky Brussels Sprouts   37
Ginger Broccoli and Carrots   169
Ginger Chicken   89
Gingered Sweet Potatoes   163
Gooey Chocolate Chip Cookie Sundae   173
Greek Navy Bean Soup   53
Greek-Shrimp with Feta Cheese   96
Greek-Style Fish   105
Greek-Style Peas   159
Green Beans with Tomatoes and Potatoes   162

H

Haddock Curry   101
Haddock Fillets with Black Beans   92
Haddock Fillets with Steamed Green Beans   96
Halibut Chowder   126
Halibut Steaks with Tomatoes   110
Halibut Steaks with Wild Rice   103
Ham and Hash   19
Ham Bone Soup   117
Ham Cheese Egg Bites   31
Ham Cheese Omelet   33
Hamburger Soup   129
Hang Wau Soup   127
Hard-Boiled Eggs   43
Hearty Minestrone Soup   161
Herb Stock   155
Herbed Lima Beans   53
Herbed Potato Salad   165
Homemade Ketchup   147
Homemade Salsa   155
Homemade Three-Bean Salad   49
Honey Sweet Potatoes   38
Hot Cauliflower Bites   39
Hot Pepper Sauce   152
Hot Wings   77

Hungarian Beef Goulash   135
Hungarian Chicken Stew   139
Hunter Chicken   87
Hyderabadi- Lentil Stew   143

I

Indian Bean Stew   139
Indian Kulambu   97
Irish Bean Cabbage Stew   137
Israeli Pasta Salad   60
Italian Beef Ragù   136
Italian Beef Stew   132
Italian Chicken   76
Italian Sausage Ragu with Polenta   72

J

Jalapeño Peppers with Cashews   46
Japanese Seafood Curry   100

K

Kentucky Burgoo   143
Key Lime Pie 177
Kidney Bean Chicken Soup 122

L

Lemon Bars   180
Lemon Eggplant in Vegetable Broth   44
Lemon Garlic Red Chard   169
Lemon Mustard Chicken with Potatoes   85
Lemony Cauliflower Rice   169
Lemony Steamed Asparagus   169
Lentil and Tomato Soup   117
Lentil Balls   42
Lentil Curry Stew   145
Lentil Vegetable Hotpot   141
Lima Bean Soup   55
Lima Bean Soup   124
Lime Chicken Wings 77
Loaded Bacon Grits 31
Lobster Bisque   124
Louisiana-Seafood Boil   99

M

Mahi-Mahi Fish with Guacamole   110
Makhani Chicken   71
Mango Sticky Rice   174
Mango-Apple Chutney   149
Maple Barbecue Sauce   151
Maple Dill Carrots   166
Maple Pecan Pears   185
Maple Steel-Cut Oats   20
Marinara Sauce   147
Marinara Spaghetti with Mozzarella Cheese   63
Marsala Fish Stew   134
Mashed Cauliflower 172
Mashed Potato and Cauliflower   38
Mashed Sweet Potatoes   172
Matzo Ball Soup   114
Mayo Shrimp Salad 111
Meatball Noodle Soup   121
Mediterranean Chicken Stew   140
Minestrone Soup   118
Minty Asparagus Soup   128
Mixed Vegetable Couscous 61
Mojo Chicken Tacos 86
Molten Chocolate Lava Cake   177
Mulligan Stew   137
Mushroom and Chicken Sausage Risotto 67
Mushroom Broth   154
Mushroom Gravy Sauce   157
Mussels in Scallion Sauce   106

Mustard–Braised Chicken   72

N

Nacho Cheese Sauce   39
Noodle Soup 118
Nut-Free Cheese Sauce   152

O

Ocean Trout Fillets   95
Oil-Free Marinara Sauce   151
Olive Chicken88
Onion Gravy 148
Orange and Lemon Marmalade   150
Orange Chicken   83
Orange Sea Bass   104
Orange Walnut Coffee Cake   184
Oyster Stew with Chorizo   144

P

Parmesan Cod with Basmati Rice   94
Pasta Primavera   59
Pasta with Chickpeas and Cabbage   62
Pasta with Marinated Artichokes   57
Peach Cobbler   179
Peanut Butter Pudding   187
Penne and Turkey Meatballs   69
Pepper Couscous Salad   58
Peppery Ground Pork Soup 124
Pina Colada Chicken83
Pinot Grigio Soup   119
Polenta with Mushroom Ragù   48
Poppy Seed Oatmeal Cups 28
Pork Broth   153
Pork Chile Verde   135
Portuguese-Fish Medley   95
Potato Chowder   125
Potato Pea Salad   37
Prawn Dipping Sauce   104
Prawns with Basmati Rice   95
Pumpkin Pie Bites   173
Pumpkin Pudding   184
Pumpkin Quinoa   27
Pureed Cauliflower Soup   163
Purple Cabbage Salad   167
Puttanesca Sauce   148

Q

Quinoa Energy Balls 42
Quinoa–Stuffed Peppers   74

R

Raspberry Steel Cut Oatmeal Bars   25
Ratatouille   166
Red Lentil Spinach Soup   126
Red Snapper in Mushroom Sauce 95
Red Velvet Cake   186
Refried Beans   35
Rich Chicken Purloo 138
Risotto with Sea Bass   111
Roasted Chicken with Tomatoes   68
Roasted Spaghetti Squash 160
Roasted Tandoori Chicken   86
Root Vegetable Casserole   29
Rotini with Red Wine Marinara   59
Rotini with Walnut Pesto   60

S

Sage Onion Soup   121
Salmon on Croissants   108
Salmon Steaks with Kale Pesto Sauce   93
Salsa Chicken   87
Salsa Verde Chicken78

Salty Edamame   50
Saucy Brussels Sprouts and Carrots   168
Saucy Clams 112
Saucy Red Snapper 107
Sausage and Bean Stew   133
Sausage and Cabbage Soup   130
Sausage and Prawn Boil   98
Sausage Pancake Bites   24
Sausage Spinach Quiche   31
Seafood Chowder with Bacon   125
Seafood Quiche with Colby Cheese   105
Seafood Soup Stock 155
Seafood Vegetable Ragout 140
Seasoned Chicken   76
Sesame Chicken   78
Shredded Chicken Breast   84
Shredded Chicken with Marinara   84
Shrimp in Tomato Sauce   91
Shrimp Salad 107
Shrimp Scampi with Carrots   103
Shrimp Vegetable Bisque   128
Simple Beet Salad   171
Simple Lentil-Walnut Dip   46
Simple Spaghetti Squash   168
Slumgullion Stew   141
Sole Fillets with Pickle   112
Sole Fillets with Vegetables   99
Southern California Cioppino   99
Spaghetti Squash with Mushrooms   161
Spaghetti with Meat Sauce 63
Spanish Olla Podrida   140
Spanish Paella   106
Spiced Coconut Chicken   68
Spiced Potatoes Dip 46
Spicy Chicken Bone Broth   146
Spicy Chicken Wings   77
Spicy Corn On the Cob   163
Spicy Thai Prawns   100
Spinach Artichoke Dip   40
Spinach Salad with Beets   171
Spinach Salad with Quinoa 170
Spinach-Stuffed Salmon   101
Sriracha Chicken   78
Steak Kidney Bean Chili   134
Steamed Broccoli   167
Steamed Cauliflower   168
Steamed Cauliflower with Herbs   165
Steamed Tilapia with Spinach   102
Strawberries Quinoa Porridge   30
Strawberry Applesauce   158
Strawberry Chocolate Chip Cakes 185
Strawberry Compote   153
Stuffed Acorn Squash   165
Stuffed Apples   179
Stuffed Baked Apple À La Mode   174
Stuffed Chicken Parmesan 71
Stuffed Turkey Breast   69
Sweet and Tangy Barbecue Sauce 147
Sweet Potato Hummus   40
Sweet Potato Kale Soup   116
Sweet Potato Soup with Swiss Chard   123
Sweet Potatoes with Maple Syrup 45

T

Tabasco Sauce   156
Tahini Soup 63
Tamari Edamame   41

Teriyaki Chicken   82
Teriyaki Fish Steaks 102
Teriyaki Wing 70
Thai Chicken 76
Thai Curry Stew   144
Three-Bean Chili   54
Tilapia Fillets with Mushrooms   91
Tilapia Fillets with Peppers 104
Toasted Couscous with Feta   61
Toasted Orzo Salad 57
Tomato Basil Sauce 157
Tomato Basil Soup   160
Tomato Soup 113
Tomato Vegetable Soup   127
Tomato, Arugula and Feta Pasta Salad   61
Traditional Polish Stew   136
Triple-Berry Jam   150
Trout Salad   91
Tuna and Asparagus Casserole   101
Tuna Fillets with Eschalots 92
Tuna Fillets with Onions   96
Tuna Steaks in Lime- Sauce   109
Tuna, Ham and Pea Chowder   94
Turkey and Basmati Rice Soup   123
Turkey Stock 154

U

Unsweetened Applesauce 35

V

Vanilla Bean Custard   179
Vanilla Bean Yogurt 22
Vanilla Crème Brulee   175
Vanilla Yogurt with Granola   33
Vegan Alfredo Sauce   156
Vegan Pottage Stew 137
Vegetable Breakfast Bowls 29
Vegetable Broth   151
Vegetable Cheese Sauce   167
Vegetable Egg White   22
Vegetable Stock   146
Vegetable Wild Rice Soup   118
Vegetarian Loaf   55
Vegetarian Ratatouille   142
Vietnamese-Fish   108

W

Walnut Brownies   188
Warm Caramel Apple Dip   183
White Bean Barley Soup   54
White Bean Cassoulet   56
White Bean Dip   41
White Bean Soup   52
White Bean Soup with Kale 56
White Chicken Chili 131
White Chocolate Crème Brûlée   178
White Chocolate–Lemon Pie   178
White Sauce 158
Wild Mushroom Soup   164
Wine Glazed Whole Chicken   75

Z

Zesty Couscous   64
Zucchini Cake   187
Zucchini Pomodoro 164
Zucchini Quinoa Soup   128

© Copyright 2021 - All rights reserved.

The content contained within this book may not be reproduced, duplicated or transmitted without direct written permission from the author or the publisher.

Under no circumstances will any blame or legal responsibility be held against the publisher, or author, for any damages, reparation, or monetary loss due to the information contained within this book, either directly or indirectly.

Legal Notice:

This book is copyright protected. It is only for personal use. You cannot amend, distribute, sell, use, quote or paraphrase any part, or the content within this book, without the consent of the author or publisher.

Disclaimer Notice:

Please note the information contained within this document is for educational and entertainment purposes only. All effort has been executed to present accurate, up to date, reliable, complete information. No warranties of any kind are declared or implied. Readers acknowledge that the author is not engaged in the rendering of legal, financial, medical or professional advice. The content within this book has been derived from various sources. Please consult a licensed professional before attempting any techniques outlined in this book.

By reading this document, the reader agrees that under no circumstances is the author responsible for any losses, direct or indirect, that are incurred as a result of the use of the information contained within this document, including, but not limited to, errors, omissions, or inaccuracies.

CPSIA information can be obtained
at www.ICGtesting.com
Printed in the USA
BVHW012102250222
630132BV00003B/26

9 781801 218566